Dictionary of Economics and Financial Markets

To my mother

Clara Mary Gilpin

in her 95th year

Dictionary of Economics and Financial Markets

Fifth edition

Alan Gilpin
B.Sc. (Econ.) (Lond.), Ph.D. (Qld.), C.Eng.,
F. Inst. E., M.I.E.Aust., F.R.S.A.
Commissioner of Inquiry, New South Wales Government, Australia. Sometime with the Central Electricity Generating Board, London, and with English local government.

London
Butterworths
1986

United Kingdom	Butterworth & Co (Publishers) Ltd, 88 Kingsway, London WC2B 6AB and 61A North Castle Street, Edinburgh EH2 3LJ
Australia	Butterworths Pty Ltd, Sydney, Melbourne, Brisbane, Adelaide, Perth, Canberra and Hobart
Canada	Butterworth & Co (Canada) Ltd, Toronto and Vancouver
New Zealand	Butterworths of New Zealand Ltd, Wellington and Auckland
Singapore	Butterworth & Co (Asia) Pte Ltd, Singapore
South Africa	Butterworth Publishers (Pty) Ltd, Durban and Pretoria
USA	Butterworth Legal Publishers, St Paul, Minnesota, Seattle, Washington, Boston, Massachusetts, Austin, Texas and D & S Publishers, Clearwater, Florida

British Library Cataloguing in Publication Data

Gilpin, Alan
Dictionary of economics and financial markets.
—5th ed.
1. Economics—Dictionaries
I. Title II. Gilpin, Alan. Dictionary of economic terms
330′.03′21 HB61

ISBN 0 406 50230 7

Typeset by Cotswold Typesetting Ltd, Gloucester
Printed and bound in Great Britain by Biddles Ltd, Guildford, Surrey

Preface to the fifth edition

Preparations for the fifth edition of my *Dictionary of Economic Terms* yielded an additional 1,000 terms, concepts and topics relating to contemporary applied economics and financial institutions with particular reference to commodity, stock, financial and futures markets. The introduction of these new items necessitated a severe pruning of the material in the fourth edition, as well as justifying a change of title to *Dictionary of Economics and Financial Markets*. The surviving material from the fourth edition has been thoroughly updated.

While much new material relates to changes in practices and institutions in Britain, a substantial number of new entries relate to the United States, Canada, Australia and the European Economic Community. The co-operation of many trade and financial institutions in several countries has been warmly appreciated, including the Federal Reserve Board and the Bank of England. Several major commodity and stock exchanges have contributed to the strengthening of the terminology of those markets in this edition.

The aim of this revised work has been to improve significantly its interest and value to a market ranging from students of economic science who are focusing on the applied side, to professional and business people wishing to have a better understanding of the terminology of the financial press and the background to developments in the economic and financial world.

A.G.
October, 1985

Preface to the first edition

This book has been inspired by my professional acquaintance with applied economics in a major industry and my experience as a lecturer in economics and allied subjects over many years.

It is intended primarily for economists and students of economics, but it is hoped that it will prove of value and interest also to planners and engineers in industry who, faced with the growing impact of positive national economic planning, are having to give more constructive thought to the long-term development of their own industries and the implications of such development for the economy as a whole.

I would like to thank my wife for scrutinising and typing the manuscript and the many organisations who have assisted by supplying information on their activities. In particular, I should like to thank the Board of Trade, the Commercial Banks, the Monopolies Commission, the National Economic Development Council, the Stock Exchange and the United Nations Organisation.

The terms in this dictionary are those used largely in the United Kingdom, but a number in use in the United States of America and other countries have also been included.

A.G.
December, 1965

A

A.A.A. A rating classification given by Standard and Poor in respect of the credit standing of outstanding corporations and companies; in this instance, an indication of considerable commercial integrity, with minimal risk of default. The concept is also applied to countries and public institutions. *See* STANDARD AND POOR'S CREDIT RATINGS.

A fortiori. May imply 'in consequence', 'with stronger reason' or 'with greater certainty'; a term frequently appearing in economic literature.

A priori. An expression commonly used in economics, it relates to speculation or reasoning which is prior to actual experience. As reasoning it proceeds deductively from cause to effect; such speculation or reasoning stands in contrast to an appeal in evidence. The term is often used as a synonym for 'on theoretical grounds'. An example of the use of the term appears in the following extract from an O.E.C.D. Report on inflation: 'With regard to costs and prices, there are *a priori* reasons for expecting a slowdown, notably the lagged effect of lower demand pressures, and the above average productivity gains in the early phase of renewed expansion.'

'A' shares *See* STOCKS AND SHARES PREFIXED OR AFFIXED 'A', 'B' ETC.

Abandoned option. A share option (q.v.) not exercised as the price is against the buyer (or taker) on declaration day (q.v.), i.e. the situation has become unprofitable.

Ability-to-pay. A principle most commonly associated with the theory of taxation which asserts that the burden of taxation (q.v.) should be carried by the individual in accordance with his ability-to-pay, and not in accordance with the benefits he may receive as a result of public expenditure. Adam Smith (1723–1790) enunciated the principle that citizens should contribute 'in proportion to their respective abilities: that is in proportion to the revenue which they respectively enjoy under the protection of the state'. The problem is to translate the principle of ability-to-pay into an actual pattern of tax distribution: whether the principle requires a regressive, proportional or progressive taxation in relation to income; or an equitable distribution through equal sacrifice; or an efficient distribution aiming at the least total sacrifice for the community.

Absolute monopoly. The control of the entire output of a commodity or service, for which there is no substitute, by a single producer or supplier. This kind of situation rarely occurs, in real life. Also called pure monopoly or perfect monopoly. The central idea is that the demand curve (q.v.) is perfectly inelastic. *See* MONOPOLY.

Abstinence. In an economic sense, the sacrifice of current consumption to increase future consumption, usually by enabling resources to be directed to the production of capital goods. As this means that in the long run the flow of consumer goods will be increased, abstinence may be regarded as the sacrifice of some current consumption in favour of greater future consumption.

Abstinence or agio theory of interest. A theory that interest (q.v.) is a payment for abstaining from current consumption. This is but a partial explanation as there are other reasons for saving. *See* INTEREST, THEORIES OF; LIQUIDITY PREFERENCE; PROPENSITIES TO CONSUME AND SAVE.

Abu Dhabi Fund for Arab Economic Development. A fund established in July, 1971, by the Government of Abu Dhabi to help other Arab countries by offering them economic aid in the form of loans or guarantees or direct participation in projects. The original authorised capital of the fund was subscribed totally by the Government of Abu Dhabi; the first loan agreement was signed in 1974. The fund is now authorised to offer aid to African, Asian and other Islamic nations. Some 30 per cent of the gross national product of Abu Dhabi now goes in aid to other countries. *See* UNITED ARAB EMIRATES.

Accelerator Coefficient. The amount of additional capital stock needed to obtain a given increase in output; the coefficient relates the level of investment to the change in output or sales:

$$I_t = V(Y_t - Y_{t-1})$$

where: I_t = investment in time; V = accelerator coefficient; and Y_t and Y_{t-1} represent output or sales in times t and t−1 respectively.

Accelerator, the. A theory that investment is determined by changes in output; the process by which changes in the demand for consumer goods bring about even larger variations in the demand for the capital equipment used to make them. The accelerator is a factor which tends to accentuate booms or slumps in the economy. The demand for capital equipment is the aggregate of two distinct demands: (a) the demand arising from the need to replace worn-out or obsolete capital equipment, and (b) the demand for the provision of additional productive capacity if there is a growing demand for goods. As an example of the effect of the accelerator, envisage a plant manufacturing 1 million units of a commodity per year. Assume that 10 per cent of the productive capacity requires replacement each year. Now if the market demand for the commodity increases from 1 million units to 1.1 million units, the productive capacity will have to be increased by 10 per cent to meet the additional demand. Thus the effect of a 10 per cent increase in consumer demand is an increase of 100 per cent in the demand for capital equipment. Conversely, if demand for the commodity fell by 10 per cent, then the producer need not carry out his normal replacement of plant at all, and the effect of this relatively small fall in demand for the commodity is to reduce the demand for capital equipment to zero. In practice, the effect may not be as sharp as this. An increase in demand, if temporary, may be met by running down stocks; there may be reserve productive capacity which can be brought into use; existing plant may be used more intensively; and the cost of durable equipment may not be great in relation to materials and labour, reducing the importance in the economy of large variations in the demand for equipment. The theory assumes a fixed capital-output ratio (q.v.). The principle received its name from the accelerating effect of a change in production or income on levels of investment—equipment or inventory.

Accelerator-multiplier model. A model of the trade cycle (q.v.) based on the interaction of the acceleration principle and the multiplier (q.v.). A change in national income determines through the acceleration principle a change in the level of investment; a change in investment causes, in turn, through the multiplier a change in the national income. The interactive effects are continuous. Professor Paul A. Samuelson (b. 1915) formulated the nature of this inter action in an article published in 1939.

Acceptance. The agreement of the drawee of a bill of exchange (q.v.) signified by his signing the bill, to carry out the order of the drawer. An acceptance may be general (i.e. without qualification), or qualified (i.e. conditional or partial). After acceptance the drawee is known as the acceptor; the acceptor acts as a guarantor.

Acceptance credit. Also known as a 'letter of acceptance', a method of payment widely used in inland and international trade. If the credit of a foreign import merchant is considered satisfactory an accepting house (q.v.) may open an acceptance credit for him in London. A purchase from a British exporter may then be financed by means of a bill of exchange (q.v.) drawn on the accepting house. The exporter can then obtain his money quickly as the bill can be easily discounted in the London discount market.

Accepting house (U.K.). A financial institution which accepts bills of exchange; with such backing the bills command a higher price. Most accepting houses were originally merchant houses engaged in trade before specialising in financial operations. In addition to accepting bills, accepting houses engage in ordinary banking business and function as investment advisers and issuing houses. *See* ACCEPTANCE; ACCEPTANCE CREDIT; ISSUING HOUSE.

Accepting Houses Committee (U.K.). Established in 1914, when merchant bankers in the City of London were faced with common problems concerning money owed to them by German nationals, the committee today is a representative body for the City's accepting houses. The committee continues to provide a forum for the discussion of matters of common interest, and provides a means of conveying the views of the accepting houses to the British Government, the Bank of England (q.v.) and others. It also has a part to play in the self-regulation of the City's activities. In 1984, the committee had sixteen members. *See*

ACCEPTANCE; ACCEPTING HOUSE; MERCHANT BANK.

Accommodating credit. A term frequently used to refer to the 'automatic financing' of deficits, e.g. when an exporter gives credit to the importer.

Accommodating movements. Transfers of gold and convertible currency abroad to meet deficits in the total balance of payments (q.v.) of a country

Accommodation bill. A bill drawn, accepted or endorsed for the sole purpose of discounting it, no goods being given or received for it, thus providing short-term cash accommodation.

Account day. The day on which all bargains (q.v.) done on The London Stock Exchange (q.v.) must be settled, being usually seven days after the close of dealings at the end of the previous account period (q.v.). Also known as settlement day, and occasionally as pay day.

Account period. A period during which transactions take place on The London Stock Exchange (q.v.). The year is divided into twenty-four account periods; these are normally fortnightly periods, but there are four three-week periods in each year to cover Christmas and other holidays. *See* ACCOUNT DAY.

Accounting costs. Costs considered as recorded costs only; economic costs may be larger or smaller when alternative costs or opportunity costs (q.v.) and external effects (q.v.) are taken into account.

Accrued interest. Interest accrued on a bond since the last interest payment was made; the buyer of the bond usually pays the market price plus the accrued interest. In this case, the bond is sold 'cum (with) interest'.

Accumulation. The action of traders who buy a commodity heavily and 'take it out of the market'.

Accumulation index. A stock market index which reveals the total return on equities over a period of time and shows the investor which sections of the market are giving the best return in terms of capital gains plus dividends.

A.C.P. countries. The 63 African, Caribbean, and Pacific countries that signed the Lomé Convention (q.v.) with the European Economic Community (q.v.). Most of these were former colonial territories of the EEC countries.

Active circulation. That part of the note issue of the Bank of England (q.v.) in circulation at any given time.

Active market. A market for a particular class of stock or shares in which there are frequent and regular dealings.

Activists. Descriptive of economists who believe in the use of monetary and fiscal policies to control the economy, and who tend to recognise and favour a large role for government in the economy. In particular, activists believe in the possibility of successful fine-tuning (q.v.). Activists reject the case for any 'rules' to govern economic policy whether by way of fixed exchange rates, a balanced budget, or a monetary rule as advocated by Milton Friedman. Instead, they believe that better economic management will result from the policy makers having complete discretion. *See* SCHOOLS OF ECONOMICS.

Activity rate. The proportion of civilian employees (employed plus registered unemployed) in a given population age group. Low activity rates may be regarded, to some extent, as an indication of 'concealed' unemployment; also known as participation rate (q.v.). *See* UNEMPLOYMENT.

Actuals. Commodities on hand, ready for shipment, storage or manufacture; the physical, or cash commodity, as distinct from commodity futures contracts.

Adding to a position. Descriptive of further purchases of a security or commodity when a person has established a favourable position in the market with prospects for future sizable price increases. It is often advocated that additional purchases should at most equal and never exceed the original purchase; indeed, that additions should be made in successively smaller amounts so that the total position takes the form of a pyramid. In this way, the bulk of the overall position has been established at the most advantageous prices, and there is a cushion against temporary sharp declines in price:

Size of fourth addition	x
Size of third addition	xxx
Size of second addition	xxxxx
Size of first addition	xxxxxxx
Size of initial position	xxxxxxxxx

When prices are rising, a position built up in successively larger units is considered very vulnerable with potentially disastrous effects for the total position:

Size of fourth addition	xxxxxxxxx
Size of third addition	xxxxxxx
Size of second addition	xxxxx
Size of first addition	xxx
Size of initial position	x

In this instance, the average price of the whole position is much closer to the price at which the last and largest addition was made; a sharp reaction in price may wipe out, therefore, all profit in the position.

Adjustable peg system. The system established under the Bretton Woods Agreement (q.v.) of currency exchange parities which were normally, but not immutably, fixed. International Monetary Fund (q.v.) members were expected to follow a uniform exchange rate policy, keeping their currency values within 1 per cent of a pre-determined par value. A change in the par value was provided for but only in the event of 'fundamental disequilibrium'. So while fixed, the rates were in the extreme adjustable to new fixed levels; hence the term 'adjustable peg'.

The system broke down in 1971, when the convertibility of the dollar was suspended and the cornerstone of the system was removed; all the major currencies then floated for the first time since the 1930s, with most of them appreciating quite sharply in terms of the dollar. This episode ended with the Smithsonian Agreement (q.v.).

The Smithsonian system itself quickly collapsed. Various efforts were made to revive it in the 1970s, but all were unsuccessful. However, adjustable pegs are an integral part of the European Monetary System (q.v.).

Administered pricing. Introduced by Gardiner C. Means in 1933, a term referred to a price which is set and kept constant for a period of time and over a series of transactions; the word 'administered' implies a degree of power over pricing which allows some discretion in setting a price regardless, at least in the short-term and perhaps in the long-term, of the precise price which would just clear the market by equating supply and demand. Administered pricing has emerged as a most common form of marketing in the twentieth century, replacing 'higgling and bargaining' within both the public and private sectors, applying to wages and salaries as much as to the prices of goods and services. Administered pricing may also be defined as pricing by 'price makers' or 'price setters', and not 'price takers' as under perfect competition (q.v.); the pricing policies of monopolistic and oligopolistic sellers. Administered prices tend to be cost determined, i.e. they are arrived at by applying various percentages to direct labour and material costs to allow for overheads and profits. These simplified pricing formulas are known as mark-up pricing, full-cost pricing, short-run profit pricing and long-run target pricing. The inflexibility of prices often means that it is production and stock which are adjusted to changes in demand; production is reduced in response to an accumulation of unsold goods, and raised in the face of a depletion. *See* PRICING.

Ad valorem. 'According to value', i.e. as a percentage.

Ad valorem tax. A duty imposed on commodities in proportion to their value, i.e. a duty expressed as a percentage and not a flat amount. It is commonly used in respect of import tariffs. In Britain values are assessed on the c.i.f. (q.v.) values, plus landing charges, or alternatively on the market value when landed. In Canada the value used is that which is considered to be the fair market value on such or like goods sold for home consumption. When a fair market value cannot be ascertained, production cost plus a reasonable mark-up is accepted.

Advance refunding (U.S.). A technique of the U.S. Treasury to hold traditional bondholders; the Treasury offers holders of expiring bonds especially attractive terms to buy its new bond issues. In this way it does not compete with private borrowers for the inflow of new savings.

Afloats. Commodities loaded on vessels and already on the way to a destination or about to be despatched; the term does not apply to cargoes already at the destination.

African Development Bank Group. A group of development financing institutions comprising the African Development Bank (A.D.B.) and its affiliates, the African Development Fund (A.D.F.) and the Nigeria Trust Fund (N.T.F.). The A.D.B. established by African independent states in 1963 is a collective instrument for promoting economic and social development in its member states. The A.D.B. provides financial and technical assistance to projects of proven economic, financial and technical feasibility. The A.D.F. and the N.T.F. have similar objectives. The A.D.F. was established with non-regional states in 1972, and the N.T.F. by the Federal Government of Nigeria in 1976. The 1982 membership of A.D.B. consisted of 50 independent African states, although membership is to be extended to non-regional states in order to mobilise funds on a more permanent basis. By far the largest portion of A.D.B. Group loans have gone into agriculture and physical infra-structure. Over 80 per cent of the softer loans from A.D.F. and N.T.F. went to the poorer members of A.D.B.

After-hours dealings. Dealings done after the official close (3.30 p.m.) of The London Stock Exchange; these dealings count as the first deals done for the following business day. Also known as early bargains.

Aggregate demand. The total effective demand

or expenditure of all purchasers of consumer and capital goods within a given market, or economic system. Keynes emphasised the role of aggregate demand. In his model, aggregate demand determined output and therefore employment; unemployment emerged as a result of insufficient aggregate demand. Hence, there was a need for active stabilisation or demand management policies. In modern macroeconomic models, aggregate demand interacts with aggregate supply (q.v.) to determine price and output. *See* ACTIVISTS; DEMAND MANAGEMENT POLICIES; KEYNESIAN REVOLUTION; KEYNESIAN SCHOOL; STABILISATION POLICY.

Aggregate demand function. A relationship between the planned level of real spending or demand for goods and the level of prices, given the quantity of money and fiscal policy; the function describes an equilibrium relationship between aggregate spending and the price level.

Aggregate supply. The total supply of goods and services in an economy available to meet aggregate demand (q.v.). The stream of goods and services comprises domestic production together with imports.

Aggregation. The bringing together or summing of primary data. For example, the national income is an aggregate, in contrast with the income of an individual. *See* AGGREGATE DEMAND.

Aggregative index. An index number which is constructed by aggregating a number of items, e.g. Laspeyres' Index (q.v.) and Paasche's Index (q.v.)

Aggregative model. An econometric model in which the variables are themselves constructed from groups of individual variables, as when a price index number is substituted for a set of prices. *See* ECONOMETRIC MODELS.

Agio. A charge for changing one currency into another, or for changing paper money into coin; the excess value of one currency over another at the prevailing official rate of exchange. Agiotage is exchange business such as stockjobbing and speculation in stocks.

Agio theory of interest. *See* ABSTINENCE OR AGIO THEORY OF INTEREST; INTEREST, THEORIES OF.

Agricultural futures contract. *See* CHICAGO BOARD OF TRADE.

Agricultural subsidies. Payments to the farmers by the British Government for the purpose of encouraging home production of foodstuffs while maintaining reasonable retail prices to consumers. *See* AGRICULTURE AND CONSUMER PROTECTION ACT 1973, (U.S.); COMMON AGRICULTRUAL POLICY; INTERVENTION PRICES; COMMON SUPPORT PRICES.

Agriculture and Consumer Protection Act 1973 (U.S.). Legislation which provides a system of assistance for United States agriculture, relying on price supports, direct-income payments and acreage restrictions in the event of the production of market surpluses in certain farm commodities. The Act was modified by subsequent legislation in 1977, 1981, and 1983.

Aldrich Commission. Arising from the Aldrich Freeland Act 1908, a commission appointed by the United States Congress to recommend the most effective monetary organisation for the nation. Early in 1912 the commission submitted its report which proposed the creation of a National Reserve Association, a voluntary affiliation of banks which would issue notes, hold deposits of member banks and make loans to them against acceptable collateral. In 1913 Congress passed the Federal Reserve Act which introduced central banking on a permanent basis, establishing the Federal Reserve System (q.v.).

Allen Committee. A committee of inquiry set up by the British Government, under the chairmanship of Professor R. G. D. Allen, to examine and report on the impact of rates on households. The Committee reported in 1965. It found that the impact of rates was regressive; while on average rates accounted for only 2.9 per cent of total disposable household income, the burden was as much as 8.2 per cent of income among the poorer households. The committee recommended that the payment of rates on a monthly basis should be permitted; this and other measures were incorporated in the Rating Act 1966.

Alligator spread (U.S.). A commodity traders' expression for a commission that is so large that it 'eats the client' or 'chews up the client's cash'.

Allonge. Slip of paper attached to a bill of exchange (q.v.) to provide additional space for endorsements, should this be required.

All-or-none order (U.S.). A market or limited price order for the purchase or sale of stocks and shares which is to be executed in its entirety or not at all. *See* FILL-OR-KILL ORDER.

Allotment. Act of allotting newly issued debentures, or shares between applicants who have responded to an offer for subscription.

Allotment letter. Letter advising an applicant how much stock or how many shares he/she has been allotted and specifying the amounts due and dates of payment in respect of them.

All-savers certificates. Authorised in the United States in 1981, certificates which gave every wage earner the chance to earn $1,000 interest tax-free. They matured in October, 1982. It was hoped through this issue to make available mortgage money for the stricken housing industry. The sales fell well short of expectations.

Amazon Pact. A pact proposed by Brazil in 1977 with a membership to include all countries in the Amazon Basin; the purpose of the pact was to develop the resources of the region in harmony, settle territorial disputes, and promote joint projects and research. The countries were Bolivia, Brazil, Colombia, Ecuador, Guyana, Peru, Surinam, and Venezuela, eight in all. The first meeting of the eight countries' representatives was in October, 1980.

American Depository Receipt (A.D.R.). A security issued by a United States bank in place of the foreign shares held in trust by that bank, thereby facilitating the trading of foreign shares in the U.S. markets.

American Federation of Labour and Congress of Industrial Organisations (A.F.L.–C.I.O.). Achieved in 1955, an amalgamation of two American rival federations of trade unions. The combined federation comprises over 100 national and international unions and over 500 local unions, with a total membership of over 14 million trade unionists. The A.F.L.–C.I.O. deals primarily with issues of public policy, international relations with foreign trade unions, and the co-ordination of activities between unions in support of common goals and objectives.

American Stock Exchange. Located in New York City, the second largest stock exchange (q.v.) in the United States of America; once known as the Curb Exchange (q.v.). Late in 1982, the exchange began trading in options on 90-day U.S. Treasury Bills, and options on 10-year U.S. Treasury Notes. The options are based not on futures but on actual instruments. In 1983, trading began in 90-day certificates of deposit and six-month bills, also based on actual instruments.

Amortisation. (a) The gradual repayment of a debt by means of a sinking fund (q.v.); (b) the annual writing down of the value of an asset by depreciation (q.v.).

Ancient Spanish Customs. A term apparently originating in the London printing industry, relating to many restrictive practices, excessive and unnecessary overtime, and work-to-rule activities of an obstructive kind.

Andean Pact. A pact agreed to in 1969 forming a common market between Chile, Peru, Bolivia, Colombia, and Ecuador; Venezuela joined the pact in 1973, while Chile terminated her agreements in 1976. The aim of the group was to set up a common external tariff and establish free trade between member countries. *See* LATIN AMERICAN INTEGRATION ASSOCIATION (L.A.I.A.).

Anticipatory pricing or hedge pricing, or inflation premium pricing. A pricing strategy by companies that allows for future anticipated cost increases both in operating and capital costs. It is an attempt in inflationary conditions to maintain profit margins. If companies believe that government policies will lead to a greater rate of inflation, then this belief will be reflected in price structures particularly in respect of goods and services to be delivered at some future time. *See* FULL COST PRICING; PRICING; TARGET RETURN PRICING.

Anti-takeover tactics. Methods used by management to make their companies less attractive to take-over bidders; often known as 'poison pill' or 'scorched earth' tactics viewed collectively. Tactics include the following: introducing a rule that a merger must be approved by two-thirds of the stockholders, in contrast to the more normal bare majority; the creation of a new class of stock to dilute shareholders' power and keep control in the hands of the management; the payment of large premiums to buy back shares from threatening suitors (known as 'greenmail'); the selling of a valuable property to a third party (perhaps a linked commercial interest) to reduce the prospective value of asset stripping (q.v.); the incurring of a substantial debt in respect of a large venture which reduces the short-term attractiveness of the company; self-tendering, whereby a target company makes tender offers for its own shares to outcompete contenders; carefully prepared arguments to stockholders that buyout offers are too low because 'great opportunities are around the corner and the stock price is likely to rise to even greater heights'; contracts for the management that contend with prospective failure calling for very large payments to individual executives (called 'golden parachutes' in case the senior management has to 'bail-out').

Anti-Trust Laws (U.S.). A series of Acts introduced by the United States Federal Government to check and control the formation of trusts (q.v.), and more generally to restrict monopolistic practices and encourage competition. The first was the Sherman Anti-Trust Act of 1890 (q.v.). The Clayton Act 1914 (q.v.) sought to check the development of monopolies by prohibiting the amalgamation of firms producing a large proportion of the total output of a commodity.

In 1984, there was a break-up of the 22 Bell operating companies. Previously all had been exclusive customers of the Bell manufacturing arm, the Western Electric Co. Subsequently, the companies became free to purchase domestic or overseas equipment on the open market.

Applied economics. Branch of economic science devoted to the study of practical problems, utilising the principles and tools of economic analysis provided by theoretical economics.

Appreciation. An increase in the value of an asset. For example, an increase in: (a) the value of property in relation to other assets during a period of growing demand; (b) the value of stocks held by merchants and manufacturers during a period of rising prices; (c) the value of a currency when its value increases in relation to the values of other currencies; or (d) the value of stocks and shares in general, or particular categories, on the stock exchange.

Arbitrage. Dealing in commodities, currencies or securities between two or more markets to take profitable advantage of any differences in the prices quoted for such commodities, currencies or securities. Arbitrage may involve the simultaneous purchase and sale of the same quantity of the same commodity in two different markets, either in the same country or in different countries, in order to take advantage of a temporary disparity in prices. The effect of arbitrage is to bring the prices of comparable commodities traded in separate markets within limits set by the cost of buying a commodity in one market and selling it in another. Arbitrage also assists in establishing relationships in the prices of commodities due for delivery at different times, such that the price for later delivery does not exceed the price for earlier delivery by more than the marginal cost of storage between the two dates, other things being equal. *See* PRICING.

Articles of association. A document which must be submitted to the British Registrar of Companies when seeking registration of a company. The articles determine the internal constitution of the company, either accepting the standard articles suggested in the Companies Act or setting out special terms of their own. Articles cover such important matters as:

(a) Issue and transfer of shares;
(b) Alteration of capital;
(c) Borrowing powers;
(d) Shareholders' meetings and voting rights;
(e) Appointment and powers of directors;
(f) Presentation and auditing of accounts.

See COMPANIES ACTS 1948 TO 1985; COMPANY, LEGAL FORMATION OF; MEMORANDUM OF ASSOCIATION.

Asian Development Bank. Founded in 1966, a bank to further development investment in Asia, to help prepare and co-ordinate development and provide technical aid. It has twenty regional members and thirteen non-regional members. The bank has its headquarters in the Philippines.

Asset backing. The net assets of a company divided by the number of issued shares. For example, if the ABC Co. Ltd. has £100,000 net assets and 10,000 shares issued, the asset backing is £10 per share.

Asset stripping. Usually the selling-off of valuable assets following a successful takeover bid for a company, profiting possibly from an under-valuation of some or all of the assets of that company.

Assets. The property of a business; they may be classified as:

(a) Current Assets, consisting of cash, stock and book debts;
(b) Fixed Assets, consisting of buildings, plant and machinery;
(c) Intangible Assets, being the value of goodwill or patents.

Assets/employee ratio. A ratio used as an indication of the capital intensity of a company; the ratio is useful for comparing the capital of companies within an industry group. *See* CAPITAL-INTENSIVE INDUSTRY.

Assets markets. Markets in which money, bonds, stocks, houses, and other forms of wealth are traded.

Assisted areas. Designated areas in Britain with particularly serious problems of unemployment and industrial decline; industry in such areas receives government assistance to encourage development and expansion. The three types of assisted areas are: special development areas, development areas, and intermediate areas.

Associated British Ports. A company, formerly the British Transport Docks Board, which runs 19 of Britain's ports; it is the largest of the British port authorities.

Association of Futures Brokers and Dealers. A self-regulatory body embracing all the London futures exchanges, offering a variety of safeguards to clients.

Association of Licensed Dealers in Securities. *See* NATIONAL ASSOCIATION OF SECURITIES DEALERS AND INVESTMENT MANAGERS (U.K.).

Association of South East Asian Nations (ASEAN). An association of the south east Asian nations of Singapore, Malaysia, Indonesia, Thailand, and the Philipines for security, diplomatic, and economic purposes. In November, 1982, the economic ministers of the member countries approved an agreement on joint industrial ventures which included 50 per cent tariff reductions for approved products.

Association of Tin-Producing Countries. An association formed in London in 1983 by the world's seven main tin-producing countries: Malaysia, Indonesia, Thailand, Nigeria, Bolivia, Australia, and Zaire. The association is concerned with ways to cut production costs as well as ways of expanding consumption. It has taken over responsibility for the International Tin Research Institute. *See* INTERNATIONAL TIN AGREEMENT.

At a discount. At a price lower than par value, or lower than normal, due to special circumstances. *See* AT PAR.

At a premium. At a price higher than par value, or higher than normal, due to special circumstances. *See* AT PAR.

At best. In relation to instructions to brokers in commodity or securities markets, an abbreviation for 'at the lowest possible price', in respect of a buying order, and 'at the highest possible price' in respect of a selling order.

At call. Description of funds invested but which can be recovered quickly, on demand.

At discretion. A term qualifying an instruction given by a client to his stockbroker (q.v.) to buy or sell stocks or shares, it gives the broker discretion as to price.

At limit. A term qualifying an instruction given by a client to his stockbroker (q.v.) to buy or sell stocks or shares, it places a specified limit on either the highest price that may be paid, or the lowest price at which a sale may be made.

At par. Stocks and shares the market price of which is the same as the nominal or face value. If new stock is issued at par, then £100 of such stock can be bought for £100.

'At the back door'. Description of assistance to the money market by the Bank of England (q.v.), which injects cash into the market by the purchase of bills when it wishes to provide the market's requirements of cash without exerting pressure upwards or downwards on the rates of interest in the market. If the Bank does not wish to provide cash in this manner, and the discount houses can obtain the cash they require in no other way, then the discount houses may borrow direct from the Discount Office of the Bank of England. This is known as assistance to the market 'at the front door'. *See* LENDER OF LAST RESORT; MONEY MARKET; 'PENAL' TERMS.

At the market. A term qualifying an instruction given by a client to his stockbroker (q.v.) to buy or sell stocks or shares, it indicates that the broker may buy or sell at about the market price prevailing at the time the instruction is given. It involves a prompt execution of the order.

Auction. A method of determining prices employed in the sale of objects which cannot be standardised, e.g. horses, fish, cattle, vegetables, etc. Specified quantities or 'lots' are open to public bids, buyers competing to complete a purchase. The general system is for the price to start low and for bidding to raise it, although there may be a reserve price below which the seller reserves the right to withdraw the goods from sale. In a Dutch auction, however, the bids come down from a high price instead of rising from a low price. This method is used extensively in Holland for the sale of agricultural commodities.

Auction market. The system of trading securities through brokers or agents on stock exchanges, such as the New York Stock Exchange (q.v.). Buyers compete with other buyers, and sellers with other sellers, for the most advantageous price.

Aussie Bonds. Australian Savings Bonds. Series 24, issued in 1983, attracted a rate of interest of 12.25 per cent. Bonds may be sold in the secondary markets before maturity.

Australian banking system. A banking system consisting of a central bank (the Reserve Bank of Australia, based in Sydney), the Commonwealth Banking Corporation, private trading banks (all joint-stock companies) and various other commercial and savings banks. The Reserve Bank is responsible for the issue of notes, regulation of bank lending, and bank interest rates, the movement of foreign currencies, and the management of government securities. Through a system of statutory deposits, the Reserve Bank regulates the liquidity of the trading banks and hence their capacity to make advances. By 1982, as a result of mergers, the four major trading banks were the Commonwealth Banking Corporations, the Westpac Banking Corporation, the National Australia Bank, and the ANZ Banking Group. The Report of the Committee of Inquiry into the Australian Financial System (Campbell Report) released in 1981 recommended that interest rates should be totally deregulated and left to be determined by market forces, and that banks should be allowed to pay interest on current (checking) accounts. A more competitive future was envisaged for the banking sector; it was argued that the banking system should be open to anyone, foreign or domestic, who could fulfill appropriate requirements. Non-bank financial institutions should also find themselves facing much greater competition. A free exchange market (without exchange controls) was envisaged. The Australian dollar floated from 12 December, 1983. In 1984, deposit maturity controls were removed to allow trading banks to compete with merchant banks for short-term funds.

Australian Loan Council. A body composed of State and Australian Government ministers which determines the amount of public borrowing that may be undertaken during the current year, and the distribution of the amounts raised between the seven governments. The Loan Council was established in 1927, following an amendment to the Constitution which permitted the negotiation of a financial agreement between the Australian Government and the States.

Australian options market. A market established on the floor of the Sydney Futures Exchange (q.v.) in February, 1976, initially in call options. The Options Clearing House, a fully-owned subsidiary of the Exchange, facilitates the processing of option trades and eliminates the requirement of a contractual tie between the buyer and seller of the option (q.v.).

Australian short term money market. A short term money market (q.v.) divided into two separate but interlocking segments, the official market and the unofficial market: (a) The official market comprises nine dealers authorised by the Reserve Bank of Australia to promote the sale of short term Australian Government securities; and (b) The unofficial market comprises a multitude of dealers, mainly merchant banks and large corporate entities, the purpose of which is to facilitate the efficient operation of Australia's financial markets generally. The bulk of deposits in this segment are unsecured and for amounts, in 1982, of not less than $100,000.

Australian Stock Exchange all-ordinaries index. A share price index calculated using the market prices of over 250 Australian companies listed on the Sydney and Melbourne stock exchanges. The market value of these companies accounts for nearly 90 per cent of the value of all shares listed on Australian stock exchanges. The index is a weighted index of the share prices of the companies included; each stock is weighted by multiplying the number of shares in the company by the price per share to give a total market value, or market capitalisation. The index is calculated continuously each day. Share price index futures are based on this index, in the Australian markets.

Austrian School of Economists. Name given to a group of 19th century economists at the University of Vienna, among whom were Carl Menger (1840–1921), Friedrich von Wieser (1851–1926) and Eugen von Böhm-Bawerk (1851–1914). Their contribution rested largely in the development of the utility theory of value, refuting the cost of production theory of value of the older Classical School of Economists. The Austrian contribution was developed in the work of Ludwig von Mises (1881–1973), Friedrich von Hayek (b. 1899), and more recently by Sir John Hicks (b. 1904). The main philosophy of the school has been that government intervention is both economically and morally evil. *See* SCHOOLS OF ECONOMICS.

Automated policy. A reliance on fixed rates of change in money and tax rates, rather than frequent discretionary changes in monetary or fiscal policy to influence the level of economic activity. An example of automated policy would be the setting of a growth rate for the money supply (q.v.) to be adhered to over a long period independent of current economic conditions.

Automated Real-time Investments Exchange (U.K.). A computerised system owned by the Accepting Houses Committee (q.v.) in which subscribers are able to 'talk' anonymously to other subscribers over a television screen. Bargains are struck by one subscriber accepting the bid of another, by-passing the stock exchanges altogether. Subscribers pay an annual rent for the equipment, plus a transaction fee. The saving on stock exchange commissions can be considerable and the jobber's turn is eliminated. Ariel came on stream in February, 1974. *See* STOCKJOBBER.

Automatic stabilisers. Those elements of the economic system, both private and public, which tend without conscious alteration to correct recessionary or inflationary tendencies. For example, direct taxes on inflating money incomes, being progressive, tend to curb excessive aggregate demand in inflationary conditions; in another instance, a tendency of people to maintain a customary level of consumption even by drawing of savings tends to retard a decline in aggregate demand in a recession (q.v.).

Autonomous expenditures. Expenditures exogenous to a model used to forecast Gross National Product (q.v.); generally regarded as autonomous are private investment, exports or net foreign balances, expenditures by the federal or national government.

Autonomous investment. Investment not influenced by such economic factors as the rate of interest, the rate of growth of sales, or the rate of return on investment.

Autonomous spending. Spending that is independent of the level of income and interest rates.

Autonomous variables. *See* VARIABLES, ENDOGENOUS AND EXOGENOUS.

Avoidable costs. Costs of production which would not be incurred if a given output was not produced; the costs avoided may be not only direct costs but also costs arising indirectly in other parts of the production system.

B

Back-to-back. A reference to offsetting loans, often made in one currency in one country against a loan in another currency in another country; it involves two parties, matching assets and liabilities in opposite directions. In the futures markets, back-to-back describes an equal number of bought and sold contracts held by one trader in the same month.

Backward sloping supply curve. *See* SUPPLY CURVES, REGRESSIVE, OR BACKWARD SLOPING.

Backward vertical operations. The securing and exploiting of raw materials by a company which would otherwise have to purchase such materials.

Backwardation. (a) A payment made by a bear (q.v.) to a bull (q.v.) for refraining from demanding delivery of shares sold by the former to the latter. Opposite to contango (q.v.).

(b) Fee paid by a bear (q.v.) on borrowing stock or shares to deliver against his sale.

(c) A market situation in which prices are progressively lower in the future delivery months than in the nearest delivery month. For example, if the wool quotation for March is $4.80 per kilogram, and that for July is $4.50 per kilogram, then the backwardation for five months against March is $0.30 per kilogram.

Balance of payments. The relation between the payments of all kinds made from one country to the rest of the world and its receipts from all other countries. For the world as a whole, imports must equal exports. In recent years, Britain's balance of payments has shown generally a deficit on visible trade wholly or partially offset by a surplus on invisible earnings (q.v.). In 1980 and 1981, however, there was a substantial improvement in visible trade resulting in the first large visible trade surpluses since 1971. As the balance on invisible transactions also rose substantially in 1981, there was a large current account surplus of over £6,000 million. However, the trade deficit on goods and services was £588 million in April, 1984, due to a reduction in exports and an increase in imported oil arising from the extended miners' strike.

Balance of trade. The relationship between the values of a country's imports and its exports, i.e. the 'visible' balance. These items form only part of the balance of payments (q.v.) which is also influenced by (a) 'invisible' items and (b) movements of capital.

Balance sheet. An ordered statement of:

(a) The economic resources or assets of a company or other business organisation, each item having a value set upon it;

(b) The financial claims of persons or organisations upon the value of these assets.

All assets are, by definition, owned by someone; consequently, the total claims equal the value of the assets.

Balanced budget multiplier. The effects of an increase in government purchases accompanied by an increase in taxes, if, in the new equilibrium, the budget deficit or surplus is exactly the same as in the original equilibrium the resulting multiplier of such a policy change is unity, i.e. 1. A multiplier of unity implies that output shifts by precisely the amount of the increased government purchases with no induced consumption spending. Higher taxes exactly offset the effect of income expansion, maintaining overall disposable income and consumption constant.

Balancing item. An item entered in the balance of payments (q.v.) accounts to make the account balance; it is the net total of the errors and omissions in other items

Baltic Exchange. *See* LONDON BALTIC EXCHANGE.

Bank accepted bill, 90-day. A bill of exchange (q.v.) being a lending and borrowing instrument used by large companies to arrange their funding requirements; essentially it is a promise to pay a specified sum on a designated date in the future, in this case 90 days from the date of issue. If a bank 'accepts' the bill, that is guarantees payment of the face value to the ultimate holder, the bill may then be sold to another company at a discount. *See* DISCOUNT YIELD FORMULA.

Bank bill. A bill of exchange (q.v.) carrying the names of two accepting houses (one a member of the Accepting Houses Committee) eligible for discount at the Bank of England (q.v.).

With a bank bill, a bank puts its name to a bill and provides credit to the drawer by granting him an 'acceptance facility'. A commission, which will depend partly on the drawer's standing, is payable to the bank which has accepted the bill and has undertaken to meet it when it is presented for payment on the agreed (due) date. Bankers' acceptances, as these bills are also called can provide temporary working capital, and many large industrial companies arrange appropriate facilities with a bank. The discount on a bank bill is usually less than that on a trade bill because of the credit standing of the bank or accepting house which has undertaken to pay it on the due date. A firm can sometimes arrange with such acceptors a line of credit (an acceptance credit) to finance a wide range of commercial transactions rather than just one specific transaction.

Bank Charter Act 1844. Following a series of banking crises during the period 1825–37, an Act introduced to control the issue of bank-notes.

The chief provisions of the Act were:

(a) The work of the Bank of England (q.v.) was to be divided into two departments: (i) Issue Department, and (ii) Banking Department;

(b) There was to be a small fiduciary issue (q.v.) of about £14 millions; all notes above this amount were to be backed by gold;

(c) No new bank was to be allowed to issue notes and existing issues were not to be increased; note-issuing powers were withdrawn from any business as soon as the number of partners exceeded six, and from any issuing bank becoming bankrupt, ceasing to carry on the business of banking, or otherwise discontinuing note issue;

(d) The Bank of England (q.v.) was to be allowed to increase its fiduciary issue by two-thirds of the lapsed issue of any other bank; and

(e) The Bank of England had to publish a weekly return for both its issue and banking departments.

In 1844 there were 72 banks of issue in England, but by 1914 the number had been reduced to 13. By 1921 the Bank of England had become sole bank of issue in England; eight Scottish Banks continued to issue notes. *See* CURRENCY AND BANK-NOTES ACTS 1928–1954.

Bank deposit. Funds placed with a bank credited to a person, firm, or institution; the bank has a legal obligation to pay the sum credited to the customer on request. The funds may have been lodged directly by the customer, or been credited from some other source including bank loans. If a deposit is payable immediately it is known as a demand deposit or checking account; if it is payable only after the expiry of a period of time, it is known as a time deposit (or as a passbook or certificate account). Demand deposits are usually withdrawn by writing a check naming the person to whom the specified amount should be transferred; the check is a negotiable instrument unless endorsed 'not negotiable'. Negotiable means retradable on a secondary market. Time deposits similarly may be either negotiable or non-negotiable. The most common type of negotiable time deposit is the neogtiable certificate of deposit (CD) (q.v.); most of the depositors in negotiable CD accounts are large corporations.

Defined in the U.K. Banking Act 1979 (q.v.) as 'a sum of money paid on terms under which it will be repaid . . .'. *See* CHECKING DEPOSITS; CHEQUE.

Bank for International Settlements (B.I.S.). Established at Basle in 1930, as a result of the recommendation of the Young Committee, the B.I.S. undertook initially certain functions in relation to the collecting and disbursing of reparations and allied war debt payments; the intention was that the bank would develop into a clearing house for central banks and eventually into a 'central bank for central banks'. These earlier hopes were not realised and since the Second World War the International Monetary Fund (q.v.) has been performing many functions which might have been performed through the B.I.S. For many years, the B.I.S. remained concerned with short-term operations between European central banks and acting as an agent for a number of international organisations. However, in 1982 the B.I.S. became heavily involved in the international debt crisis, playing an increasingly prominent role in co-ordinating central bank bridging loans.

Bank giro. A scheme for the improvement of money transfer services offered by the British clearing banks; the improved services include direct debiting arrangements, a particularly useful service for large organisations receiving frequent payments from the holders of bank accounts. *See* GIRO SYSTEM.

Bank Merger Act 1960. A U.S. Act which requires bank regulatory agencies to weigh the possible competitive effects of proposed mergers and acquisitions when considering applications.

Bank of Canada. The central bank of Canada responsible for regulating 'credit and currency in the best interests of the economic life of the nation'. The Bank implements its monetary policy primarily by varying the amount of cash reserves available to the banking system. The minimum rate at which the Bank is prepared to make advances to the chartered banks is called the Bank Rate. The Bank acts as fiscal agent for the Government of Canada and has sole right of issue of bank notes for circulation in Canada. *See* CHARTERED BANK.

Bank of England. The British central bank. Its functions and duties are as follows:

(a) It carries out the monetary policy (q.v.) of the Government;
(b) It has the sole right in England and Wales to issue bank notes (the Scottish and Northern Ireland banks have limited rights to issue notes);
(c) It is the bankers' bank. The commercial banks (q.v.) keep about 50 per cent of their reserves with the Bank of England;
(d) It is the Government's bank. It receives the proceeds of taxation and makes payments on behalf of the Government. It manages the National Debt (q.v.) and floats new loans for the Government. By 'ways and means advances' (q.v.) it lends money direct to the Government;
(f) It is the 'lender of last resort' (q.v.);
(g) It carries on a little ordinary banking business.

The Bank of England was established as a joint-stock company in 1694. The Bank Charter Act of 1844 (q.v.) gave the Bank a virtual monopoly of note issues. In 1946, the Bank was nationalised, the capital being acquired by the state.

Section 4 of the Bank of England Act 1946 formalised many informal understandings which had grown up in the past. With some qualifications, the Treasury is able to direct the Bank, and the Bank is able to direct any or all of the commercial banks. However, the House of Commons Select Committee on Nationalised Industries 1969–70 concluded that moral suasion (q.v.) was 'much the most important control exercised by the Bank over the monetary system . . .'. In 1971 the Bank brought into operation Competition and Credit control Measures which introduced a uniform system of minimum ratios. Since 1981,

(i) Each institution in the monetary sector (see (ii) below) has been required to keep half a per cent of its eligible liabilities in a non-operational account at the Bank of England. This provision does not apply to institutions with eligible liabilities below £10 million and is set at only a quarter per cent for banks in Northern Ireland.
(ii) A new 'monetary sector', somewhat broader than the old 'banking sector', has been defined to include all recognised banks and licensed deposit takers (as defined in the 1979 Banking Act), the National Girobank, banks in the Isle of man and Channel islands participating in the cash ratio scheme, the Banking Department of the Bank of England, and the trustee savings banks.
(iii) Eligible liabilities have been calculated in a uniform fashion for all institutions with a few exceptions and are subject to spot checks between the monthly reporting days to deter artificial manipulation.
(iv) The scheme whereby the Bank of England may call for 'special deposits' as a percentage of eligible liabilities has been retained, applying to all institutions with eligible liabilities of £10 million or more.
(v) The list of institutions whose acceptances are eligible for discount at the Bank of England has been widened and now includes non-Commonwealth banks for the first time (mainly American, French and Japanese). Eligible banks must agree to maintain an average of 5 per cent of their eligible liabilities in the form of secured loans with the discount market.
(vi) The reserve asset ratio has been suspended.
(vii) The Bank of England no longer publishes a minimum lending rate (q.v.). However, it retains the option to reveal in advance the rate at which it will operate in the market, for a short period ahead, when a more positive indication of official policy is desired. The aim of the Bank of England is to conduct its money market operations by reference

to an unpublished band of very short-term interest rates, unpublished so as to allow market forces' influence on the structure of interest rates to be as large as possible.

Bank of issue. A bank, authorised by statute to issue bank notes. *See* BANK CHARTER ACT 1844; CURRENCY AND BANK NOTES ACTS 1928–1954.

Bank of Japan. The central bank of Japan, created in 1882. Originally privately owned, it is now required by statute to be at least 55 per cent in public ownership.

Bank of North Dakota (U.S.). The only commercial bank in the United States of America owned and operated by a state. Most of its loans are to state agencies.

Bank overdraft. In Britain, a widely used type of short-term finance. It is particularly used to provide short-term working capital to tide over the production cycle; finance for seasonal requirements; and bridging loans for the purchase of property or plant with repayment coming from the realisation of another asset. Advantages to a business include the following:

(a) The system is simple, and arrangements can be negotiated and set up very quickly;

(b) The system is flexible: there is no minimum level, and sums can be drawn or repaid within the agreed limit at any time entirely at the option of the borrower and without prior notice;

(c) The system is usually one of the cheaper forms of borrowing; interest is payable only on the amount outstanding each day, building up and being charged at the end of the quarter or half-year; arrangement fees, service charges, and commitment fees on undrawn facilities may be charged, but are generally small; and

(d) A facility, once agreed, is generally renewable, subject to the creditworthiness of the borrower and any special factors. The overdraft has never been used in the United States.

Bank Rate. The minimum rate at which the Bank of England (q.v.), acting as 'lender of last resort' (q.v.) would discount first class bills or make advances to a discount house against 'eligible paper'. Bank rate governed the movement of market rates of discount, although these remained somewhat below bank rate. By custom, bank rate also governed the movement of many administered interest rates, e.g. the rates on commercial bank deposits and advances, and the rates of lending by the Exchequer to local authorities and nationalised industries. Until 1972 the Bank Rate was announced every Thursday by the Court of Directors of the Bank of England.

The effect of raising the bank rate was to check or reduce bank advances; lowering the bank rate meant that borrowing was cheaper and an expansion of credit was encouraged. It was thus a monetary instrument for influencing the activity of the economy; its effectiveness was often assisted by 'open market operations' (q.v.).

At one time bank rate fluctuated frequently, but between 1932 and 1951, save for a short period in 1939, it remained steady at 2 per cent; this was the era of 'cheap money'. In 1951 the bank rate was raised to 2½ per cent, and in March 1952 to 4 per cent. After this it rose to higher levels, varying between 5 and 8 per cent. Apart from its effect on the Treasury Bill discount rate, the influence of Bank rate in the past to a large extent depended on the fixed links maintained between it and the clearing bank interest rates. From 16th September 1971, these fixed links were terminated as a result of abandoned agreements. In October, 1972, after 270 years of existence, the bank rate was replaced by the minimum lending rate (q.v.).

Bank wire. A pioneer payments system in the United States; in 1982, it was in use by about 250 banks in over 75 American cities. In addition to making transfers, the system provides information on loans and account balances.

Bankers' acceptances. Bills endorsed by a major bank and used to finance trade between the United States and the rest of the world, as well as trade among foreign countries; federal agency securities issued by institutions such as the Federal National Mortgage Association; federal funds or banks' excess reserves which are borrowed, usually for one day only, by banks with a temporary reserve deficiency; and brokers' loans or loans made by banks to brokers and dealers for purchasing and carrying securities.

Banking Act 1935 (U.S.). An Act which made several important changes to the Federal Reserve System (q.v.): it established the Federal Open market Committee (q.v.) as a statutory body to decide the System's policy in respect of open-market operations; the Board of Governors was given the authority to change the percentages of deposits which member banks must hold as reserves up to a maximum of twice the original percentages; the System's role as a lender of last resort was enhanced by giving it the ability to make loans to member banks, secured to the satisfaction of the Federal Reserve Banks (q.v.); and the composition of the Board of Governors was amended.

Banking Act 1979. An Act under which the Bank of England (q.v.) supervises the banking system in the United Kingdom; institutions which accept deposits from the public must be authorised to do so and accept legal supervision, with the exception of bodies such as building societies. There are two kinds of authorisation: (1) The Bank may grant a licence to a deposit-taking business if satisfied that it is financially sound and competently managed. In 1984, there were 308 of these institutions; (2) The Bank may grant recognition to an institution as a bank, providing it has a high reputation and standing in the financial community, and provides either a wide range of banking services or highly specialised banking services. Only a 'recognised bank' may call itself a bank. In 1984, there were 290 recognised banks. The award of a licence or the grant of recognition is a matter for the judgment of the Bank of England (q.v.). The Act also set up a Deposit Protection Fund to which recognised banks and licensed deposit-takers are required to contribute; if a contributor goes into liquidation, the Fund covers some of the losses. The powers and duties of the Bank under the Act apply to all U.K. banks and deposit-taking institutions, whether domestic or foreign-owned. *See* LICENSED DEPOSIT-TAKING INSTITUTIONS (U.K.).

Banking and Currency Schools. Following a series of banking crises during the period 1825–37, two schools of thought which developed on the best form of parliamentary intervention to control the issue of bank notes. The Currency School believed that strict measures were needed to restrict the note issues of the banks and that the entire note issue should be fully backed by gold. If a fiduciary issue (q.v.) was permitted, then it should be kept very small. The Banking School believed that the note issue should be flexible and made to suit the needs of business at any time. The Bank Charter Act of 1844 (q.v.) was a victory for the Currency School. Neither group at that time could foresee the future development of the cheque (q.v.) as a money medium much more flexible than bank notes.

Banking sector. Term used by official statisticians in Britain to describe a group of institutions whose balance sheets they consolidate as a preliminary to measuring the total stock of certain financial assets, notably the money stock, and monitoring the circulation of capital funds through the financial markets and financial intermediaries; the banking sector includes both private-sector and some government-owned institutions. The former include the deposit-taking banks, though not savings banks; along with the banks are also included the discount houses. The latter includes the Banking Department of the Bank of England (q.v.) and the National Girobank. After November, 1981, the term 'banking sector' tended to be superseded by a more widely defined 'monetary sector' (q.v.).

Banking system. A network of commercial banks co-ordinated, influenced and controlled by statutory regulation and a central bank. *See* AUSTRALIAN BANKING SYSTEM; BRITISH BANKING SYSTEM; CANADIAN BANKING SYSTEM; CENTRAL BANK; COMMERCIAL BANKS; FRENCH BANKING SYSTEM; ITALIAN BANKING SYSTEM; UNITED STATES BANKING SYSTEM; WEST GERMAN BANKING SYSTEM.

Bargains. Deals done on the London Stock Exchange (q.v.). Every day, *The Times* and other newspapers print a list of 'bargains marked'. The term bargain does not imply 'cut-price'.

Barometric price leadership. *See* PRICE LEADERSHIP.

Barter tax avoidance systems. The exchange of goods and services between merchants, traders, and workers, in respect of which no record is kept and no tax is paid. Such direct exchanges may involve a points system of mutual obligations, expressed in monetary terms but without actual payment.

Base drift. Descriptive of a problem when the money supply of a country grows beyond its nominated ceiling.

The choice lies in planning from the higher finishing point, or so scaling down the permitted increase in the second period that over two years the overall intended growth target is achieved.

Base rate. Usually, the basic rate for lending by a bank.

'Basic' balance of payments. That part of a nation's balance of payments (q.v.) covering the balance on current account and long-term capital flows. It excludes often volatile short-term capital movements, thus being a better indicator of a nation's fundamental balance-of-payments position.

Basis. The price difference between the actual or spot commodity and the futures market.

Basis grade. The specified grade or grades of a commodity named in the futures contract of an exchange; other grades than this are tenderable, but at a price differentiation from the basis, or 'contract grade'.

Basis point. One gradation on a 100-point scale representing 1 per cent; used especially in expressing variations in the yields of bonds. Fixed income yields vary often and the basis point scale easily expresses these changes in hundredths of 1 per cent. For example, the difference between 12.83 per cent and 12.88 per cent is five basis points.

Basle Concordate on Banking Supervision. An agreement first drawn up in 1975, in the wake of the Herstatt Bank collapse, by the Bank for International Settlements (q.v.) to improve the supervision and monitoring of banking operations; it is the only international pact in respect of banking supervision.

Bear. A person who, believing prices are about to fall, sells shares in the hope of buying them back again at a lower price thus making a profit. If the bear does not possess the securities he sells he is said to have 'sold short'; to complete his manoeuvre he must purchase them again within the same account period. If a bear does possess the securities he sells, he is known as a 'protected' or 'covered' bear. *See* BACKWARDATION; BULL; CONTANGO.

Bear covering. The act of buying back a speculative short position on a steady or rising market, despite the original intention to await a market decline.

Bear market. A market in which prices are falling.

Bear spread. A market strategy involving buying a nearby contract and selling a deferred contract, to take advantage of a weakening market. In a declining market, the deferred month contract will usually fall in price faster than those expiring earlier.

Bear straddle. In futures markets, selling nearby months while buying distant months. *See* BULL STRADDLE.

Bearer stocks or bonds. Securities (q.v.) the ownership of which can pass from one person to another without formal deed of transfer (q.v.) or re-registration of ownership by the company concerned.

Bearish and bullish. Descriptive of contrasting market situations; when conditions suggest lower prices a bearish situation is said to exist, while if higher prices appear warranted the situation is said to be bullish.

Bed and breakfast (U.K.). Descriptive of stock purchased and held overnight only, before resale.

Beggar-my-neighbour policies. In international trade, national policies which attempt to secure an advantage, usually temporary, at the expense of other nations; the effect is often to invite retaliation.

Behavioural theory of the firm. *See* PROFIT MAXIMISATION.

Beneficial owner. The ultimate owner of a security, regardless of the name in which it is legally registered. *See* SECURITIES.

Benefit-cost analysis. *See* COST-BENEFIT ANALYSIS.

Benefits, social. *See* SOCIAL BENEFITS.

Benelux. A customs union established between Belgium, Luxembourg and the Netherlands in successive stages between 1944 and 1948. The purpose of the union was to abolish tariff duties within the union and to apply a common tariff to imports from other countries. A final treaty of economic union was ratified in 1960. Belgium, Luxembourg and the Netherlands are members of the European Economic Community (q.v.). On 1 July 1968, the common external tariff of the European Economic Community replaced the separate Benelux tariff.

Beta factor. A measure of the historical volatility of a particular stock or group of stocks; the beta factor for the market as a whole is 1.0. If a stock has a high beta factor (exceeding 1.0) this means that in the past the stock has been, on average, more volatile than the market as a whole. If a certain stock has a beta factor of 1.1, this means that the stock has tended to move in the past in the same direction as the whole market, but that the magnitude of this movement averaged about 10 per cent more than the market's movement. Beta factors may be, of course, less than 1.0. By weighting the beta factors of shares in a portfolio, a beta factor for the whole portfolio may be calculated. The beta factor is a guide to probable future behaviour.

Bid. (a) On the stock exchange (q.v.), the price at which a person is prepared to buy the securities concerned; the lower of the two prices quoted by a stockjobber (q.v.). (b) On the commodity markets, an offer to buy a definite quantity of a commodity at the (bid) price stated; usually the offer is subject to immediate acceptance.

Bid and asked. Often referred to as a quotation or quote, the bid is the highest price anyone has declared that he or she is prepared to pay for a security at a given time, while the asked is the lowest price anyone will take at the same time.

Bid-filing. After a contract has been allotted, an arrangement whereby firms who competed for the contract notify a central agency of the prices submitted on tender. These prices are subsequently circulated to all members of the agency.

Big board. The display of the New York Stock Exchange on which the shares of more than 1,550 business corporations are listed; also a synonym for the New York Stock Exchange (q.v.) itself.

'Big Four', The. Barclays, Lloyds, Midland, and the National Westminster Banks.

Big Seven, The. *See* WILLIAMSBURG ECONOMIC SUMMIT.

Bilateral exchange rate. A conventional concept of a currency exchange rate, such as the dollar price of sterling, yen, or Deutsche marks.

Bilateral monopoly. A market structure (q.v.) in which single seller faces a single buyer.

Bilateral oligopoly. A market situation in which a few sellers confront a few buyers.

Bilateral trade. Trade between two countries; strictly interpreted the value of the goods and services exported by country A to country B must be exactly matched by the value of the exports from country B to country A. The development of bilateral, as distinct from multilateral, trade dates largely from the Great Depression (1929–35) (q.v.). In the post-war years it has tended to recede with increasing efforts to remove barriers to international trade by commercial treaties such as the General Agreement on Tariffs and Trade (q.v.).

Bill Finance (U.K.). Bills of exchange widely used to finance both exports and imports, and also to provide working capital. Bills can be offered as security for an advance. They are traditionally for 90 or 91 days, but are often for 30 days. They may also be for as long as 180 days. It is possible to use them for the settlement of any suitable commercial transaction between two parties, provided the definition expressed in the Bills of Exchange Act is followed in drawing up documents. Most banks can advise how to draw up a bill, and the discount houses are specialists in this field. There are two main types of bill: trade bills and bank bills. *See* BANK BILL; BILL OF EXCHANGE; TRADE BILL.

Bill of exchange (U.K.). Defined by the Bills of Exchange Act 1882 as 'an unconditional order in writing addressed by one person (the drawer) to another (the drawee), signed by the person giving it, requiring the person to whom it is addressed to pay on demand, or at a fixed or determinable future time, a sum certain in money to, or to the order of, a specified person or to bearer'. The ownership of a bill of exchange payable to bearer passes with delivery, and that of a bill made payable to a specified person by that person's signature on the back of the bill (legally known as an indorsement), and delivery.

Delivery of a bill transfers all legal rights; this attribute makes a bill of exchange a negotiable instrument. A purchaser may buy bills of exchange without having to register ownership of the bills, as would be necessary in the case of, for example, gilt-edged stocks.

Bills that are drawn by commercial companies are known as commercial bills. Typical self-liquidating bill transactions include the finance of exports prior to payment by the foreign importer, and the finance of raw materials whilst they are being manufactured into finished products and sold.

After a bill of exchange has been written by the drawer it must be presented to the drawee for acceptance. In accepting the bill by signing the face of the bill, the drawee affirms that he will pay the bill on maturity. If the drawee is a bank, the bill is known as a bank bill (in contrast to a trade bill drawn by one trader on another). An arrangement to draw bills on a bank is known as an acceptance credit facility. On the maturity of the bill the bank will pay the holder of it and debit the customer's account.

Following the acceptance of a bill it is returned to the drawer who can sell it in order to obtain funds immediately rather than wait until its maturity. The bill will be sold at below its maturity value; this difference is expressed as a percentage of the maturity value known as the discount rate. The principal purchasers of bills are banks and discount houses; there is also a market for bills outside the banking system. In the course of money market intervention, the Issue Department of the Bank of England (q.v.) will purchase bills from the discount houses, but will only purchase commercial bills that have been accepted by a bank that is on its list of recognised banks whose bills are eligible for discount at the Bank of England. In 1982, there were 103 such banks. *See* CHEQUE.

B.I.S. The Bank for International Settlements (q.v.).

Black economy. *See* CASH ECONOMY.

Blackboard trading. A form of trading used on exchanges such as the Chicago Mercantile Exchange (q.v.) for commodities sold in relatively small quantities. Prospective buyers place their bids on the buying side of the board, while sellers place their offers on the offering side of the board for the appropriate contract months. If and when a bid is sold or an offer bought, the action is posted on a sales panel and becomes a binding futures contract. If at any time trading becomes very heavy, dealings are immediately transferred by Exchange officials to the appropriate pit where pit trading (q.v.) rules apply automatically; in this event all board-posted bids and offers become null and void.

Block trading. Trading involving blocks of 10,000 or more shares in a single transaction; block trading is now a major force in the securities industry. These massive trades often account for half the volume of business on exchanges. Such heavy trading is engaged in by corporations, banks, insurance companies, and pension funds.

'Blown up' price. Descriptive of the final price of a good following a rise in the price of basic materials and fuel; the effect of the rise is passed through the various stages of production into the final price with an exaggerated impact—it becomes 'blown up' on the way by a succession of percentage additions to prime costs amounting to an increase in cash margins at each stage. This mechanism illustrates that a rise in commodity prices (which are demand-determined) can have a very powerful inflationary effect operating on the cost side (industrial prices often being cost-determined).

'Blue Button'. An Unauthorised Clerk on the floor of The London Stock Exchange (q.v.).

Blue chip. High class industrial share; originally an American term, derived from the highest valued chip used in poker.

Blue chip rate. The lowest interest rate payable by borrowers having the highest credit rating (q.v.). The rate may be only one-half to 1 per cent above base rate.

Blue sky laws. A popular description for laws enacted in various States of the United States of America intended to protect the public against security frauds. The term is thought to have originated when a judge ruled that a particular stock had about the same value as 'a patch of blue sky'.

Blue sky prices. Booming prices in real estate, which present to the vendors a clear, blue, and unclouded sky of unrestrained prosperity. Late in 1982, however, an Australian newspaper carried the headline: 'Blue sky prices disappear and quick sales are rare'.

Bodgies. Individuals and teams who engage in work contracts on a cash only basis; they may work under 'bodgie' or false names. *See* CASH ECONOMY.

Body hire. A system in which workers, particularly labourers, are recruited at unofficial pick-up points in the early hours of the morning by labour supply firms which deliver them to various sites; the workers are paid in cash only without records or tax payments, and are encouraged to stay on unemployment relief. No provision is made for workers' compensation, sick pay, vacation pay, annual loading, long-service leave, public holidays, or wet weather. *See* CASH ECONOMY.

Boiler room (U.S.). A room lined with desks or cubicles, each with a telephone, containing salesmen engaging in high-pressure peddling over the telephone of company stocks and shares of dubious value.

Bolton Committee. A committee of inquiry set up by the Board of Trade in 1968, under the chairmanship of Mr. John Bolton to examine and report on the role of small firms in the British economy. The committee reported that there were one-and-a-quarter million small firms in Britain contributing some 24 per cent of the net output of the private sector, or 19 per cent of the Gross National Product (q.v.); the small-firm sector was in secular decline, however, both in the number of firms and in respect of its share of economic activity. The decline in the small-firm sector was considered to be due to increasing taxation, the increasing role of the state, the emergence of the large corporation, improved transport and communication, changes in techniques, and the growing importance of marketing economies. As a result of a recommendation of the Committee, a small-firms division was established in the Department of Trade and Industry to monitor the well-being of the small-firm sector.

Bond. A debt instrument, representing a financial claim that the holder (or creditor) has against the issuer (or debtor); it is a written promise to pay a certain sum of money (known as the principal) at a definite date in the future or in a prescribed manner over the period of the loan. Usually, the issuer promises to pay the holder a fixed rate of interest on specified dates. Bonds are issued by governments, public bodies, corporations and companies; the terms of repayment are usually printed upon the bond. A bond may be secured or unsecured, and the date of maturity varies considerably though usually the minimum period is 10 years. Some bonds are undated and irredeemable. *See* CORPORATION BOND; STATE AND LOCAL GOVERNMENT BONDS; SECURITIES; TREASURY SECURITIES.

Bond rating agencies. Private business firms that provide informed and considered judgments on the quality of corporate, municipal and other bonds for those interested in the merits of particular issues. Ratings are essentially a ranking of bond issues according to the probability of default, i.e. the likely failure of the issuing body to meet interest or sinking fund payments or repay the principal on maturity. The credibility of the rating organisations depends in substantial part on their independence from external pressures. As part of this, agencies must not engage in the market or be connected with investors or issues.

The first rating agency in the United States was that of John Moody who included security ratings in his 1909 *Analyses of Railroad Investments*. Moody's today undertakes the rating of over 1,300 corporate bonds and over 15,000 municipal bonds. Standard and Poor began rating corporate bonds in 1923 and municipal bonds in 1940; today the company undertakes the rating of over 1,700 corporation bonds and over 8,000 municipal bonds. Moody's and Standard and Poor's rating categories are similar. A triple A rating (Moody's Aaa, Standard and Poor's AAA) signifies the highest quality bonds, the issues having only the remotest prospect of not meeting their obligations. *See* STANDARD AND POOR'S INDEXES.

Bond-stock ratio. A Wall Street measure of equity value by comparing bond yields with corporate earnings yields. In December, 1983, the ratio reached a peak of 1.50, the highest since 1926; this was taken to mean that equities had become overvalued relative to the corporation bond (q.v.).

Bonded warehouse. Warehouse in which dutiable articles may be stored without previously paying duty. Thus, if the goods are re-exported, the duty need not be paid at all. On the other hand, if goods are removed to be consumed in the country, i.e. taken out of bond, duties are then payable.

Bonus issue. *See* SCRIP OR BONUS ISSUE.

Bonus-penalty contract. A type of contract under which the contractor is guaranteed a bonus, usually a fixed sum of money, for each day the project he has undertaken to construct is completed ahead of a specified date, while he agrees to pay a penalty for each day of delay in completing the works after the specified date.

Boom. A period of expansion of business activity. Opposite of slump or recession. A boom reaches a peak when the economy is working at full capacity.

Borrowing. On a commodities exchange, buying a commodity for a nearby date and simultaneously selling a date further forward.

'Borrowing short to lend long'. Incurring short-term liabilities to purchase long-term assets.

Boston Stock Exchange. A U.S. regional exchange, providing facilities for trading in the equity securities of over 800 national and international corporations; the exchange has about 200 members representing specialist firms, and regional and national retail firms. The trading floor consists of 72 posts where specialists maintain continuous markets in assigned securities. The Exchange is controlled by a 22-member Board of Governors, elected by the membership. The exchange is small compared with other regional exchanges and has had a history of difficulties; however, 1984 witnessed a resurgence assisted by block trading (q.v.).

Bottom-of-the-harbour tax avoidance schemes. Tax avoidance schemes as developed in Australia (the harbour is Sydney Harbour), whereby smart business operators sell companies, strip the assets, fail to pay outstanding taxation debts, and then transfer ownership of what is left to an unsuspecting buyer or to a person paid to take over the property. Some thousands of companies went to the bottom-of-the-harbour, finishing in the possession of derelicts, druggies, and the mentally backward. Between 1972 and 1982 immense fortunes were made in Australia by these tactics, and a new breed of accountant emerged: the tax avoidance consultant. In 1982, the Australian Government began to consider whether steps could be taken against the powerful and influential elements involved in these gigantic schemes. A report by investigators Patrick McCabe and David Lafranchi was made to the Victorian Government in November, 1981, which stated that more than 900 companies had been sold to a particular group, that the companies had not paid any tax, and that all of them had been sent to the bottom-of-the-harbour during the 5 years 1973 to 1978. In all cases the companies' shells had finished up with sham directors; the sham directors included a number of pensioners and unemployed people who had no hope of ever being able to pay the tax owed by the companies. As a result of the sales the companies were dumped and the taxation liability avoided or evaded. The consequential loss of revenue to the Australian (federal) Government was massive, the report stated.

Bought deal. Descriptive of an arrangement whereby a securities house with a strong selling network and a great deal of capital applies for and obtains the privilege of buying and distributing a whole new issue of shares. *See* INVESTMENT BANK; SHELF REGISTRATION.

Bourse. The name of the Paris stock exchange, but also a generic name for all stock exchanges. *See* STOCK EXCHANGE.

Boutiques. Specialised brokers' offices or specialist financial institutions offering services such as research, corporate finance advice, and investment counselling.

Branch banking. A feature of the British and Australian banking systems in that relatively few large banks maintain a large number of branch banks throughout the country. In Britain there are over 14,000 branches. Branch banking has shown considerable development in the United States of America in recent years, but the basic pattern is one of a very large number of banks each possessing only a very small number of branches. The United States still possesses over 14,000 separate banks. Almost 6,000 banks are members of the Federal Reserve System; of these 4,700 are national banks and the remainder State banks. *See* COMMERCIAL BANKS.

Brandt Commission. A commission set up in 1977 at the instigation, among others, of the World Bank (q.v.); the 20 members were drawn from rich northern industrial countries, oil producers, and the poor south. The purpose of the Commission was to recommend an emergency programme in respect of international imbalances and longer-term reforms. The 1980 report of the Commission, *North-South: A Programme for Survival*, envisaged a large transfer of resources to the less developed countries to reach 0.7 per cent of the rich countries' G.N.P. by 1985, and 1.0 per cent by 2000, together with increased lending by the World Bank and other measures; a global food programme in the form of aid to agriculture and larger food stocks; and major reforms in the international economic system. The report proposed a new institution – A World Development Fund – with universal taxes flowing into its coffers.

Break. A sharp decline in prices on a stock or commodity exchange.

Break-even analysis. Analysis undertaken by a business to establish the point at which the volume of sales yields revenues equal to the total expenses of the business; at that point profit (and loss) is zero. The calculations take account of the fixed costs (costs that do not vary with output) and the contributing margin per unit of sale, being the selling cost minus the variable costs (costs that vary directly with output). Break-even charts represent linear approximations of costs and revenues; as projections, they assume sellings prices and costs over a range of output not yet tested. *See* FIGURE 1.

Bretton Woods Agreement. An agreed statement of aims for post-war monetary policy which resulted from an international monetary and financial conference held at Bretton Woods, New Hampshire, U.S.A., in July, 1944.

These aims were:

(a) to make all currencies freely convertible and thereby encourage multi-lateral trade;
(b) to keep exchange rates stable; and
(c) to provide some means of assisting a country with temporary difficulties with its balance of payments (q.v.).

It was recognised that during the immediate post-war years a degree of exchange control would have to be accepted. A direct result of the Agreement was the creation of two institutions, the International Monetary Fund (q.v.) and the International Bank for Reconstruction and Development (q.v.). The Bretton Woods Agreement was essentially a compromise between two plans, one advanced by Lord Keynes of the British Treasury and the other by Mr. White of the American Treasury.

The Bretton Woods Agreement tended to operate under strain. The system envisaged a change in exchange rates only when a fundamental disequilibrium had become apparent after the use of stop-gap measures. By then the fundamental disequilibrium would be clear to all, and the known direction of the prospective change in the exchange rate offered ample scope for profitable speculation.

On 15 August 1971, the Bretton Woods system effectively collapsed with the Nixon Administration decision to suspend the convertibility of the dollar into gold. *See* ADJUSTABLE PEG SYSTEM.

British banking system. *See* BANK OF ENGLAND; BANKING ACT 1979; 'BIG FOUR'; BRANCH BANKING; CLEARING BANKS; COMMERCIAL BANKS; DISCOUNT HOUSE; GIROSYSTEM; LENDER OF LAST REPORT; MERCHANT BANKS; MINIMUM LENDING RATE; NATIONAL SAVINGS BANK; OPEN MARKET OPERATIONS.

British Depository Receipt (B.D.R.). Introduced in 1984, with the consent of the U.S. Treasury, an instrument for the purchase of U.S. Treasury bonds which does not necessitate next day settlement in New York; the purchases may be settled in London, an easing of the previous situation.

British government stock or British Funds; issues of British government stock include the following:

$13\frac{1}{4}$% Exchequer Stock 1987
$6\frac{1}{2}$% Funding Stock 1985–1987
$7\frac{3}{4}$% Treasury Stock 1985–1988

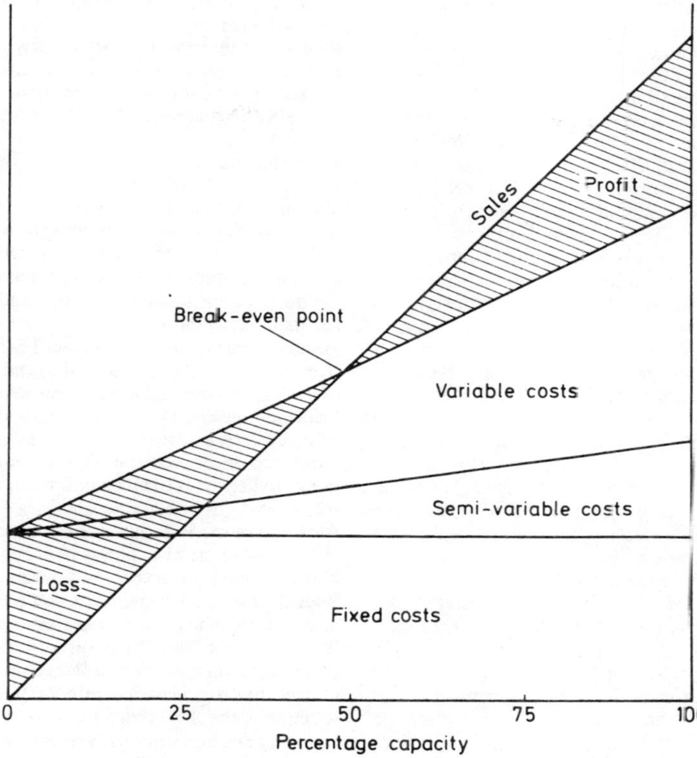

Figure 1 Break-even chart

2% Index-Linked Treasury Stock 1988
British Transport 3% Stock 1978–1988
10½% Treasury Stock 1989
5% Treasury Stock 1986–1989
13% Treasury Stock 1990
2% Index-Linked Treasury Stock 1990
8¼% Treasury Stock 1987–1990
11¾% Treasury Stock 1991
5¾% Funding Stock 1987–1991
12¼% Exchequer Stock 1992
13½% Exchequer Stock 1992
6% Funding Stock 1993
13¾% Treasury Stock 1993
14½% Treasury Stock 1994
9% Treasury Stock 1994
12% Treasury Stock 1995
12¾% Treasury Stock 1995
9% Treasury Stock 1992–1996
15¼% Treasury Stock 1996
13¼% Exchequer Stock 1996
3% Redemption Stock 1986–1996
13¼% Treasury Stock 1997
8¾% Treasury Stock 1997
6¾% Treasury Stock 1995–1998
15½% Treasury Stock 1998
9½% Treasury Stock 1999
12¼% Exchequer Stock 1999
9% Conversion Stock 2000
13% Treasury Stock 2000
14% Treasury Stock 1998–2001
13¾% Treasury Stock 2000–2003
3½% Funding Stock 1999–2004
12½% Treasury Stock 2003–2005
2% Index-Linked Treasury Stock 2006
8% Treasury Stock 2002–2006
2½% Index-Linked Treasury Stock 2011
5½% Treasury Stock 2008–2012
7¾% Treasury Stock 2012–2015
2½% Index-Linked Treasury Stock 2016
4% Consols
3½% War Stock
3½% Conversion Stock

2½% Treasury Stock, 1975 or after
2½% Consols } *Dividends paid quarterly*
2½% Annuities
2¾% Annuities

See GILT-EDGED STOCK.

British Steel Corporation. A public corporation formed on 27 April 1967, to implement the Iron and Steel Act 1967, and assume ownership and control of fourteen major British steel companies and their subsidiaries. The aims of the corporation are: (a) to strengthen the marketing and technological position of the nationalised steel industry as a whole; (b) to provide British industry with products that are competitive in price, quality and service; and (c) to ensure the efficient and socially responsible use of human resources. The corporation intends to retain substantial planning and policy-making authority at the centre, while allowing the four groups into which the industry is divided the greatest degree of operating autonomy. A common system of pricing is maintained throughout the nationalised steel industry, although the groups compete with each other on costs, service, quality and productivity.

British Steel Corporation (Industry) Ltd. Formed by the British Steel Corporation (B.S.C.) (q.v.) specifically to help create jobs in the areas of the main steel closures. It can provide advice and certain incentives itself, in addition to the regional assistance available from the Government and local authorities and to financial aid from the European Coal and Steel Community. At some of the closure sites it provides workshops in converted B.S.C. buildings which are suitable for very small businesses.

British Technology Group (B.T.G.). Formed in 1981, to combine the work of the National Enterprise Board (N.E.B.) (q.v.) and the National Research and Development Corporation (N.R.D.C.) (q.v.).

British Telecommunications Act 1981. Legislation which finally separated the British Post Office from British Telecom. The Act also opened the way for the licensing of private consortia to run commercial networks offering the business community high speed transmission services.

British Transport Commission. A body set up in 1947 to take over and control the railways, docks and inland waterways, road transport, London transport, and hotels owned and operated by the railways. The Transport Act 1962 replaced the Commission by four Boards – the British Railways Board, the London Transport Board, the British Waterways Board and the British Transport Docks Board.

Broker. An intermediary between two or more persons engaged in a business transaction. Brokers include import brokers, issue brokers, insurance brokers and stockbrokers. *See* STOCKBROKER.

Brokerage. Commission charged by a broker for selling or buying shares, commodities or insurance on behalf of a client.

Broker-trader. A firm or organisation which is a member of the London International Financial Futures Exchange (q.v.) and acts in the dual role of broker (q.v.) and trader (q.v.) for its own account.

Brokers' loans. Money borrowed by brokers from banks or other brokers; the funds may be used by specialists to finance stock inventories, by brokerage firms to finance the underwriting of new issues of securities, or to help finance the purchase of securities for customers who prefer to use the broker's credit when they buy securities.

Buddy gangs. Self-employed workers who work from home but operate in groups, e.g. as building sub-contractors or 'subbies'.

Budget and Accounting Act 1921. An Act which established the Bureau of the Budget (q.v.) to assist the President of the United States in the preparation of the annual federal budget and to conduct administrative studies to enable the President to achieve greater economy and efficiency in the executive branch of government. The Budget and Accounting Procedures Act 1950 amplified the basic Act by providing for a performance budget, improved administration of executive agencies, integration of statistical activities, and a continuous program for the improvement of accounting and financial reporting throughout the United States Government.

Budget deficit. An excess of government expenditures over revenues; a negative budget surplus. The size of a budget deficit (or surplus) is affected by the government's fiscal policy variables, e.g. government investments and purchases, transfer payments, and direct and indirect tax rates. A deficit may be allowed to expand as a means of boosting demand and stimulating the economy in a time of recession.

By the end of 1982, Britain's budget deficit was about 2 per cent of gross domestic product (q.v.), compared with Canada's 6.4 per cent, and West Germany's 4.1 per cent.

Buffer stocks. Stocks of raw materials and commodities held for the purpose of reducing fluctuations in the prices of primary products. Buffer stocks may be used to match the supplies coming on to a market with the current demand in order to narrow the movement of prices. Usually a 'ceiling' and a 'floor' price is fixed for a commodity; when the floor price is reached stocks are increased. Such schemes, which are generally international in scope, are only suitable for commodities which can be stored cheaply and with little risk of deterioration. Schemes in the past have been run solely for the benefit of producers, but the larger schemes now provide for consumer representation.

Nicholas Kaldor (b. 1908) has argued strongly that the most promising line of action for introducing greater stability into the world economy would be to create international buffer stocks for all the main commodities, and to link the finance of these stocks directly to the issue of international currency, such as SDRs, which could thus be backed by, and directly convertible into, major commodities comprising foodstuffs, fibres and metals. The very existence of these buffer stocks over a sufficiently wide range of commodities would, he has asserted, provide a powerful self-regulating mechanism for promoting growth and stability in the world economy.

Bufferstock facility. A facility extended by the International Monetary Fund (q.v.) for the purposes of providing loans for countries wanting to finance commodity stocks. Only SDR 79 million was borrowed between 1974 and 1980.

Building society. A society which is a source for the provision of long-term loans on the security of houses and land, and a channel for the investment of small personal savings; the building society in Britain enables large numbers of people to buy their own houses. Building societies are regulated by the Building Societies Act 1962; over three hundred societies are members of the Building Societies Association. The investment facilities offered to the public take the form of 'shares' and 'deposits'. The shares are not dealt in on the stock exchange (q.v.) and carry a rate of interest which may be varied from time to time. In 1984, a government green paper proposed the granting of new powers to building societies to compete in the financial services industry.

Bull. A person, who believing prices will rise, buys shares with a view to selling them at a higher price. A 'tired' or 'stale bull' is a person who has made a purchase but has found no early opportunity to sell at a profit. *See* CONTANGO, CARRY OVER, CONTINUATION.

Bull market. A market in which prices are rising.

Bull spread. A market strategy of going short on a nearby month and long on a distant month. A bull spread is used when an investor is optimistic about the stock market; in a period of upward trending prices, the distant month contracts are likely to rise in price faster than those with earlier expiration dates.

Bull straddle. In futures markets, buying nearby months while selling distant months. *See* BEAR STRADDLE.

Bulldog bond. A fixed-interest security denominated in sterling and issued by a non-resident in the United Kingdom domestic fixed-interest market.

Bullet loan. A single-repayment loan with no amortisation; that is, a loan which is not paid off in instalments.

Bullion. Name given to gold and silver in bulk, whether in the form of bars or lumps of refined metal, or coins, medals or dust.

In Great Britain, until 1925, anyone taking gold bullion to the Royal Mint had the right to have it made into coins free of charge.

This right was abolished, but even up to 1931 anyone could still sell gold to the Bank of England (q.v.) at fixed prices.

Bullion market. A market in which gold bullion is bought and sold. The London bullion market comprises five firms of bullion brokers who meet daily to fix an official price; dealings are also carried on between banks and authorised dealers.

Buoyant. A stock or commodity market in which prices have a tendency to rise easily with a considerable show of strength.

Bureau of the Budget. A bureau created by the Federal Budget and Accounting Act of 1921; the Act provided the first comprehensive national budget system and gave the Bureau the authority 'to assemble, correlate, revise, reduce, or increase the requests for appropriations of the several departments or establishments'. The Act also safeguarded the President's role in the budget by forbidding Federal agencies to seek funds from Congress directly, except at legislative request. The Bureau was also authorised to make any detailed administrative studies which would help in 'securing greater economy and efficiency in the conduct of the public service'.

Business Council of Australia. A national business research and lobby group, formed in 1983, as a result of a merger of the Australian Industries Development Association and the Business Round Table. One purpose of the new body was to remove the fragmentation of industrial representation in Canberra, the seat of the federal government.

Business cycles. *See* JUGLAR CYCLE; KITCHIN CYCLE; KONDRATIEFF CYCLE; KUZNETS CYCLE; TRADE CYCLE.

Business Expansion Scheme (B.E.S.) (U.K.). Introduced in 1983, as a successor to the Business Start-Up Scheme, a means of assisting the flow of funds to businesses; investing in companies offers considerable tax benefits under the scheme. Investment must be held for 5 years.

Business finance. The provision of funds at the time they are needed to assist a business during an adverse period of lack of identity between payment and receipts; a situation particularly acute during the setting-up of a business when there there may be no receipts for a considerable period of time. The sources of finance, short-term and long-term, are as follows:

Short-term finance

(1) *Trade and consumer credit.* The purchase of supplies and materials on credit from other firms is a form of finance, the debts being recorded simply as 'accounts payable'.

(2) *Liquid financial assets.* A firm may increase its internal sources of finance by running down liquid financial assets accumulated during more profitable periods.

(3) *Invoice discounting* (q.v.).

(4) *Inventories review.* Inventories may be reviewed and selectively reduced to provide more internal finance.

(5) *Intercompany loans.* These may be arranged where there are several companies in the group.

(6) *Tax funds.* Funds set aside to meet future tax commitments may be tapped in the short-term.

(7) *Internal cash flow.* Accumulated internal funds arising from company cash flow may be available for immediate or early use. These retained profits ensure a certain self-financing ratio when a new project is launched.

(8) *Increased short-term debt.* The commercial banking system, finance houses, and U.S. Government agencies may provide additional short-term finance by way of lines of credit (q.v.), revolving credit agreements (q.v.) and term loans (q.v.).

(9) *commercial paper* (q.v.). Short-term unsecured promissory notes may be sold in the open market by the larger financial and non-financial corporations.

Long-term finance

(1) *Corporate bonds and mortgages.* The issue of corporate bonds has been a dominant source of long-term finance for manufacturing and public utility corporations. Mortgages have also been an important source of funds for financing real property acquisitions such as office buildings, shopping centres, and apartment blocks. *See* BOND; COMMON STOCK; DEBENTURES; ISSUING HOUSE; MORTGAGE BONDS; OFFER FOR SALE; PLACING; PREFERRED STOCK; PUBLIC ISSUE; RIGHTS ISSUE; SECURITIES; SHARE; STOCK EXCHANGE INTRODUCTION; STOCKS AND SHARES.

(2) *Euro-dollar financing.* Domestic financial markets may be augmented by external markets for dollar-designated loans. *See* EUROBONDS; EURO-DOLLARS.

(3) *Leasing arrangements.* Leasing is often used as a substitute for long-term financing. *See* FINANCE LEASE; LEASE-BACK AGREEMENT; LEASE LENDING; LEASING ARRANGEMENTS; LEASING COMPANIES; LEVERAGED LEASING; OPERATING LEASE; TAX BASED LEASE. *See also* HIRE PURCHASE.

(4) *Tax exempt financing.* Some forms of development project investment attract special tax concessions, which become a form of subsidy.

(5) *Redevelopment and relocation subsidies.* Some state governments offer special concessions and subsidies, many of a long-term nature, to attract industry to certain locations either for decentralization purposes or to achieve balanced development, or to boost a declining area.

(6) Socialization of losses (q.v.).

Butterfly straddle. A sophisticated form of transaction, used especially in the U.S. treasury bill and silver futures markets, involving taking simultaneous and identical long and short positions in contracts of different months. There are many permutations. The ideal butterfly straddle gives the investor a capital gain in six months on his long position and a loss by covering his short position. The short-term loss can be used as a direct offset against income for tax purposes.

Buy back. An offsetting purchase to cover or liquidate a short sale. *See* SHORT.

Buy in. To cover, offset, or close out a short position.

Buy on close. An instruction to buy at the end of the trading session of an exchange at a price within the closing range.

Buy on opening. An instruction to buy at the beginning of a trading session on an exchange at a price within the opening range.

Buy-out financing. *See* LEVERAGED BUY-OUTS.
Buy-outs. Company acquisition by staff or management who often raise finance by way of a co-operative scheme.
Buy stop. *See* STOP ORDER.
Buyers' market. A market in which producers, suppliers and dealers experience difficulty in selling the goods which are available.
Buying hedge or long hedge, a hedging transaction in which futures contracts (q.v.) are bought to provide protection against the possible increased cost of commodities.
Buying-in. (a) In respect of currency, the buying by a government of its own currency in order to maintain its international value; (b) A procedure adopted by the Stock Exchange to assist a seller who is unable at the due date to deliver shares sold, by buying an equivalent amount of stock in the market, charging the cost and extra expenses to the seller.

C

Calendar spread. *See* OPTION SPREAD.

Call loan. A loan which may be terminated or 'called' at any time by the lender or borrower.

Call option. An option (q.v.) in which the buyer (taker) acquires the right to sell a futures contract at a basis (or strike) price agreed at the time of concluding the contract. The buyer pays the seller (granter) a premium for this.

Call, to. To buy.

Callable. A bond issue, all or part of which may be redeemed by the issuing corporation under specified conditions before maturity; the term also applies to preferred shares that may be redeemed by the issuing corporation.

Callable preferred stock (U.S.). Preferred stock (q.v.) which can be called in for payment at a stated price.

Calls. Instalment payments on new shares. A company does not necessarily require immediately the full amount on the shares it has issued, and may instead call-up the additional capital as it requires it.

Cambridge School or neo-Keynesian school. A convenient description for a body of influential economists centred at the University of Cambridge, England, who were deeply involved in the Keynesian Revolution (q.v.) of the 1930s or in the development of Keynes' basic ideas. The school has been associated with the names of Joan Robinson, Nicholas Kaldor, Luigi Pasinetti, and Piero Sraffa. Also important in the work of the neo-Keynesian economists has been the Polish economist, Michel Kalecki. Although the views of the school tend themselves to be somewhat discordant, the main body of opinion interprets Keynes differently to orthodox Keynesians. While stagflation (q.v.) has tended to undermine orthodox Keynesianism, the neo-Keynesians claim a solution to this, favouring, in addition to fiscal policies, an incomes policy to curb price inflation (q.v.). The quantity of money is not regarded as a strategic factor in policy, as it is in monetarism (q.v.). The neo-Keynesians have developed a macro-economic theory of income distribution, in marked contrast to the neo-classical micro-economic theory of income distribution. Investment is regarded as a strategic element in the distribution of income between wages and profits, the 'degree of monopoly' directly affecting income distribution. The neo-Keynesians have much in common with the classical economist David Ricardo (1772–1823) and with the socialist Karl Marx (1818–1883); hence they are sometimes referred to as the neo-Ricardian or neo-Marxian school. *See* NEO-CLASSICAL ECONOMICS; SCHOOLS OF ECONOMICS.

Cambridge theory of money. A 'cash balance' form of the quantity theory of money (q.v.) developed by Cambridge economists such as Marshall, Pigou, and Robertson (the early Cambridge School) and contained in the equation:

$$M = kPT$$

where M = the amount of money (bank notes, etc. plus bank deposits); k = the reciprocal of the velocity of circulation; P = the general price level; and T = the value of output. If the velocity of circulation of money is four times in a given period, then k is one-quarter of expenditure; k is the proportion of the community's expenditure on goods and services which on average is held as cash during the period. There are no fundamental differences between Fisher's quantity theory of money and the Cambridge theory of money, but the 'cash balance' approach emphasises that changes in the demand for money (k) may be as important as the quantity of money (M) in determining the general price level (P). The influences determining the general level of prices are more complex than both forms of the quantity theory envisaged. *See* LIQUIDITY PREFERENCE; SCHOOLS OF ECONOMICS.

Campbell Report (Aust.). The report of the

Committee of Inquiry into the Australian Financial System, chaired by Mr. Keith Campbell, which was released in 1981. The key recommendation of the Committee was that interest rates should be totally deregulated and left to be determined by market forces. A less-controlled, more competitive future, was envisaged for the banking sector. Participation in the banking system would be open to anyone, foreign or domestic, who could fulfil the appropriate requirements. Areas which would remain the monopoly of the banks would be the cheque issuing facility and foreign exchange; banks would have to maintain a reserve asset ratio and subsidiaries would be consolidated to form banking groups. Non-bank financial institutions would find themselves facing much greater competition. Banks would be enabled to pay interest on current accounts, thus opening up a battle to attract small dollar depositors. There would be a progressive but rapid move to a free exchange market; exchange controls should be largely abolished. Financial institutions that did not perform would be allowed to fail.

Canadian Bank Act, 1980. Passed at the end of 1980, after a gestation period of 6 years, an Act intended to stimulate more competition among Canada's five large commercial chartered banks. Reserve requirements were reduced. The banks lost their traditional control of the cheque clearing system. The biggest change related to foreign banks, in being able to apply for the first time for federal bank charters.

Canadian banking system. A banking system consisting of a central bank (the Bank of Canada), together with commercial banks known as chartered banks, and various other savings and loans institutions. The central bank is responsible for regulating 'credit and currency in the best interests of the economic life of the nation'. The bank implements its monetary policy in part by varying the amount of cash reserves available to the banking system. The bank also acts as fiscal agent for the Government of Canada and has the sole right of issue of bank notes for circulation in Canada.

There are ten chartered banks incorporated under the provisions of the Bank Act with about 6,700 branches throughout Canada. The 'Big Five' chartered banks hold about 90 per cent of all banking assets and 60 per cent of all deposits. The bank charters expire and need renewal every 10 years. The statutory banks must maintain a statutory cash reserve in the form of reserves with the Bank of Canada; a secondary reserve in treasury bills and government bonds has also been required. The Canadian Bank Act 1980 was intended to stimulate more competition among the chartered banks, while reserve requirements were reduced. The banks lost their traditional control of the check clearing system. Foreign banks became able to apply, for the first time, for federal bank charters.

Canadian loan companies are savings banks that take deposits and make mortgage advances; in 1982, some 80 per cent of their business was in mortgages. There were then 33 federal loan companies, and 16 provincial loan companies.

Canadian trust companies also take deposits and make loans mainly in the form of first mortgages. In 1982, there were 32 federal trust companies, and 67 provincially chartered trust companies.

Canadian loan companies. Savings banks that take deposits and also make mortgage advances; in 1982, some 80 per cent of their business was in mortgages. There were 33 federal loan companies, and 16 provincial loan companies.

Canadian trust companies. Companies originally formed to handle trusts or estates which evolved into near-banks, taking deposits and making loans mainly in the form of first mortgages; commercial or personal loans exceeding 7 per cent of the trusts' assets have been forbidden. In 1982, there were 32 federal trust companies, and 67 provincially chartered trust companies.

Canons of taxation. *See* TAXATION, ADAM SMITH'S CANONS OF.

Capacity. The estimated maximum level of production from a plant on a sustained basis, allowing for all necessary shut-downs, holidays, etc.

Cape scrip. Union of South Africa shares.

Capital. One of the factors of production (q.v.) and may be defined as 'wealth used for the production of further wealth', or simply a commodity used in the production or other goods and services, e.g. such as plant or equipment. It represents current consumption forgone in order to obtain future production and future consumption; it enhances the productivity of labour and land. Capital is described as 'real' when it consists of machines, factories, railways, stocks of raw materials, etc. Real capital may be subdivided into:

(a) *Fixed capital*—factories, warehouses, offices, shops, and other buildings used in industry and trade; plant and machinery and equipment; means of transport and communication;

(b) *Floating or circulating capital*—raw materials, fuel, goods in process of manufacture, stocks held by producers or traders. Alfred Marshall described circulating capital as 'fulfilling the whole of its office in the production in which it is engaged by a single use';

(c) *Specific capital*—equipment which cannot normally be used for any other purpose than that for which it was originally designed and constructed;

(d) *Non-specific capital*—equipment which can be used in a variety of processes.

The term 'capital' is commonly used for the money subscribed by shareholders or stockholders, or lent by banks, for use in a business. This is more correctly described as business finance, although Adam Smith argued that 'a person's capital is that part of his stock from which he expects to derive an income'.

Capital account. An element in the balance of payments (q.v.) account which deals with financial transactions, the buying and selling of securities, investment abroad and non-residents' investment in the U.K.

Capital accumulation. An increase in man-made equipment such as machinery, tools, buildings and other structures, and stocks of goods, used for or capable of being used for the production of goods and services.

Capital allowances. Deductions from gross business profits for the purpose of covering the depreciation of assets permitted by the tax authorities when calculating taxable income.

Capital – authorised, nominal or registered. Synonymous terms for capital fixed by the Memorandum of Association (q.v.) of a company.

Capital charges. Charges which include interest on the amount of capital employed, and provision for depreciation or repayment of principal.

Capital consumption. *See* CAPITAL FORMATION AND DEPRECIATION; DEPRECIATION.

Capital cost component. In relation to the total production cost of each unit of output, the capital cost component given by:

$$\frac{\text{Capital Charges}}{\text{Units of Output}}$$

where the capital charges are the sum of the annual interest charges on capital employed (q.v.) and the annual depreciation charges, and the units of output relate to the year under consideration.

Capital cost of. The cost of obtaining the total capital employed (q.v.) by a business, expressed as a rate of interest.

Capital employed. The capital in use in a business; it consists of the total assets *minus* the current liabilities. Current liabilities are those liabilities providing resources for less than a year; their exclusion helps avoid fluctuations in total assets which might otherwise impair comparisons based on several years' trading. *See* CAPITAL EMPLOYED, RETURN ON.

Capital employed, return on. The relating of profit to the estimate of average capital employed (q.v.) to give a ratio, commonly called the primary ratio, as follows:

$$\frac{\text{Profit}}{\text{Capital}}$$

It is essential that the long-run return on capital employed in a business should be sufficient to ensure a fair return to shareholders, provide for the normal expansion of the business, attract new capital when required and retain the confidence of creditors and employees.

Capital expenditure. Expenditure of a non-recurrent nature resulting in the acquisition of assets.

Capital formation and depreciation. Capital formation in a given time period is the expenditure on fixed capital assets (buildings, plant and machinery, vehicles, etc.) either for replacing or adding to the stock of fixed assets. Expenditure on repairs and maintenance is excluded. During a year fixed capital resources are also used up, or 'consumed', due to wear and tear, obsolescence, etc. Thus from the value of gross capital formation, there must be deducted the value of capital consumption or depreciation, thus leaving a value for net capital formation. *See* DEPRECIATION.

Capital gains. Profits made from the sale of investments or property, due allowance being made for any decline in the value of money during the period which elapsed between buying and selling.

Capital gains tax. A tax imposed by the Government on capital gains (q.v.). Previously untaxed in Britain, the Finance Act of 1962 introduced a short-term capital gains tax on the purchase and sale of property (including shares) excluding personal belongings and owner-occupied houses, if the sale took place less than six months after the purchase (three years in the case of land and buildings). In 1965, the law was extended to cover capital gains realised over any period of time, but with similar exceptions from the tax. In the early Seventies, the distinction between short-term and long-term capital gains tax was abolished.

Individuals are taxed at a flat rate of 30 per cent on gains over £3,000 a year (£1,000 prior to the 1980 budget); and trusts on gains over £1,500. Assets transferred at death are not subject to capital gains tax.

Capital gearing. The ratio of fixed interest capital including prior charges to ordinary share capital. If a company's capital contains a large proportion of fixed interest stocks, the company is described as 'highly-geared'. In these circumstances a small change in profits can make a large difference to the amount available for distribution to ordinary shareholders; yields may be well above or well below the average yield on the whole capital involved. *See* LEVERAGE (U.S.).

Capital goods. Goods made for the purpose of producing consumer goods (q.v.), and other capital goods, e.g. machinery of all kinds. Synonymous with 'producer goods'.

Capital growth, real. In financial investment markets, descriptive of a return to an investor by way of growth in capital value and income which, together, are greater than the negative effects of inflation and taxation; in the economy an increase in real assets or capital (q.v.) more than offsetting the depreciation of such assets.

Capital-intensive industry. Industry in which the ratio of capital input to labor input is higher than the average ratio for industry as a whole. The capital input may be measured by the depreciation costs of plant and equipment. Examples of capital intensive industries include petroleum refineries, chemical works, primary metal smelters, and open-cut mining. *See* LABOUR-INTENSIVE INDUSTRY.

Capital levies. Once-for-all capital taxes. Death duties (q.v.) are a form of capital levy.

Capital, marginal efficiency of. *See* MARGINAL EFFICIENCY OF CAPITAL.

Capital market. A market comprising institutions which deal in the purchase and sale of securities, e.g. the new issue market and the stock exchange (q.v.).

Capital market instruments. Financial instruments such as company shares and bonds, long-term government bonds (called 'gilts' in Britain), and local government bonds. These instruments may be bought and sold in a secondary market between the time they are issued (first sold in the primary market) and the time they mature. This gives them the important quality of liquidity.

Capital movement. The movement of money capital from one country to another. *See* HOT MONEY.

Capital-output ratio, incremental. For a given industrial technique, the ratio of the capital cost of the technique to the value added by the additional output. If the ratio is 3:1 then a £300 addition to capital equipment will yield a £100 increase in output per annum. Thus, if an economy invests 12 per cent of its income, and has a capital-output ratio of 3:1, it can expect a 4 per cent increase in output per annum.

Capital recovery. The process by which the original investment in a physical asset is recovered over its economic life. In the absence of inflation (q.v.), capital recovery is achieved through depreciation allowances.

Capital, risk. *See* RISK CAPITAL.

Capital, security. *See* SECURITY CAPITAL.

Capital, social. *See* SOCIAL CAPITAL.

Capital stock (U.S.). Shares in the proprietary interest in a corporation (q.v.).

Capital structure. The types and numbers of stocks and shares which are to be issued, or have been issued by a company.

Capital surplus (U.S.). The amount paid by stockholders in excess of the par value of each share.

Capital, theory of. An area of economic theory concerned with the analysis of the formation of capital, the role of inputs, the role of time and intertemporal planning, and the mechanism of resource allocation between consumption and investment. *See* CAPITAL; CAPITAL FORMATION AND DEPRECIATION; DISTRIBUTION.

Capital transactions. The lending or borrowing of sums of money, or the transfer of assets accumulated in the past.

Capital transfer tax, (U.K.). A tax designed to replace estate duty as a much more effective method of taxing large accumulations of wealth. It applies to lifetime transfers made after 26 March 1974, and to transfers on death on or after 13 March 1975. The tax applies broadly to all gratuitous transfers of personal wealth (or 'gifts') whether they take place during a person's lifetime or on his death. There is a lower scale of rates for lifetime transfers than for transfers on death. The rates on death are considerably lower than the old estate duty. Gifts and bequests to charities made a year or more before death are exempt without limit. Under the old estate duty, all wealth given away 7 years or more before death escaped all tax. Tax avoidance was also possible through the use of trusts. The effectiveness of estate duty was much reduced by these means. Under the new tax, there is a major change in that gifts between husband and wife in life and on death are exempt.

In 1982, the threshold at which capital transfer tax became payable, on gifts made during the donor's lifetime and on death, was £50,000.

Capitalisation. The total amount of the various securities issued by a company or corporation; it may include bonds, debentures, preferred and common stock.

Capitalisation issue. *See* SCRIP OR BONUS ISSUE.

Capitalisation of reserves. The process whereby money from a company's reserves is converted into issued capital, which is then distributed to shareholders as new shares, in proportion to their original holdings, in a capitalisation issue; also known as a free, or scrip or bonus issue of shares (q.v.).

Capitalisation ratios. The proportions of each kind of security issued by a company. *See* CAPITAL STRUCTURE.

Capitalised value. The capital equivalent of an annual payment. Capital values are determined by the rate of interest and the rent produced. Thus, if the prevailing rate of interest for investments is 10 per cent and a parcel of land has a rental of £5000, the capitalised value will be £50,000. If the rate of interest falls, then the capital value increases, the rent still being regarded as corresponding to the current rate of interest. If the site has prospects of development, however, the market value may greatly exceed the capitalised rental value.

Capitalism. A social system in which the means of production, distribution and exchange are wholly or substantially owned by private persons. *See* INDIVIDUALISM.

Capitalist development, Schumpeter's theory of. A theory developed by Professor J. A. Schumpeter (1883–1950); it starts out from the circular flow of economic life where producers and consumers all function in a state of equilibrium, all adjustments and adaptations having been made; into this circular flow Schumpeter introduces a shift in the production function (q.v.) which generates a sequence of alterations in the behaviour of the economic actors – bank credit expands and eventually a secondary wave of investment activity is imposed on top of the primary wave as the expectations of the enlarged business community are influenced by the evidence and by the consequences of business expansion.

Capitalist ethic. Descriptive of the sustaining drives of industrial development based upon private ownership of the means of production, distribution and exchange. The capitalist ethic sanctions and gives dignity to work; the quest for material success and the accumulation of wealth is applauded; respect and prestige are accorded to the successful. Idleness, waste and indifference are condemned. More broadly, there is a belief that multiple-centres of decision-making contribute to the health of society and constitute the soundest basis for stability, flexibility and progress, as well as for the development of creative and responsible individuals; these qualities are also regarded as the basis of political democracy. While economic planning by the state is recognised, it should not substitute authority for responsibility but provide a framework in which private initiative can be exercised. A contrary view of the capitalist ethic holds that the pursuit of profit as an end encourages exploitation of man by man and promotes bitter competition; hence anti-social qualities such as unscrupulousness, duplicity and the cult of force prosper. Karl Marx (1818–1883) described what he considered to be the weaknesses and evils of the capitalist system, arguing that a socialist economy would eliminate these features and avoid repeated economic crises. However, it is clear beyond reasonable doubt that other forms of society based on public ownership do not eliminate the less attractive features of human nature. *See* MARXIST SOCIALISM; SOCIALIST ECONOMICS.

Capitation tax. Also known as a poll tax, a tax levied on each member of the community equally irrespective of wealth or income.

Captive market. A market in which the supplier of a good or service is in a monopolistic position, the consumer being unable to obtain suitable substitutes or to do without. For many years, the gas industry, using no other raw material save coal, was a captive market for the National Coal Board (q.v.).

Car. A loose term used on commodity exchanges to describe a contract, e.g. 'a car of bellies'. The term is derived from the historical fact that the quantities specified in contracts used to correspond closely to the capacity of a railroad car.

Cargo cult. A belief among New Guinea natives that the spirits of ancestors will soon arrive bringing cargoes of food, tobacco, and other good things. The term finds occasional use in economic journalism; in a review of the year, the Australian Financial Review commented, 'Summing up 1982, it is clearly enough the year when the great cargo cult of the Australian resources boom was laid to rest'.

Caribbean Basin Initiative (C.B.I.). Adopted in 1982, a programme to assist Caribbean nations; an immediate grant of aid was dispensed to 8 Caribbean countries. The package also involved the removal of certain American import restrictions on goods from the

Caribbean region, and grants and credits for investment in the Caribbean. The programme has been described as a mini-Marshall Plan for the area; the principal partner has been the United States, but other members of the Caribbean Group for Co-operation and Economic Development (q.v.) have participated.

Caribbean Common Market (CARICOM). A free trade area based upon an agreement which came fully into effect in May, 1974; twelve territories, all former colonies of Great Britain, are members of the market. These are Antigua, Barbados, Belize, Dominica, Grenada, Guyana, Jamaica, Montserrat, St. Kitts, Nevis and Anguilla, St. Lucia, St. Vincent and Trinidad and Tobago. The objectives of the agreement are to promote the expansion and diversification of trade in the region, to encourage balanced and progressive economies in the area, and to eventually proceed towards political union. The total population of the CARICOM region is estimated at about 4.5 million.

Caribbean Group for Co-operation and Economic Development (C.G.C.E.D.). Established in the late 1970s, a body concerned with the economic development of the Caribbean; members include the European Economic Community (q.v.), Canada, Venezuela, Mexico, the United States of America, the International Monetary Fund (q.v.), the International Development Bank, the World Bank (q.v.), the United Nations Development Programme, and the Caribbean Development Bank. *See* CARIBBEAN BASIN INITIATIVE (C.B.I.).

Carrying. A general term used for both borrowing (q.v.) and lending (q.v.) on commodity futures markets.

Carrying charge. Charges associated with the storage of a commodity, e.g. warehouse charges, insurance and other incidentals often including an interest charge and estimated values in respect of the loss or gain in weight. A 'full carrying charge market' refers to a situation in the futures markets when the price differential between the futures months reflects the full costs of carrying the commodity.

Carry. The purchase of a commodity for delivery on a given date combined with the sale of an identical amount for delivery at a later date.

Cartel. An arrangement among formerly competing producers to charge the same or similar prices. It may or may not include an agreement to set up a central selling organisation, or to share out the market either geographically or by production quota. The members of a cartel agree, in effect, to operate as a monopoly. The Organisation of Petroleum Exporting Countries (O.P.E.C.) (q.v.) is an outstanding example of an oil cartel. The Queensland Sugar Industry is organised as a cartel by Queensland State Government legislation. Air fares for international travel are fixed by agreement through the International Air Transport Association, an agreement which includes sharing the market between national carriers. The European Economic Community has set up an iron and steel cartel, Eurofer (q.v.). The attitude of governments to cartels may vary from disapproval and positive measures to restore competition, to positive approval with active support.

Cash and carry. A market situation in which the contango (q.v.) may widen to the point where banking operations are attractive; funds may be invested by buying a cash commodity (q.v.) and simultaneously selling forward where, after costs, it yields better returns than the prevailing money markets.

Cash commodity. An actual physical product as distinguished from a 'future' commodity. *See* FUTURES CONTRACT.

Cash economy. A sector of the economy in which individual tradesmen, trade teams, or small builders, deal directly with customers for cash or cash cheques; customers may include other tradesmen, builders or subcontractors. The basic characteristic is payment in untraceable cash as a lump sum, sometimes by-passing union awards, and payroll and income taxation. These illicit aspects are referred to as the underground economy, hidden economy, black economy, or moonlight economy.

Cash flow. The passage of money into and out of a business enterprise. The term is used by American and Canadian companies to describe net earnings, plus depreciation and other allowances, expressed as an amount per share.

Cash generation. The net cash flow (q.v.) arising from an investment by a business enterprise, assuming this to be positive.

Cash in hand system. A system in which workers are paid on, say, an hourly basis for labour only, receiving cash in payment on which income tax has not or will not be paid; such payments may be received in conjunction with tax-free dole payments. *See* CASH ECONOMY.

Cash management systems. Sophisticated systems aiming to reduce the amount of money companies and corporations leave idly floating in low-earning accounts. *See* CASH MANAGEMENT TRUSTS.

Cash management trusts. Trusts which enable the smaller investor to use the short term money market (q.v.). By aggregating small deposits and purchasing money market instruments, these trusts have made it possible for small investors to earn a rate of interest comparable with that available to the major corporations and other participants.

Cash market. A market for the immediate delivery of, and payment for, commodities.

Cash price. The price in the market place for a cash commodity (q.v.) (or spot commodity) to be delivered through normal market channels.

Cash settlement. A procedure for settlement of contracts by automatic close-out at a cash price designated by the clearing house (q.v.) in futures markets which make no provision for delivery, e.g. U.S. dollars, All Ordinaries Share Price Index.

Cashless society. A society either so primitive that exchanges take place through barter alone; or so controlled that goods and services are provided on vouchers only; or so sophisticated through the use of credit cards and instant debiting that bank notes and cash become redundant. In the 1970s it became fashionable for Americans to proclaim that they had forgotten what money looked like; however, in reality, even in America, the displacement of cash for transactions still appears to be many steps beyond the horizon, and it may well be cheques that are eliminated.

Category three banks. Banks in the United States with 'operational weaknesses', yet with 'failure a remote possibility'. The Comptroller of Currency has a 'Richter Scale' of one to five in respect of bank performance and the need for support and regulation.

Census of population. An enumeration of inhabitants. A census of the population of the United Kingdom has been taken every tenth year since 1801, with the exception of 1941. From 1966 a census has been taken every 5 years. Estimates of population for the intervening years are made by the Registrar-General. The modern census is a means of obtaining a great deal of information about people, their occupations and their social conditions.

The last census was in April, 1981. It revealed that population growth over the decade had been very small, less that 0.25 per cent. Many large cities lost population, notably London (inner and outer), Glasgow, Liverpool, Manchester, Salford, Birmingham, Nottingham and Newcastle-upon-Tyne. Only one sizeable British town grew at all, Plymouth.

In the United States, the 20th enumeration of the nation's population was conducted in 1980. The decennial census revealed profound changes in the growth, distribution, and composition of the U.S. population and in the lifestyles of the American people. The census revealed that there were 226,504,825 persons residing in the United States on 1 April 1980; this represented an increase of 11.4 per cent over the number counted in 1970, although the rate of growth of population continued to decline.

Central bank. A bank which in any country is (a) banker to the Government, (b) banker to the commercial banks and (c) implements the currency and credit policy of the country. Examples of central banks are:

United Kingdom	Bank of England
France	Banque de France
West Germany	Deutsche Bundesbank
Italy	Banca d'Italia
Norway	Norges Bank
Sweden	Riksbank
Canada	Bank of Canada
U.S.A.	Federal Reserve Banks
Brazil	Banco Central da Republica do Brasil
U.S.S.R.	State Bank
China	People's Bank
Japan	Nippon Ginko
South Africa	Central Reserve Bank
Australia	Reserve Bank
New Zealand	Reserve Bank

Central banks are generally established by statute, are publicly accountable and usually publicly owned. They implement the monetary policy of the country in a broadly similar manner, e.g. by varying minimum ratios, requiring special deposits (q.v.), and providing the credit basis of the banking system. *See* BANK OF ENGLAND; FEDERAL RESERVE SYSTEM.

Central Electricity Generating Board (C.E.G.B.). Established under the Electricity Act of 1957, which reorganised the electricity supply industry, the Board's statutory responsibilities are 'to develop and maintain an efficient, co-ordinated and economical system of supply of electricity in bulk for all parts of England and Wales'. The Board undertakes the planning and construction of new generating and transmission capacity.

At the end of 1981, Britain had 65,000 MW of installed electricity generating equipment. Steam power accounted for 85 per cent of electricity generation, and nuclear power for 13 per cent. The industry consumed 110 million tonnes of coal equivalent. Eleven power stations had a capacity of 2,000 MW or more.

Central Gilts Office Service (U.K.). A computer based transfer and settlement system developed by the Bank of England (q.v.) and The London Stock Exchange (q.v.). A statutory basis for the service was provided in the Stock Transfer Act 1982.

Certificate of deposit (C.D.). Introduced in 1961 by Citibank, New York's largest bank, a fixed-term deposit which can be bought and sold in a secondary market. C.D.s are only available in large denominations. A similar sterling instrument was created in London in 1968.

Certified stocks or certified supplies. Those supplies of commodities which have been approved as deliverable grades. Such gradings hold good for a specified period of time and perhaps in some cases indefinitely. They are stored at delivery points designated as 'regular' or 'acceptable for delivery' by the appropriate commodity exchange.

Ceteris Paribus. 'Other things being equal', i.e. the holding of other factors constant. That is normally done in economic analysis so as to isolate the impact of a particular variable on another, e.g. in demand theory income and taxes are held constant so as to isolate the effect of price changes on the quantity of a good produced.

Chamberlinian monopolistic competition. *See* MONOPOLISTIC COMPETITION.

C.H.A.P.S. *See* CLEARING HOUSE AUTOMATED PAYMENTS SYSTEM.

'Charging what the traffic will bear'. A system of charging based upon the upper limit of what any particular traffic can afford to pay, subject to the lower limit of what a transport system can afford to carry it for. In practice, this means that some rates are so low as to barely cover running expenses, while other rates are sufficiently high, not only to cover running costs but also to leave a surplus available as a contribution towards the unapportioned expenses of the low class traffic. Essentially, a businessperson's term for equating marginal revenue with marginal cost. This principle also forms the basis of the system of taxation which aims, not at equality of payment by each taxpayer, but rather equality of burden or sacrifices.

Charter party. A contract to convey goods by sea to a special place for a stated sum.

Chartered Bank (Can.). A Canadian commercial bank incorporated under the terms of the Bank Act. In 1984 there were ten such banks, operating about 6,700 branches in all throughout Canada. They are one of the major sources of finance in Canada, while offering customers a wide range of other services also. The chartered banks are required by law to maintain cash reserves in the form of deposits with the central bank, the Bank of Canada, equal to 12 per cent of demand deposits and 4 per cent of notice deposits. The 'Big Five' chartered banks have 90 per cent of all banking assets in Canada and 60 per cent of all deposits of accepting institutions. *See* BANK OF CANADA; CANADIAN BANKING SYSTEM.

Cheap money. Any period of low interest rates or policy aiming at low interest rates; a description applied to money in the United Kingdom when the Bank Rate (q.v.) was low. Between 1932 and 1951, save for a short period in 1939, the Bank Rate was kept down to 2 per cent in order to stimulate borrowing. The use of the Bank Rate as a flexible instrument of monetary policy was restored in 1951.

Check trading. A method of consumer credit financing whereby a company sells a voucher or check on credit. The purchaser repays the debt by agreed regular instalments and with interest. The check is exchanged for goods at specified shops.

Checking deposits (U.S.). Demand deposits held by commercial banks; the largest element in the supply of money. The system of demand deposits enables payments to be made by cheque (q.v.). *See* TIME DEPOSIT.

Check-off arrangements. Arrangements in Britain whereby employers collect union dues on behalf of the unions; most employers charge a small fee for the service. The effect, apart from the convenience of unions in the collection of dues, is to shift the responsibility for closed shop industries from the unions to the management.

Cheque (U.K.). A bill of exchange (q.v.) drawn on a banker and payable on demand; an instruction to a banker to pay without delay a stated sum of money to the person to whom the cheque is payable. If payable to the 'bearer' a cheque is a negotiable instrument (q.v.); but it is not negotiable if it is endorsed 'not negotiable'. If a cheque is 'crossed', having two lines drawn parallel across its face, the amount will be paid only into the payee's account. If 'open' or uncrossed, a banker will pay cash to the person presenting the cheque. A cheque is not legal tender (q.v.). Banks honour cheques by reducing the deposit of the person writing the cheque and increasing the deposit of, or paying cash to, the person in whose favour the cheque is written.

Chervonets. A quarter-ounce coin of Russian

gold, offered by the Soviet Union and advertised in capitalist countries. Chervonets are offered as a 'personal gold reserve', or even as a 'contribution to a loved one's nest-egg'; it is argued that gold is no longer the 'privilege of the privileged few'. The coin carries the slogan, in Russian, 'Proletarians of all countries unite!'

Chicago Board of Trade (C.B.T.). The oldest established commodity exchange (q.v.) in the United States, where active trading takes place in wheat, corn, oats, soyabeans, soyabean meal, soyabean oil, and metals; it is the world's largest commodity futures exchange, with over 48 million futures contracts being traded on the floor in 1982. Futures trading is conducted in trading areas called 'pits' on the exchange floor. There is a different pit for each commodity, but the method of trading is the same in all the pits. Every offer to sell and every bid to buy a futures contract must be called or cried out publicly. The exchange has been trading in metals only since 1968; interest rate futures were introduced in 1975 and energy futures in 1982. A 5,000 ounce silver futures contract was introduced in 1969, with a 1,000 ounce contract following in 1971. A one kilogram gold futures contract is also offered. *See* CHICAGO BOARD OF TRADE CLEARING CORPORATION, *and* TABLE 1.

Chicago Board of Trade Clearing Corporation. A body separate from the Chicago Board of Trade (q.v.) whose task is to match scores of thousands of individual sales and purchases made on the exchange; for a 'trade' to clear the reported purchase and reported sale must correspond in every essential detail. The Clearing Corporation plays a role as the 'other party' in every futures transaction. As soon as a trade is made between a buyer and a seller, the Clearing Corporation legally substitutes itself as the buyer to every seller and the seller to every buyer. The relationship between the original buyer and seller is totally and permanently severed; the contracts of the buyer and the seller are with the Clearing Corporation. The Corporation provides financial integrity to the transactions.

Chicago Board Options Exchange (C.B.O.E.). An offspring of the Chicago Board of Trade (q.v.), operating the largest stock and index trading markets in the United States.

Chicago Mercantile Exchange (C.M.E.). A commodity exchange (q.v.) first organized in 1919; it grew out of the Chicago Butter and Egg Board which had been established in 1898. The initial function of the C.M.E. was to provide a national marketplace for trading in cash and futures contracts in various agricultural commodities. In recent years, trading has been almost entirely in futures, the only exceptions being a cash call in butter on the final day of each week's trading, and daily trading in options on futures on the Standard and Poor's 500 stock index. The C.M.E. is the second largest organized futures exchange in the world. Its member firms have offices in every state in the Union, as well as in many other countries. Trading accounts for about 30 per cent of the total volume of business on the 11 U.S. futures exchanges. With the listing of futures in seven foreign currencies in 1972, the Exchange instituted trading in financial instruments; an International Money Market was established. An Index and Option Market was opened in 1982. A 24-member Board of Governors exercises control of the Exchange. In 1983, the Exchange had more than 2,600 full individual members; memberships are sold by members from time to time at market prices. *See* TABLE 1.

Chicago School. Name applied to a group of economists who, among other things, believe that changes in the money supply are a major determinant of short-run changes in the level of economic activity, and the most important of the policy instruments available to a federal or national government for affecting short-run changes in economic activity. The members of this school generally advocate reliance on automated policy (q.v.). The school emphasises the desirability of individual freedom and competitive markets. The philosophy and methodology of the school found early expression in the work of Frank H. Knight (1885–1973) who became professor of economics at the University of Chicago in 1928; he published his famous *Risk, Uncertainty and Profit* in 1921. Milton Friedman, Professor of Economics at Chicago 1947–79, viewed competitive markets as the 'only means so far discovered of enabling individuals to co-ordinate their economic activities without coercion'. Competitive markets are also regarded as the most efficient, while business cycles are attributed primarily to swings in the rate of growth in the money supply. Members and supporters of the school are critical of most types of governmental regulation of the economy believing it has undesirable effects on both economic efficiency and individual freedom. George J. Stigler has been another prominent member of the school. *See* MONETARIST SCHOOL; SCHOOLS OF ECONOMICS.

C.H.I.P.S. *See* CLEARING HOUSE INTER-BANK PAYMENTS SYSTEM.

TABLE 1
COMMODITY QUOTATIONS

CHICAGO BOARD OF TRADE		*How quoted*	*Months**	*Times (N.Y.)*	*Increment value*
Oats	5000 Bu	cents/Bu	HKNUZ	10.30–2.15	$\frac{1}{4}$¢=$12.50
Corn	5000 Bu	cents/Bu	HKNUZ	10.30–2.15	$\frac{1}{4}$¢=$12.50
Wheat	5000 Bu	cents/Bu	HKNUZ	10.30–2.15	$\frac{1}{4}$¢=$12.50
Soyabeans	5000 Bu	cents/Bu	HKNUZ	10.30–2.15	$\frac{1}{4}$¢=$12.50
Soyabean meal	100 tons	dollars/ton	FHKNQUVZ	10.30–2.15	10¢=$10
Soyabean oil	60,000 lbs	cents/lb	FHKNQUVZ	10.30–2.15	.01¢=$6
Western plywood	76,032 sq ft	$/1000 sq ft	FHKNUX	10.00–2.00	10¢=$7.603
G.N.M.A.	$100,000	pts+32nds/100%	HMUZ	9.00–3.00	1/32=$31.25
Treasury bonds	$100,000	prs+32nds/100%	HMUZ	9.00–3.00	1/32=$31.25
CHICAGO MERCANTILE EXCHANGE					
Live cattle	40,000 lbs	cents/lb	GJMQVZ	10.05–1.45	2.5/100¢=$10
Feeder cattle	42,000 lbs	cents/lb	FHJKQUVZ	10.05–1.45	2.5/100¢=$10.50
Live hogs	30,000 lbs	cents/lb	GJMQVZ	10.10–2.00	2.5/100¢=$7.50
Porkbellies	38,000 lbs	cents/lb	GJKNQ	10.10–2.00	2.5/100¢=$9.50
Lumber	130,000 bd ft	$/1000 bd ft	FHKNUX	10.00–2.05	10¢=$13

**Key to months*

January	F	April	J	July	N	October	V
February	G	May	K	August	Q	November	X
March	H	June	M	September	P	December	Z

(Source: Chicago Board of Trade)

Choice. A fundamental principle underlying all market activity. The individual must decide on the distribution of his/her income between expenditure and saving and the distribution of expenditure between different goods and services; the business person must decide on what it is intended to produce, the method of production to be adopted, the location of the production facilities, and the methods of marketing; the State must decide how the resources of the nation are to be best deployed. All these decisions often involve difficult choices between alternatives. John Maynard Keynes commented in his *General Theory* (1936) that the best safeguard of personal liberty is a wide field for the exercise of personal choice, which ensures variety – 'the most powerful instrument to better the future' (p. 380).

C.I.F. Cost, insurance and freight. Term used of goods shipped where the price includes shipping and insurance charges. A C.I.F. quotation means that the seller must ship the goods, meeting all charges up to 'on board' and paying freight, insurance, etc. The seller must supply the buyer with all the documents required to enable the goods to be imported. The buyer must pay all expenses, customs duties, etc. on arrival of the goods at the port of destination. *See* F.O.B.

Circuit velocity. *See* VELOCITY OF CIRCULATION.

Circular flow of incomes. The flow of payments from households to firms and back again, within a community; money paid for factor services becomes income for households, while the money paid by households for commodities and services becomes the income of firms.

'City, The'. The City of London, commonly known as the 'Square Mile'. Hobson has defined the four fundamental functions which the City performs:

(a) The City provides a mechanism by which payment of any sum of money, large or small, may be made with safety and dispatch, without the use of actual notes or coins;
(b) The City provides the money which enables foodstuffs and raw materials to be produced, to be transported about the world, and to undergo processes of manufacture until they are finally sold as finished, consumable articles;
(c) The City collects the country's savings and provides for their investment;
(d) The City provides a mechanism, consisting of the Foreign Exchange market, assisted by the Gold Bullion Market by which the money of one country can be exchanged into the money of another.

The City of London accounts for about one-quarter of international bank lending and rather more of the Eurobond market. London still leads the world in insurance and reinsurance, and shipping and cargo contracts. It remains a prominent centre for commodity trading and futures markets.

The term is also used as a reference to the whole financial community in the United Kingdom.

Classical real wage doctrine. A doctrine which holds that, in the long-run, there is no trade-off between unemployment and price increases as is implied by the Phillips Curve (q.v.); it has been taken to indicate that a rising price level will not affect permanently the level of unemployment.

Classical School. Appellation for a group of writers on economics during the second half of the 18th century and the first half of the 19th century. They were the first to formulate a systematic body of economic principles, seeking to explain uniformities in economic activity which are not the result of deliberate design by a central planning body, but the product of interplay of separate decisions by individuals and groups. In general they supported the philosophy of laissez-faire (q.v.) in opposition to mercantilism (q.v.) prevalent in the early part of the period. Their doctrines became the philosophical basis of the Manchester School (q.v.) which was ardent in support of free trade between nations. The principal members of the group included:

ADAM SMITH (1723–1790). Professor of logic and moral philosophy at Glasgow University. In 1759 he published his *Theory of the Moral Sentiments*. This was followed in 1776 by his great work *An Inquiry into the Nature and Causes of the Wealth of Nations*. This was the first comprehensive treatment of the subject, examining the forces through which the market process directed the distribution of resources between different industries and the manner in which competition produced a kind of order based on specialisation and division of labour. He explained the value of commodities in terms of the quantity of labour employed in their production and examined the three elements which entered into price—wages, profit and rent. Smith's philosophy was individualistic, seeing self-interest as a proper criterion of economic action. Thus, the pursuit of self-interest would contribute to the public interest. Nevertheless, he introduced some important exceptions to the doctrine of laissez-faire (q.v.), for example, state administration of the post office and compulsory elementary education. He strongly advocated freedom of trade and sharply criticised the restriction of competition whether by government regulation or by combination of producers.

THOMAS ROBERT MALTHUS (1766–1834). In the year 1798 Malthus became curate of Albury in Surrey. In the same year appeared his *Essay on the Principle of Population* in which he argued that population tended to increase beyond the means of subsistence and that checks on this increase were necessary. The *Essay* re-appeared as a second edition in 1803 embodying somewhat less dismal conclusions. The work caused a storm of controversy. *See* MALTHUSIAN THEORY OF POPULATION.

DAVID RICARDO (1772–1823). After making a fortune on the London Stock Exchange, Ricardo devoted himself to a study of economics. With James Mill (1773–1836) he founded modern economic theory, although his work was somewhat impaired by building on Smith's theory of value. In 1817 he published his main work, *Principles of Political Economy and Taxation*, a work largely concerned with the causes determining the distribution of wealth. In it he developed his famous theory of rent. *See* RENT, RICARDO'S THEORY OF.

NASSAU WILLIAM SENIOR (1790–1864). Professor of political economy at Oxford University, 1825–30 and 1847–52. In addition to important political articles, he published *An Outline of the Science of Political Economy* in 1836. Senior stands somewhat outside the orthodox classical tradition.

JAMES MILL (1773–1836). Although educated for the ministry, Mill became a journalist. In 1818 he published his *History of British India*, and, subsequently, obtained a high post with the East Indian Company. He was closely associated with Jeremy Bentham and David Ricardo, helping to found modern economic theory. In 1821 his *Elements of Political Economy* appeared. This was followed by his *Analysis of the Human Mind* in 1829. Mill was the father of John Stuart Mill.

JOHN STUART MILL (1806–1873). Son of James Mill. He formed the Utilitarian Society and in 1825 edited Jeremy Bentham's *Treatise upon Evidence*. In 1843 he published his *System of Logic*; and in 1848 his *Principles of Political Economy*, which became the most influential book on the subject during the second half of the 19th century. Subsequently, in 1859, appeared his essay *On Liberty* and in 1873 his autobiography.

Other members of the school included John Elliot Cairns, John Ramsey McCulloch, Jean Baptiste Say, David Hume and Robert Torrens. The name of Karl Marx is sometimes included also, as his economics was essentially that of the classical school, and he owed much to the work of David Ricardo; however, his conclusions were vastly different. *See* MARXIST SOCIALISM; SCHOOLS OF ECONOMICS.

Clayton Act 1914 (U.S.). An Act which prohibits certain discriminatory and acquisitive practices when the effect can be shown to suppress competition. This Act was subsequently strengthened by the Robinson-Patman Act 1936 and the Celler-Kefauver Act 1950. *See* SHERMAN ANTITRUST ACT 1890.

Clean float. The introduction of a floating exchange rate in which the monetary authority of the nation does not intervene in the money market; this is an ideal situation rarely if ever achieved in practice. *See* DIRTY FLOAT.

Clearing bank base rates. Interest rates set by the London clearing banks for their advances according to the supply and demand for funds. The actual rates charged an individual customer depend upon his status and the nature of the requirements, but most lending is currently at between 1 per cent and 5 per cent higher than base rate. Base rates were introduced in October, 1971. However, in December, 1973, the clearing banks announced that, to curb arbitrage transactions (that is, the movement of funds to profit from differing rates of interest in different investments) they proposed that for certain customers—especially local authorities and other banks—future advances would be linked to market rates instead of base rates. The three Scottish clearing banks and the four Northern Ireland banks have similar arrangements

Clearing banks, London. Twelve banks who are members of the London Bankers' Clearing House, an institution which originated in the late 18th century for clearing or settling inter-bank transactions. Inter-bank payments are limited to net deficits arising from each day's business. Much of the domestic banking business of England and Wales is in the hands of four banks, which are Barclays, Lloyds, Midland, and the National Westminster.

On 20 August 1981, the London clearing banks' $1\frac{1}{2}$ per cent cash ratio (the percentage of eligible liabilities they had to maintain in non-interest-bearing accounts at the Bank of England) was cut to $\frac{1}{2}$ per cent.

Clearing house. An agency connected with a commodity exchange through which all futures contracts are reconciled, settled, guaranteed, and later offset or fulfilled through delivery of the commodity and through which financial settlement is made. A clearing house may be a separate fully chartered corporation, or a division of the exchange itself.

Clearing House Automated Payments System (C.H.A.P.S.). A payments system which came into operation in London, England, in 1983 to enable London clearing banks to engage in international transfers using the latest computer and communications techniques.

Clearing House Inter-bank Payments System (C.H.I.P.S.). A system which processes some 90 per cent of all international dollar transfer transactions. Based in New York, over 90 banks participate in the system; of these 56 are the New York branches of foreign banks. C.H.I.P.S. is a computerised telecommunications system that substantially eliminates cheques in the movement of funds. It was devised by the New York Clearing House Association and became operational in 1970.

Clearing member. A member of a clearing house (q.v.) by whom fulfilment of all contracts, registered in the member's name, is guaranteed.

Close, The. The period at the end of the trading session on a commodity exchange.

Closed economy. No imports or exports: an assumption that may be made for the purpose of economic analysis.

Closed shop. A condition imposed by trade unions or employers that all employees of a firm shall be members of the appropriate trade unions. Closed shop arrangements spread rapidly in the 1970s from their traditional strongholds in shipbuilding, steel and heavy industries, to textiles, clothing, and food, drink and tobacco. By 1981, they covered about one-third of Britain's factories (45 per cent of blue-collar and 10 per cent of white-collar workers). Many employers have welcomed closed shops; closed shops ensure that unions and shop stewards represent the whole work-force. It is claimed that they also stabilise relations between managers and workers.

Closed shops are illegal in West Germany and France. In Sweden, the employers' association forbids its members to make closed shop agreements; only about 5 per cent of Swedish workers are covered by closed shops. In the United States of America, closed shops are illegal in about 20 'right-to-work' states.

Closed-end investment companies. Investment companies whose shares are purchased by investors; these closed-end funds do not redeem their shares at prices that reflect the day-to-day value of their security holdings; instead, closed-end fund share prices fluctuate according to supply and demand, often selling at market discounts compared with their per-share net asset values.

Close-out. To withdraw from or terminate; for example, 'do not be in a hurry to close-out a winning position for a profit-in-hand'.

Closing a position. Making a balancing transaction in the opposite direction; thus a purchase of 500 shares opens a position, which may be closed by a sale of the same amount during the same account period (q.v.).

Closing quotations. Bids and offers being made at the close of stock exchange business; these are recorded by stock exchange staff and appear in newspaper reports.

Closing range. The high and low prices recorded during the period designated as the official close on a commodity exchange (q.v.).

Cobb-Douglas production function. A production function (q.v.) developed by Cobb and Douglas in the 1920s for the purposes of attempting to explain the relative constancy of the shares of capital and labour in the national income. It may be written in the form:

$$Q = b_o X_1^{b_1} X_2^{b_2} \cdots X_n^{b_n}$$

where: Q is output; $X_1 X_2 \ldots X_n$ are factors of production; and $b_o b_2 \ldots b_n$ are parameters. This production function appears to have fitted the facts of American experience quite well. The function, often in a special form, has been widely used in economics not only in the theory of income distribution, but also in the theories of production and economic growth.

Cobweb diagram. A diagram which illustrates reactions in unstable markets, e.g. housing and agricultural markets. The cobweb diagram (Figure 2) shows that if bad weather or a strike reduces supply from Q* to Q_1 then, in the next period, prices will move up to A_1. The effect of this will be to stimulate a greater supply, B_2, which will find enough buyers only if prices are brought down to A_2. Supply then contracts to B_3; the process continues until equilibrium is finally restored. This model assumes a tendency towards stable equilibrium rather than continually widening swings in both price and production.

Collateral. Securities or other property pledged by a borrower to secure repayment of a loan.

Collateral trust bond. A bond (q.v.) secured by collateral (q.v.) deposited with a trustee.

Collective good or service. A good or service, such as defence, from which the benefits accrue to all or none.

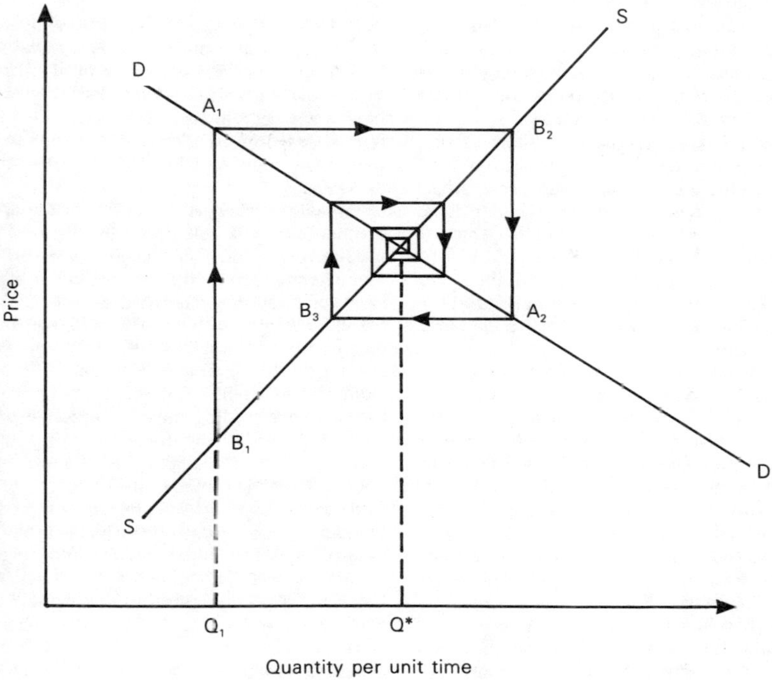

Figure 2 Cobweb diagram

Collusive tendering. A restrictive practice (q.v.) in which firms tendering for a particular job agree to submit a common price, or to allow one of their number to submit a lower tender, thus allocating orders between themselves.

Coming out price. The price at which new shares are issued.

Command economy. Descriptive of an economic system dominated by central planning, as distinct from a free enterprise economy with a minimum of state interference. Command economy characteristics are not restricted to socialist economies; systems which encourage free enterprise maintain a powerful apparatus of central control and influence although much of it may be of an indirect character through the use of monetary and fiscal policies.

Commercial banks. Joint-stock banks whose principal function is to receive deposits and make loans. These loans are often for a short-term nature and mainly required as working capital (q.v.) in businesses; however, long-term housing finance may also be provided. In addition to ordinary banking business, the commercial banks offer many ancillary services, e.g. executor and trustee services, foreign currency transactions, bill discounting, investment management services, personal loans, credit cards, and custody of valuables. The United States has over 42,000 deposit-taking institutions; these comprise 14,700 commercial banks and 27,500 thrift institutions (4,000 savings and loan associations, 500 mutual savings banks, and 23,000 credit unions or consumer finance co-operatives).

The Glass-Steagall Act (U.S.) 1933 (q.v.) erected a wall between commercial and investment banking by prohibiting banks which take deposits, or their affiliates, from underwriting or dealing in corporate bonds, corporate equities, and some types of municipal securities. Britain does not have any legislation separating commercial and investment banking, and for that reason some commercial banks are referred to as investment banks.

Commercial economy. An economy comprising industrial production, agriculture carried on for sale beyond the immediate neighbourhood, the trade through which these products are distributed and the transport, communications, construction and services related to these processes. Such an economy is dynamic, growing and spreading, developing new institutions while adapting the old.

Commercial paper market. A non-bank short-term money market in which corporations lend their surplus cash directly to each other, cutting out intermediate financial institutions. Commercial paper outstanding in America grew from $48 billion at the end of 1975 to almost $115 billion at the end of 1979. No commercial paper market exists in Britain; the nearest equivalent is the bankers' acceptance (q.v.).

Commission broker. A partner of a member firm of a U.S. Stock Exchange, e.g. the New York Stock Exchange. A broker executes orders for customers, and for his/her services charges a commission. The equivalent of an English stockbroker (q.v.). Also, a broker (q.v.) who, as a member of the London International Financial Futures Exchange (q.v.), executes orders for members and non-members for the purchase and sale of financial futures contracts.

Commission house (U.S.). A business house that buys and sells actual commodities or futures contracts for the accounts of customers.

Commitment. The assuming of an obligation by a commodity exchange member to accept or make delivery on a futures contract (q.v.).

Committee for Middle East Trade (C.O.M.E.T.). Created in 1963, an autonomous but government-sponsored body made up of leading British industrialists and senior Government officials from the Department of Trade, the Foreign Office and the Export Credits Guarantee Department (q.v.). Its purpose is to provide advice to the British Government on boosting exports to the Middle East. By 1983, the Middle East had become the third largest trading area for British companies.

Committee on Banking Regulations and Supervisory Practices. A committee which meets at the Bank for International Settlements (q.v.) in Basle, bringing together supervisors from the Group of Eleven (q.v.) major industrialised countries and Luxembourg. The supervisors discuss their approach to the supervision of banks. In 1983, a revised Concordat or set of principles governing supervision responsibilities in respect of banks' foreign establishments was published.

Commodity. Any tangible good or product which can be traded or used for commercial purposes. Commodities which are suitable for trading on futures markets must possess certain special characteristics; the product must be capable of division into standard units, each of which is virtually identical to any other, and it must conform to the specifications in respect of grade and quality. *See* COMMODITY EXCHANGE.

Commodity exchange. A market for the open, competitive, bulk sale and purchase of commodities including financial instruments, for immediate and forward delivery often in the form of a futures contract. In the United States, a commodity futures exchange must receive official designation as an approved market by the Commodities Futures Trading Commission (q.v.); futures contracts proposed for exchange trading must also receive prior approval. The leading domestic grain futures exchanges are in Chicago, Minneapolis, and Kansas City. In Canada, an important grain futures exchange is the Winnipeg Commodity Exchange. Leading cotton and wool exchanges are in New York. Sugar, cocoa, potatoes and metals also have futures markets in New York City. Beef cattle, porkbellies and egg futures markets are in Chicago. Commodity markets in the United States are, like the stock exchanges, membership organisations; each exchange has its own governing board. All prices are established through open trading around the trading rings or pits provided by the exchanges. The London Commodity Exchange, England, provides a market for many commodities, while several specialised exchanges are to be found in the City of London. Other important exchanges are the Baltic Mercantile and Shipping Exchange for shipping and aircraft charter markets, and the London Metal Exchange (q.v.). *See* CHICAGO BOARD OF TRADE; CHICAGO BOARD OPTIONS EXCHANGE; CHICAGO MERCANTILE EXCHANGE; KANSAS CITY BOARD OF TRADE; LONDON BALTIC EXCHANGE; LONDON COMMODITY EXCHANGE; LONDON GOLD FUTURES MARKET; LONDON GOLD MARKET; LONDON INTERNATIONAL FINANCIAL FUTURES EXCHANGE; LONDON METAL EXCHANGE; MID-AMERICA COMMODITY EXCHANGE; MINNEAPOLIS GRAIN EXCHANGE; NEW YORK COMMODITY EXCHANGE; NEW YORK FUTURES EXCHANGE; NEW YORK MERCANTILE EXCHANGE; SINGAPORE INTERNATIONAL MONETARY EXCHANGE; SYDNEY FUTURES EXCHANGE; SYDNEY INTERNATIONAL OPTIONS MARKET.

Commodity futures contract. A legally binding commitment to buy or sell a precisely defined quantity and quality of a commodity in a given month, the price of which is determined by the participants at the time of transaction.

Commodity Futures Trading Commission (C.F.T.C.). Created by the United States Congress in 1975, a body with wide discretionary powers to regulate the country's eleven commodity exchanges. The Commission sets rules under which the exchanges operate, e.g. rules preventing the cornering of markets by speculators. It may levy fines. The Commission reports directly to the Congress. It seeks to be a parallel body to the Securities and Exchange Commission (q.v.). In 1983, the Commission introduced a $10,000 fee for each application for new contract markets; the fee was intended to cover the time commission staff must spend examining and processing contract proposals.

Commodity mutual fund. A firm that sells shares to the public and invests the proceeds in the commodities markets.

Common Agricultural Policy. The agricultural policy adopted by the European Economic Community (q.v.). The principle that the Common Market was to extend to agricultural products was enunciated in the Treaty of Rome. The aims have been to increase agricultural productivity, ensure a reasonable standard of living for the agricultural population, stabilise markets, and ensure sufficient supplies at fair prices to the consumer. Early steps involved the removal of existing tariffs and other barriers to trade between members, and their replacement by levies to offset internal price differences. On 1 February 1973, the United Kingdom adopted the Common Agricultrual Policy. The financial aspects of the policy are handled by the European Agricultural Guidance and Guarantee Fund.

The 'Ten' recognise it is uneconomic to keep so many people on the land, so farm incomes are supported at a level which slows down but does not reverse drift from rural areas into towns and cities. The aim is to make the pace of economic change tolerable, not to defy such change. Minimum guaranteed prices are known as common support prices (q.v.).

The common agricultural policy supports farmers in five ways: high support prices; import levies; export subsidies; supplementary and fixed-rate aids; and structural aid.

More than 70 per cent of farm output benefits from markets controlled to maintain prices at politically determined levels. The Ten's agricultural ministers meet every spring to fix prices for cereals, milk, sugar, beef, veal, pork, some fruits and vegetables, and table wine. About 25 per cent of common market output (flowers, some cereals, good wines, some fruit and vegetables) has no intervention price, relying solely on tariff protection. Import levies raise import prices to E.E.C. levels, while export subsidies make up the difference between E.E.C. and world prices to enable farmers to sell on the world markets.

In 1958, the present 10 E.E.C. members had 20 million people working on the land; in 1982, the numbers were down to 8.7 million or 8.2 per cent of total employment.

The central problem with the policy is that it tends to subsidise inefficient mainly French farmers at the expense of all others.

Common fisheries policy. A policy adopted by the European Economic Community (q.v.) in respect of fisheries towards the end of 1982; a fisheries policy had become necessary because fewer and fewer fish were being chased by too many fishermen. The adopted common fisheries policy had four main elements:

(a) The total allowable catch for each species in each region would be set, and then shared out between countries according to pre-fixed quotas. Britain would get the largest slice, about 36 per cent, of the main species;

(b) Britain would get exclusive rights in a six-mile strip around its coasts, and there would be only limited access to other E.E.C. boats between six and twelve miles. The limited access zone would be much wider off northern Scotland;

(c) Rules on mesh sizes for nets and the type of equipment which may be used, in order to conserve fish stocks; and

(d) Finance to help fleets adjust capacity and equipment to the new circumstances, that is fishing inshore rather than deep sea.

Common Market, European. *See* EUROPEAN COMMON MARKET; EUROPEAN ECONOMIC COMMUNITY.

Common pricing. The fixing of identical prices for goods by agreement between otherwise competing firms selling through wholesale or retail channels of distribution.

Common Property Resource. *See* FREE GOODS.

Common Stock (U.S. and Can.). Shares representing ownership of a business, with the common stockholders sharing all distributed earnings after the prior claims of the bondholders and preferred stockholders, if any, have been met; the equivalent of British ordinary shares. *See* ORDINARY SHARES.

Common stock ratio (U.S.). The ratio of common stocks to the total of all bonds and stocks issued by a corporation.

Common support prices. The system of pricing for agricultural produce maintained under the Common Agricultural Policy (q.v.) of the European Economic Community (q.v.). A 'target price' is decided by the European Commission (q.v.) for each product, the aim being to keep the market price throughout the Community at the level of the target price so that individual farmers may plan their production on this basis. The 'intervention price' is the floor price for the commodity, always being above the actual costs of production but below the target price. If the market price should fall to the intervention level, then national agencies are obliged to buy produce in order to maintain this minimum. The market is protected from movements on the world market by three measures. First, a 'threshold' price is established for imports from non-member countries, which is lower than the target price, but is fixed in such a way that after adjusting for transport costs they cannot be sold for less than the target price. Secondly, if stocks in the Community are thought to be too high but the world price is below the Community price, export restitutions (or subsidies) may be offered to enable exports to be made at world prices. Thirdly, when world prices are higher than Community prices, exports may be prohibited to conserve supplies for the Community market. All monies spent by the Commission on supporting product prices come from the European Agricultural Guidance and Guarantee Fund (F.E.O.G.A., as it is known by its French initials).

The United Kingdom fixed threshold and intervention prices for all relevant commodities, but these were initially lower than Community levels. They were raised in six equal steps to equal Community prices by 1978. An intervention board was set up to administer the support programme and the phasing out of deficiency payments began.

Community Land Act 1975 (U.K.). An Act which empowered local authorities to acquire land by compulsory purchase; its aim was 'to restore to the community the increase in the value of land arising from its efforts' and clearly envisaged local authorities becoming by stages monopoly landowners in development land.

Community Reinvestment Act 1977. An Act the purpose of which is to encourage financial institutions to meet the 'credit needs of their local community or communities'. The Act requires the several supervisory agencies, including the Federal Reserve System (q.v.), to take into consideration compliance with this Act when dealing with applications relating to merging, establishment of branches, creation of bank holding companies, and other measures.

Companies Acts 1948 to 1985. Laws establishing the fundamental rules for the establishment and conduct of businesses in Britain. The Companies Act 1948 revised and consolidated company law in Britain, giving legal force to most of the recommendations of the 1945 Report of the Cohen Committee on Company Law Amendment (Cmnd. 6659). The Act introduced 'consolidated accounts' which lump together all subsidiary companies with the parent company. It created the 'exempt' private company which was exempt under certain conditions from filing accounts annually with the Board of Trade. Over 70 per cent of registered companies were in this category. In 1962 the Jenkins Committee reported its findings leading to further amendments of company law embodied in the Companies Act 1967. This Act abolished the exempt private companies and has compelled companies to reveal much more information than hitherto. The additional disclosures which must now be made include: (a) the naming of each subsidiary company and its country of incorporation (if other than Britain); (b) trade investments, if more than 10 per cent of the capital of a company; (c) the naming by subsidiaries of the country of ultimate holding company; (d) the Chairman's pay, the Directors' pay in income 'bands' and shareholdings, and the pay of highly-paid employees; (e) turnover, profits and allocation between different activities; (f) charitable and political payments; (g) number of people employed and average pay; (h) exports. In addition, the Act requires that new insurance companies will need to seek Board of Trade permission to start business, and any permission granted may be subject to conditions. The Companies Act 1980 provided for new arrangements for the classification and registration of companies in Britain, and their capital structure and distribution of profits and assets. After registration under the Act, a public company must put Public Limited Company or PLC after its name. The Act laid down new criteria for public companies and rules concerning the conduct of company directors. It made illegal share dealings that depended upon certain privileged kinds of information. The Companies Act 1981 set out the statutory framework for the disclosure of company accounts, altered the law controlling company names and business names, and introduced other changes.

The Companies Acts 1948–1981 became consolidated in the Companies Act 1985, and other concurrent legislation relating to business names and insider dealings.

Company issued option. An option by a company to buy the underlying stock at some time in the future; the only fundamental difference between a company option and an exchange traded call option with the same amount of time to run, is that a company option is created by the issuer of the underlying stock. *See* SHARE OPTIONS.

Company, legal formation of a (U.K.). A legal process requiring the completion of two documents, the Memorandum of Association (q.v.) and the Articles of Association (q.v.), followed by registration of the Company. An application for registration should be addressed to the Companies' Registration Office of the Board of Trade in respect of a business to be registered in Great Britain, or to the Ministry of Commerce in respect of a business to be registered in Northern Ireland. The Memorandum of Association and the Articles of Association should accompany the application, together with certain statutory declarations and certificates. Upon issue by the Registrar of a Certificate of Incorporation the company becomes a legal entity. On the issue of this Certificate a private company can start business at once; a public company requires an additional document known as a 'Trading Certificate'. The Registrar may refuse to register a company if its objects are illegal, or the proposed name is that of some other Company or is otherwise undesirable or misleading.

Company taxation. In Britain, taxes charged on the trading profits of a company, whether distributed as dividends or retained as reserves. Formerly, companies paid two taxes on their profits:

(a) Profits tax at 15 per cent; and
(b) Income tax at the current standard rate.

Thus company taxation absorbed about half of a company's taxable profits. Beginning in the tax year 1966–67, profits tax and income tax were replaced by a 'corporation tax'. This tax falls on the whole of the taxable profits of a company whether distributed as dividends or not. Corporation tax does not distinguish between distributed and undistributed profits.

Since 1973, British company tax has been based on the 'imputation system'. Tax is levied at a single rate (52 per cent for large companies, 40 per cent for smaller firms) on all taxable profits. When profits are distributed to shareholders, normally as dividends, a proportion of the company's tax is imputed to the shareholder (the company effectively deducts the 30 per cent basic rate tax from the gross dividend and pays this to the Inland Revenue as advance corporation tax (A.C.T.). Shareholders then receive a corresponding tax credit. In 1983, corporation tax was levied at the standard rate of 52 per cent though the rate fell to 40 per cent on smaller profits. However, owing to carried-forward tax losses, the Inland Revenue estimated in 1982 that only about one-third of British companies regularly pay mainstream corporation tax, while another third slip in and out of tax liability from year-to-year.

In 1984, it was proposed to reduce corporation tax to 35 per cent over the following 3 years.

Company taxation, The Economist's canons of. *The Economist*'s criteria for a good company tax are:

(a) It should be easy and cheap to administer and to comply with;
(b) It should not distort firms' investment and fund-raising decisions;
(c) The burden of the tax should be eased according to companies' ability to pay; and
(d) Tax liabilities should be clear-cut.

(*The Economist*, London, England 29 January 1983, p. 72). *See* TAXATION, ADAM SMITH'S CANONS OF.

Comparative advantage, theory of. In international trade, a statement that countries tend to specialise in the production of those goods and services which they can make or provide most profitably. Let us assume that Country A can produce two commodities more cheaply that Country B. Country A will still specialise in that commodity in which it has the greater comparative advantage and let country B specialise in the other. It is a mutually profitable arrangement.

Comparative cost method. A method of comparing the profitability of alternative projects. The method takes account of the initial cost of alternative projects only; it is possible to use this method only where the output and life of each competing scheme is the same.

Comparative static analysis or comparative static equilibrium analysis. Analysis based on a comparison of two positions of equilibrium, the second differing from the first as a result of the introduction, for example, of a tax or a change in the conditions of demand.

Compensation Fund or guarantee fund. A fund maintained by an organisation, e.g. The London Stock Exchange (q.v.) or Lloyds to recompense losers should a member firm fail to meet its obligations.

Compensation principle. A criterion for judging the desirability of an economic policy which states that if those who gain from the policy could fully compensate those who lose, and still remain better off, then the policy should be implemented. The compensation is hypothetical and not actually paid. This compensation principle was first put forward by Nicholas Kaldor (b. 1908) in an attempt to deal with cases which cannot be assessed by the Pareto criterion, i.e. cases in which there are losers as well as gainers. However, this guideline may serve in practice as only a contribution to policy-making, for explicit value and political judgments about the distribution of social welfare and its proposed redistribution cannot be ignored. A public policy resulting in the well-to-do becoming better off, while the poor became worse off, even if overall the gains exceeded the losses could have unfortunate repercussions both of a social and political kind. *See* PARETO CRITERION OF ALLOCATIVE EFFICIENCY.

Compensatory financing facility. A facility extended by the International Monetary Fund (q.v.) for countries whose export earnings temporarily fall (e.g. because of a crop failure). During the period 1974–80 some SDR 4.5 billion was lent.

Competition. In an economy, a voluntary trading process in which individuals or business units freely exchange goods and services through markets, with a view to mutually beneficial exchanges, buying and selling being normally assisted and separated through the functions of money. The degree, character, and intensity of competition in markets is strongly influenced by the nature of the participants and their negotiating strength. Situations may range from a market with many sellers and many buyers (*see* PERFECT COMPETITION) to one in which there are few sellers, or few buyers (*see* OLIGOPOLY; OLIGOPSONY). A competitive element disappears in a situation of absolute monopoly on the selling or buying side, an uncommon but not rare situation.

In a competitive situation, each trader may accept or reject the terms offered; any consent or refusal must be freely decided. All are free to pursue gain and avoid loss, motivation based on self-interest being socially and politically acceptable. Competition is generally regarded as the key to the success of capitalist and mixed economies. The countervailing view is that co-operation for the common good is a superior form of activity to competition. *See* IMPERFECT COMPETITION; MONOPOLY; MONOPOLISTIC COMPETITION; MONOPSONY.

Competition Act 1980 (U.K.). An Act which provides a procedure for the investigation of practices ('Anti-competitive practices') which restrict, distort or prevent competition in the production, supply or acquisition of goods or services in the U.K. or any part of it. Restrictive agreements already controlled by the Restrictive Trades Practices Act are excluded. Unlike the powers to investigate monopolies under the Fair Trading Act 1973 (q.v.), the Competition Act makes it possible to investigate specific practices of named individual firms without requiring an investigation of all the major suppliers in the market. Under Competition Act procedure the Director General of Fair Trading may undertake a short preliminary investigation to determine whether there is an anti-competitive practice. He then has to publish a report explaining his findings and stating whether he thinks a reference to the Monopolies and Mergers Commission (q.v.) is appropriate. References are subject to the Secretary of State's veto. If a reference is made and the Commission finds that a practice is against the public interest, the Secretary of State has powers to remedy or prevent the adverse effects specified; these include asking the Director General to seek undertakings from the parties involved and the power to make an order.

Competition and Credit Control Measures 1971. Measures introduced by the Bank of England (q.v.) to regulate credit through the market mechanism in the context of a more competitive banking system, while at the same time giving the authorities more effective control over the banking system as a whole by bringing within its influence the non-clearing banks which had been expanding rapidly under comparatively light control.

Complementary goods. Goods which are necessarily used in conjunction with each other, e.g. pen and ink, knives and forks, petrol and motor-cars. A rise in the *price* of A, *reduces* the demand for B.

Composite demand. The total demand for a product which arises when it is required for a number of different purposes, e.g. steel is demanded by the engineering, construction and shipbuilding industries.

Composite supply. The total supply of a number of products which satisfy a particular demand, e.g. tea, coffee, lemonade and beer, provide a composite supply of beverages.

Concentration. A situation in which the control of economic activity within a market (q.v.), whether on the supply or demand side, has moved into the hands of one company or a small number of companies.

Concentration ratio. A measure of the concentration (q.v.) of an industry, e.g. the extent to which the largest sellers control the bulk of the sales of the industry. Concentration ratios may be expressed as the percentage of value of sales accounted for by the largest firms in the industry, e.g. the largest 4, largest 8, largest 20 firms. The concentration ratios for different industries assist in assessing their positions in the spectrum ranging from pure competition to pure or absolute monopoly.

Confederation of British Industry (C.B.I.). Founded in August, 1965, the representative organisation of British Industry. The Confederation combines the roles previously played by the British Employers' Confederation, the Federation of British Industries and the National Association of British Manufacturers. The Confederation seeks to express the views of industry as a whole and to offer advice to the Government on all aspects of Government policy which affects the interests of industry. Membership of the C.B.I. consists of some 14,000 companies and 300 trade associations and employers' federations. In addition to these full members the nationalised industries and commercial undertakings are able to apply for associate membership. The governing body of the C.B.I. is the Council which is assisted by some 30 expert standing committees. There is also a Regional Council for each industrial development region in the United Kingdom. The C.B.I. provides its members with a wide range of services and practical advice. Member companies pay subscriptions, the amount varying with the numbers employed.

In 1982, the C.B.I. published a strategy aimed at cutting the number of unemployed people in Britain by up to 1.5 million (from 3.3 million) within 5 years.

Conference Board Inc. Initially formed in 1915, a non-profit, non-political group, which undertakes research, reviews worldwide management practices, makes short-term forecasts of the gross national product of North America, and conducts conferences and seminars. Financial support for the work of the Board is obtained from the voluntary contributions of over 4,000 organizations including large corporations, labour unions, government agencies, universities and consultants. The Board publishes many research reports.

Confirming houses. Agencies in Britain through which overseas buyers may import goods. A confirming house will usually pay a producer for his goods and then attend to the necessary documentation and shipment. A confirming house in Britain normally acts solely in the interests and under the instructions of principals overseas.

Congestion. On an exchange, a period of repetitious and limited price fluctuations.

Conglomerate merger. A combination of firms possibly without horizontal or vertical elements, i.e. a combination which does not necessarily bring together firms producing the same or similar products, or merge suppliers and customers in the production process. A conglomerate merger achieves diversification, combining independent risks. Risk reduction is of interest to management while motives of prestige and power cannot be excluded; diversification may also appeal to shareholders, although shareholders can always achieve risk reduction through a diversification of shareholdings. The U.S. Federal Trade Commission classifies conglomerate mergers into four groups: product extension mergers, in which the firms may have some degree of functional relationship in either product or distribution; market extension mergers, with firms in the same product line, but selling in different geographical markets; unrelated combinations, the companies engaging in diverse activities without vertical or horizontal elements; and conglomerates in which firms combine activities with similar specific functions such as research, engineering or marketing. The advantages and disadvantages of conglomerates in the economy have been a matter of controversy for some years.

Congressional Budget and Impoundment Control Act 1974 (U.S.). An Act revising Congressional budgetary procedures. It established a joint Congressional Committee on the Budget composed of a 23-member standing committee from the House of Representatives and a 15-member committee from the Senate. These committees consider the budget, singly and jointly. This avoids a situation in which the final budget is the outcome of the independent actions of several committees. The Act represents the most radical revision of procedures since the Budget and Accounting Act

1921. A Congressional Budget Office was created also to service Congress with information pertaining to the budget and related financial matters.

Connected lending. Loans to companies or persons connected with the institution lending the funds, its managers, directors or controllers. In 1983, the Bank of England (q.v.) expressed the view that 'such lending can be justified only when undertaken for the clear commercial advantage of the lending institution and should be negotiated and agreed on an arms length basis'.

Conscious parallelism. Firms co-ordinating sales and output policies one with another without formal or indeed informal understanding or agreement.

Consideration. The money value of a stock exchange (q.v.) transaction (for example, the number of shares multiplied by the price per share) before adding commission, stamp duty and taxes.

Consolidated Fund Standing Services. An item in the British Budget consisting of expenditures which have been authorised by specific legislation and which do not have to be voted annually by parliament but which are otherwise similar to Supply Services. By far the greater part of this item consists of interest payable on the National Debt.

Consolidated Loan Funds. An item in the British Budget covering expenditures which do not have to be voted annually by Parliament, although the total sums that can be advanced to particular categories of borrowers are usually limited by statute. These loans are distinguishable from Consolidated Fund Standing Services (q.v.) by the fact that statutes authorising the loans also empower the Treasury (q.v.) to borrow for the purpose.

Consols. Funded Government securities or stock which the Government need not repay until it wishes. The term is an abbreviation for 'consolidated annuities'. The purchase of £100 nominal of $2\frac{1}{2}$ per cent Consols brings a perpetual annuity of £2.50, subject to the Government's right to redeem it at its discretion. An investor in Consols can however sell them at prices reflecting the yield on securities of comparable security.

Consortium banks. Defined by the Bank of England (q.v.) as a bank owned by other banks but in which no one bank has more than 50 per cent ownership and in which at least one shareholder is an overseas bank. On this definition there are over 27 consortium banks in London. Consortium banks may engage in full-fledged commercial banking as well as international loan business. The first consortium bank was the Midland and International Banks Ltd. (M.A.I.B.L.) formed in 1964. Another early example was the Rothschild Intercontinental Bank formed in 1967 with 11 shareholding banks from the United States, Japan and Europe; it has now been taken over. Other examples are the European Banks International Company, the Western American Bank (Europe), the Saudi International Bank, the United Bank of Kuwait, United International, and the Euro-Latin American Bank. Not all consortium banks are multi-national. Most of the largest banks of the world are directly, or indirectly through subsidiaries, members of consortia.

Constant returns. Description of a situation in which all the productive services can be increased in a given proportion, the amount of product being increased in the same proportion. Factor substitutions and qualitative changes are not introduced.

Consumer Advisory Council (U.S.). Part of the Federal Reserve System (q.v.), a council composed of 28 members from all parts of the United States; its membership includes a broad representation of consumer and creditor interests. It advises the Board of Governors on its responsibilities under such laws as Truth in Lending, Equal Credit Opportunity, and Home Mortgage Disclosure. Established by Congress in 1976, the Council confers with the Board of Governors four times each year.

Consumer behaviour, principles governing. The generalisations made in economic analysis relating to the behaviour of a consumer in distributing a limited personal income amongst an infinite variety of goods and services available. It is assumed that:

(a) the consumer will so arrange expenditure that the relative marginal utility of all the goods consumed will be in the same proportion to their relative prices;
(b) a fall in the price of a good or service, other things being equal, will increase consumption of it, while a rise in its price will have the opposite effect; and
(c) a rise in real income will normally result in an increased consumption of goods and services, a fall in real income having the opposite effect.

While exceptions to these generalisations do occur, and people vary enormously in the efficiency with which they spend their incomes, the principles are of sufficient validity to be regarded as reasonable assumptions for analysis.

Consumer credit. Defined by the Federal

Reserve Board as 'short and intermediate-term credit extended to individuals through regular business channels, usually to finance the purchase of consumer goods and services or to refinance the debts incurred for such purposes'. This definition excludes such categories as mortgage financing and borrowings against the cash value of life insurance policies. The two main classes of consumer credit are non-installment credit and installment credit. Non-installment credit is consumer credit due to be repaid in a lump sum such as charge accounts, 30-day accounts with retailers, medical and hospital bills. Installment credit involves the payment of regular installments; it is much the more popular form of consumer credit. A rapidly growing form of installment credit has been revolving credit (q.v.).

Consumer Credit Act 1974 (U.K.). An Act embodying many of the recommendations of the Crowther Committee (q.v.), consolidating and amending consumer protection legislation. It introduced a licensing system for all agencies connected with consumer credit, e.g. credit and hire firms, finance houses, banks, credit brokers, and debt collectors. Licences are issued by the Office of Fair Trading (q.v.) under the Fair Trading Act 1973 (q.v.). *See* HIRE PURCHASE.

Consumer durable. A commodity (q.v.) of reasonably long life, such as a refrigerator or piece of furniture; as distinct from, say, foodstuffs.

Consumer goods. Products in the actual form in which they will reach domestic consumers.

Consumer preference, theory of. Used in modern economics, a theory of consumer preference in which the consumer is asked if he/she 'prefers' one set of goods to another, or is 'indifferent' between them. The theory is not concerned with by *how much* the consumer prefers one set of goods to another. *See* REVEALED PREFERENCE THEORY; UTILITY.

Consumer price index, (U.S.). A retail price index conducted by the U.S. Labour Department; it is an all-urban consumer price index which embraces the purchases of about 80 per cent of the population. It was long criticised for overstating the speed with which prices rise. In 1981, it was announced by the bureau of labour statistics, which actually calculated the C.P.I., that changes would be made in the home-ownership component of the index, to take effect prior to 1985. The index had allowed for the interest payments on a typical new fixed-interest mortgage on a typical new house. The Index overstated inflation when interest rates were rising rapidly, because of the gap between what new purchasers were paying and what average home-owners actually paid. The Bureau of Labour statistics proposed to switch to an index which used a rent-equivalent as a substitute for the home-ownership component of the C.P.I.

Consumerism. A widespread movement concerned with the quality and safety of consumer goods, with harmful advertising, and the conduct of businesses in a manner harmful to the consumer. In the United States, the movement has been greatly stimulated by the work of Ralph Nader. His work has also included scrutiny of those regulatory agencies set up to monitor business activities.

Consumers' sovereignty. The influence of consumers exercising freedom of choice in a free market over the activities of producers of goods and services. To succeed in business, producers must direct their activities to meeting precise consumer requirements; the consumer passes judgment by buying or not buying, and in varying the amounts bought. In times of national emergency, such as the Second World War, the consumer loses sovereignty and must buy just what is available. It has been argued by Professor John Kenneth Galbraith (b. 1908) that the assumption of consumer sovereignty underlying modern micro-economic theory is invalid due to the power and influence of the major firms, and that the theory is no longer relevant to much of the economic system. *See* PRICE MECHANISM.

Consumer's surplus. The excess of the price which a person would be willing to pay rather than go without an article, over that which he/one actually does pay; it may be called consumer's rent. The consumers' surplus is measured by the area under the demand curve which represents the additional aggregate payment consumers would pay in excess of the amount actually paid for a good at the going price. A perfectly discriminating monopolist leaves no surplus.

Consumption. The use of goods and services for the satisfaction of wants. Consumption was described by Keynes as 'the sole end and object of all economic activity'.

The act of economic consumption does not destroy the elements that enter into production, these becoming solid, liquid and gaseous wastes. Robert U. Ayres and Allen V. Kneese argue that waste disposal is so general and so massive in modern society that it should be considered an integral part of the production and consumption process of the economy as a whole, that it should be placed within the framework of general equilibrium analysis.

Consumption function. A Keynesian concept, a schedule that relates aggregate consumption expenditure to the level of disposable income; called also the schedule of 'propensity to consume', or sometimes the schedule of 'intended consumption'. The statement that the consumption expenditures of the community are determined principally (but not solely) by the level of disposable income in the community is a central proposition of the theory of income determination.

Consumption goods, collective. Goods and services provided collectively by the community and paid for out of taxes, e.g. national defence, police protection, public health measures and other public works, etc.

Contango. A market situation in which prices are progressively higher in the future delivery months than in the nearest delivery month. Contango is the opposite of backwardation (q.v.).

Contango broker. Broker (q.v.) who lends to other brokers who need money for settlement of accounts. A loan is not advanced, however, in the ordinary way; for a consideration the shares in question are 'carried over' until the next settlement day.

Contango, carry-over, continuation. Synonymous terms for a charge levied on a 'bull' (q.v.) for deferring payment for stocks and shares bought from one settlement day to the next. *See* BACKWARDATION.

Contango or making-up day. The last dealing day of the account period (q.v.). Contango is the charge made for postponing payment.

Contract. An agreement, either oral or in writing, whereby one party undertakes to do something for the other party to the contract. Also a term of reference describing a unit of trading for a commodity futures contract (q.v.).

Contract grades. Those grades of a commodity which have been officially approved by an exchange as deliverable in settlement of futures contracts. *See* FUTURES CONTRACT.

Contract month. The month in which delivery is to be made in accordance with a futures contract (q.v.).

Contract trading volume. The total number of contracts traded in a commodity or commodity delivery month, during a specified period of time.

Contract unit. The actual amount of a commodity designated in a given futures contract (q.v.).

Contractual savings institutions. Institutions such as life insurance companies and pension funds, whose schemes and policies are characterised by regular contributor payments and by defined obligations for future payments in respect of such events as retirement or death. With liabilities that are predictable, these institutions are able to invest in longer-term securities than ordinary deposit-type financial intermediaries. Bonds and common stock have been traditional areas of investment, but since the 1970s investments have embraced real estate, commercial loans, mortgage loans, and many others.

Contributing share. A share (q.v.) which is partly paid, i.e. the par value is not fully paid; usually refers to shares in no liability (q.v.) companies. *See* CALLS.

Convenient social virtue. A description by Professor John Kenneth Galbraith of virtues which are held up as eternally desirable yet serve the ends of the more powerful members of the community. Merit is ascribed to any pattern of behaviour, however uncomfortable and unnatural for the individual involved, that serves the comfort or well-being of, or is otherwise advantageous for, the more powerful and influential members of the community. The moral commendation of the community then serves as a substitute for proper pecuniary compensation. Inconvenient behaviour becomes deviant behaviour and is liable to the righteous disapproval of the community. The concept of convenient social virtue can ensure the charitable and compassionate services of nurses, and of social workers, all at a greatly reduced cost. In time of war or national emergency, cheerful military service is ensured at rates well below the market price. Above all, says Galbraith (in his *Economics and the Public Purpose*, 1974), the 'ultimate success of the convenient social virtue has been in converting women to menial personal service'. According to Thorstein Veblen (in his *The Theory of the Leisure Class*), in 'the ideal scheme of the pecuniary culture, the lady of the house is the chief menial of the household'.

Conversion issue. Issue of new stock by Government or other borrower, offered to holders in exchange for an existing stock which is, or will shortly become, due for repayment. *See* ADVANCE REFUNDING (U.S.).

Convertibility. The freedom to exchange any currency for another currency at the ruling rate of exchange.

Convertible debentures. Bonds that the holder may convert into the preferred or common stock (q.v.) of the same corporation at the option of the holder. The terms of the conversion are specified at the outset of the issue and include the conversion ratio (that is, how many shares of stock the holder will receive for each bond that is converted).

Convertible gilt-edged stock. Issued by the Bank of England (q.v.) in 1981; an example was 12 per cent Exchequer Convertible Stock 1985 which gave investors the right to convert into a longer-dated (1992) stock at pre-determined prices on any one of five dates over 2 years beginning in September, 1981. It enabled investors to lock-in to a fixed interest rate in the future, but left them with the hope that in the event of a fall in market rates a capital gain would be made.

Convertible notes. A special issue by companies as a means of raising finance; the holder has an option to convert the holding into ordinary shares at some future date, or to be paid out in cash on the maturity of the note. Notes carry a fixed rate of interest.

Convertible preferred stock (U.S.). Preferred stock (q.v.) which may be exchanged, under certain terms and conditions, for common stock (q.v.). For example, after a stated date each share of the convertible issue may be exchangeable for, say, three shares of common stock.

Co-operative banks. Small local institutions, usually, organised by a group of individuals with a common bond or purpose. Designed to give members easier and cheaper access to credit, these institutions tend to remain small. As an exception, in France, Crédit Agricole is a large umbrella organisation for a huge number of local agricultural co-operative banks; it is the largest bank in the country. *See* CREDIT UNION.

Co-ownership firm. A firm in which control and ownership is largely in the hands of the employees of that firm. An example in the retail field is the John Lewis Partnership. This company is controlled by a central council, 80 per cent of the membership of which is elected by the employees and 20 per cent by the management. An example in the manufacturing field is Scott Bader. This company is controlled by a community council comprising employee representatives. In both firms there are highly developed systems of information sharing and channels for employees to influence management. Both concerns have been operating in democratic form for more than 30 years and have been commercially successful.

Co-partnership in industry. Schemes introduced by individual firms to give employees a bigger stake in the prosperity of the firms they work for. Full co-partnership is made up of three main elements:

(a) Machinery for joint-consultation by means of which information and ideas can flow freely between employers and employed;

(b) The granting to employees of a share of a pre-determined portion of the net profits of the firm, in accordance with a scheme which has secured the prior agreement of all concerned; and

(c) The enabling and encouragement of employees to acquire capital in the firm which employs them

Besides full co-partnership incorporating all these features, some schemes are confined to employee-shareholding or profit-sharing.

Coreper. A group comprising the ten ambassadors of the European Economic Community (q.v.); all European Commission (q.v.) proposals go first to Coreper for detailed study and reconciliation, if possible, of national interests. Proposals go then to the Council of Ministers.

Corner. The buying up of the whole or the larger part of the stocks of a commodity with a view to selling at a higher price from a monopolistic position.

Corporate income tax (U.S.). A tax on the earnings of business corporations imposed by the U.S. Federal Government and most of the States. Tax yields from this source account for about 15 per cent of the revenues of the Federal Government.

Corporate paper. Notes sold by large corporations in the money market as a means of obtaining funds; such notes are secured by the general credit standing of the corporation. Corporate paper appeared on Canadian money markets in substantial amounts during the 1950s when the cost of corporate borrowing from the chartered banks became relatively high. A market developed for corporate paper and firms with excess funds have tended to make these available to the money market rather than to hold them as bank deposits. *See* PROMISSORY NOTE.

Corporate planning. An approach to top level management problems which emphasises: (a) the need for an organisation to decide exactly what its objectives are; and (b) the need for long-term planning in every part of the organisation to achieve these objectives

Corporation. A contemporary form of business organisation in the United States of America and elsewhere, with two distinct characteristics: it is a legal entity separated from its owners, the stockholders; and it is usually on a scale much too large for the sole proprietor or partnership to manage or fund. In the United States corporations are chartered under state laws; in general these charters include the right of the common stockholder to amend the charter, adopt and amend byelaws made under the charter, elect the directors of the corporation, change the amount of authorised stock, enter into mergers, share in the residual assets in the event of dissolution, sell shares, and inspect the corporation's books. The stockholders' liability is limited to the investment they have in the corporation, while ownership can be transferred relatively easily by the sale of stock. The corporation has become the principal agency for the conduct of business and economic expansion in all industrial nations in the non-communist world.

Corporation bond. Bonds issued by corporations; owing to tax deductions they often provide a less expensive method of raising funds than equity financing. Corporate bonds may be secured (mortgage bonds) or unsecured (debentures). In the former case, the corporation executes either a mortgage pledging specific assets as security, or a blanket mortgage which establishes a lien as security against all the real property owned by the corporation. Debentures are secured by all the corporation's unpledged assets. The ultimate security of a corporation bond rests in the corporation's earning ability.

Corporation tax. *See* COMPANY TAXATION.

Cost. The amount of expenditure incurred in obtaining the services of a factor of a production (q.v.). Cost was once explained by economists in terms of real effort and sacrifice. The approach to cost is now in terms of the opportunities or alternatives foregone; this approach regards the cost of producing or acquiring certain goods and services as the value of the alternative goods and services that could have been obtained instead. *See* OPPORTUNITY-COST.

Cost-benefit analysis. A systematic comparison between the cost of carrying out a service or activity and the value of that service or activity, quantifying, as far as possible, all costs and benefits whether direct or indirect, financial or social. It is of particular value and relevance where public services are involved, involving both cost and benefit to the general public; thus a public service may be justified in circumstances which a private organisation would regard as 'uneconomic'.

The theory and practice of cost-benefit analysis (or benefit-cost analysis, the American term) was developed in the United States in response to a legal requirement imposed in 1936 on the water resource projects of the Federal Government; this requirement specified that projects be undertaken only '. . . if the benefits to whomsoever they may accrue are in excess of the estimated costs . . .'. (U.S. Flood Control Act 1936). Efforts to implement this requirement led to the preparation of a *Green Book* by a Federal interagency committee composed of the representatives of the major water-resource agencies. This report embodied the general principles of economic analysis as they were to be applied in the formulation and evaluation of Federal water-resource projects. The principles of cost-benefit analysis have since been applied to a wide range of projects and to the design of public policies in various areas. The principles have been applied, despite the inherent difficulties, to pollution control, transportation, urban development, electric power, health, education and welfare, and in social issues such as equity, income distribution, and unemployment.

Cost-benefit analyses proceed by adding-up total money costs and benefits (reduced to present worth), generally disregarding who incurs the costs and receives the benefits. If the money aggregate is positive, this is taken to indicate that the gainers could compensate the losers and still be better off after the project is completed. If the net monetary gain is negative, the compensation test fails. Net monetary gains are generally held to measure the efficiency effects of government projects (or policy changes) in this sense. If gainers can more than compensate losers, the change will realise a potential Pareto improvement (q.v.).

Cost-benefit ratio. A ratio calculated:

$$\frac{\text{Gross Benefits (present value)}}{\text{Gross Costs (present value)}}$$

The gross costs and benefits are discounted over the life of the project by a selected annual rate of interest. The difference between the two amounts is the present value of net benefits. The ratio of the two amounts is the gross cost-benefit ratio. Both considerations are relevant in choosing between projects.

Cost coefficient. The cost of a unit of output, e.g. the cost of processing a kilogram of material or the cost of mining a ton of coal. A concept useful in comparisons between processes of a similar charater.

Cost control. The procedure by which the management accountant evaluates the actual cost of a capital project or a manufacturing operation for the purpose of comparison with the authorised estimates or cost standard; in the event of marked deviation, appropriate action can then be taken.

Cost curve. A graph showing by means of a curve the expenses which a firm will incur in achieving any given volume of output.

Cost marginal. *See* MARGINAL COST.

Cost of sales (U.S.). All costs incurred in a factory in converting raw materials into a finished product; such costs include raw materials, labour, and factory overheads.

Cost of service principle. A basis for charging for services, regard being had to the costs of producing a particular service rather than the value of the service to the consumer. In conditions of perfect competition charges would tend to correspond to costs, including normal profit. In a public utility, the principle may be adopted as a deliberate policy. To apply the cost of service principle accurately is a very difficult matter, however, involving elaborate costing techniques. An initial difficulty is that the phrase itself is ambiguous—it may mean simply the short-run marginal cost, or it may mean the additional cost plus a fair share of the overhead costs of the undertaking. Assuming the latter, there is still much scope for disagreement as to what is a 'fair share' of overhead costs in a particular case. Some have claimed that the system cannot be applied in practice except in a very rough and ready manner. *See* PRICING; VALUE OF SERVICE PRINCIPLE.

Costigan Royal Commission (Aust.). The Australian Royal Commission on the Federated Ship Painters and Dockers' Union, chaired by Mr. Frank Costigan, Q.C., which uncovered in the course of its inquiries into union activities much evidence of financial malpractice in other areas, particularly in respect of 'bottom-of-the-harbour' tax avoidance schemes (q.v.). In 1983, it uncovered multi-million dollar criminal income tax frauds and recommended that controls over foreign exchange, taxation, banking and company records should be radically tightened to stop organised crime flourishing.

Cost-push inflation. *See* INFLATION, COST-PUSH.

Costs, long-run average. The lowest practicable average cost of producing a commodity, within the current state of technical knowledge and managerial ability, after adequate time has been allowed to make all the necessary adjustments.

Costs of production. Expenditure incurred by way of payments for rent, mortgages, interest on loans, dividends, salaries and wages, buildings, plant and machinery and raw materials, in the production of a commodity or a service, including development and marketing costs. Accountancy costs are the expenses incurred in producing commodities or services; costs may be divided into fixed costs or overhead costs (those which are incurred even at zero output), and variable costs (those which vary with the level of output). Costs may also be divided into the following categories:

(1) Total Cost (T.C.). The sum of fixed and variable costs at any given level of output.
(2) Average Cost (A.C.). T.C. at output Q, divided by Q.
(3) Total Variable Cost (T.V.C.). T.C. at any given level of output minus fixed costs.
(4) Average Variable Cost (A.V.C.). T.V.C. at output Q, divided by Q.
(5) Marginal Cost (M.C.). At any given level of output, the addition to total cost of producing one more unit of output.

See FIGURE 3.

Council for Mutual Economic Assistance (Comecon). An organisation established in January, 1949, by several eastern European countries for the purpose of centralising arrangements for trade, credit and technical assistance among the members. The members now comprise the Soviet Union, Bulgaria, Cuba, Czechoslovakia, Hungary, Poland, Rumania, the German Democratic Republic and the Mongolian People's Republic. The Bank of Socialist Countries, founded under the auspices of Comecon, began to operate on 1 January 1964. In June, 1962, the Council recommended that the individual development plans of the members should be co-ordinated at the draft stage, envisaging far-reaching economic integration and an end to autarkic tendencies. However, the application of this policy soon met with opposition within the Council, particularly from Rumania.

Council for the Securities Industry (C.S.I.). Formed in 1978, a voluntary body which co-ordinates regulation in the square mile of the City of London. The membership includes The Stock Exchange Council and the Issuing Houses Association together with representatives of the licensed dealers in securities. *See* 'CITY, THE'.

Council of Economic Advisers (C.E.A.). A three-member Council which advises the President of the United States on national economic policy. The Council was established under the Employment Act 1946, its charter being revised under the Full Employment and Balanced Growth Act 1978 (the Humphreys-

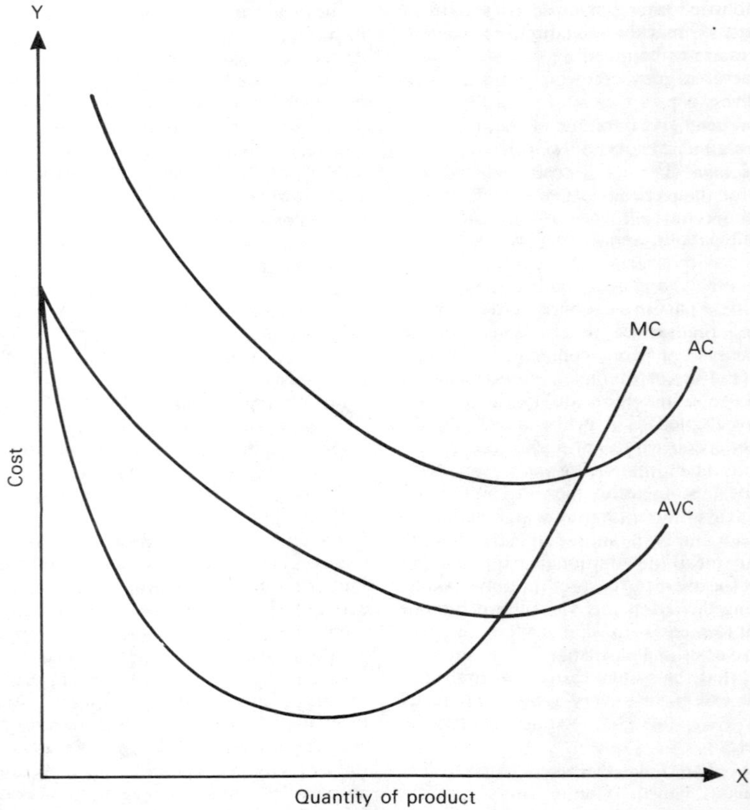

Figure 3 The relationship of the average total cost, average variable cost, and marginal cost curves

Hawkins Act). More specifically, the Council's role is to: advise the President on macro-economic policy, fiscal policies, regulation and regulation reform, energy policies, and international economic policies; to prepare economic forecasts; to assist in the development and implementation of national economic policies designed to achieve the government's objectives for employment, output, and price stability; to assist the President in the preparation of an annual economic report; gather information on economic conditions; appraise economic programmes and activities of the Federal government; and carry out special economic studies for the President.

Countervailing duty. Or matching duty. A situation achieved when an excise duty (q.v.) on an article produced at home equals the customs duty (q.v.) imposed on a similar article imported from abroad, neither the home-produced or imported product being given an advantage. For example, excise duty on British manufactured beer is matched or 'countervailed' by a customs duty of virtually the same level on imported beer. Also a tariff imposed to offset a foreign subsidy, or to counter dumping (q.v.).

Countervailing power. A concept developed by Professor John Kenneth Galbraith (b. 1908), envisaging restraint being placed on the freedom of action of monopolists or oligopolists by the existence of opposing power in the purchasing market, or in the labour market. For example, the buying power of large retail firms almost certainly curbs any tendency to monopolistic pricing on the part of their suppliers. Firms selling to large vehicle manufacturers are constrained by the fact that the manufacturers may decide to make the part themselves.

Coupon bond. A bond (q.v.) with interest coupons attached; the coupons are clipped as they become due and are presented by the owner for the payment of interest.

Coupon interest rate. The interest rate attracted by the coupons attached to a bond (q.v.).

Coupon rate. The coupon value divided by the face value of a bond multiplied by 100; if £25 is paid for a bond with a coupon value of £2,50, then the yield or coupon rate is 10 per cent.

Cover. (1) The cancellation of a 'short' position in any future by the purchase of an equal quantity of the same future; (2) Collateral deposited as security against an open position (q.v.); (3) The amount of money a company has available for distribution as dividend (q.v.), divided by the amount actually paid. If this results in a figure of 1 or more, the dividend is that number of times covered; if the result is less than 1, the dividend is uncovered. *See* DIVIDEND COVER.

Covered bear. A person, who, believing prices will fall, sells securities with a view to repurchasing them later at a lower price. He does not, however, deliver the securities sold hoping to save expense on repurchasing; if, however, prices rise he is in a position to deliver stock without paying inflated prices.

Covering. Buying a security previously sold short. *See* SHORT COVERING.

Crawling peg. Descriptive of a compromise arrangement between a fixed exchange rate and a floating exchange rate (q.v.), where the exchange value of a currency is allowed to alter over time but only by some agreed-upon percentage each year.

Credit. A loan made either directly, or indirectly, through deferred payments for goods received; thus credit may be extended by a creditor (lender) to a debtor (borrower) either through the transfer of cash with the promise of future repayment, or through the sale of goods to be paid for later in an agreed manner. The creditor may require interest payments over the period of the loan. The widespread use of credit facilities has provided another avenue for the transfer of purchasing power from savers to investors and consumers. *See* CREDIT RATING.

Credit insurance. A type of insurance affording indemnity to merchants and manufacturers against the risk of loss due to the insolvency or protracted default of customers to whom goods are sold on credit. When applied to export credits, the term may embrace facilities outside normal insurance underwriting. *See* EXPORT CREDITS GUARANTEE DEPARTMENT.

Credit rating. An evaluation of the soundness of an individual or business firm as a credit risk. It is usually based on the three 'C's' of credit: (a) character, or integrity; (b) capacity, or earning power; and (c) capital, or the overall financial status of the applicant. *See* CREDIT.

Credit sale. A procedure for purchasing goods under which the purchaser pays a deposit on receipt of the goods followed by a number of instalments until the debt is cleared. Generally the goods become the property of the purchaser immediately who may sell or otherwise dispose of them at any time, the liability for the outstanding debt remaining. If a purchaser defaults on the repayment of his debt he may be taken to court; a court order may then be made requiring him to pay the debt. Interest charges are usually expressed as a flat rate per annum. *See* HIRE PURCHASE.

Credit sales system. A credit sales system, which may be offered as an alternative to hire-purchase, under which ownership is obtained at the outset. The borrower must, of course, continue to make the agreed payments. In the credit sales arrangement, the lender's security is the borrower's written promise to repay.

The advantages of instalment credit include the flexibility of the repayment terms (which can be arranged to suit a firm's cash flow pattern), the absence of legal fees, and the widespread availability of the facilities.

Credit union. A group of people engaging in organised self-help who save their money together and make low-interest loans to each other. The loans are usually short-term consumer loans, but may extend to loans for farm or small business enterprise purposes. The directors and management committee are chosen by the members from among their own numbers. Credit unions operate under government charters: there appear to be over 28,000 credit unions in existence, located mainly in the United States of America and Canada. *See* CREDIT.

Creditwatch list. An early warning system introduced by Standard and Poor whereby corporations and companies engaging in unusual behaviour such as a marked deviation in a company's established mode of operation are 'listed'; a listing, which is public, indicates that the company has come under surveillance. The event may be regarded as having positive or negative tendencies; to be listed with negative indications is clearly 'bad news' for a company, as the market is placed 'on notice'. Listings are normally dealt with within a 90-day time frame; but this may be extended in special cases. The United States corporation of Standard and Poor is one of the world's 'big two' of credit rating organisations, the other being Moody's. *See* STANDARD AND POOR'S INDEXES.

Creeping inflation. Descriptive of the slow inflationary trend which characterised the western economies during the 25 years immediately following the Second World War. In the 14 years 1953–67 in 11 leading industrial countries it averaged just over 2 per cent a year. From about 1968, the rise in labour costs per unit of industrial output began to accelerate in all industrial countries, followed by rapidly rising commodity prices in 1970–72 which in turn preceded the fourfold rise in oil prices following the Arab-Israeli war. All this resulted in an unprecedented inflation in consumer prices in all countries.

Cross. To buy and sell simultaneously in the same contract month for the same commodity.

Cross-section analysis. The analysis of a series of records of economic data for different groups of people, firms or countries, at the same moment or in broadly the same period of time; it contrasts with time series analysis which measures the changing situation at successive points in time.

Cross-subsidisation. The transfer of earnings from remunerative individual plants or products to unremunerative plants or products within the same enterprise, including transfers of earnings between peak and off-peak outputs. The Committee of Inquiry into the Electricity Supply Industry (the Herbert Committee), reporting to the British Government in 1956, criticised cross-subsidisation in electricity supply on the grounds that it may cause a misallocation of resources; the Committee favoured a detailed relating of prices to costs on individual services as the most fair and efficient approach.

Crowding-out. Descriptive of any group being pushed out of a market; specifically the term has been used to describe ways in which the demand for credit by the private sector may be 'crowded-out' of the financial markets by the stronger and inflexible demand of the public sector. In the notion of 'crowding-out' public expenditure is cast in the role of retarding the expansion of the economy, rather than in the more frequently attributed role of over-stimulating it. In practice, depending on circumstances, either characteristic may temporarily dominate the market, as the public and private sectors compete for funds.

Crowther Committee (U.K.). The Committee on Consumer Credit set up under the chairmanship of Lord Crowther in 1968, its report being published in March, 1971. The committee recommended that the confused array of different Acts relating to credit be abolished and replaced by a single body of law, based on a clear recognition that all credit was essentially the same. It recommended the introduction of a licensing system for all agencies connected with consumer credit. *See* CONSUMER CREDIT ACT 1974.

Cum. Latin for 'with'. *See* CUM ALL; CUM BONUS; CUM DRAWING; CUM INTEREST; CUM RIGHTS.

Cum all. With-all advantages. A description which may be attached to the sale of a security, implying that any dividend, interest, rights, bonus or other benefit, just declared or current is not being withheld. *See* EX-ALL.

Cum bonus. With bonus just declared. A condition which may be attached to the sale of a security.

Cum drawing. With benefit of the current drawing (q.v.). If there is no benefit, it means with the liability for loss of drawing. A condition that may be attached to the sale of a security.

Cum interest. With current interest. A condition which may be attached to the sale of a security.

Cum rights. With 'rights' recently issued. A condition which may be attached to the sale of a security.

Cumulative preference share. A preference share (q.v.) entitling the holder to receive not only the current dividend but also any unpaid arrears, before any dividend is paid to ordinary shareholders.

Cumulative preferred stock (U.S.). Preferred stock (q.v.), the dividends on which, if unpaid, continue to accumulate until paid. *See* NON-CUMULATIVE PREFERRED STOCK.

Curb exchange (U.S.). Former name of the American Stock Exchange (q.v.), second largest exchange in the United States; the term comes from the origin of the exchange on the streets of downtown New York.

Currency and Bank-Notes Acts 1928–1954. The chief provisions of these Acts were:

(a) The Bank of England (q.v.) to take over the Treasury (q.v.) issue of notes (during the period 1914–28 the Treasury issued notes in denominations of £1 and 10s.);
(b) The fiduciary issue (q.v.) to be increased by the 1928 Act to £260 million. All

notes above this to be backed £1 for £1 by gold. The fiduciary issue to be varied only with the consent of the Treasury;
(c) Under the 1954 Act the size of the fiduciary issue to depend entirely on the decision of the Government.

See FIDUCIARY ISSUE.

Currency-deposit ratio. The ratio of the public's holdings of currency to its holdings of deposits at banks. In the United States, in early 1980, the ratio was 0.38 (i.e. $109 billion currency as a proportion of $283 billion demand deposits), using the M1–B (q.v.) definition of the money stock.

Currency hedge market. A currency market providing hedging (q.v.) against future currency rates of exchange. Consider an exporter who expects to receive $U.S. 25 million in 6 months' time and who wishes to fix his price for the transaction in Australian dollars. With a present exchange rate of U.S. 94 cents for an Australian dollar, let us assume that a hedge dealer quotes a rate for 6 months forward at U.S. 91 cents, and the exporter accepts that rate. In 6 months' time, the exporter receives his $U.S. 25 million; however, the spot rate of exchange may have moved up or down during that time. At the agreed exchange rate of 91 cents, the Australian exporter would receive in terms of Australian dollars the sum of $A 27,473,000. However, if the spot rate had changed to 95 cents, the exporter would only be credited with $A 26,316,000; to settle the hedge, the dealer would send him a cheque for the difference of $A 1,157,000. If the spot rate had moved to say 87 cents, the exporter would be credited with $A 28,736,000 and he would owe the dealer the sum of $A 1,263,000. The exporter gets an exchange rate of 91 cents to the Australian dollar no matter what happens to the rate before he settles. The final adjustments are settled by arrangement with his trading bank.

Current assets and liabilities. Current assets are those assets of the company which are reasonably expected to be realised in cash, or sold, or consumed during the normal operating cycle of the business. Such assets include cash, bonds, inventories, and money due within 1 year. Current liabilities, on the other hand, consist of money owed and payable by a company, usually within one year.

Current cost accounting. A system of inflation accounting in which assets are recorded in the accounts of a company at their 'value to the business', i.e. the loss the business would suffer if the asset were destroyed, in money terms. Accounts then reflect the effect of relative price changes on the business. In practice the system resembles replacement cost accounting, but with no adjustment for monetary items. For example, the company charges against revenue the amount it would have had to pay to buy stocks at the time they were sold, rather than the amount they actually cost when they were bought earlier. Plant and machinery is valued at replacement cost. In the balance sheet, all non-monetary items are revalued annually at current costs. The balance sheet becomes then a statement about values instead of simply historic costs which have become increasingly irrelevant because of inflation. The Sandilands Committee on Inflation Accounting recommended in its 1976 report a similar approach. *See* HISTORIC COSTS.

Customs Co-operation Council. An international council comprising the Comptrollers-General of Customs from around the world; inter alia, the Council seeks to maintain a uniform trade classification. During the early 1980s, the classification system was greatly enlarged and incorporated for the first time such items as freight forwarding, insurance and travel.

Customs duty. Revenue protective or preferential duty imposed on goods imported from abroad, e.g. customs duty on leaf tobacco imported into Britain, varying with source and moisture content. Imported hydrocarbon oils and beer are also subject to customs duty. *See* EXCISE DUTY.

Cut a dividend. Pay a smaller dividend (q.v.) than the previous one.

Cyclical stocks. Stocks and shares (q.v.) of those companies which are sharply affected by 'feast or famine' swings in their respective industries.

D

Daisy chain schemes. Commercial schemes in which the ownership of a commodity is transferred through the hands of a chain of subsidiaries, tax-haven companies, affiliates, and other companies; a commodity may be sold at a low price for export and re-imported later for sale at a higher world price, leaving offshore a substantial untaxed mark-up.

Damping. In economics, a reducing effect. For example, at low levels of market demand some people may withdraw from the labour market, thus damping the rise in unemployment figures. *See* ACTIVITY RATE.

Dated securities. Bonds, bills of exchange, and other securities which have a stated date for repayment (redemption) of their nominal (face) value. Securities without a redemption date are known as 'undated' or 'irredeemable' securities.

Day order. An order given by an investor to a stockbroker (q.v.) which holds good for 1 day only.

Day trader. A speculator (q.v.) who takes positions in the futures market and then liquidates them before the close of the same trading day.

Dead horse. Work which has been paid for but has yet to be completed; a situation in which services and goods are paid for in advance of performance or production.

Deadweight debt. That part of the National Debt (q.v.) not covered by real assets, in contrast to Reproductive Debt. Most of the National Debt is of this type.

Dealer. (a) A person carrying on a business of selling goods, whether by wholesale or by retail, or engaging in the buying and selling of shares. *See* STOCKJOBBER; (b) An individual or firm dealing in securities acting as a principal rather than as an agent. Typically, a dealer buys for his own account and sells to a customer from his own inventory.

Dealing within the account. Buying and selling the same security within the same account period (q.v.); this means that no stocks or shares need to be delivered and the investor either pays or receives the cash difference involved.

Death duties. Duties payable when a property passes at death. Death duties are often progressive, increasing in proportion with the value of the estate.

Debentures. Long-term fixed interest loans to companies. Interest is payable by a company on these stocks whether a profit is earned or not. Debenture stockholders rank as creditors of the company; if the interest is not forthcoming, the debenture holders can sell up the company and repay themselves (capital and interest due) out of the proceeds. Debenture stocks may be bought or sold in any amounts, subject to any special restrictions imposed by a company. The interests are relatively low, but the capital is usually very secure. There are three main types of debenture:

(a) Mortgage debentures. These are secured by the mortgage of a particular fixed property (land or buildings) owned by the company.
(b) Income debentures.
(c) Guaranteed debentures, usually incorporating a third party guarantee.

In the case of liquidation of the company, mortgage debentures rank ahead of other types up to the value of the properties on which they are secured. All debenture creditors rank ahead of any shareholder, preferred or ordinary. Debentures may be issued at par (q.v.), at a discount on par, or at a premium on par. *See* INCOME BONDS AND DEBENTURES.

Debt. A sum of money, or quantity of goods or services, owed by one individual or body to another. *See* DEADWEIGHT DEBT; FLOATING DEBT; NATIONAL DEBT.

Debt/equity ratio. Total borrowing less cash as a percentage of capital employed. The Bank of

England (q.v.) has calculated that the top 250 companies in Britain had a debt/equity ratio of 27 per cent in 1981, after eliminating the effects of inflation.

Debtors' repayment period. A measure of the average length of time taken for debtors to pay their accounts; a warning signal over a number of years if it takes longer and longer to retrieve accounts from debtors. It is calculated by dividing trade debts by sales turnover and multiplying by 365 days.

Decasualisation. The abolition of the casual employment of workers; casual employment was for many years a notorious characteristic of the London docks. Lord Beveridge (1879–1963), who first used the expression 'decasualisation' recommended permanent employment and guaranteed minimum wages for docks employees. *See* DEVLIN REPORT.

Decentralisation. A conscious policy of relocating some parts of an organisation in outlying regions, away from metropolitan areas, or guiding new organisations into those regions. As an aspect of state regional development policy, it often involves providing incentives to firms to locate in centres which would not otherwise have been chosen. A general system of incentives is often ineffective, and the tendency in some countries is to offer incentives in relation to selected centres only; this is known as selective decentralisation. It is also recognised that incentives of a permanent character introduce economic inefficiency, and the tendency is to offer incentives of a temporary character, e.g. to overcome the initial disadvantages only that firms might encounter by moving.

Decimal currency. Metallic and paper currency in which each successive denomination is ten times the value of that next below it; commonly the basic unit of currency is divided into 100 cents. The United States of America was the first country to adopt the decimal system, coining both gold and silver money in 1792; many other countries have adopted the same principle. The system enjoys two main advantages: (a) the ease with which the relationship of the value of the various notes and coins can be computed; and (b) the convenience for arithmetic purposes of stating sums of money as multiples of the unit of account.

In Britain, the Halsbury Committee reported in 1963 on the most convenient and practical form which a decimal coinage might take, if adopted, a majority of the Committee favouring the retention of the pound, the standard unit being divided into 100 sub-units. The Decimal Currency Act 1967 provided for a decimal system based on the pound sterling, the pound being divided into 100 new pence. The new system took effect from 15 February 1971

Declaration day. The latest day or time by which the buyer of an option (q.v.) must indicate to the seller his intention to exercise or abandon the option.

Decreasing cost industry. An industry in which the average cost curve of a typical firm tends to fall with an expansion of output.

Decreasing costs, law of. The tendency towards falling average costs of production in taking advantage of the economies of scale, over the long period. Sir Roy Harrod (b. 1900) described the form of the long-period cost curve as the envelope of the short-period cost curves. It was assumed that an initial choice of size of plant would be made from an array of plant sizes, each with its own parabolic cost curve, arranged in descending order of minimum average cost according to the economies of scale. The long-period curve was defined as the locus of the lowest possible average cost of production for any given output, on the assumption that the right size of plant was chosen to secure that cost. This locus was then shown to be the envelope of the cost curves of the plants providing the lowest possible cost for the given outputs. The implication was that each plant would, at that output, be operating below capacity.

Decreasing returns to scale. A possible response of total output to changes in the scale of the production process: when the employment of all factors of production is doubled, total output is less than doubled.

Deduction. The method of reasoning from principles to facts, from the general to the particular. It is a method which begins by investigating the principal forces determining a given class of phenomena, and the general laws in accordance with which these forces operate. It then goes on to trace the consequences which ensue from their action and interaction under specified conditions. Alfred Marshall expressed the opinion that in economics, at any rate in dealing with concrete cases, there is no scope for long chains of deductive reasoning. Nevertheless, he took the view, that 'induction and deduction are both needed for scientific thought as the right and left foot are both needed for walking'. There is no one method, therefore, which can be properly called the method of economics. *See* INDUCTION.

Deed of transfer. A formal agreement under seal bearing a government revenue stamp and signed by both the buyer and the seller of, for example, shares. Upon the registration of the deed of transfer the holder receives in due course a certificate which, in conjunction with his registration in the company's books, confirms his ownership of shares. *See* BEARER STOCKS OR BONDS.

Deep discount bonds. Loan bonds or stocks on which a very low coupon interest rate (q.v.) is payable (or in the case of a zero coupon bond, nil) but which have an issue price of only a fraction of the eventual redemption value. The capital gain or uplift over the life of the bond compensates for the low, or non-existent, income over the period. In the Eurobond market, zero coupon bonds have been issued at a price of $8 for redemption in 20 years' time at $100. *See* ZERO COUPON BOND.

Deferred, founders' or management shares. Shares which have to wait for their dividend until all other classes of share have participated in the profits. Often taken by the founder as promoter of the company. These are generally entitled to the whole or a very large portion of the surplus profit after payment of all prior claims.

Deferred futures. The most distant months of a futures contract (q.v.).

Deferred ordinary share. A share which ranks for dividend after the preferred ordinary share (q.v.).

Deferred rebates. Rebates granted on the charge for some service, or on the price of goods, on a deferred basis as a means of encouraging customers to buy exclusively from a particular firm or from members of an association over a period of time. This technique has been employed, for example, by Shipping Conferences (q.v.). Schemes differ in detail, but usually if goods are shipped in Conference ships during a prescribed period (perhaps 6 or 12 months) a rebate is earned. If, during a further similar period, all goods are again so shipped, the rebate is actually paid or credited. Also called aggregated rebates.

Deferred (D.D.) shares. Shares quoted as 'D.D.' being the result of a reconstruction of the company's share capital where shareholders have surrendered old scrip (q.v.) to the company, but the company has yet to issue new scrip. Shareholders who wish to sell must do so on a 'D.D.' basis so buyers know that they cannot yet expect delivery of scrip.

Deficit blow-out. An unexpected and unplanned enlargement of a Government budget deficit due to a combination of unforeseen and unforeseeable events. In Australia, in 1982, a deficit blow-out occurred due to drought assistance measures, poor economic growth associated with lower tax receipts, and a steep rise in the number of people receiving unemployment benefits.

Deficit financing. The financing of a budget deficit by the Government by means of borrowing against the issue of Government securities, that is by increasing the National Debt (q.v.). A budget deficit is incurred as a means of stimulating the economy through increased Government expenditure.

Deflation. A situation in which prices and money incomes are falling, accompanied by an increase in the value of the monetary unit.

De-industrialisation (U.K.). Descriptive of the loss of 4 million jobs, amounting to 34 per cent of the industrial workforce, in Britain between 1966 and 1982. Between 1966 and 1979, while gross domestic product increased by 29 per cent, manufacturing output grew by only 11 per cent. Thus the collapse of industrial output in 1979–81 followed a long period in which the manufacturing share of total economic activity had been steadily shrinking.

Deliverable types. *See* CONTRACT GRADES.

Delivery month. The month in which a futures contract (q.v.) matures, resulting in, for example, the delivery of the specified currency or fixed interest commitment.

Delivery Not Enforceable (D.E.L.) shares. Shares quoted as D.E.L. being the result of a new issue for which the scrip (q.v.) has not yet been issued. These shares sell for slightly less than the existing shares to compensate for the delay in scrip delivery.

Demand. The amount of a commodity or service which will be bought at any given price per unit of time. In society, the two main components of demand are consumption (q.v.) and investment (q.v.). Aggregate demand curves slope down from left to right, with real income increasing as prices fall. *See* ELASTICITY OF DEMAND; SUPPLY; SUPPLY AND DEMAND, LAWS OF.

Demand, cross-elasticity of. The responsiveness of the demand for a commodity or service to changes in the prices of other commodities. It is calculated:

$$\frac{\text{Percentage change in demand for commodity X}}{\text{Percentage change in price of commodity Y}}$$

If commodities are complementary they have negative cross-elasticities. i.e. if X and Y are complementary a fall in the price of Y will lead to an increase in demand for both X and Y. The changes in the quantity of X and the price of Y will have opposite signs. Substitutes have positive cross-elasticities, i.e. a fall in the price of Y will increase the quantity of Y consumed, but will reduce the quantity of X consumed. Changes in the price of Y and the quantity X will have the same sign. *See* COMPLEMENTARY GOODS; ELASTICITY OF DEMAND.

Demand curve. A graphical presentation of demand function, $x = \phi(p)$, showing how much of a commodity will be bought per unit of time at any given price, providing that the other influences governing demand remain unchanged, i.e. that the incomes of consumers and their tastes remain constant, and that the price level of closely related commodities remains constant. The demand curve is referred to axes OY and OX along which prices and demands are respectively measured. It is an economic convention that demand curves are referred to a vertical price axis. In normal demand curves x decreases as y increases, i.e. the demand function, $x = \phi(p)$, is monotonic decreasing. The shape is generally concave, but the precise form will depend on the commodity and the elasticity of demand. In the case of common salt, for example, a considerable fall in price will not be likely to result in a large increase in sales. The elasticity of demand depends upon a number of parameters such as the number of consumers, their incomes and tastes, and the price of other goods generally and of close substitutes in particular. Figure 4 depicts a demand curve. In exceptional circumstances demand curves may be regressive, or backward sloping, indicating that over a limited period the fall in price of a commodity may be followed by a fall in demand, e.g. due to an expectation that price will fall even lower. The terms 'expansion' and 'contraction' of demand are reserved for changes in demand attributable to changes in the price of the commodity only; the amount demanded at any given price remaining constant. The terms 'increase' or 'decrease' in demand are reserved for changes in demand attributable to changes in the state of demand; more or fewer goods being demanded at any given price than formerly.

Changes in demand are shifts or movements of the entire demand curve; a shift to the right means an increase in demand, while a leftward shift of the curve means a fall in demand. An

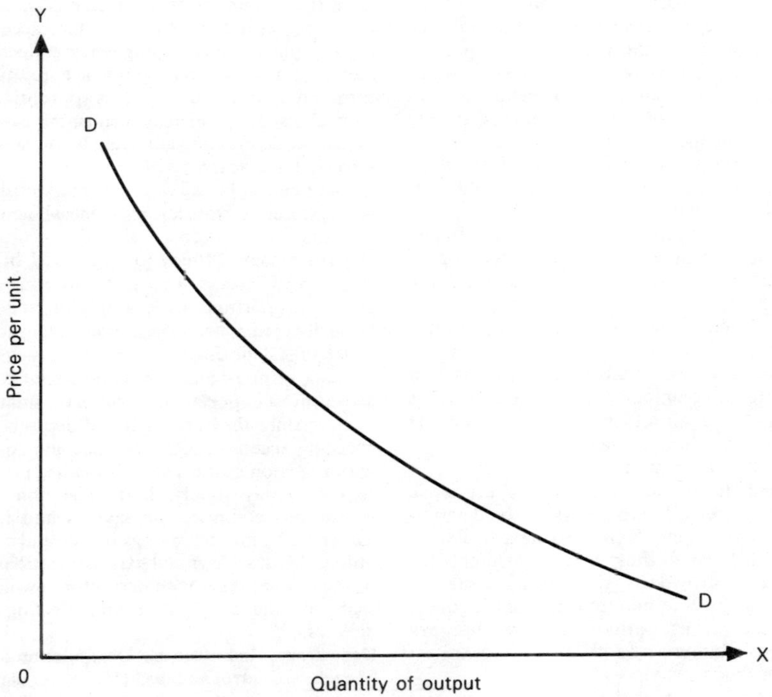

Figure 4 Demand curve

exception is 'inferior goods'. As income rises the demand for inferior goods falls at any given price. That is, increases in consumer incomes, ceteris paribus, cause the downward sloping demand curves for inferior goods to shift to the left, not right. *See* INFERIOR GOODS.

Demand function. The relationship between the quantity of a good which a consumer wants to buy, and all the quantitative factors which determine his/her demand, e.g. the price of the good, the price of complementary goods, the price of substitutes, the consumer's income, and methods of payment. If all factors are held constant, save one, it is possible to study how demand will vary with changes in that one element. *See* DEMAND, THEORY OF; SUPPLY AND DEMAND, LAWS OF.

Demand price. The price (q.v.) which buyers are prepared to pay for a given quantity of a good or service.

Demand management policies. Keynesian policies of pursuing an activist, stabilisation course by regulating aggregate demand (q.v.) so as to minimise unemployment and curb inflation.

The concept of demand management is applicable to areas other than the economy as a whole. The demand for water, for example, can be greatly influenced by the policies adopted in respect of such matters as water charges, restrictions on peak demands, and unrestricted use of treated water. A steeply rising schedule of water charges may be adopted for those periods of the year when demand tends to be greatest. Considerable cost savings can be made if peak demands are not allowed to rise unhindered. Demand management in this area requires the metering of supplies to individual consumers, including households.

Demand-pull inflation. *See* INFLATION, DEMAND-PULL.

Demand schedule. A table giving the demand (q.v.) for a commodity or service at various prices, while all other factors determining demand remain unchanged.

Demand-shift inflation. *See* INFLATION.

Demand, theory of. A branch of economic theory concerned with analysing the determinants of a consumer's choice of a particular set of goods from all those that are available for purchase, particularly with how a consumer's tastes and income, and the prices of the goods, influence his/her pattern of purchases. *See* DEMAND CURVE; INDIFFERENCE ANALYSIS; INDIFFERENCE CURVE.

Demographic transition. A fundamental change in the characteristic trends of a population, e.g. a transition from high birth rates and high death rates to low birth rates and low death rates. Much of Europe and North America has passed through this demographic transition. Japan is now experiencing the same transition characteristic of the Western world; the growth rate of the population of Japan has declined to about 1 per cent per annum, similar to that of North America.

Demurrage charges. The monetary penalty paid to compensate for the delaying of a ship or freight car due to a consignee's failure to load, unload or sail within an allotted amount of time.

Department of Trade and Industry (U.K.). A department with responsibilities for overseas trade policy; promotion of exports; industrial policy and consumer protection (embracing the Office of Fair Trading (q.v.) and the Monopolies and Mergers Commission (q.v.)); science, technology and research; administration of company legislation; and the Business Statistics Office. *See* EXPORT CREDITS GUARANTEE DEPARTMENT.

Depletion accounting. An accounting practice consisting of charges against earnings based upon the amount of an asset taken out of the total reserves in the period for which accounting is made. A bookkeeping entry, it does not represent any cash outlay nor are any funds earmarked for the purpose. It is appropriate to natural resources, such as metals, oil, gas and timber, which conceivably can be reduced to zero over the years.

Deposit banks. Banks whose primary business is the receipt, transfer and encashment of deposits.

Deposit money. Money (q.v.) created by the commercial banks (q.v.) constituting the greater proportion of the supply of money.

Deposit-type financial institutions. Institutions which take deposits from the public; they may be bank or non-bank. The commercial banks are the most important element in the financial system; since they hold demand deposits (i.e. checking account funds) they account for the major portion of the narrowly defined portion of the money supply, M-1. The non-bank institutions comprise the savings and loans associations, mutual savings banks, and credit unions. Most savings and loan associations are of the mutual type, with depositors owning a share of the association and electing the directors.

Depository Institutions Deregulation and Monetary Control Act 1981 (U.S.). Legislation aiming to give the Federal Reserve System (q.v.) greater powers over the money supply by requiring regular reports to the 'Fed' by some 5,000 savings and loan associations (the equivalent of British building societies), 22,000 credit unions, and all the 14,500 commercial banks. Unlike the 5,500 members of the Federal Reserve System, these other bodies did not have to keep reserves against money that could be easily withdrawn; the new Act required them to do so.

The Act also began dismantling controls over the interest that may be paid on savings, and over the type of business that the various institutions could undertake. The Act allowed all commercial banks, and the savings and loans associations, to offer 'negotiated order of withdrawal' (N.O.W.) accounts; these are chequing (i.e. current) accounts on which interest can be paid. Until 1981, N.O.W. accounts were permitted only in the New England states, New York and New Jersey.

Depository or warehouse receipt. A document issued by a bank or warehouse, or a clearing house, indicating ownership of a commodity stored in a depository or warehouse. In the case of some commodities deliverable against futures contracts, transfer or ownership of an appropriate depository receipt may effect contract delivery.

Depository Trust Company (D.T.C.). A central securities certificate depository through which members effect security deliveries between each other via computerised bookkeeping entries thereby reducing the physical movement of stock certificates.

Depreciation. (a) In respect of the exchange rate, an increase in the domestic currency price of foreign exchange. If foreign money becomes more expensive in terms of domestic money, then domestic money has depreciated and foreign money appreciated. *See* APPRECIATION; (b) the diminution in the original value of an asset due to use and/or obsolescence. Depreciation can be calculated at 'historical cost' (the price which was actually paid for the asset at the time of purchase) or at 'replacement cost' (the amount that it would take to replace the asset at the present time). Historical cost is the method normally adopted, but economists tend to favour the second method. *See* DEPRECIATION FUND METHOD; DIMINISHING BALANCE METHOD; FIXED INSTALMENT METHOD; SINKING FUND.

Depreciation fund method. A method of calculating and allowing for the depreciation of an asset. The asset is allowed to stand in the company's books at its original cost and then a fixed amount, known as the 'sinking fund instalment', is debited to the profit and loss account each year and a corresponding amount of cash is invested in securities, the amount being enough to accumulate at compound interest to the sum required to replace the asset. *See* DEPRECIATION; DIMINISHING BALANCE METHOD; FIXED INSTALMENT METHOD; SINKING FUND.

Depression. A prolonged and severe slowing-down of economic activity exemplified by mass unemployment and a level of national income well below its potential level; more severe and long-lasting than a recession (q.v.).

Derived demand. The demand for a commodity not required for its own sake, but for its contribution to the manufacture of another commodity.

Developed nations or industrial nations, those countries which have achieved substantial manufacturing and service capability in addition to advanced techniques in agriculture and raw material extraction. *See* DEVELOPING NATIONS.

Developing nations. Countries which are in the process of building up industrial capacity, but have economies dominated by agricultural and possibly mineral extraction activities. *See* DEVELOPED NATIONS.

Development. The application of human, financial, living and non-living resources to satisfy human needs and improve the quality of human life; inevitably development involves a modification of the biosphere some aspects of which may detract from the quality of life locally, regionally, nationally, or globally. The benefits and disbenefits of development came sharply into focus in the 1970s.

Devlin Report. The report of a committee chaired by Lord Devlin which investigated decasualisation and the causes of dissension in the Port of London; the committee reported in 1965 recommending the complete decasualisation of the dock labour force. The recommendation was put into effect in September 1967. *See* DECASUALISATION.

Diagonal spread. *See* OPTION SPREAD.

Diamond Commission. The Royal Commission on the Distribution of Income and Wealth, set up in 1974 under the chairmanship of Lord Diamond to make 'a thorough and comprehensive inquiry into the existing distribution of income and wealth and to study past trends'. The Commission produced several reports on various aspects of the subject for the British Government.

Differential. The difference between physical price and futures price. *See* FUTURES CONTRACT.

Dillon round. The first international round of

bargaining in respect of the liberation of world trade, conducted in 1962. *See* KENNEDY ROUND; TOKYO ROUND.

Diminishing balance method. A method for calculating and allowing for the depreciation of an asset. In the diminishing, or declining, balance method a constant percentage of the remaining book value of an asset is written off each year. The amount to be written off each year may be calculated from the formula:

$$\frac{P-CD}{n}$$

where P is the initial asset cost; CD the cumulative depreciation charged in previous years; and n the plant life expressed in years. As the method is that of a geometric progression, it cannot provide for the complete depreciation of the plant. It is therefore necessary at a certain point to switch to the fixed instalment, or straight-line method in order to reach a point where P – CD becomes zero. *See* DEPRECIATION; DEPRECIATION FUND METHOD; FIXED INSTALMENT METHOD; SINKING FUND.

Diminishing returns, law of. A generalisation that while an increase in some inputs relative to other fixed inputs in a productive process may, in a given state of technology, cause total output to increase there will come a point where the extra output resulting from the same additions of extra inputs is likely to diminish. This falling off in extra returns is a consequence of the fact that the additional doses of the varying resources must work with smaller proportions of the fixed resources. In the extreme, the process of additions will become counter-productive.

D.I.N.G.O.S. *See* DISCOUNTED INVESTMENT IN NEGOTIABLE GOVERNMENT OBLIGATIONS.

Dirty float. The introduction of a floating exchange rate, while the monetary authority continues to intervene in the market; continued intervention represents a dirty float. *See* CLEAN FLOAT.

Disappreciation. A movement of prices which, while downward in direction, was merely a correction of a previously excessive rise.

Discount. (a) A reduction in a previously determined price granted to a customer or class of customers; (b) the difference between the price at which a security was issued and the price at which it now stands, if the latter is the lower than that of May; (e) the rate charged sometimes used to refer to the price differences between futures of different delivery months, as in the phrase 'July at a discount to May', indicating that the price of the July future is lower than that of May; (e) the rate charged member banks on their loans from the Federal Reserve Banks. *See* BILL OF EXCHANGE; DEFERRED REBATES; DISCOUNT HOUSE; DISCOUNT RATE; FUTURES CONTRACT.

Discount House (U.K.). A business institution which will buy acceptances from their owners for less than their face value and hold them to maturity. The difference between the price paid and the face value, expressed as a percentage per annum, is called the 'discount rate'. Discount houses borrow 'at call' from banks and other financial institutions; such funds may be called in by the banks at short notice. Money borrowed is invested in British Government Treasury bills, commercial bills of exchange, British Government securities with a life of up to 5 years, and to a limited extent local authority bonds. Discount houses also provide an active market in commercial bills; when a bill, bought on the London market, is sold by a discount house it is endorsed, i.e. the discount house adds its name to the bill thus assuming responsibility for the payment of the bill at maturity in the event of default. The twelve members of the London Discount Market Association have a right to borrow from the Bank of England (q.v.) as 'lender of last resort' (q.v.) should they become short of money as a result of the calling in of loans by the commercial banks (q.v.) In October, 1980, the Bank of England discontinued the practice of quoting prices for the purchase of eligible bank bills, and of Treasury Bills from January, 1981 of more than 1 month to maturity. Discount houses were obliged to put forward their own prices if they wished to offer bills to the Bank. *See* ACCEPTANCE; ACCEPTING HOUSE; BILL OF EXCHANGE; LONDON DISCOUNT MARKET; TREASURY BILLS.

Discount rate. The rate charged member banks on their loans from the Federal Reserve Banks (q.v.); changes in the discount rate have several important effects on credit conditions and hence on the United States economy as a whole. An increase in the rate makes it more costly for banks to borrow at the Reserve Banks; this higher cost may encourage them to sell short-term securities rather than use the discount route. Such sales lower the prices of short-term securities and raise short-term interest rates. The higher cost of funds may force banks to screen loan applications more carefully and to slow the growth in their loan portfolios. Conversely, a reduction in the rate reduces the incentive to sell short-term securities as a substitute for borrowing at the discount window. As a result prices of short-term securities tend to be higher, and interest rates on these securities correspondingly lower than would otherwise be the case. Apart from these influences, changes in the discount rate can have important psychological effects on the attitudes of both lenders and borrowers. These effects react on market expectations and often influence both the timing of borrowers' demands for funds and the willingness of lenders to lend. If the market interprets an increase in the rate as the beginning of a sustained program to tighten credit, the tightening effects can be quite dramatic. Lenders may tend to cut back commitments awaiting more attractive rates. Some borrowers will attempt to complete their borrowing before the expected higher rates occur. A reduction in the rate tends to produce entirely opposite effects. These effects sometimes occur before the actual change in the discount rate takes place; when a change in the rate is fully anticipated (or 'discounted' as the market describes it) the actual change may have little or no effect on credit markets. Changes in the discount rate are initiated by the boards of directors of the individual Reserve Banks, but the Board of Governors must approve all changes which ensures co-ordination. A discount rate is a deduction from the amount loaned, having an equivalent effect of a rate of interest.

Discount window lending. Historically, direct lending by the Bank of England (q.v.) to the discount houses, as an alternative to open-market operations in bills; known as 'through the window' lending. Under the Monetary Control Act 1981 the U.S. Federal Reserve System (q.v.) is directed to open its discount window to any non-member depository institutions that maintain transaction accounts or non-personal time deposits, on the same basis as banks which are members of the system. Advances may be for brief periods or to meet a longer term need for funds.

Discount yield formula. A formula used to discount bills of exchange (q.v.), e.g. a bank accepted bill (q.v.). The formula is:

$$\frac{365 \times \text{Face Value}}{365 + \left(\dfrac{\text{Yield} \times \text{Days to Maturity}}{100}\right)}$$

By this formula the face value of a bill may be discounted to a price which is governed by two variables: The interest rate (yield) and the term to maturity.

Discounted cash flow method. A method of comparing the profitability of alternative projects. This method may be sub-divided into (a) yield method, and (b) net present value method. Both of these techniques utilise as a measure of the 'rating' of an investment the present cash value of a sum to be received at some future date, discounted at compound interest. The present value or worth of a sum to be received at some future date is such an amount as will, with compound interest at a prescribed rate, equal the sum to be received in the future. The yield method is based upon the assumption that the best investment is that from which the proceeds would yield the highest rate of compound interest in equating the present value of the investment with future proceeds. In the net present value method an appropriate percentage rate is stipulated, the present value of the cash inflow is determined using this percentage, the original cost of the investment is subtracted therefrom, and the resulting surplus is the net present value of the investment. Both the yield and net present value methods give reliable guidance to the profitability of alternative schemes, on the assumptions that may be used. However, errors of a serious nature may occur in the assumptions made regarding capital costs or trading returns.

Discounted Investment in Negotiable Government Obligations (D.I.N.G.O.S.). A form of zero coupon bond (q.v.), an investment in Commonwealth of Australia Treasury Bonds. D.I.N.G.O.S. are created by physically separating the interest coupons from the bond certificates; the two component parts are then called principal D.I.N.G.O.S. maturing at a specified future date, and coupon D.I.N.G.O.S. maturing every 6 months throughout the life of the bond. D.I.N.G.O.S. of both types are sold to investors with interest returns incorporated in the difference between the initial outlay and the value on maturity. In effect, D.I.N.G.O. bond holders receive all interest returns on maturity, the rate of interest being determined by the discount on the initial investment.

Discretion. The amount by which a broker, on his client's instructions, may vary the price at which his client wishes to deal. the 'discretion' may vary from a few cents to a few dollars, depending upon the price of the security.

Discretionary policy. Fiscal, monetary, or other government policy which may be consciously altered to produce a desired economic effect; in contrast with policies which operate either automatically or according to a fixed rule and are not subject to intervention to meet changed circumstances, at least not in the short-term.

Dishoarding. The desire on the part of individuals to hold few assets in the form of money, thus reducing 'idle balances'. The concepts of 'hoarding' and 'dishoarding' form part of John Maynard Keynes' liquidity preference theory. *See* LIQUIDITY PREFERENCE.

Disinflation. The removal of inflationary pressure from the economy in order to maintain the value of the monetary unit. If Government measures to achieve this go too far, the result may be deflation (q.v.). Disinflation is achieved by direct restriction of consumers' expenditure; methods have included hire purchase controls, the creation of a budget surplus, the raising of interest rates and credit squeezes.

Disintermediation. A process of cutting out the financial middle man, both in short term money markets and long-term (capital) markets.

Disinvestment. Or negative investment, as for example when businesses reduce their stocks or inventories, or allow capital goods to depreciate without replacement.

Distribution. Branch of economics (q.v.) which examines the determination of payments made to the factors of production for their share in the work of production, these being known as rent, wages, interest and profits.

Distribution, marginal theory of. A theory seeking to demonstrate that the price of each factor of production depends upon its marginal productivity.

Ditchley group. A group of bankers who met informally at Ditchley Park, London, England, in 1982 to discuss problems facing the banking industry; bankers attending the meetings were from North America, Western Europe, and Japan. The outcome of the Ditchley meetings was the creation of an international banking institute; financing of the new institute was undertaken by the 31 banks participating in the first two meetings. Initially the institute would serve only the private sector, though central banks were expected to work closely with the institute. The need for an institute to collect and distribute for its members lending risk information arose following liquidity problems which had engulfed many Latin American countries, most notably Mexico, Brazil and Argentina.

Dividend. The portion of a Company's profits which the shareholders each year decide to distribute to Ordinary Shareholders. This is usually expressed as a percentage of the nominal value of the shares. An interim dividend is a dividend declared part of the way through a company's financial year, authorised solely by the directors; a final dividend, covering the last part of a company's year, is recommended by the directors but authorised by the shareholders at the annual general meeting.

Dividend cover. The number of times a dividend is covered by a company's earnings. If the net profits attributable to the ordinary shareholders of a company amount to 40 per cent of the ordinary capital, then a dividend of 10 per cent would be described as '4 times covered'.

Dividend mandate. An order to a company by a shareholder to pay all dividends to a third party.

Dividend per share. The cash payment or distribution made by a firm to shareholders on a per share basis; it is calculated by adding declared interim and final dividends in terms of cents per share.

Dividend stripping. A technique of tax avoidance, e.g. a private company may be brought under a public company 'umbrella' and its affairs so arranged that dividends do not have to be paid and undistributed profits tax is also avoided.

Dividend warrant. Payment of a dividend to an investor by means of a cheque. It is accompanied by a tax voucher showing the gross amount of the dividend, and the net amount payable after deduction of income tax.

Division of labour. The specialisation of labour, which inevitably accompanies agricultural, industrial and commercial development. Its advantage lies in the fact that individuals gain greater skill and dexterity by doing one job, rather than several. It permits the exploitation of individual aptitude and encourages the use of machinery. The result is an increase in productivity and an improvement in quality. A serious implication of the system is that the community becomes more vulnerable to the strike threats of minorities holding 'key' jobs. In addition, labour through becoming very specialised or 'specific' faces difficult problems if suitable forms of employment decline.

Documentary credits. A method of paying an exporter for goods despatched. Under this arrangement the importer requests his bank to send a letter to the exporter undertaking to pay the exporter as soon as it receives the shipping documents. In this way, an exporter receives a bank's assurance of payment. A documentary credit is usually irrevocable.

Dole bludger (Aust.). A person who makes greater use of unemployment relief than is necessary, or even relies upon it as a way of life; a term of denigration used by Australians against some or all who are on unemployment relief. Between 1975 and 1982 a massive publicity campaign was undertaken against dole bludgers aimed in part at the exposure of abuses, and also as a means of minimising the true nature of the unemployment problem; the campaign also served to deflect public attention from massive tax avoidance schemes and swindles. *See* BOTTOM-OF-THE-HARBOUR TAX AVOIDANCE SCHEMES.

Dollar (or pound) cost averaging. A system of buying securities at regular intervals with a fixed dollar amount. Under this system, the investor buys by the dollar's worth rather than by the number of shares. If each investment is of the same number of dollars, payments buy more securities when the price is low, and fewer when it rises. Thus temporary downswings in price benefit the investor if he continues periodic purchases in both good times and bad, and the price at which the securities are sold is more than their average cost.

Dollar overhang. During the 1960s, the difference between the millions of dollars held in the reserves of many countries and the limited supply of assets (mainly gold) held by the United States as backing for them. The confidence of foreign holders of dollars that they had a gold-backed asset was undermined. As the Vietnamese War intensified the outflow of dollars increased. Partly because of this, exchange rate relationships became more precarious in the second half of the 1960s. A persisting lack of confidence in the dollar finally precipitated the suspension of dollar convertibility in August, 1971.

Dominant future. That future on a futures market (q.v.) having the largest volume of open contracts. *See* FUTURES CONTRACT.

Double coincidence of wants. A feature of barter in which A offers x to B, and B offers y to A. For an exchange to take place x must appear more desirable to B than y, and y must appear more desirable to A than x. The wants must coincide. In a money economy, the two sides of a transaction can be separated, i.e. the buying and selling can take place at different times and with different people, and change can readily be given.

Double option. A combination of a 'put' option and a 'call' option which may be exercised in either respect at the specified price before the expiry date. *See* SHARE OPTIONS; STRADDLE OPTION.

Douglas Amendment to the Bank Holding Act 1956. A U.S. Act which prohibited a bank holding corporation, which has headquarters in one state, from acquiring a bank in another state unless the second state specifically permits the acquisition.

Dow Jones averages. An index of United States security prices. The Dow Jones transportation and industrial averages have been regarded as significant indicators of both price and business trends. Historically, the index has been based upon 30 industrial, 20 transportation, 15 utility, and 65 composite averages. However, in addition to the 30 blue-chip industrial average, there is a wider 225 blue-chip industrial average. *See* DOW THEORY; FIGURE 5.

Dow theory. A theory of market analysis based upon the performance of the Dow Jones industrial and railroad stock price averages. According to the theory the market is in a basic upward trend if one of these averages advances above a previously important high, accompanied or followed by a similar advance in the other. When the averages both dip below previously important lows, this is considered an indication of a basic downward trend. The theory does not attempt to predict how long either trend will continue. Dow theory consisted originally of the analysis of the stock market trends by Charles H. Dow (1851–1902), founder with Edward D. Jones of the financial news agency Dow, Jones & Co. and one of the owners of 'The Wall Street Journal'. *See* DOW JONES AVERAGES.

Drawback. The repayment of certain customs and excise duties in respect of materials, components and goods exported after duty has been paid. For example, cigarettes made from duty-paid tobacco would attract drawback when exported.

Drawing. A method of determining the order in which creditors are to be paid off. Provisions for the repayment of capital invested in a project may incorporate a scheme for drawing lots to determine the order in which capital is to be paid off. *See* CUM DRAWING; EX-DRAWING.

Drysdale crash. The collapse of the United States corporation Drysdale Government Securities on 17 May 1982, when it failed to pay a $160 million interest bill to the Chase Manhattan Bank. The securities firm had grown rapidly in the previous 3 months from a broking firm called Drysdale Securities.

Dual capacity. *See* LONDON STOCK EXCHANGE; STOCKBROKER; STOCKJOBBER.

Dual economy. A term descriptive of an economy undergoing important developments in say both primary and secondary industry. In the case of Japan, dualism refers mainly to the concomitance, in the same areas of the country and often within the same industry sector, of

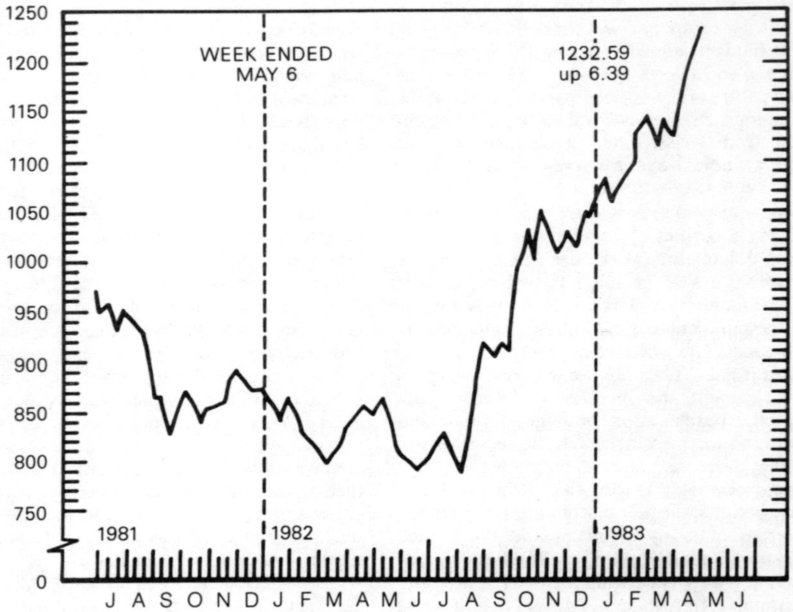

Figure 5 The Dow Jones Industrial Average (source: The Asian Wall Street Journal)

very advanced large-scale firms and small low-productivity establishments (not infrequently employed as sub-contractors by the larger companies).

Dumping. The sale of a good on a foreign market at a price below its marginal cost. The practice of dumping is prohibited within the European Economic Community (q.v.) by the Treaty of Rome. Dumping may be engaged in as a means of breaking into new markets, using goods as a 'loss leader', or to eliminate competition, or simply to dispose of surplus stocks overseas rather than upset prices on the domestic market. Export prices lower than domestic prices are not in themselves conclusive evidence of dumping, though often interpreted as such by the media.

For example, Japanese goods sometimes sell more cheaply in suburban London, England, than in suburban Tokyo. The goods may leave Japanese factories at the same price for sale either overseas or at home. However, they may suffer a larger mark-up in moving a few kilometres through the inefficient Japanese distribution network than in crossing half the world and moving through Britain's efficient distribution system.

Duopoly. A market situation in which there are only two sellers, neither seller being able to ignore the actions and reactions of the other. Duopoly is the simplest case of oligopoly (q.v.).

Duopsony. A market situation in which there are only two buyers of a particular good or service. *See* DUOPOLY.

Dutch auction. A form of auction (q.v.) in which the seller offers goods initially at a high price which is progressively lowered until a buyer accepts. Once a buyer accepts no further bidding can take place; there is no outbidding as in normal auctions.

Dutch disease. Descriptive of an alleged undermining of the competitiveness of Dutch industries as a consequence of the substantial contribution made by natural gas to the Dutch balance-of-payments over many years; the consequent featherbedding of the Dutch economy has suggested to some observers the possibility of a serious economic decline as the gas field approaches exhaustion.

E

Early Cambridge School. *See* MARSHALLIAN ECONOMICS.

Early warning system. Any technique adopted which provides an early indication of an economic problem likely to lie ahead. For example, some members of the Organisation for Economic Co-operation and Development (q.v.) have developed 'early warning systems' for providing advance information on important changes in the demand for labour. Such systems rest upon the study of trends and the analysis of future probabilities. In Britain an arrangement exists whereby employers and trade unions voluntarily notify the Government in respect of all wage and salary claims and proposed settlements which are regarded as significant and, in any case, all those covering 100 or more workers.

Earnings before interest and tax (E.B.I.T.). A company's total earnings including both operating and non-operating income, but excluding non-normal surpluses and losses. The figure is a measure of a company's performance and is frequently used in preference to net profit because it excludes the effect of different gearing structures and the ability to take advantage of taxation benefits and adjustments.

Easier, dull, soft and flat prices. Stock exchange (q.v.) terms meaning prices are falling.

Easy money. A monetary policy (q.v.) regarded as stimulating economic activity; defined by some as a policy of promoting low interest rates; by others, falling interest rates; by others, a rapid rate of growth of the quantity of money; and by others, an acceleration in the rate of growth of the quantity of money. Opposite of tight money.

E.B.I.T. *See* EARNINGS BEFORE INTEREST AND TAX.

Econometric models. Pioneered by Klein, mathematical models designed to assist in forecasting (q.v.) the needs and demands of the national economy some years ahead. Models can be constructed for static or dynamic economic situations, and the interaction of forces (i.e. the in-built economic assumptions) can be isolated and studied. Among many others, a model has been built and developed by the Department of Applied Economics of Cambridge University. It permits the computation for each industry of output, input, investment, manpower, imports and exports, etc., at different rates of projected growth in consumption. Professor Richard Stone has stated that 'Such a model takes the form of a system of equations suitable for computing, but its purpose is very similar to that of engineering models of hulls or aerofoils—built to test the reliability of the design before the real ship or aircraft is built'. Both Lawrence Klein and Sir Richard Stone were awarded Nobel Prizes for their work. *See* NOBEL PRIZE IN ECONOMICS.

Economic anthropology. The comparative study of the relations between the system of management and allocation of the economic resources of societies of various types, and the structure and values of those societies; a branch of social anthropology.

Economic appraisal. The study of the economic implications of a project, as a first step in assessing its acceptability.

Economic behaviour. The way in which people pursue their material well-being, individually and collectively. Economic conduct seeks to bring resources under control with a minimum of effort, and to redistribute them in a manner which will give the greatest satisfaction. Thus, economic behaviour consists in the exercise of choice, choice being made in many instances at the margins of expenditure. Equilibrium is reached for the individual when there is no way by which a shift in expenditure from one thing to another could improve material well-being.

Economic Commission for Europe (E.C.E.). A commission set up in 1947 by the Economic and Social Council of the United Nations to initiate action to raise the level of European economic activity and for maintaining and strengthening the economic relations of European countries, both among themselves and with other countries. The members consist of the European members of the United Nations and the U.S.A.

Economic Development Committees ('Little Neddies'). Committees set up by the national Economic Development Council (q.v.) to study Britain's major industries, consider ways in which each industry might improve its efficiency and to formulate reports and recommendations. Each of the Committees includes representatives of management, trade unions, the National Economic Development Office, the Government departments concerned with the industry being examined, and up to three independent members. The E.D.C.s have no executive power and no powers of compulsion. Their primary task is to identify the problems within their industries and devise and recommend ways of putting them right. Having agreed on the course of action that should be taken it is up to members of the E.D.C.s to persuade the relevant bodies to take action. Another task of the E.D.C.s is to examine the prospects and plans of the industry, assess from time to time the progress of the industry, and provide information and forecasts to the National Economic Development Council. The creation of the E.D.C.s began in 1964; there are now over twenty at work covering most of Britain's major industries.

Economic disturbances. Shifts in aggregate demand or aggregate supply, or shifts in money demand or supply, that cause output, interest rates, or prices to fluctuate or diverge in such a manner as to move the economy off-course.

Economic dynamics. A subject area defined by Sir Roy Harrod (b. 1900) as being concerned with the determinants of rates of change of both traditional micro and macro variables; Harrod considered the domain of economic dynamics as being narrower in scope than that of growth economics. He always distinguished sharply between statics (or the conditons of stationary equilibrium) and dynamics. *See* HARROD-DOMAR MODEL.

Economic efficiency. The efficiency with which scarce resources are used and organised to achieve stipulated economic ends (q.v.). In competitive conditions, the lower the cost per unit of output, without sacrifice of quality, in relation to the value or price of the finished article, the greater the economic efficiency of the productive organisation. The concept of economic efficiency ignores considerations of equity or fairness, because market prices already imply a particular underlying distribution of wealth which neoclassical writers tended to take as given. *See* PARETO OPTIMALITY; PRODUCTIVITY.

Economic ends. The objectives of economic activity. Ends are both quantitative and qualitative, but with the nature of ends economics has no direct concern; economics is concerned only with the number of ends and with their degree of relative intensity.

Economic friction. Influences, natural or deliberate, which tend to impede the full or rapid operation of economic laws. For example, ignorance or habit may inhibit the movement of resources into their most profitable lines of activity; Government measures may be introduced to protect individuals against the harsher aspects of the operation of economic laws in the fixing of minimum wages and in other ways. Conversely, Government measures may be taken to reduce economic friction where this is though desirable by, for example, making it easier for workers to move between jobs or providing special advisory services to exporters. *See* EXPORT CREDITS GUARANTEE DEPARTMENT; MINIMUM WAGE LEGISLATION.

Economic growth. The growth per head of the population in the production of goods and services of all kinds available to meet final demands, e.g. goods and services for domestic consumption, capital goods for accumulation, export goods to pay for imports. An acceleration of economic growth requires as much emphasis on such elements as better management, better training of labour and improved education, as on higher capital investment. Furthermore, the quality of investment may count almost as much as the quantity of it. Capital investment, though important, is but one significant factor in the growth rate of an economy. The 'growth rate' is the annual growth usually expressed as a percentage over the previous year, of productive capacity in a community. Figure 6 illustrates the effect on the national income of a range of growth rates from 1 to 10 per cent per annum.

The period between the end of the Second World War and about 1970 was characterised by economic growth and prosperity in the leading industrial countries of the world; living standards rose while unemployment remained very low.

However it became stagnant in 1974 and fell

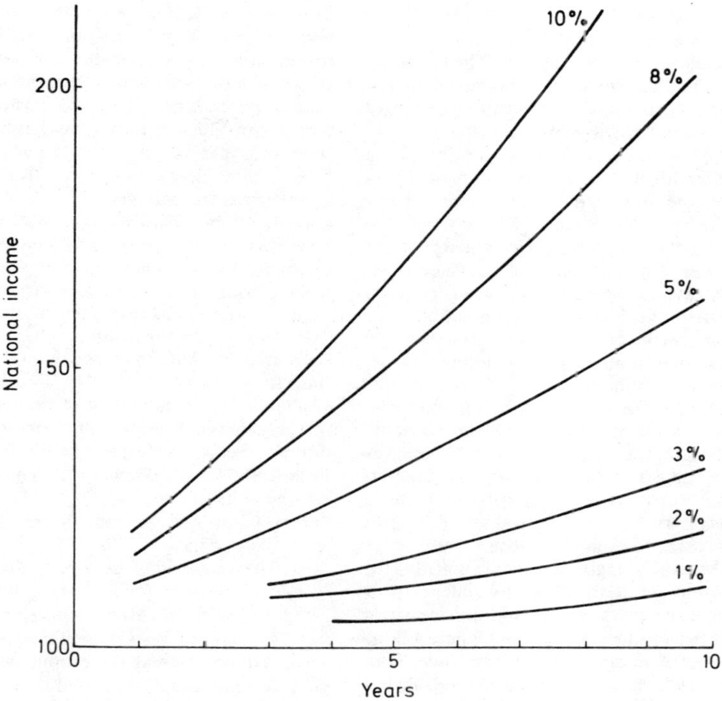

Figure 6 Rates of growth, per cent per annum

by 10 per cent in 1975, accompanied by unemployment levels not experienced since the 1930s.

Economic growth, stages of. Five stages of economic growth in society distinguished by Professor W. W. Rostov. All societies, in their economic dimensions, lie within one of these five categories; the traditional society, the preconditions for take-off, the take-off, the drive to maturity, and the age of high mass-consumption.

A traditional society is defined as one whose structure is developed within limited production functions, based on pre-Newtonian science and technology, and on pre-Newtonian attitudes towards the physical world. While this concept is in no sense static and would not exclude increases in output, there is a ceiling on the level of attainable output per head. The term embraces the dynasties of China; the civilisation of the Middle East and the Mediterranean; the world of medieval Europe; and post-Newtonian societies which, for a time, remained untouched or unmoved by man's new capability for regularly manipulating his environment to his economic advantage.

The second stage of growth embraces societies in the process of transition; that is, the period when the pre-conditions for take-off are developed. This period witnesses major changes in both the economy itself and in the balance of social values together with the building of an effective centralised national state. The idea spreads not merely that economic progress is possible, but that economic progress is a necessary condition for some other purpose, judged to be good—be it national dignity, private profit, the general welfare, or a better life for the children.

The take-off is the interval when the resistances to steady growth are finally overcome and the forces making for economic progress expand and come to dominate the society. Growth becomes its normal condition. During the take-off the rate of effective investment and saving may rise from say 5 per cent of the national income to 10 per cent or more, and new industries expand rapidly. The economy exploits hitherto unused natural resources and methods of production; revolutionary changes take place in agricultural productivity.

The drive to maturity takes the form of a long interval of sustained if fluctuating progress, as the now regularly growing economy drives to extend modern technology over the whole front of its economic activity. Some 10–20 per cent of the national income is steadily invested, permitting output regularly to outstrip the increase in population. The make-up of the economy changes unceasingly as technique improves, new industries accelerate, older industries level off; the economy finds its place in the international economy. Maturity is the stage in which the economy demonstrates the capacity to move beyond the original industries which powered its take-off and to absorb and to apply efficiently over a very wide range of its resources the most advanced fruits of modern technology.

In the age of high mass consumption, the leading sectors of the economy shift towards durable consumers' goods and services; real income per head rises to a point where a large number of persons gain command over consumption which transcends basic food, shelter and clothing. The proportion of urban to total population increases; and also the proportion working in offices or in skilled factory jobs. Society ceases to accept further extensions of modern technology as an overriding objective; the emergence of the welfare state is one manifestation of a society's moving beyond technical maturity.

Economic indicators. Statistics which are sensitive to changes in the state of industry, trade and commerce. United Kingdom economic indicators include the statistics of unemployment and unfilled vacancies; bank advances, gold reserve, basic materials and fuel prices, and retail prices; wage rates, retail sales, H.P. debt; terms of trade and industrial output; imports, exports and imports surplus; output of steel, cars and commercial vehicles, man-made fibres, houses, furniture, bricks, cement, hosiery, radios and television sets, machine tools, petroleum; orders on hand in the engineering, electrical and textile industries; consumer spending. Indicators may be classified into three types; 'leaders'—offering advance pointers; 'coincidents'—moving in tandem with business conditions; and 'laggers'—showing delayed results.

Economic interpretation of history. A theory developed by Karl Marx (1818–1883) which asserted: (a) The forms or conditions of production are the fundamental determinant of social structures which in turn breed attitudes, actions and civilisations; and (b) The forms of production themselves have a logic of their own, that is to say, they change according to necessities inherent in them so as to produce their successors through their own working. It appears to be acknowledged by many that both propositions contain a large amount of truth, provide invaluable working hypotheses, while working less satisfactorily in some cases than in others. However, Marx also argued that new political institutions could create new economic institutions and economic base. *See* MARXIST SOCIALISM.

Economic law. A statement of what will occur in the economic world under specified conditions. George J. Stigler, in his 'Theory of Price' offers the following statement of an economic law:

If: (a) An entrepreneur seeks maximum profits;
(b) His marginal cost curve does not fall so fast as (or more rapidly than) his marginal revenue curve;
(c) The curves are continuous.

Then: He operates at the output where marginal revenue equals marginal cost.

Alfred Marshall's view of economic laws was that 'there are no definite and universal propositions in economics which can compare with the Laws of Gravitation and of Conservation of Energy in physics. But there are many which rank with the secondary laws of those natural sciences which resemble economics in dealing with the complex actions of many heterogeneous and uncertain causes. The laws of biology, for instance, or, to take an example from a purely physical science, the laws of the tides, like those of economics vary much in definiteness, in range of application—and in certainty. An economic law is then nothing but a general proposition, or statement of uniformity, more or less certain, more or less definite.'

As the specified condition for the operation of a law may not be fully complied with in any real-life situation, the law may appear not to operate. In other situations, the operation of a law may be masked by other events. Hence, economic laws are often referred to as 'tendencies'. For example: 'In a free market price *tends* to equate the supply of, and the demand for, an article.'

Economic nationalism. Often a concomitant of political nationalism; also a reaction to the frustrations of multinational solutions to common trade problems leading to unilateral measures to protect the national interest, most narrowly defined.

Economic problem. A problem of ensuring that all available resources are used to the best possible effect, in the resolving of which decisions must be made as to which ends are to be satisfied first and perhaps which wants will have to be left unsatisfied.

Economic quantities or aggregates. The subject matter of macro- and micro-economics, economic quantities or aggregates include such diverse items as the amount of a commodity produced, stored and consumed; the volume of employment and unemployment; the price of butter; the interest on bank loans; the wages of brick-layers; the price of houses; taxes on tobacco or spirits; the surcharge on imported raw materials, etc. The main task of economic analysis is the explanation of the magnitude of economic quantities.

Economic Recovery Tax Act 1981. A United States Act which enabled corporations to effectively sell unused tax allowances on the purchase of plant and machinery to a third party, providing such deals were completed before November, 1981. The beneficiaries of such tax-benefit selling were small companies with no income against which to·offset their tax allowances.

Economic rent. A payment to a unit of a factor of production (q.v.) which is in excess of the minimum amount necessary to keep that unit in its present occupation. A firm may pay a wage sufficient to retain its present staff. In attempting to increase its staff, however, the firm may find it necessary to raise wages and attract workers from other employment. The increase in wage now enjoyed by the original staff is economic rent. A perfectly elastic supply yields no economic rent as such an assumption implies an unlimited supply available at stable prices; a situation not experienced, or experienced for long, in real life. Economic rent can be enjoyed indefinitely by a factor whose supply is relatively fixed; land enjoys this distinction. Successful opera singers, barristers, and pop-stars enjoy an economic rent; there is a very marked contrast in these cases in the earnings of the successful compared with the less talented. In writing some authors enjoy a high economic rent while most earn very little. *See* QUASI-RENT.

Economic summits. *See* NATIONAL ECONOMIC SUMMIT (AUST.); TOKYO ECONOMIC SUMMIT MEETING; WILLIAMSBURG ECONOMIC SUMMIT.

Economic system, functions of an. The functions of an economic system which may be defined as follows:

(a) generally, to match supply to the effective demand for goods and services in an efficient manner;
(b) to determine what goods and services are to be produced, and in what quantities;
(c) to distribute scarce resources among the industries producing goods and services;
(d) to distribute the products of industry among members of the community;
(e) to provide for maintenance and expansion of fixed capital investment;
(f) to fully utilise the resources of society.

In a free enterprise system, the fulfilment of these six economic functions is left to the profit motive and the price mechanism (q.v.) working within a framework of social safeguards. In a socialist society all the operations required are consciously planned by salaried officials; there are no private investors. Britain operates a mixed system, splitting the economy into public and private sectors, the activity of the whole being influenced by direct and indirect planning measures.

Economic welfare. Defined by A. C. Pigou as 'that part of social welfare that can be brought directly or indirectly into relation with the measuring rod of money'; in other words, those aspects of social welfare which are concerned with material as distinct from bodily, moral or spiritual well-being, although obviously these are inter-related in some ways. Pigou stressed that there is no precise line between economic and non-economic satisfactions. Economic or material satisfactions are derived from the consumption of both goods and services; and it is this which is the subject matter of economics. Pigou warned that economic welfare will not serve for a barometer or index of total welfare; this is because an economic cause may affect non-economic welfare in ways that cancel its effects on economic welfare. Non-economic welfare is liable to be modified by the manner in which income is earned and also by the manner in which it is spent—'Of different acts of consumption that yield equal satisfactions, one may exercise a debasing and another an elevating influence.'

Economics. A social science concerned with how people, either individually or in groups, attempt to accommodate scarce resources to their wants through the processes of production, substitution and exchange. it is not as a science concerned with the problems of what ought to be, but with the explanation and understanding of what already exists. There have been many definitions of economics in the past. The earliest definitions envisaged economics as the study of wealth. Adam Smith (1723–1790), the founder of modern economics, entitled his great work *An Inquiry into the Causes of the Wealth of Nations*. Nearly 70 years later, John Stuart Mill (1806–1873) in his *Principles of Political Economy* defined economics as 'the practical science of the production and distribution of wealth'. The Victorian economist, Alfred Marshall (1842–1924), in his *Principles of Economics* defined economics as 'a study of man's actions in the ordinary business of life; it inquires how he gets his income and how he uses it. It is on the one side a study of wealth and on the other part of the study of man'. In more recent years, Lionel Robbins, in his *Essay on the Nature and Significance of Economic Science*, has defined the subject more precisely as 'the science which studies human behaviour as a relationship between ends and scarce means which have alternative uses'.

These earlier definitions stressed only the alternative and competitive uses of resources, while focussing on choices between alternative points on a stationary production–possibility boundary. Today, the science is regarded as concerned with the allocation of the resources of society among alternative uses; the distribution of output among individuals and groups; the ways in which production and distribution change over time; and the efficiencies and inefficiencies of economic systems.

Economies of scale. The gains by way of reduced average costs of production per unit of output often arising from increasing the size of a plant, business or industry. In suitable circumstances, large-scale production leads to important economies in the use of (a) Land—it is most unlikely that a doubling of production requires twice as much land; (b) Labour—persons with specialised knowledge and skill may devote all their time to the tasks they perform most efficiently; (c) Capital—specialised units of equipment may be brought into use and fully employed; (d) Marketing—advertising costs per unit may be less; (e) Buying—raw materials may be bought more cheaply by buying in bulk; (f) Finance—a large firm can usually raise new capital more easily and cheaply than a small firm; (g) Research—development costs are spread over many more units. All forms of production at various periods experience the operation of the laws of increasing, constant and diminishing returns. Firms may attempt to increase profits and spread risks by diversifying activities, producing a wide range of products sometimes of a very contrasting nature. Horizontal and vertical integration of processes may be sought in order to achieve greater economies. *See also* EXTERNAL ECONOMY; VARIABLE PROPORTIONS, LAW OF.

Economist. A social scientist who has become an expert in dealing with the economic aspects of social phenomena. He may specialise in theoretical or applied economics. As John Maynard Keynes commented: '. . . the ideas of economists and political philosophers, both when they are right and when they are wrong, are more powerful than is commonly understood. Indeed the world is ruled by little else. Practical men, who believe themselves to be quite exempt from any intellectual influences, are usually the slave of some defunct economist. Madmen in authority, who hear voices in the air, are distilling their frenzy from some academic scribbler of a few years back. I am sure that the power of vested interests is vastly exaggerated compared with the gradual encroachment of ideas . . . soon or late, it is ideas, not vested interests, which are dangerous for good or evil.' (*General Theory*, p. 383–4).

Economist-Extel Index. An index of industrial share prices compiled by *The Economist* in association with the Exchange Telegraph Company. It is calculated twice daily. The indicator has the unique feature of combining 50 stocks in an unweighted arithmetic average of their price relatives, rebased each year and then linked back to the original base of the indicator, namely, the average of mid-monthly prices in 1953. Each year end, the constituent shares of the index are reviewed and revised where necessary.

Edge Act (U.S.). An Act passed by Congress in 1919, it permits United States commercial banks to set up corporations outside their own States but only for the purposes of engaging in international business. Interstate branch banking is normally prohibited. Such organisations are called Edge Banks.

E.E.C. laws. The laws of the European Economic Community (q.v.) which take precedence over national laws and regulate such disparate matters as equal pay for women, pollution standards, the labelling of supermarket goods, and competition between corporations. E.E.C. Directives are laws that are binding on all member states as regards the result to be achieved, but leave each member state to decide how best to implement the directive. E.E.C. Regulations are laws made by the Council (or, in rare cases, by the Commission) that further define the scope of the Treaty of Rome 1957; Regulations are equally binding on all member countries and apply directly, like national laws. Case law has been most influential also in defining the Rome Treaty.

Effective demand. Demand measured by spending on consumption (goods and services more or less used up immediately); on investment (plant, buildings, equipment, stocks); and on the difference between exports (which adds to demand for output at home) and imports (which satisfies home demand without adding to home output).

Effective exchange rate index. An index for the dollar price of a basket of foreign currencies, each currency being given a particular weight. The index serves as a summary measure of the 'average' cost of foreign exchange, the index being influenced by the number of foreign currencies included and the weights given to each particular currency. Commonly used effective exchange rate indexes are based on a basket containing fifteen to twenty major currencies. *See* SPECIAL DRAWING RIGHTS.

Elasticity of demand, income. The response of the demand for a commodity to changes in the real income of consumers. Its computation is as follows:

$$\frac{\text{Percentage change in quantity demanded}}{\text{Percentage change in income}}$$

For most commodities, increases in income lead to increases in demand, income elasticity being positive. In respect of 'inferior goods' or Giffen goods (q.v.) a rise in income leads to a fall in demand for the commodities concerned, income elasticity being negative. Condensed milk has been regarded in some countries as an inferior substitute for fresh milk; an increase in income gives rise to reduced purchases of condensed milk, income elasticity being negative. Tea consumption appears to vary hardly at all as income varies. If the income elasticity of demand for water for household purposes is estimated to be 0.4, then if the average real income per head is rising at 2 per cent per annum the demand for water will rise by 0.8 per cent per annum. In Britain, it has been estimated that every 1 per cent increase in real personal incomes leads eventually to an increase of about 3½ per cent in the electricity consumption of domestic consumers, i.e. the income elasticity of demand for electricity for domestic purposes is about 3½.

Elasticity of demand, price. The response of demand to a change in the price of a commodity. It is measured:

$$\frac{\text{Percentage change in quantity demanded}}{\text{Percentage change in price}}$$

If the price is lowered, the amount demanded will normally be increased. Where a percentage increase of the amount demanded is greater than the percentage reduction of price, the demand is described as 'elastic'; if it is less, 'inelastic'. If a given percentage reduction of price leads to an equal percentage increase of the amount demanded, the elasticity of demand is unity.

If a fall of 1 per cent in selling price is accompanied by an increase of 5 per cent in demand, then the elasticity of demand is 5. If a fall of ½ per cent in price expands sales from 100 to 110, the elasticity of demand at the price is 20. If the price elasticity of demand for water for household purposes is 0.5, this means that the price of water will have to rise by 2 per cent to achieve a 1 per cent reduction in consumption.

When the elasticity of demand is unity, the total receipts from selling different amounts of a commodity at higher or lower prices remain the same. When demand is elastic a fall in price accompanied by an expansion of demand causes total receipts to increase. A fall in price when demand is inelastic causes total receipts to fall. Conversely, a rise in price when demand is elastic causes a fall in receipts. A rise in price when demand is inelastic causes an increase in receipts.

Many factors influence the elasticity of demand for a commodity. A commodity having no close substitutes is likely to have an inelastic demand; conversely, a commodity having close substitutes will have an elastic demand. The demand for a commodity which commands only a small share of consumers' total expenditure is likely to have an inelastic demand. In the case of a durable commodity, the replacement of which can always be readily deferred, demand is likely to be elastic (i.e. to fall sharply) if price rises, and equally elastic (i.e. to increase rapidly) if price falls. Much depends on the circumstances of the commodity concerned.

It is generally accepted that the elasticity of demand for commodities increases with time. Thus a 1 per cent increase in price may lead to only ½ per cent fall in demand in the short-term but later the quantity may decrease by 2 or more per cent. There are various reasons for this. A consumer may leave matters for a time to see how other prices change. For example, if the price of a particular fuel increases by 10 per cent he would need to be sure that this was a permanent relative change in the price of fuels before considering changing any of his heating appliances. Then again, it may be found that the theoretical saving in running costs may not be sufficient to justify the cost or the upheaval of installing new appliances. A change would be delayed, therefore, until a normal replacement had to be made.

For many years it was held that the price elasticity of energy amounted to about -0.25 (that is, a real price rise of 1 per cent would reduce energy demand by 0.25 per cent); more recent work has suggested much higher price elasticity effects in the long term, about unity for transport and housing and about 0.8 for industry. The significance of higher price elasticities could be much reduced estimates for primary energy demand in the year 2000.

Elasticity of substitution. A measure of the ease or difficulty of substituting between commodities (by consumers) or between factors of production (by producers). The elasticity of commodity substitution may be measured as follows:

$$\frac{\text{Percentage change in the ratio in which two commodities are combined}}{\text{Percentage change in the ratio of their marginal utilities}}$$

A high value, indicating that substantial changes in the proportions of commodities combined would produce little change in relative marginal utilities, would indicate a high degree of substitutability, and *vice versa.* The elasticity of factor substitution may be measured as follows:

$$\frac{\text{Percentage change in the ratio in which two factors are combined}}{\text{Percentage change in the ratio of their marginal physical productivities}}$$

Again a high value indicates a high degree of technical substitutability between factors, and *vice versa.* The result indicates how far one factor may be substituted for another (more expensive) factor before the benefits are nullified by changes in the relative productivities of the two factors.

Elasticity of supply. The response of supply to a change in the price of a commodity. If the price rises, the amount supplied will normally be increased. The elasticity is calculated as follows:

$$\frac{\text{Percentage change in quantity supplied}}{\text{Percentage change in price}}$$

Thus if a 1 per cent rise in the price of a commodity results in a 2 per cent increase in the quantity supplied, the elasticity of supply is 2. If the price falls, the supply will normally shrink. There are some important exceptions to the 'normal', however, particularly in the international commodity markets (*see* PRICE MECHANISM). The supply of a commodity is likely to be elastic if a given increase in the output of single firms produces only a small increase in the marginal costs of production, and if it is relatively easy for new firms to enter the industry. A supply will tend to be inelastic (elasticity less than unity) for a time in respect of an industry using highly specialised capital or labour, the quantities of which cannot be readily increased. If the proportional change in the quantity supplied equals the proportional change in price, then elasticity is unity. *See* ELASTICITY OF DEMAND, INCOME; SUPPLY CURVE.

Eligible liabilities. In Britain, the sterling deposit liabilities of the banking system as a whole, excluding deposits having an original maturity of over 2 years, plus any sterling resources obtained by switching foreign currencies into sterling. Between 1971 and 1981, the banks observed, day-by-day, a uniform minimum reserve ratio of 12½ per cent of 'eligible liabilities' and placed such special deposits with the Bank of England (q.v.) as were called for from time to time.

Eligible margin. The cash or other collateral which a commodity exchange (q.v.) specifies that members may accept from their customers for the purpose of satisfying initial and variation margin requirements. *See* MARGIN.

Employment, Classical theory of. A theory held by the Classical School (q.v.) of economists, based on two fundamental postulates:

(a) The wage is equal to the marginal product of labour; and
(b) The utility of the wage when a given volume of labour is employed is equal to the marginal disutility of that amount of employment, i.e. the real wage is just sufficient to induce the volume of labour actually employed to be forthcoming.

Postulate (a) represents the demand schedule for labour, and postulate (b) the supply schedule for labour. The theory is compatible with frictional or voluntary unemployment; but is not compatible with involuntary or mass unemployment. The Classical view was that, if workers agreed to a reduction of money-wages, more employment would be forthcoming and involuntary unemployment would disappear. John Maynard

Keynes (1884–1946) did not deny the proposition that a reduction in money-wages accompanied by the same aggregate effective demand as before will be associated with an increase in employment. But, a general reduction of wages is ineffective if it results in, and is accompanied by, a fully proportionate reduction in the aggregate effective demand for goods and services. Keynes argued that a reduction in money-wages will have no lasting tendencies to increase employment, except by virtue of its repercussions either on the propensity to consume for the community as a whole or on the schedule or marginal efficiency of capital (q.v.), or on the rate of interest. He recognised that the unemployment which characterises a depression is not due to the refusal of labour to accept a reduction of money wages. Indeed, he recognised that, with wages and prices falling simultaneously, there may exist no expedient by which labour *as a whole* can reduce its *real* wage to a given figure by making revised *money* bargains with the entrepreneurs. He argued that if the propensity to consume and the rate of new investment result in a deficient effective demand, the actual level of employment will fall short of the supply of labour potentially available at the existing real wage, and the equilibrium real wage will be greater than the marginal disutility of the equilibrium level of employment. The insufficiency of effective demand will inhibit the process of production in spite of the fact that the marginal product of labour still exceeds in value the marginal disutility of employment. Keynes rejected the belief, springing from Classical theory, that a flexible wage policy is capable of maintaining a state of continuous full employment.

The employment theory of the classical school has been revived by the New Classical School (q.v.).

Employment subsidies (U.K.). Subsidised schemes in Britain to help moderate the rise in unemployment. In 1982, there were six such schemes covering a total of about 700,000 people. The two largest, affecting 600,000, were the Youth Opportunities Programme (work experience and training) and the short-time working compensation scheme. Employers are paid half the wage costs for those whom they put on to short-time working rather than making them redundant. The six programmes were budgeted to cost £1 billion in all in 1981–82.

Energy computer models. Computer models of the energy sector of an economy, which have been developed largely in the United States of America and Europe; the models consider both the sector itself in detail and its relationship with the national economy. Modelling activity in this field developed from about 1970, as the necessary mathematical tools and computers became available, and the impact of the 1973 oil price rises was felt. Most models are concerned with the medium-term (5–15 years) and the long term (15–50 years). Two basic types of energy analysis have evolved: one focusing on the technical side of the energy system and the other on economic analysis. Models developed in the United States can be used separately or collectively to study a wide range of economic and energy problems. A model has been developed at the U.S. National Centre for Energy Analysis, Brookhaven National Laboratory. The Brookhaven Energy System Optimization Model (B.E.S.O.M.) is a linear programming model in which the total cost of satisfying a given set of national energy demands is minimised. An input-output model developed by the Brookhaven National Laboratory and the Centre for Advanced Computation at the University of Illinois gives the output of the energy sector in physical units (British thermal units).

Energy futures. *See* NEW YORK MERCANTILE EXCHANGE (N.Y.M.E.X.).

Energy stocks. Stocks and shares in companies operating in the energy sector of the national economy, notably in oil, shale oil, natural gas, manufactured gas, uranium, coal mining, coke, briquettes and electricity. Companies may be engaged in exploration, processing, mining, drilling, treatment, transmission, generation, storage, transport or distribution.

Engel's law. A generalisation that the proportion of income spent on food tends to decline as income grows, with given tastes or preferences. This law or tendency was formulated by Ernst Engel (1821–96) in a paper published by him in 1857.

Enterprise zones. Designated areas in Britain in which businesses pay no rates for 10 years and escape most of the red-tape of planning permission procedures; by 1982, the British Government had designated eleven zones. In November, 1982, it was announced that the number of enterprise zones would be doubled.

Entitlement issue. A method of raising finance (q.v.), usually employed by no liability (q.v.) companies, whereby existing shareholders may buy new shares in the company usually below the current market price. Shares are usually issued in a pre-determined ratio, e.g. one new share for every four shares held. Unlike a rights issue (q.v.), an entitlement issue cannot be sold or transferred, i.e. it is non-renounceable.

Entrepreneur. A business organiser whose aim is profit. His responsibilities comprise:

(a) risk and uncertainty bearing;
(b) making decisions on what goods and services will be produced, how the factors of production (q.v.) will be combined for this purpose, and the scale of production; and
(c) marketing of these goods and services.

It is commonly assumed, for the purpose of economic analysis, that an entrepreneur will always seek to maximise his profit. This is a useful generalisation, although business organisers are human and this may modify the concept in practice. Some may be content to sustain a customary standard of living; others may be motivated by thoughts of power and prestige; others may sacrifice profit in the short-run to keep prices low and drive competitors out.

The term 'entrepreneur' may be readily applied to the owner-manager of a small enterprise; it is also applied to boards of directors and sometimes to the general body of shareholders. *See* PAPER ENTREPRENEUR.

Environmental economics. A recognised field of specialisation in the economics discipline with a number of journals, such as the *Journal of Environmental Economics and Management*. It embraces the issues of pollution control and protection of the natural environment; issues in the resolution of which markets have played little or no part, but in which immense common property resources need to be allocated sensibly to the overall public good.

Equal Credit Opportunity Act 1974 (U.S.). An Act proscribing credit discrimination on the basis of an applicant's 'race, colour, religion, national origin, sex, marital status or age . . .'. The Board of Governors of the Federal Reserve System (q.v.) has the responsibility for the administration of this Act, including the prescribing of regulations. The Act created a Consumer Advisory Council (q.v.) to furnish the Board with advice.

Equal pay. Equal material reward for men and women doing equal work. The vexed question of equal pay was examined by a British Royal Commission, whose findings in the form of majority and minority reports were published in 1946. The Majority Report ascribed the difference in the earnings of men and women to the greater physical strength and greater efficiency of men; the higher sickness rate and more absenteeism among women; and further declared that women generally had less ambition and showed less initiative in a crisis. The Minority Report affirmed that women were equally efficient as men, except where physical strength was required, but that employers were prejudiced against the employment of women in new spheres and afraid of fermenting trouble among their male employees.

As a result of equal pay legislation and the Sex Discrimination Act 1975 women in Britain have to be paid the same wages and granted the same conditions as men if they are performing the same or broadly similar work. In Canada, eight provinces and the Federal Government have enacted legislation prohibiting discrimination between men and women in rates of pay.

As long ago as 1884, Federick Engels in his *Origin of the Family, Private Property and the State* concluded: 'The emancipation of woman will only be possible when woman can take part in production on a large, social scale, and domestic work no longer claims anything but an insignificant amount of her time.'

In Britain, between 1951 and 1979 the proportion of 'economically active' women rose from 35 per cent to 44 per cent of the workforce. The additions to the labour force have been predominantly married women, especially those returning to the workforce after rearing families.

Equal service. A concept often employed in making inter-plant comparisons, e.g. inter-power station comparisons, which implies not only an assumed identical aggregate output from each plant but an identical time pattern of supply.

Equilibrium. A concept of an economic system at rest and in which no one has an incentive to behave differently. It is not a state, however, that necessarily affords the maximum possible economic benefit to the community at large. An individual's expenditure is in equilibrium when the ratio of the prices of any two goods purchased equals the marginal rate of substitution between them. A firm is in equilibrium when the maximum profit is being earned, i.e. when marginal cost equals marginal revenue, and there is no incentive to increase or decrease output. An industry is in equilibrium if there is no tendency for firms to enter or leave the industry. A market is in equilibrium when at the ruling price the amount of commodities being offered for sale is just equal to the amount consumers wish to buy.

Equilibrium may be stable or unstable,

partial or general. Stable equilibrium implies that any temporary movement in the factors involved, arising from an outside cause, would be offset after a time by a movement in the opposite direction until the initial situation was restored. In unstable equilibrium any movement in the factors involved will result in the situation departing increasingly from the initial position while showing no tendency to return to it; it will tend to settle down in some quite different position. Professor Gerard Debreu has described the theory of general equilibrium as 'an attempt to show how the many agents of economic systems make economic decisions and how those decisions are consistent with each other'. *See* COMPARATIVE STATIC ANALYSIS.

Equilibrium analysis. *See* GENERAL EQUILIBRIUM ANALYSIS; PARTIAL EQUILIBRIUM ANALYSIS.

Equilibrium price. A price at which the quantity demanded equals the quantity supplied; the market is said to be cleared.

Equi-marginal returns, law of. A basic theorem describing the way in which consumers with limited resources divide their expenditure between the innumerable different goods and services they could enjoy, based on the assumptions that consumers wish to obtain the maximum utility (q.v.) from their income and that they act rationally in seeking that end. The theorem asserts that people generally will distribute their expenditure between various commodities so as to ensure that the marginal utility (q.v.) obtained from every commodity purchased is in the same relationship to price, i.e. that the marginal rates of substitution should be everywhere equal to relative prices. As the pattern of prices changes, so the consumer will shift his pattern of expenditure.

Equipment trust certificate. A type of security generally issued by a railway to pay for new equipment. The title to the equipment, such as a locomotive, is held by a trustee until the notes are paid off. An equipment trust certificate is usually secured by a first claim on the equipment.

Equities. The ordinary shares of a limited company. They carry the right to the residue of a company's assets after it has paid all its creditors, and share in the distribution of profits, if any, after interest has been paid to preference share-holders and debenture holders each year. *See* DEBENTURES; PREFERENCE SHARE.

Equity.

(a) Another name for ownership; often used to describe a share in a company. *See* EQUITIES.

(b) The residual value of the total initial and variation margins in a futures trading account, assuming its liquidation at the current market price. *See* MARGIN.

(c) Or fairness, a concept with an interface with economics in the sphere of supplies and tariff-making; it means that no group of consumers feels that it has been 'unfairly treated' or 'discriminated against' in relation to these matters. Thus, an equitable electricity supply tariff might be regarded by some as a standard charge for all electricity whenever and wherever the demand occurs, i.e. country people would pay no more than town people, even though it costs more to supply them. Undertakings may look for equity in the framing of tariff proposals in order to avoid too much criticism and retain goodwill. However, what is and what is not 'equity' depends on the point of view. W. A. Lewis has remarked in his *Overhead Costs* (George Allen and Unwin, London, 1949) that in this field equity is the mother of confusion and that economists who are interested in costs, not equity, are pre-disposed to the view that the most equitable charge is that which corresponds to cost.

Equity leasing. Leases under which the lessor contributes the entire capital cost, unlike leveraged leasing (q.v.) where the lessor contributes only a minor portion of the capital. *See* LEASE; LEASE BACK AGREEMENT; LEASE LENDING; LEASING COMPANIES; TAX BASED LEASES.

Equity trust. *See* UNIT TRUST.

Erratic. Descriptive of a market when it moves rapidly, changes direction quickly, and is irregular in its action.

Essentialist arguments. Arguments in economics concerned with correct definitions, labelling, and classification, rather than facts.

Estate Duties Investment Trust ('Edith'). Formed in 1953, an investment trust which buys and holds minority shareholdings in family business and small public companies; the facility is used by executors and trustees holding shares in such companies and who are faced with estate duty liability who wish to avoid losing control or selling out.

Eurobonds. Bonds denominated in the currency of one country but issued in some other country or countries. The first Eurobonds were dollar denominated fixed rate bonds issued in

Europe rather than in the United States so as to escape the Interest Equalisation Tax (I.E.T.) imposed in 1963 on foreign bond issues in the United States domestic market. Dollar denominated Eurobonds have since then been issued on an increasing scale, even though the I.E.T. was abolished in January, 1974. During the 1970s, Eurobonds issues denominated in other currencies became increasingly important, especially during periods when the U.S. dollar has been weak in the exchange market. Floating rate notes have been issued during periods of rising interest rates. In 1978, gross new issues of Eurobonds amounted to $U.S. 15.9 billion equivalent, not far short of half the value of new issues of all international bonds in that year.

Euro-currencies. The currencies of the European Economic Community (q.v.), together with euro-dollars (q.v.).

Euro-dollars. U.S. dollars held by residents outside the United States, serving a dollar market in Europe; hence the term 'Euro-dollar market'. This international money market was created in 1957 when, as a result of the Suez crisis, restrictions were placed on ordinary sterling credit facilities to finance non-British trade, London bankers sought to overcome the difficulties of meeting traders' demands for credit by tapping the pool of dollars held by residents outside the United States. The market is no longer confined to dollars, but embraces European currencies also; it has become one of the world's largest markets for short-term funds. Outside the direct control of any national central bank it is a free, competitive and flexible market. A wholesale market it deals only in large amounts. Concomitant with the Euro-dollar market is the Euro-bond market, a source of long-term capital. *See* REGULATION Q.

Eurofer. The steel cartel of the European Economic Community (q.v.), officially formed in December, 1976. It is governed by a fifteen-man board elected by the steel associations of the Community. Quotas, directly administered through Eurofer, are set for the thirty different groups of steel makers within the Community. The British Steel Corporation (q.v.) counts as one group. The secretariat of Eurofer is based in Luxembourg. One advantage of the cartel is that it is able to negotiate with powerful overseas groups such as the six large Japanese steel producers which act in a co-ordinated manner.

Euronotes. Short-term marketable debt issued by companies and often bought by other companies; the European response to the commercial paper market (q.v.) which has flourished elsewhere. In 1984, Euronotes worth $7 billion were issued; the market was dominated by banks selling their own notes to each other, although other Euromarket private and institutional investors were involved, notably European and American companies.

European Coal and Steel Community. A Community for the creation of a common market for coal and steel established by a Treaty, signed in Paris on behalf of Belgium, France, the German Federal Republic, Italy, Luxemburg and the Netherlands ('the Member Countries') on 18 April 1951, and ratified in all of them with effect from 23 July 1952. The Treaty is for a period of 50 years. The creation of the Community, to which other European countries may be admitted, was the first step taken by the member countries towards European integration and facilitated the establishment in 1958 of the European Economic Community ('the Common market') (q.v.) for all products other than coal, steel and nuclear energy, and of the European Atomic Energy Community ('Euratom'). Each of these three communities constitutes a separate entity.

The powers of the Community in respect of the coal and steel enterprises under its jurisdiction were initially vested in the High Authority, subject in certain stipulated circumstances to the concurrence of a Special Council of Ministers and subject to a right of appeal to the Court of Justice of the European Communities ('the Court'). The decisions of the High Authority under the Treaty were binding on the member countries. Twenty-four countries, among them the United States of America, have established diplomatic relations with the European Coal and Steel Community. *See* EUROPEAN COMMISSION.

European Commission. A single European Commission which on 1 July 1967, replaced the Coal and Steel High Authority, the Euratom Commission and the Common Market Commission; thus the executives of the three European Communities were merged. The Commission has three main functions:

(a) to prepare and submit new policies to the Council of Ministers;
(b) to issue regulations for the community as a whole in respect of decisions made by the Council of Ministers;
(c) to police the customs union and its rules for the free movement of labour; administer Common Market farm policy;

and act as a European monopolies commission.

European Common Market. *See* COMMON AGRICULTURAL POLICY; COMMON FISHERIES POLICY; COMMON SUPPORT PRICES; EUROFER; EUROPEAN COAL AND STEEL COMMUNITY; EUROPEAN COMMISSION; EUROPEAN COURT OF JUSTICE; EUROPEAN CURRENCY UNIT (E.C.U.); EUROPEAN ECONOMIC COMMUNITY; EUROPEAN INVESTMENT BANK; EUROPEAN MONETARY SYSTEM.

European Court of Justice. Located in Luxembourg, a body created to assist in interpreting and applying the principles of the Treaty of Rome and the European Economic Community (q.v.); in 1982 the Court had 11 judges and 462 permanent staff. The Court enforces E.E.C. laws on companies and countries, for community law overrides national law. In 1979, France was found guilty by the Court of illegally blocking free trade in lamb. However the enforcement of decisions against countries presents the greatest problem.

European currency snake. *See* SMITHSONIAN AGREEMENT.

European Currency Unit (E.C.U.). A basket of fixed amounts of European Economic Community (q.v.) currencies, to facilitate transactions in the Community. Its initial composition was the same as that of the European unit of account previously in use within the Community; but the amounts of each currency in the basket may be changed in future by agreement of the Council of Ministers. At the end of September, 1979, the dollar market value of the E.E.C. currencies made one E.C.U. equal to about $U.S. 1.43.

The E.C.U. performs two functions: (a) it is a denominator for expressing debts and claims as between central banks. An exchange rate risk is unavoidable whenever there is the possibility of an exchange rate adjustment. However, by denominating debts and claims in the E.C.U., the European Monetary System (q.v.) has introduced the concept of Community Burden-sharing in respect of the exchange rate risk, in that the risk is no longer borne wholly by the debtor nor wholly by the creditor; and (b) it is an instrument of settlement between the Community central banks. E.C.U.s acquired by central banks are held in reserve and used primarily as a means of settling debts arising from official market intervention in Community currencies. *See* TABLE 2.

European development fund. (E.D.F.). *See* LOMÉ CONVENTION.

European Economic Community. Popularly known as the European Common Market, a free trade organisation created by the Treaty of Rome, 1957. Its members comprised France, West Germany, Italy, Belgium, the Netherlands and Luxembourg, although the Treaty allows for the admission of other countries at a later date. With the signing of the

TABLE 2
INITIAL COMPOSITION OF THE EUROPEAN CURRENCY UNIT

	Amount of each currency in basket	*Approximate weight of currency at end-March 1979** %
Deutschmark	0.828	33
French franc	1.15	20
Pound sterling	0.0885	13
Dutch guilder	0.286	10
Italian lira	109	10
Belgian franc	3.66	10
Luxembourg franc	0.14	
Danish krone	0.217	3
Irish punt	0.00759	1
		100

*The exact weight of each currency depends on its current exchange rate, and changes continually.

Treaty, the 'Six' became combined in three distinct but interlocked functional communities; the European Coal and Steel Community (q.v.) formed in 1952, the European Atomic Energy Community ('Euroatom') and the European Economic Community. The total population of the Community, about 186 million, was only slightly less than that of the United States.

The purpose of the Treaty was to permit goods to travel freely, without custom duties or quota restrictions, throughout the area of the Six, and thus to permit manufacturers to invest on the scale that modern technology makes possible and necessary: to permit work-people to move wherever wages and conditions are best for them; and to permit free competition to eradicate waste and inefficiency. Progress was rapid. By July, 1968, virtually all remaining customs duties between members were abolished and a common external tariff completed. The common tariff raised Benelux and German tariffs, greatly reduced French and Italian. A considerable degree of mobility of labour and capital among members has been achieved. Progress in abolishing internal tariffs on agricultural products has been less rapid than for industrial goods.

On 2 May 1967, the British Government decided to apply for membership of the European Economic Community. Denmark, the Irish Republic and Norway also decided to apply for membership. On 30 June 1970, the British Government reiterated its acceptance of the Treaties establishing the three European Communities and the decisions which had flowed from them, subject to satisfactory solutions being found to certain problems.

A Government motion recommending in principle that the United Kingdom should seek to proceed to membership of the European Community on the terms negotiated earlier in 1971 was approved by both Houses of Parliament on 28 October 1971. A transitional period of 5 years was agreed for Britain to adopt the rules of the Community in the fields of industry, agriculture, movement of capital and fiscal harmonisation. On 22 January 1972, the United Kingdom, Ireland and Denmark signed the Treaty of Accession to the European Economic Community. Britain acceded to the Community on 1 January 1973. As a result of this enlargement, the population of the Community increased from 186 million to 253 million. Norway did not proceed with her application. The nine-nation common market accounted for over 40 per cent of world trade.

In 1974 Britain sought to renegotiate the terms of entry particularly in respect of Common Market budgetary contributions, the Common Agricultural Policy (q.v.) and the problem of greater access to markets for Commonwealth countries. On 5 June 1975, the first national referendum was held in Britain on the question of continued membership of the Community; two-thirds of those voting supported continued membership.

Article 237 of the Treaty of Rome states: 'Any European state may apply to become a member of the Community'. Greece applied for full membership of the Community on 12 June 1975, having been an 'associated state' since November, 1962, becoming the tenth member of the Community in January, 1981. In June, 1985, Spain and Portugal joined the Community, the original 'Six' becoming 'Twelve'.

In 1981, the E.E.C. budget represented 0.9 per cent of the E.E.C. countries joint gross domestic product, and equal to 2.7 per cent of national spending. The budget is financed from four sources: customs duties, agricultural levies, value-added tax, and direct national contributions. In 1980, Britain and West Germany paid more into the budget than the E.E.C. spent in their countries.

European Free Trade Association (E.F.T.A.). Originally an association of seven western European states (Austria, Denmark, Norway, Portugal, Sweden, Switzerland and the United Kingdom), who have agreed to gradually eliminate tariffs and restrictions on trade with each other. Proposals for such a free trade area were first made in July, 1956, at the Council of Ministers of the Organisation for European Economic Co-operation. Subsequently, an O.E.E.C. committee reported that such an Association was technically feasible. The United Kingdom supported the proposals with the proviso that foodstuffs should be excluded from their scope. The Association was formed in 1960. It was often referred to as 'the outer seven', a description arising from the geographical position of the members in relation to the Common Market 'Six'. Finland is now an associate member of E.F.T.A. Industrial trade between the E.F.T.A. countries was substantially freed from protective customs and tariffs from January, 1967. Iceland joined E.F.T.A. as a full member on 1 March 1970. A former member, Britain withdrew from the European Free Trade Association on entry into the European Economic Community. The surviving members of the Association are Austria, Finland,

Iceland, Norway, Portugal, Sweden and Switzerland. On 22 July 1972, a treaty between E.F.T.A. and the E.E.C. (q.v.) sought to abolish tariffs on industrial goods between the groups over a period of 5 years.

European Fund. *See* EUROPEAN MONETARY AGREEMENT (E.M.A.).

European Investment Bank (E.I.B.). A bank established by the European Economic Community (q.v.) in 1958 to assist economic development within the Community. It is an independent public body, set up under Articles 129 and 130 of the Treaty of Rome. Projects may qualify for loans if they will help to develop less advanced regions; if they will modernise or convert existing undertakings to more effective use; if they will promote new types of activity which become necessary or desirable within the Community; or if they will serve an interest common to several of the member states. The bank has supported such infrastructure schemes as the Paris–Brussels motorway, and the electrification of the Moselle railway line. It has assisted nuclear power station schemes in the Federal Republic of Germany and the building of gas pipelines linking member countries. Projects in less developed regions have included irrigation schemes in Sicily and Languedoc, power stations in Campania, the Messina–Catania motorway, telephone networks in Southern Italy and France, and manufacturing capacity in Lower Saxony. The European Airbus scheme has received help. The E.I.B. finances its operations by borrowing on capital markets both inside the Community and elsewhere. The loans are intended to supplement rather than replace funds from other sources. In Britain's assisted areas projects may qualify for E.I.B. loans and for financial help under the Industry Act 1972. A loan has been made to the British Steel Corporation towards its investment programme on Teesside.

By 1982, the bank was financing projects in the 10 member countries of the European Economic Community, and in more than 70 other countries in the Mediterranean, Africa, the Pacific and the Caribbean.

In September, 1982, the E.I.B. lent £52 million to Lancashire's County Council in England for 12 years, at an interest rate of 10.35 per cent, for a project to improve sewage treatment and strengthen Blackpool's sea wall.

European Monetary Agreement (E.M.A.). An Agreement concluded in August, 1955, by the members of the Organisation for European Economic Co-operation (O.E.E.C.). The E.M.A. came into operation in 1958, replacing the European Payments Union (E.P.U.) which had been in operation since 1950. The general objective of the Agreement is to foster the achievement and maintenance of full multilateral trade and convertibility in Europe by providing a framework for monetary co-operation between governments and between central banks. Its more specific objectives are:

(a) to lay down certain basic rules concerning the foreign exchange transactions of member countries;
(b) to discourage any relapse into bilateralism in international relations between member countries; and
(c) to provide a source of financial assistance for the purpose of helping member countries to overcome temporary balance-of-payments difficulties.

The E.M.A. has two main parts: (a) the European Fund, to which members contribute, which can grant credit to member countries additional to credit facilities they could obtain from the International Monetary Fund (q.v.), and (b) the Multilateral System of Settlements, under which each member country's central bank is assured of obtaining settlement in dollars, at an exchange rate known in advance, of its holdings in other members' currencies. This arrangement is designed to back-up the efficient operation of the foreign exchange markets. The Execution of the Agreement is supervised by the Board of Management of the E.M.A., which consists of a small group of financial experts nominated by member countries and appointed by the Council of the Organisation for Economic Co-operation and Development (O.E.C.D.) (q.v.). The E.M.A. is the only financial institution linking three groups of European member countries—the European Economic Community (q.v.), the European Free Trade Association (E.F.T.A.) (q.v.) and the remaining countries. As such it can be used for mutual support between, as well as within, these three groups.

European Monetary Co-operation Fund. A fund which began operations within the European Economic Community in April, 1973, managing existing short-term credit lines between member countries and concerned with the central bank co-operation necessary for the joint float of currencies.

European Monetary System (E.M.S.). A scheme of quasi-fixed exchange rates among European Economic Community (q.v.) currencies which float freely against those of non-members; the scheme has operated since March, 1978. Under the E.M.S., central banks are required to work together to smooth the exchange market, and have set up facilities for swapping credit. Initially, it was proposed to extend the E.M.S. to create a European central bank, common exchange reserves and, eventually, a common currency; this second stage has been postponed, despite the decision of the six heads of government in 1969 to seek economic and monetary union by 1980.

In March, 1983, all eight currencies involved in the European Monetary System were revalued against the European currency unit central rate. In particular, the margin between West German and French currency was widened by 8 per cent. Britain has not participated in the exchange rate mechanism.

Eurosterling bond. A bond denominated in sterling not necessarily on the United Kingdom capital market or by a resident of the United Kingdom; it is essentially an international instrument.

Euroyen money market. A money market fund established by the Nikko Investment Bank in 1984; it is based in Luxembourg.

Evening up. Buying or selling to offset an existing market position (q.v.).

Ex. Without or minus.

Ex-all. Without everything that has just been declared payable or detachable from a security.

Ex ante. 'From beforehand'; thus an ex ante definition of saving means saving as it is expected to be in the future in the light of present plans. Ex post or actually realised saving may diverge from that expected for a variety of reasons. Ex ante and ex post savings and investments are important in determining changes in the level of national income.

Ex-bonus. Without the bonus just declared. Shares are sold either ex-bonus or cum-bonus (q.v.).

Ex-capitalisation (ex-cap). Description of a share when the buyer is not entitled to the 'capitalisation issue' attaching to the share. *See* SCRIP OR BONUS ISSUE OF SHARES.

Ex-coupon. Without the coupon (q.v.) just paid.

Ex-dividend. Without the current dividend (or interest); a term used with the price of a share to indicate that the seller will take the current dividend or interest.

Ex-drawing. Without the benefit of the current drawing (q.v.). If there is no benefit but a loss on drawing, it is without the loss. A term used in connection with the sale of securities.

Ex-new. *See* EX-RIGHTS.

Ex-post. *See* EX ANTE.

Ex-rights. Description of a share when the buyer is not entitled to the 'rights issue' (q.v.) attaching to the share.

Excess capacity. Or unused capacity, a situation in which the firm could expand its output and produce more cheaply, but refrains from doing so for it would be unprofitable; the loss in revenue would exceed the reduction in costs.

Exchange. The act of accepting one thing for another, e.g. as in barter or in a transaction involving money (q.v.). *See* COMMODITY EXCHANGE; STOCK EXCHANGE.

Exchange control. The control of movements of funds and of purchases of currency by a government. Exchange control may be utilised in support of any of the following objectives:

(a) to keep exchange rates stable;
(b) to keep the currency undervalued to stimulate exports;
(c) to keep the currency overvalued to handicap exports and encourage imports.

In Britain, exchange control arose out of the circumstances of the Second World War with the need to restrict the movement out of the country of money and assets. Varying degrees of control have been exercised continuously since then, the Treasury having powers bestowed upon it by the Exchange Control Act 1947.

Britain's exchange controls were finally abolished in 1979; residents were then free to acquire foreign currency for any purpose including direct and portfolio investment overseas. Non-residents were free to acquire sterling for any purpose. Gold could also be freely bought and sold. *See* BRETTON WOODS AGREEMENT; CONVERTIBILITY; FLOATING EXCHANGE RATE; INTERNATIONAL LIQUIDITY; INTERNATIONAL MONETARY FUND; SMITHSONIAN AGREEMENT.

Exchanges for physical (E.F.P.s). Facilities by which, for example, futures contracts at the London Gold Futures Market (q.v.) may be exchanged for gold in other locations or markets.

Exchequer. The central account of the Government, kept by the Treasury at the Bank of England (q.v.). The exchequer and Audit Departments Act 1866 provides that all moneys received by the central Government must be paid into, and all payments authorised by Parliament must come out of, the Exchequer.

Exchequer return. A weekly Treasury statement showing the ordinary revenue and expenditure for the week in respect of the Exchequer (q.v.) together with cumulative figures for the financial year.

Excise duty. A revenue duty imposed on goods and services produced in Britain, e.g. excise duty on whisky and beer made in Britain, and on betting and gaming. *See* CUSTOMS DUTY.

Exclusive dealing agreement. An agreement between two or more firms to deal exclusively with each other and refuse to deal with other parties in respect of a commodity or service, or class of commodities or services, or in respect of a specified technology or class of technology.

Execution. On The London Stock Exchange (q.v.), the completion of a bargain (q.v.).

Executive. Defined by Peter F. Drucker as a knowledge worker, manager, or individual professional, who is expected by virtue of his position or his knowledge to make decisions in the normal course of work which have significant impact on the performance and results of the organisation he serves.

Exercise price or striking price; the price at which a security may be bought or sold by the exercise of an option. *See* SHARE OPTIONS.

Exogenous variable. *See* VARIABLES, ENDOGENOUS AND EXOGENOUS.

Expenditure-dampening policies. Government measures designed to reduce the aggregate demand for goods and services in the community. The measures may consist of raising taxes (q.v.), lowering government expenditure, or curtailing hire-purchase or other credit facilities. *See* EXPENDITURE-SWITCHING POLICIES.

Expenditure recoupment tax avoidance schemes. Schemes where it is made to appear as if some money has been spent, but the cash finishes up back in the hands of the tax avoider.

Expenditure-switching policies. Government measures designed to influence the pattern of expenditure by the community, leaving output intact. For example, the taxing of imported goods may effect a switch of expenditure from imported to home-produced goods; devaluation of the nation's currency may have the same effect as imports become more expensive. *See* EXPENDITURE-DAMPENING POLICIES.

Experimental economics. A body of experimental research being conducted in the United States to simulate human behaviour, or find enlightening parallels in other branches of the animal kingdom. For example, rats representing consumers are allowed to find their way through mazes in an attempt to prove the universality of economic man.

Explicit costs. Costs in the form of a payment either in cash or in kind. *See* IMPLICIT COSTS.

Export Credits Guarantee Department. A British Government department which gives insurance against a wide range of losses that an exporter might incur, such as losses due to the insolvency of a buyer; a buyer's failure to pay, within 6 months of the stipulated date, for goods which he has accepted; a buyer's default on a contract; action by a Government which prevents or interferes with payments; the cancellation of licences or the introduction of new licensing systems; war or civil disturbance; and losses due to any other cause, not within the control of importer or exporter, which is not normally insurable with commercial insurers.

Export Earnings Stabilisation Scheme (S.T.A.B.E.X.). A scheme introduced as a consequence of the Lomé Convention (q.v.) to provide aid by way of loans and grants to member countries suffering losses on export earnings; in 1982, some 44 commodities were listed ranging from palm oil to coffee in respect of which claims could be made. The object of the scheme is to stabilise incomes in the face of fluctuating commodity markets. Stabex applies only to A.C.P. country exports to the European Economic Community.

Export houses (U.K.). Export agencies which operate a variety of services, particularly for the small to medium-sized exporter. They can broadly speaking be grouped under three headings: as export merchants (buying the export outright and selling them on their own account); as export agents/managers (dealing with all the mechanics of exporting the goods while not actually owning them); and as confirming houses (working for the overseas buyer, but seeing that the exporter receives payment when the goods are shipped). Although some of the larger export houses may cover the full range of facilities mentioned above, most of them tend to specialise in particular types of product or in certain markets.

Export-Import bank. A United States government agency established in 1934 for the purpose of encouraging U.S. trade by supplying credit and financial guarantees to overseas countries. By the early 1980s, the Export-Import Bank in Washington, D.C. was lending some $5 billion a year to encourage foreigners to buy American.

Export incentives. Financial support and preferential treatment offered by governments to their exporters, compared with firms selling at home; the support includes special credit facilities, direct subsidies, taxation concessions, and export credit insurance. Export finance and support schemes grew rapidly in the 1950s as many potential customers for goods were developing nations short of foreign exchange. Initially support took the form of direct guarantees from government export-import departments to commercial banks who then provided loans for exporters selling on medium-term credit. During the 1960s, it became common practice for governments to offer some form of official support for most medium-term and long-term credit for exports, subsidising interest rates and loans. In 1980, official support was behind 18 per cent of all American, 34 per cent of all French, 35 per cent of all British, 39 per cent of all Japanese, and 14 per cent of all West German exports. *See* EXPORT CREDITS GUARANTEE DEPARTMENT; EXPORT-IMPORT BANK.

Extended fund facility. Created by the International Monetary Fund (q.v.) in 1974 to assist countries needing longer periods for repayments than the normal 1 or 2 years; repayments can be made over periods as long as 8 years.

External balance. The balance in a country's international payments.

External Economy. A fall in the cost of any of the materials and services which a firm requires, which are obtained from outside sources. These materials and services comprise raw materials, labour, fuel and power, transport services, and the services of specialised firms and selling agencies. Where large quantities of, say, fuel and ores are used then any change in their prices may have a marked effect on costs of production without any change in the internal economy of a firm. An external economy is external to a firm but internal to an industry. *See* ECONOMIES OF SCALE.

External effects or 'externalities'. Flows of some goods and services that come to the consumer and business whether wanted or not, and without charge; a change in the output of one economic unit (a firm or consumer) which necessarily affects the inputs (and hence the output) of another economic unit. For example, an increase in the output of a cannery may increase stream pollution, which in turn necessitates downstream firms or communities spending more money to clean up the water they use; they have experienced an unwanted increase of certain inputs, i.e. in this instance, pollutants. In other cases, the external effects may be beneficial, e.g. the use of electricity eliminates a great deal of air pollution in residential districts through displacing more-polluting forms of heating by fossil fuels and their derivatives. *See* PUBLIC GOODS.

External inflexibilities. Inflexibilities external to an organisation which impede progressive planning; they relate to the social, technological and economic environment. For example, the attitude of governments to an economic situation may have an effect which is quite significant. *See* INTERNAL INFLEXIBILITIES.

F

Face value. The nominal value, as distinct from the market value, of a security or share. Consols (q.v.) have a nominal value and a fixed rate of interest; the market value may vary considerably from the nominal value to give a yield comparable with other securities. If new stock is issued at par (q.v.) then £100 of such stock can be bought for £100; subsequently a nominal £100 of such stock may command a higher or lower price according to market conditions. A gold coin may command a market price much higher than its nominal or face value, that is the amount stamped upon it.

Factor cost. Price net of indirect taxes and subsidies, being the amount received by the factors of production (q.v.) during the manufacture of a good. National income is equal to the incomes received in the economy valued at factor cost.

Factor demand curve. A curve which represents the quantities of a factor of production that business firms will want to purchase or hire at various hypothetical prices per unit of the factor.

Factor incomes. Incomes accruing to the factors of production (q.v.); wages, salaries, profits, interest and rent. Such incomes consist of both transfer earnings and economic rent (q.v.); in limiting cases all earnings may be either transfer earnings or economic rent.

Factor markets. Markets in which factors of production (q.v.) or inputs are bought and sold, e.g. the labour market, the capital market.

Factor mobility. The ease or difficulty with which factors of production (q.v.) can move between uses. *See* ELASTICITY OF SUBSTITUTION.

Factor payments. *See* FACTOR INCOMES.

Factor price equalisation theorem. *See* HECKSCHER-OHLIN LAW.

Factor supply curve. Curve representing the quantities of a factor of production that factor-owners will be willing to sell or hire to business firms at various hypothetical prices per unit of the factor.

Factorage. *See* FACTORING.

Factoring.

(1) A system designed to eliminate payment risks in overseas sales and to ensure that the seller receives prompt settlement. The exporter attends to the selling and shipment of goods, invoices being sent to both the buyer and the factor. The factor pays the exporter and in due course the buyer pays the factor.

(2) Also applied to the purchasing of invoices from businesses, at a percentage discount. This improves the cash flow of the business concerned, which also avoids the need to follow up unpaid invoices and bills. The business enjoys a prompt release of cash, while the factor for a prescribed percentage charge takes on, in effect, a function of the business. The factor enables the invoice to become a marketable asset.

The commission earned by the factor is called factorage.

Factors, non-specific. Factors of production which are not specialised and can be put to alternative uses, e.g. most land, unskilled labour, raw materials.

Factors of production. The various agents which combine to produce goods and services. Land, labour and capital are the traditional categories; organisation or enterprise is sometimes added as a fourth category. There are many types for each factor; although not perfect substitutes for each other one factor can often be substituted to a large extent for another, e.g. capital for labour. The tendency today is to classify factors as specific and non-specific. They may be classified also as either complementary or competitive, since an increase in the usage of one factor may either increase or decrease the marginal product of another factor. The factors of production are often referred to as 'inputs'. *See* FACTORS, NON-SPECIFIC; FACTORS, SPECIFIC.

Factors, specific. Factors of production of a specialised kind which cannot easily be adjusted to serve an alternative purpose, e.g. skilled labour, intricate machinery.

Fair Credit Reporting Act 1970, and Fair Debt Collection Practices Act 1978 (U.S.). Acts which deal, respectively, with procedures for rectifying errors made in respect of a person's credit record, and with practices used to collect debt incurred for personal, family, or household purposes when the collector is acting for another person and under another name. The implementation of these Acts is the responsibility of the Board of Governors of the Federal Reserve System (q.v.).

Fair Trading Act 1973 (U.K.). A British Act which superseded the Monopolies and Restrictive Practices (Inquiry and Control) Act 1948, and the Monopolies and Mergers Act 1965, though incorporating much of that earlier legislation. It established the position of Director General of Fair Trading with powers to monitor and investigate trading activities. A monopoly is deemed to exist when the market share is one quarter, compared with one third in the 1948 Act. The new Act extended monopoly legislation to nationalised industries and other statutory undertakings. The Act created a Monopolies and Mergers Commission (q.v.). It enabled the Secretary of State to act reasonably quickly against new forms of unwelcome trade practices by using statutory orders. The Act also set up a Consumer Protection Advisory Committee.

Fannie Maes (U.S.). Securities issued by the Federal National Mortgage Association, an independent U.S. agency that buys mortgages from banks, mortgage companies, savings and loan associations and insurance companies, helping the provision of home finance. *See* GINNIE MAES.

Farm price review. *See* AGRICULTURAL SUBSIDIES; COMMON AGRICULTURAL POLICY; COMMON SUPPORT PRICES.

Father of economics. A role and title assigned to Adam Smith (1723–1790) by the leading expositors of the English classical version of the history of political economy including McCulloch and John Stuart Mill; they regarded Smith as the supreme founding father of the subject. Karl Marx (1818–1883) on the other hand regarded Sir William Petty (1623–1687) as 'the founder of modern political economy'.

Featherbedding. A derogatory term sometimes used in respect of industries or groups receiving special support or subsidies. It has been used from time to time in respect of subsidies paid to British agriculture. In another instance, while praising the Temporary Employment Subsidy *The Economist* said 'The unions love it, naturally. It has kept well over 100,000 of their members off the dole. But it also featherbeds Britain's over-manned, low-productivity industries.'

Fed, the. *See* FEDERAL RESERVE SYSTEM.

Fed wire. The funds transfer system of the Federal Reserve Board (q.v.); in 1982 it was used by over 800 banks, handling over 60 per cent of American domestic transactions.

Federal Acquisition Institute. *See* OFFICE OF FEDERAL PROCUREMENT POLICY.

Federal Advisory Council (U.S.). A Council composed of twelve representatives of the Federal Reserve Banks (q.v.), which advises the Board of Governors of the Federal Reserve System on the views of member bankers.

Federal budget (U.S.). A centrally prepared national budget covering all the important activities of the executive branches of the United States Government, subject to direct presidential scrutiny and congressional review. The Budget and Accounting Act 1921 established the first centrally prepared federal budget; previously each agency prepared its own budget which was presented to Congress by the Treasury Department without substantive review. The Act of 1921 established the Bureau of Budget; in 1970 this was replaced by the Office of Management and Budget (O.M.B.) (q.v.) with enlarged responsibilities.

Federal Cartel Office. An agency of the West German Government, located in West Berlin, charged with protecting and furthering competition in the republic, supervision of market dominating enterprises, control of mergers, and banning of cartels (with some exceptions such as export and import cartels, and 'crisis cartels' for industry adjustment, and other cartels deemed to be in the public interest). It has the power to impose administrative fines.

Federal Deposit Insurance Corporation (F.D.I.C.). A regulatory body created in the United States in the 1930s as a response to massive bank failures and runs on banks; the purpose of the new institution was to insure bank deposits, ensuring that depositors got paid even if their bank failed. Deposit insurance reduces the likelihood that depositors will cause a run on a bank, as well as insuring against loss. The F.D.I.C. was established as part of the New Deal package of the Roosevelt administration.

Federal Funds Market. A market in which American banks with surplus or reserve assets (non-interest bearing deposits with the Federal Reserve System) sell them to other banks who do not have enough. In Britain, this smoothing out is done through the inter-bank money market (q.v.).

Federal Open Market Committee. A committee of the Federal Reserve System (q.v.) which controls the purchases and sales of federal government securities. The Committee consists of the seven members of the Board of Governors, together with the heads of five of the twelve Federal Reserve Banks (q.v.) including the head of the New York Reserve Bank which is always represented. The Committee meets every 3 weeks; at these meetings decisions are made in respect of open market operations (which are executed by the securities department of the New York Reserve Bank). A purchase of securities by the Reserve Bank adds to the cash reserves of member banks; a sale of securities reduces the cash reserves of the member banks. The Federal Open Market Committee sets the U.S. Federal Reserve monetary policy; for example, the twelve members decided on a 6–9 per cent increase in the money supply M-2 for 1982 (M-2 includes M-1, savings accounts and new money market deposit accounts at banks and thrift institutions and tax-exempt money market funds).

Federal Reserve Banks. The equivalent in the United States of the central banks of other countries. The Federal Reserve Act of 1913 divided the United States into twelve regions or Federal Reserve Districts, each of which has a Federal Reserve Bank. The most important is the Federal Reserve Bank of New York. The Federal Reserve Banks hold the cash reserves of the member banks, rediscount bills for them, and provide clearing facilities. The activities of the twelve banks are controlled and co-ordinated by a Federal Reserve Board (q.v.). The Board can prescribe the minimum reserve ratio to be preserved between the cash deposits of the member banks at the Reserve Bank and customers' deposits at the member banks; and fix discount and other interest rate charges.

The twelve Federal Reserve Banks are located in Boston, New York, Philadelphia, Cleveland, Richmond, Atlanta, Chicago, St. Louis, Minneapolis, Kansas City, Dallas, and San Francisco. The board of directors of each Reserve Bank is composed of nine members; six are elected by the stockholding, member banks, while three are appointed by the Board of Governors. The Reserve Banks receive and hold on deposit the reserve or clearing account deposits of depository institutions. These banks are permitted to count their vault cash as part of their required reserve. The Reserve Banks issue Federal Reserve Notes, which constitute the bulk of money in circulation.

Federal Reserve Board or Board of Governors. The governing body of the United States central banking system. It comprises seven full-time members appointed by the President by and with the advice and consent of the Senate. The Chairman of the Board of Governors is, by Executive Order, a member of the national advisory council on international monetary and financial policies. The Board determines general monetary, credit, and operating policies for the Federal Reserve System (q.v.) as a whole and formulates the rules and regulations necessary to carry out the purposes of the Federal Reserve Act. The Board's principal duties consist of exerting an influence over credit conditions, supervising the Federal Reserve Banks (q.v.) and member banks, and regulating the implementation of certain consumer credit protection laws.

Under the Depository Institutions Deregulation and Monetary Control Act 1981 (q.v.), the Board has been given the power, within statutory limitations, to fix the requirements concerning reserves to be maintained by depository institutions of transaction accounts or non-personal time deposits and the power to determine the maximum rate of interest that may be paid by member banks on their time and savings deposits. Another important instrument of control is found in open market operations. The Board of Governors reviews and determines the discount rates charged by the Federal Reserve Banks on their discounts and advances. The Board supervises the Federal Reserve Banks. It also has jurisdiction over the admission of State banks and trust companies to membership in the Federal Reserve System (q.v.). *See* FEDERAL OPEN MARKET COMMITTEE; INTERNATIONAL BANKING ACT 1978.

Federal Reserve System. Central banking system of the United States of America, established by the Federal Reserve Act 1913. The system consists of six parts: the Board of Governors in Washington; the twelve regional Federal Reserve Banks (q.v.) with their twenty-five branches and other facilities situated throughout the country; the Federal Open Market Committee (q.v.); the Federal Advisory Council (q.v.); the Consumer Advisory Council (q.v.); and the member commercial banks which include all national banks and State chartered banks that have voluntarily joined the system.

It is the responsibility of the Federal Reserve System to promote the full use of human and capital resources in the United States, promote the growth of productivity, restrain inflation, achieve equilibrium in the nation's international balance-of-payments, and help maintain a commercial banking system that is responsive to the nation's financial needs and objectives. The system influences the lending and investing activities of commercial banks and the cost and availability of money and credit. *See* FIGURE 7, and FEDERAL RESERVE BOARD; INTERNATIONAL BANKING ACT 1978.

Federal Trade Commission (F.T.C.). A United States government agency created by the Federal Trade Commission Act 1914; the F.T.C. became an independent administrative agency in 1951. The functions of the F.T.C. have broadened over the years and may be summarised as follows: the promotion of free and fair competition in interstate commerce through the prevention of trade restraints, including price-fixing; the elimination of false or deceptive advertisements; the discouragement of price discrimination, arrangements which reduce competition, or measures which promote monopoly; the regulation of packaging and labelling; the protection of trademarks held by U.S. firms; the licensing and supervising of associations of American exporters; the promotion of consumer protection legislation generally; and the gathering and publication of statistical information.

Fiat money. Money which the State declares to be legal tender, although its content value may be little or nothing. Most of fiat money consists of notes, although token money may also be included in the term.

Fiduciary issue. That portion of the bank-note issue which is not backed by gold; nearly the whole of the bank note issue of the United Kingdom has become fiduciary. Originally, under the Bank Charter Act 1844 (q.v.), all notes except for a very limited amount were to be backed £1 for £1 by gold. The amount not covered amounted to £14 million and was known as the 'fiduciary issue'; these notes were backed by Government securities. In 1928, the fiduciary issue was increased to £260 million. Today the fiduciary issue depends entirely on the decision of the Government acting within the terms of the Currency and Bank Notes Act 1954.

Fill-or-kill order (U.S.). A market or limited price order for the purchase or sale of stocks and shares which is to be executed in its entirety as soon as it is represented on the floor of the stock exchange, and if not so executed is to be regarded as cancelled. *See* ALL-OR-NONE-ORDER.

Final products. Goods used by consumers in the act of consumption, as distinct from goods used by firms as input into processes which may be regarded as intermediate products. Some goods such as milk and cocoa may fill a role as final products on the one hand, and as intermediate products on the other.

Finance. The provision of money at the time it is needed. *See* BUSINESS FINANCE; CONSUMER CREDIT; CREDIT; HIRE PURCHASE.

Finance Act 1982 (U.K.). An Act which amended the National Loans Act 1968 to allow the Treasury to borrow, where necessary to maintain sound monetary conditions, even if such borrowing causes funds to be accumulated in the National Loans Fund (q.v.) in excess of the working balance previously permitted under the 1968 Act.

Finance Bill. A bill not involving goods, simply promising to pay a specified sum of money on a specified date. *See* TREASURY BILLS.

Finance Corporation for Industry Ltd. (F.C.I.). A corporation set up in 1945 by the insurance companies, investment trust companies and the Bank of England (q.v.) to provide capital for the rationalisation and the re-equipment of industries in cases where the existing financial facilities were inadequate. Superseded in 1983 by Investors in Industry (q.v.).

Finance corporations. Specialised financial institutions established to provide medium and long-term finance (q.v.) where it cannot be provided easily from traditional sources. *See* FINANCE CORPORATION FOR INDUSTRY LTD; FINANCE FOR INDUSTRY LTD; INDUSTRIAL AND COMMERCIAL FINANCE CORPORATION LTD; INVESTORS IN INDUSTRY.

Finance for Industry Ltd. Formed in November 1973, a holding company in respect of the two private sector lending corporations: Finance Corporation for Industry Ltd. (q.v.) and Industrial and Commercial Finance Corporation Ltd. (q.v.). These institutions retained their identity. The shareholders of Finance for Industry Ltd. were the English and Scottish Clearing Banks who owned 85 per cent of the equity, the Bank of England (q.v.) holding the remaining 15 per cent. The group represented an important private sector source for medium and long term finance.

Finance house. A financial institution engaged in the provision of hire purchase (q.v.) and

Federal Reserve System

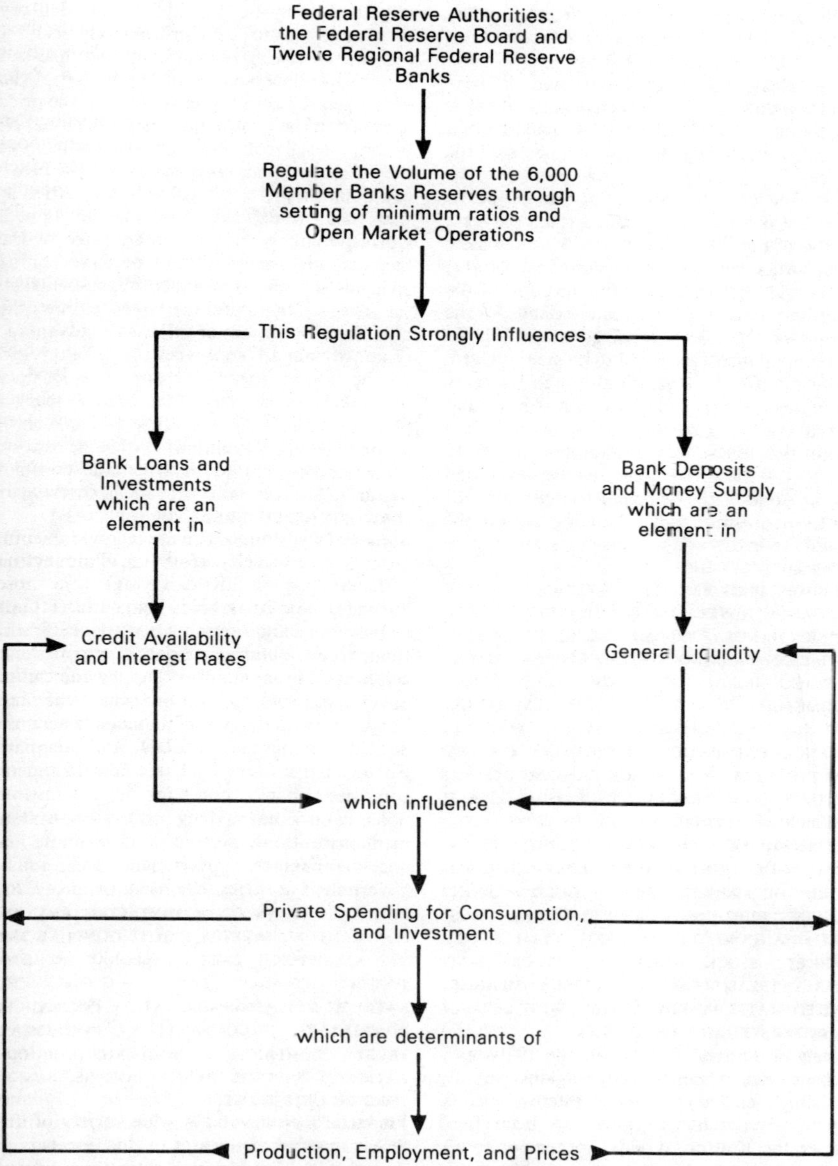

Figure 7 The influence of the Federal Reserve System

other forms of instalment credit. Also called finance companies, hire purchase finance houses (q.v.), and industrial banks.

Finance lease. Sometimes known as a 'full payout lease', a contract between lessor and lessee for the hire of a specific asset selected from a manufacturer or vendor of such assets by the lessee. The lessor retains ownership of the asset. The lessee has possession and use of the asset on payment of specified rentals over a period of time. Though the lessor remains the legal owner, the lessee is given exclusive rights to the use of the asset for the duration of the contract; the contract normally extends for the period of the asset's expected useful life. In general, finance leases tend to be medium term (typically around 5 years) although for large plant installations and items such as ships and aircraft, which generally have a much longer useful life, leases normally range from 10–15 years. By the 1980s the finance lease had become one of the principal sources of funds for the acquisition of capital equipment in the United Kingdom and other countries. *See* LEVERAGED LEASING.

Finance markets. *See* AMERICAN STOCK EXCHANGE; AUSTRALIAN BANKING SYSTEM; BILL OF EXCHANGE; BRITISH BANKING SYSTEM; CANADIAN BANKING SYSTEM; CENTRAL BANK; CHICAGO BOARD OF TRADE; 'CITY, THE'; COMMERCIAL BANKS; COMMODITY EXCHANGE; EUROPEAN INVESTMENT BANK; FINANCE; FINANCE CORPORATION FOR INDUSTRY; FINANCE FOR INDUSTRY LTD; FRENCH BANKING SYSTEM; FUTURES CONTRACT; INDUSTRIAL AND COMMERCIAL FINANCE CORPORATION LTD; INTERNATIONAL MONETARY FUND; LEASE; LONDON DISCOUNT MARKET; LONDON FOREIGN EXCHANGE MARKET; LONDON GOLD MARKET; PLACING; PUBLIC ISSUE; RIGHTS ISSUE; SAVINGS; SELF-FINANCING RATIO; SHORT TERM MONEY MARKET; STOCK EXCHANGE; STOCKS AND SHARES; TREASURY BILLS; TRUSTEE COMPANIES; UNITED STATES BANKING SYSTEM; WEST GERMAN BANKING SYSTEM; WORLD BANK.

Financial futures. Created in the 1970s as a vehicle with which to hedge against rapidly moving exchange and interest rates. Previously, exchange rates had been fixed under the Bretton Woods Agreement (q.v.), and there had also been reasonably stable interest rates. The Bretton Woods Agreement collapsed in the aftermath of President Nixon's decision to cut the link between the dollar and gold in August, 1971; also inflation began to accelerate in the West.

Financial futures contract. A futures contract for a financial instrument which commits the seller to deliver and the buyer to take delivery of it at the contracted price. Under such a contract, if the market price of the financial insrument concerned should be higher at the date when it has to be delivered than the price specified in the contract, or its yield should be lower, the seller in effect undertakes to meet the difference; and by collecting this the buyer can obtain a price or yield which is settled at the time when the contract is agreed. Correspondingly, if the market price of the financial instrument should be lower or its yield higher than is specified in the contract, the seller will gain and the buyer will lose the difference; but the latter still has the advantage of knowing in advance what the price or yield will be. Entering into a futures contract does not guarantee the buyer the current market price or yield, since the seller will take into account before agreeing to it what he expects the price or yield to be when the contract matures. *See* FORWARD EXCHANGE CONTRACT; FORWARD (OR FUTURE) RATE AGREEMENT.

Financial institutions. Private or governmental organisations which perform the vital function of facilitating the flow of savings from those businesses and households with surplus funds to businesses and households with insufficient funds to meet immediate needs, or perform a central role in the supply of money and credit. Savers are provided with financial assets and borrowers with the type of financing assistance needed to purchase goods and services. Financial institutions include central banks, commercial banks, non-bank deposit institutions, contractual savings institutions, investment institutions, personal and business finance companies, government and quasi-government agencies. *See* BANK OF ENGLAND; BUSINESS FINANCE; COMMERCIAL BANKS; CONTRACTUAL SAVINGS INSTITUTIONS; CREDIT UNION; DEPOSIT BANKS; FEDERAL RESERVE SYSTEM; FINANCE HOUSE; GOVERNMENT NATIONAL MORTGAGE ASSOCIATION; INSURANCE; INVESTMENT COMPANY; INVESTMENT TRUST COMPANIES; MORTGAGE BANKS; NATIONAL SAVINGS BANK; SAVINGS BANKS; THRIFTS; UNIT TRUST.

Financial instruments. A wide variety of different types of certificates or documents concerned with the financial obligations of one party to another. *See* BANKERS' ACCEPTANCES; BOND; COMMERCIAL PAPER MARKET; COMMON STOCK; NEGOTIABLE CERTIFICATES OF DEPOSIT; REPURCHASE AGREEMENTS; TREASURY BILLS; TREASURY NOTES.

Financial instrument contracts. Frequently describes contracts in share price index futures; bank bills futures; currency contracts; metals futures; and agricultural-based futures.

Financial intermediaries. Non-bank financial institutions which borrow from individuals and other institutions in order to make loans or other investments; these bodies include building societies, hire purchase finance houses (q.v.), insurance companies, savings banks, investment trusts, and pension funds.

Fine-tuning. The careful manipulation of monetary and fiscal policies by a government to achieve specific objectives, e.g. growth at a certain rate or a reduction in the rate of inflation. The use of the term 'fine-tuning' by a government is most likely when it appears to have command of the economy and only some small adjustments are necessary; it is quite inappropriate when a government is patently not in control of the economy, and even major measures are proving ineffective.

Members of the Monetarist School (q.v.) argue that monetary policy should not be used in a discretionary fashion to try to fine-tune the level of economic activity, as there are long and variable lags associated with such operations which may result in destabilisation rather than stabilisation.

Finest rate of discount. Lowest rate of discount.

Firm. A unit of management operating under a trade name organised either to extract minerals, produce or manufacture goods, or to sell goods or services, or to engage in two or three of these activities simultaneously. A firm may be a sole proprietorship, a partnership, a private or public limited company, or a state-owned enterprise. It is important to distinguish between a firm as a legal entity and as an operating unit. A large conglomerate may be a single firm for the purposes of company law, but will contain several operating units managed quite separately.

Firm, theory of the. The theory of the ways in which prices are determined and resources allocated among different uses in respect of the products of the individual firm.

First call. The first demand for payment of the initial instalment due on shares after allotment.

First mortgage bond (U.S.). A fixed interest loan repayable on a given date; similar to debenture (q.v.). The term 'first mortgage' means that the bond holders have a claim before other creditors on the assets of the corporation (q.v.).

First notice day. On a commodities exchange, the first day on which notice may be given or received of the intention to deliver actual commodities against futures market positions. These vary with each commodity and exchange.

Fiscal dividend. The increase in federal or national revenues which results from a rise in the Gross National Product (q.v.) at any given level of tax rates.

Fiscal drag. Descriptive of the restraining effects upon growth and demand of increasing effective rates of taxation; this may occur under conditions of inflation (q.v.) when increased wages and salaries bring people into higher tax brackets.

Fiscal policy. Generally, the policy adopted by a government for raising revenue to meet expenditure and for influencing the level of business activity; more specifically, the use of government spending and taxes to achieve macro-economic objectives. Modern fiscal policy has been a comparatively recent development, being in essence an outgrowth of Keynesian economics; only since the end of the Second World War has either a passive or countercyclical fiscal policy been generally accepted practice in the United States. It has superseded the concept of a balanced federal budget. Passive fiscal stabilisers are those built-in fiscal elements which, without any explicit policy decisions by government, move the budget towards a larger deficit, or smaller surplus, during a recession; in turn, these built-in stabilisers tend to shift the budget towards a smaller deficit, or larger surplus, during inflationary periods. Thus social security and unemployment benefits tend to rise in a recession creating a deficit in relation to government revenue, which itself may tend to shrink, while in a boom these outgoings fall while revenue from earned income and purchases tends to expand. Indeed, during a recession federal government spending may be boosted by increased unemployment benefits, various welfare programs, and accelerated early retirement.

An active, or discretionary, fiscal policy introduces more marked changes in spending programmes or in the taxation structure in order to combat recession or inflation, or simply to stimulate economic growth. This concept emerged only as recently as the Kennedy–Johnson administrations and has not gained general acceptance; in the early 1970s, the Nixon administration reverted to strictly passive fiscal policies. A central problem has been the growing inadequacy of static neo-Keynesian countercyclical fiscal policy in the presence of the concurrent problems of unemployment and inflation; high unemployment might suggest fiscal stimulation, while excessive inflation would suggest fiscal restraint. In consequence, new policy approaches have been called for including various forms of incomes policies.

Fiscalists. Those who believe that fiscal policy (q.v.) is the most important means available to the government for influencing the level of economic activity.

Fisher's Ideal Index. An index based on a formula devised by the American economist Irving Fisher (1867–1947). It is intended to be a 'true' index, the Laspeyres' index (q.v.) giving an upper limit and the Paasche index (q.v.) a lower limit to this 'true' index; it is in fact an index of the geometric mean of the Laspeyres' and Paasche indices. The formula is:

$$\left[\frac{\Sigma P_n q_o}{\Sigma P_o q_o} \times \frac{\Sigma P_n q_n}{\Sigma P_o q_n}\right]^{\frac{1}{2}}$$

where P_o = price in the base-year; q_o = quantity in the base-year; P_n = price in the year being considered; and q_n = quantity in the year being considered.

Fixed costs. Production costs which tend to be unaffected by variations in the volume of output. Once the Central Electricity Generating Board has constructed a power station, it incurs considerable annual fixed capital charges irrespective of the amount of electricity generated. Also known as 'supplementary costs' or 'overhead costs'.

Fixed exchange rates. Exchange rates among national currencies which are fixed by governments, and are not free to vary in response to market forces. *See* INTERNATIONAL MONETARY FUND.

Fixed instalment method. A method for calculating and allowing for the depreciation of an asset. The fixed instalment, or straight-line, method distributes the cost of an asset uniformly over its depreciable life. The amount to be set aside each year may be calculated from the formula:

$$\frac{P - L}{n}$$

where P is the initial asset cost, L the expected salvage value at the end of the useful life of the asset and n the plant life expressed in years. *See* DEPRECIATION; DEPRECIATION FUND METHOD; DIMINISHING BALANCE METHOD; SINKING FUND.

Fixed interest securities. Debentures and kindred securities issued by a public company, being known by a variety of names, e.g. mortgage debentures, secured debentures, secured notes. These are all loan liabilities requiring the payment of specified rates of interest and the repayment of the principal at the date of maturity. Holders of these securities are creditors of the company, and the interest and principal payments are legally enforceable. *See* DEBENTURES.

Fixed throttle policy. A policy associated with the name of Professor Milton Friedman (b. 1912) of steadily increasing the money supply by 3–5 per cent per annum in order to support non-inflationary economic growth.

Fixed trust. A type of unit trust (q.v.) whose trust deed specifies a portfolio of securities for the investment of trust monies.

Flat. A description of bonds being sold in default, since no interest is being paid.

Flat income bond. The price at which a bond is traded which includes consideration of all unpaid accruals of interest. Bonds which are in default of interest or principal are traded flat; all other bonds are usually traded with interest, which means that the buyer pays to the seller the market price plus interest accrued since the last payment date.

Flat-rate broker. A stockbroker that charges a flat or fixed fee for transactions in one stock on a single day, irrespective of value.

Flexible exchange rates. Exchange rates among national currencies which are free to vary in response to market forces, without government attempts to maintain a fixed exchange rate at which one currency is exchanged for another. Flexible exchange rates create greater uncertainty for traders and this can be minimised by an active forward market. Foreign exchange markets depend upon a confidence that obligations will be met.

Flexible-system production. A production system in which traditionally separate business functions (design, engineering, purchasing, manufacturing, distribution, marketing, and sales) are merged into a highly integrated organisation that can respond quickly to new opportunities. Flexible-system production has an advantage over high-volume, standardised production whenever solving new problems is more important commercially than the solution of problems associated with old routines. Flexible systems enable industrialised countries to move towards higher-valued and technologically more sophisticated business (speciality steel, special chemicals, synthetic fibres, and precision engineering), allowing lower-skill standardised segments of production to migrate to developing countries. Flexible-system production requires an organisation designed for change and adaptability; while high-volume, standardised production, needs an organisation geared to stability.

Flight to quality. The buying of 90-day U.S. Treasury Bill futures and the selling of bank certificate of deposit futures, by market traders. The interest on government securities is traditionally lower than that offered by the banks, banks offering a somewhat higher risk. However, for the same reason, T-Bill futures are expected to trade at a higher price or at a premium, compared with C.D. futures. This is because in a time frame of months, bank risks appear magnified. When a sufficient difference in the futures prices occurs, a flight to quality occurs in the selling of C.D.s and the buying of T-Bills.

Float. The initial raising of finance (q.v.) by public subscription to securities (q.v.).

Floaters. First-class bearer securities.

Floating capital. Capital which circulates, leaving a business by way of expenditure on materials and wages, and returning by way of receipts from sales.

Floating debt. That part of the National Debt (q.v.) which involves short-term borrowing; it consists of Ways and Means Advances (q.v.) and Treasury Bills (q.v.). It amounts to about one-fifth of the internally held National Debt.

Floating exchange rate. A market situation in which the exchange rate between currencies is free to change from day-to-day in response to supply and demand; the opposite to fixed parity.

Floor broker. A member of a United States stock exchange who executes orders on the floor of the Exchange to buy or sell any listed securities.

Floor member. Brokers represented on an exchange trading floor; they act for themselves or their clients.

Floor trader. A registered employee of a floor member (q.v.) of an exchange; the floor trader may transact all business for the floor member on the trading floor of the exchange.

Flow of funds. In the economy, the transfer of money between the different sectors; the money inflows and outflows by 'transaction group'. Flow of funds accounts are social accounts giving an overall picture of the financial relationships between the various sectors of the economy; they throw light on the processes of economic expansion and contraction. *See* FLOW OF FUNDS ACCOUNT.

Flow of funds account. A component of the British national accounts system which shows the financial transactions between broad sectors of the economy, thus linking the saving and investment aggregates in other components of the national accounts with their associated lending and borrowing activities. Flow of funds accounts are essential for any comprehensive analysis of capital market behaviour, because they help to identify both the role of finance in the generation of income, savings and expenditure, and the influence of economic activity on financial markets.

Flow of funds tax. A form of company tax recommended in the 1978 report of Sir James Meade's committee on tax reform prepared for the Institute of Fiscal Studies; the tax would be levied on the excess of inflows over outflows of funds due to both real and financial transactions, whether on current or capital account. The tax would make it unnecessary to distinguish between current spending and revenue, and capital spending.

F.O.B. Free on Board. Term used of goods shipped where the price does not include shipping or insurance charges; opposite to C.I.F. (q.v.). An F.O.B. quotation means that the exporter will deliver the goods free on board a ship in accordance with the contract at the port named; he pays all expenses up to that point. From then on the buyer must take responsibility, paying for freight, insurance, and all subsequent expenses.

F.O.B.T. Free on Board, trimmed. The price at which a loose cargo (coal, wheat, alumina, etc.) is not only loaded into a ship, but is also levelled-off in a condition ready for sailing.

F.O.Q. Free on quay. A quotation term where goods are to be delivered to a quay, but the loading expenses are to be borne separately by the buyer.

F.O.R. Free on rail (cf. F.O.B.)

F.O.T. Free of tax.

Footloose industry. Or mobile industry; industry of all kinds which is not 'tied' to existing locations by virtue of its relative independence in respect of specific transport links or markets.

'For the Account'. On The London Stock Exchange (q.v.), implies that the bargain will be completed (i.e. the stocks or shares handed over and paid for) on the next account day (q.v.). Most dealing is 'for the Account'.

Force majeure. Forces beyond the control of a company preventing it from fulfilling a contract; a company unable to deliver in these circumstances may declare *force majeure*. For example: 'Queensland Mines, the focal point of the Australian uranium share boom, yesterday declared *force majeure* on its first uranium supply contract. This means it is unable to deliver.' (*Business Age*, Melbourne, 24 March 1977).

Forced draught expansion. Economic expansion accelerated by special government measures or strong external influences.

Forced saving. Saving achieved through an enforced reduction in the consumption of consumers' goods by the community. A Government may achieve this by raising additional finance for investment purposes through increased taxation. On the other hand the same result may be achieved, though through an inflationary process, by the Government creating money to finance investment.

Forecasting, economic. The use of collected and analysed data derived from the present and the past to predict future economic, business or sales developments. In recent years the services of the economist have been increasingly used for this purpose by national and business organisations. The art of economic and business forecasting, in the long-term as well as in the short-term, enhances the background of information against which realistic budgets and the most advantageous plans can be prepared. While it has, on the whole, proved a valuable aid to policy-making and business management, it cannot be a substitute for sound judgment based on past experience.

Foreign aid. Assistance given by wealthier countries to aid the less fortunate, often being funnelled through the World Bank (q.v.) and other multilateral development banks. While in 1960, some 17 donors being members of the Organisation for Economic Co-operation and Development (q.v.) contributed on average 0.51 per cent of their gross national products in aid, this had declined to 0.35 per cent by 1981. This was due largely to a decline in American aid which amounted to 0.53 per cent of gross national product in 1960, but to only 0.20 per cent in 1981. Other donors maintained or increased their shares in 1981.

Foreign currency options. Options (q.v.) in foreign currencies offered from November, 1982, experimentally in Amsterdam, followed by a fully fledged market in the Philadelphia Stock Exchange trading initially in five foreign currency options: D.M., sterling, yen, Swiss francs, and Canadian dollars. Options give the right to buy or to sell and can be exercised at any time during their life, or be allowed to lapse. To take out an option, an investor pays a deposit which is the most he can lose. Foreign currency options appeal to those who may receive monies from abroad in the future and who wish to hedge against an adverse shift in exchange rates.

Foreign trade multiplier. The net effect on a country's foreign trade following an increase in spending at home after taking into consideration (a) the additional spending on imports to serve the increase in home demand, and (b) the effect of the increase in imports on the income of the exporting countries and the influence this increase in income may have on the demand for the exports of the country concerned.

Forestalling policies. Government measures to correct disturbing trends in the economy which might otherwise lead to a disruption of declared objectives, e.g. full employment, steady growth or stable prices.

Forex markets. Foreign exchange markets, including forward foreign exchange markets.

Forward contract. A futures contract (q.v.) to buy or sell a specific physical commodity at some time in the future.

Forward exchange contract. A futures contract (q.v.) which allows a customer to fix the price of a foreign currency for delivery at a future date, irrespective of the market rate at that time. This type of contract is available for most currencies, often for terms of 5 years or even longer.

Forward option deal. A more sophisticated version of a forward exchange contract (q.v.); it allows the customer to complete the deal during an agreed period rather than on a specific date. This type of contract is widely used in the United Kingdom though not in most other countries.

Forward (or future) rate agreement. Interest rate hedging (q.v.); an agreement between a bank and its customer on the terms of a notional deposit or loan to begin on a future date. The transaction is not actually completed on the due date, but a payment is made to reflect the difference between the original interest rate and the market rate on the agreed date. Thus, a customer may hedge any major currency interest rate, for quite large amounts without variable margin payments.

Forwardation. *See* CONTANGO.

Franchise. (1) An authorisation or permit to sell products in a particular area; (2) A most important yet least tangible element in the make-up of a successful corporation or bank, the perceived ability in the mind of the client to deliver top-quality services. It distinguishes top firms from the also-rans. Franchise determines the ability to attract and hold important customers and first-class staff.

Franked income (U.K.). Income which has already been subject to corporation tax.

Free depreciation (U.K.). An arrangement

whereby an industrialist who goes to the expense of putting in modern plant and machinery is granted a 100 per cent first-year allowance against tax for the investment. This arrangement was introduced by the Local Employment Acts of 1960 and 1963 to encourage the development of industry in the Development Districts, and in 1972 was extended to the whole of Britain.

Free exchange rates. Exchange rates which depend upon the supply and demand for a currency on the foreign exchange market, without official intervention.

Free goods. In economics, those attributes of the natural world which are valued by society but are not in individual ownership and do not enter into the processes of market exchange and the price system. Usually the marginal benefit equals zero, so the good cannot be sold. Notable among such resources are the atmosphere, watercourses, ecological systems, and the visual properties of the landscape. In reality in developed economies they are common property resources of great and increasing value presenting society with important and difficult allocational problems, which exchange in private markets cannot resolve.

Free issue. *See* CAPITALISATION OF RESERVES; SCRIP OR BONUS ISSUE OF SHARES.

Free market. A market (q.v.) in which the forces of supply and demand operate unimpeded by government regulation or the power play of large economic units.

Free reserves. The excess of member-bank reserves over borrowings from the Federal Reserve System (q.v.), plus reserves legally required against bank deposits.

Free trade. Trade which is unimpeded by tariffs, import and export quotas and other devices which obstruct the free movement of goods and services between countries. The formation of a free trade area by two or more countries, however, does not preclude the retention by those participating countries of tariffs against non-member countries. *See* EUROPEAN ECONOMIC COMMUNITY; EUROPEAN FREE TRADE ASSOCIATION; LATIN AMERICAN INTEGRATION ASSOCIATION.

French banking system. A banking system consisting of a central government bank (the Banque de France), together with deposit banks. The three largest deposit banks are the Société Générale, Banque Nationale de Paris and Crédit Lyonnais. These are state-owned and in aggregate account for about 60 per cent of all deposits in registered banks. The deposit banks are required to maintain a 'retention ratio' in the form of holdings or rediscountable medium-term bills or bonds. The banks are also required to keep in 'non-remunerative accounts' with the central bank a proportion of total sight and term deposits, which may be up to 15 per cent. Following the 1967 Wormser Report, deposit banks were sharply distinguished in law from investment banks, or *Banques d'affaires*. Reforms removed the restriction which prevented the deposit banks from accepting deposits for terms longer than 2 years, and the investment banks from taking deposits on current account.

Frictional unemployment. *See* UNEMPLOYMENT, TYPES OF.

Friendly societies. Traditional mutual aid societies which operate medical, hospital and funeral funds as well as dental clinics, physiotherapy clinics, and pharmacies. They often offer investment products, such as single premium investment bonds.

Front end loading.

(1) A characteristic of loan repayments during periods of inflation; high repayments in real terms are incurred in the early years, with lower repayments in real terms towards the end. This front end loading increases as the inflation rate rises. The higher the inflation and interest rates, the more a borrower has to put aside in the early years to service a loan, with less being available for consumption.

(2) Often called a service fee, the cost to an investor of buying into a unit trust or purchasing other securities. In respect of a unit trust, the front end load may be as high as 8 per cent of the value of the unit purchased, depending on the company.

Frustration hypotheses. A hypothesis which asserts that the higher the actual rate of growth of real income relative to the long-run expectations of the workforce the lower will be the sense of frustration and the less likely the workforce will push for higher money-wages. New Cambridge theorists argue that trade union power develops via this frustration hypothesis. In a situation of less than full employment, with expectations dampened, at some threshold there would be a fall in the rate of wage, and hence price, inflation.

Full cost pricing. The fixing of the prices of goods by a manufacturer on the basis of average direct costs in labour and materials plus an allowance for overheads. The overheads, or average fixed costs, are calculated on the assumption of less than full capacity operation of the plant to allow for fluctuations in production activity; this calculated figure then becomes the normal or standard for the purpose of costing. Firms may adopt an even simpler procedure by adding a uniform percentage mark-up above direct costs to a wide variety of products without any careful assessment of the fixed costs properly attributable to each line. It has been argued that full cost pricing shows that firms do not attempt to maximise profits; instead there is a philosophy that there is a *right* price that ought to be charged in periods of both good and bad business. *See* MARGINAL COST PRICING; PRICING.

Full employment. A situation in which all those persons seeking work in a community are able to find suitable work fairly readily, with the consequence that a very high proportion of the working population is actually in work at any one time. To achieve this in practice, the number of unfilled vacancies must exceed the number of persons seeking work as in any locality some vacancies may not be suitable for local applicants. Furthermore, the number of vacancies in a country should be distributed according to local needs, otherwise an excess of vacancies may occur in one locality and a deficiency in another.

Lord Beveridge defined full employment as a situation in which the number of those unemployed did not exceed 3 per cent of the total working population. In the 1960s, in the United States, an unemployment rate of 4 per cent of the labour force was thought by many to constitute full employment; since the 1970s the benchmark for unemployment has risen to exceed 5 per cent. *See* NATURAL RATE OF UNEMPLOYMENT.

Full employment surplus (deficit). The surplus or deficit which would occur in a federal or national government budget if the economy was functioning with full (or high) employment. This concept is relevant to the national accounts because the actual amount of taxes collected (and certain expenditures such as unemployment compensation) depends upon the level of economic activity, once the government has set the tax and expenditure rates.

'Full line forcing'. A situation in which a company will not supply certain types of goods or machinery (in which it may have an important monopoly) to dealers who do not order also certain other specified types of goods or machinery which the company manufacturers. The company thus ensures the sale of its full line of products.

Funded debt. Usually the interest-bearing bonds or debentures of a company, and may include long-term bank loans; the term does not include short-term loans, preferred or common stock.

Funding. The conversion of short-term debts into long-term debts. The sale of long-dated securities by the monetary authorities.

Funds, the. Collective name for British Government stocks.

Futures. A term used to designate all standard contracts covering transactions in financial instruments or physical commodities for future delivery on an exchange.

Futures commission merchant. A firm or person engaged in soliciting or accepting and handling orders for the purchase or sale of futures contracts, and accepts money or securities as margin (q.v.) on any resulting trades or contracts.

Futures contract. A commitment to deliver (in the case of a sold contract) or to take delivery of (in the case of a bought contract) a specified weight or quantity of a standard grade of a commodity at a fixed price and for a specified delivery date or period, at an agreed location. Futures contracts are mainly utilised by the producers and users of commodities who wish to avoid the uncertainty which fluctuations in the prices of commodities brings. Buyers prefer to know how much they will be paying for a certain commodity in several months' time, while primary producers are keen to establish, ahead of time, the price they will receive for their future output. The futures market (q.v.) operates by bringing these buyers and sellers together in one place where they agree on the price at which certain commodities will change hands at given future dates. At the cost of foregoing the possibility of exceptional profit, the hedger is able to avoid unfortunate loss. An example of a futures contract is as follows:

Suppose a wool grower in May wishes to set a price for his October wool clip. He carefully calculates his total costs and concludes that he would like to sell his wool for at least 500¢ a kilogram clean to ensure a reasonable profit on his year's output of 45 bales. He notes that December wool futures are selling at 558¢ a kilogram clean and instructs his broker to sell three December contracts at this price. The order is executed and the wool grower then has an agreement to sell 4,500 kilograms of wool (each contract covering 1,500 kilograms or about 15 bales) in December at 558¢ a kilogram clean.

By October we will assume that the price of wool in the auction system has fallen to 525¢ a kilogram clean while December futures are now selling at 528¢ a kilogram. The grower decides to sell his wool at auction and buy back on the futures market. He receives 525¢ a kilogram clean at auction and shows a profit of 30¢ a kilogram on his futures trade, giving him an effective selling price for his wool of 555¢ a kilogram clean. His hedge, presented schematically, looks as follows:

Cash market	*Time*	*Futures market*
Cost of production plus profit margin: 500¢ a kilogram clean	May	Sells December futures at 558¢ a kilogram clean
Sells wool at auction for 525¢ a kilogram clean	November	Buys December futures at 528¢ a kilogram. Profit on futures: 30¢ a kilogram clean.

Outcome: 30¢ futures profit added to 525¢ received at auction gives an effective selling price of 555¢ a kilogram clean.

Apart from hedging, the futures contract is also used by speculators, and in a minority of cases as a means of making and taking physical delivery of a commodity. *See* FIGURE 8.

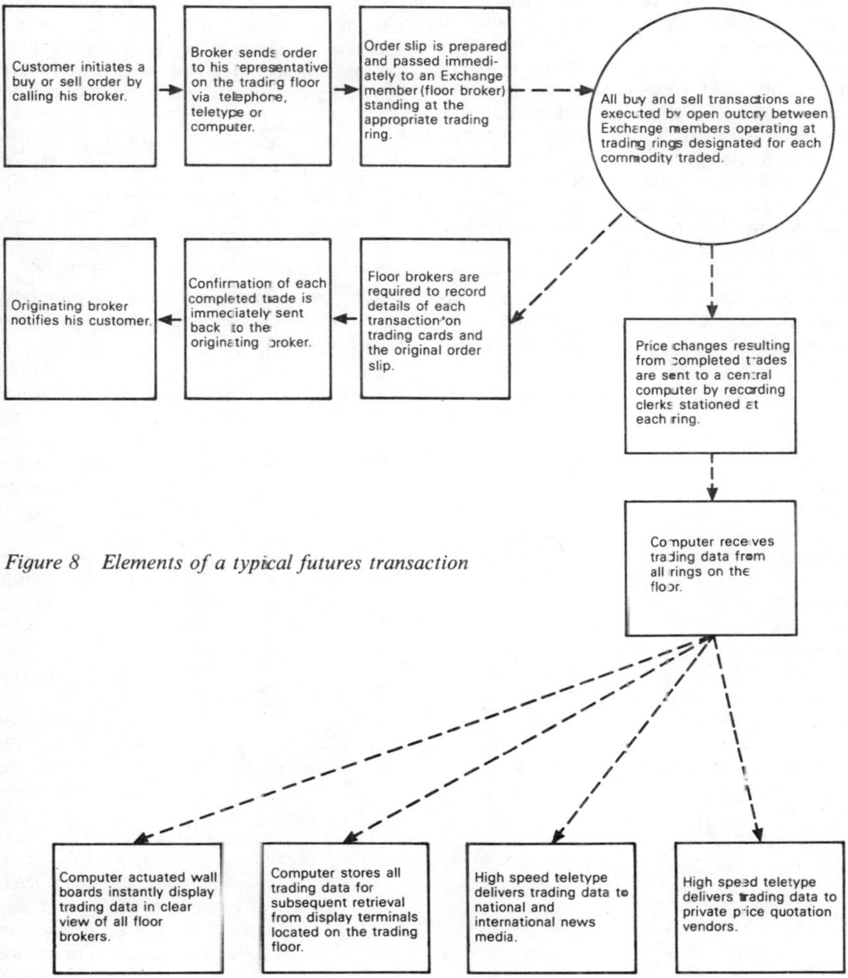

Figure 8 Elements of a typical futures transaction

Futures market. A market in which goods are sold for delivery at some future date, say in 3 months' time. Historically, futures were foreshadowed by the type of agreements made at mediaeval fairs in Flanders and the Champagne district during the 12th century. These agreements, called *lettres de faire*, were made on the basis of samples from which merchants sold their wares ahead of their arrival by ship. The price of the goods was settled at the time the agreement was struck, so that the seller was protected against any price fall between the time of the sale and the time of delivery. Later in 16th century Japan, a system was evolved of issuing tickets representing entitlements to rice crops growing in the fields. These would be bought by merchants in expectation of their future rice needs; they were in fact futures contracts that could be bought and sold. Rules were made specifying the time of the delivery of the rice, establishing standard grades and quantities for each contract, and stipulating that traders must have credit with a clearing house, through which all tickets were traded. When trading in grains and cotton between the United States and Europe began in the 19th century, a similar system to the *lettres de faire* was needed because of the time required to ship goods from one side of the Atlantic to the other. Goods were bought and sold at agreed prices while they were still afloat. Large commodity exchanges became established in Chicago, London and other European centres. *See* COMMODITY EXCHANGE.

Futures market margins. Margins which are of two types: (a) an initial margin which is a fixed amount payable at the outset on each open contract; it can range from 0.2 per cent to 3 per cent of the value of a contract, and (b) a variation margin, the amount of which differs considerably between exchanges, which is the sum that may have to be paid to the clearing house daily as the day's profit or loss is calculated. As a consequence of this arrangement, the exchange is able to guarantee all contracts. The system of buying contracts on margin makes the futures market attractive to speculators. The gearing element is considerable and the profits on what is a relatively small outlay may be very large.

Futures options. An option is a contract that gives a buyer the right, but not the obligation, to buy something at a stated price within a certain time; an option on a future gives an investor the right to buy or sell a futures contract covering a commodity. *See* COMMODITY FUTURES TRADING COMMISSION.

Futures price. The price of a given commodity unit determined by open outcry (q.v.) on a futures exchange.

G

G.A.T.T. anti-dumping code. A code introduced by the General Agreement on Tariffs and Trade (q.v.) setting out the criteria for the investigation of complaints of alleged dumping (q.v.) and the imposition of appropriate remedies.

Gazumping. The practice of raising the price of a home after accepting a deposit from a prospective buyer; the buyer is told by the real estate agent to pay the increase or miss out on the sale. Between placing a deposit and discovering that a house has been sold to someone else, a person may have engaged a solicitor, arranged finance and incurred expenses such as a valuer's fee. The practice becomes more commonplace when the housing market is buoyant and buyers have little resistance against smart operators.

Gearing. The relationship between ownership and borrowing; the higher the use of borrowing, the higher the gearing. The higher the gearing, the greater the risk of loss or potential for profit. *See* CAPITAL GEARING.

G.E.M.M. A gilt-edged market maker (q.v.); a company functioning as a primary dealer in the gilt-edged market.

General Agreement on Tariffs and Trade (G.A.T.T.). An international commercial treaty which came into force on 1 January 1948. Some 88 governments, accounting for over 80 per cent of world trade, had by 1982 become contracting members of the Agreement. Two-thirds of the membership is made up of developing countries. The basic principle of G.A.T.T. enshrined in Article 1 of the Agreement is that trade should not be discriminatory; what applies to one partner should apply to all. Exemptions from the rules granted to some branches of agricultural trade have been gradually extended so that G.A.T.T. rules apply largely to industrial products. Furthermore, the trading system embodied in Gatt has been progressively undermined by non-tariff protectionist measures, such as national subsidies, import restraint agreements, and free trade agreements restricted to two or a few countries.

In 1982, the 88 members of G.A.T.T. held their first ministerial meeting in 9 years. The meeting made little progress in the matter of reducing trade barriers, or even reducing the threat of protective reprisals. While all participants paid lip service to the need to combat protectionism, most countries argued for their own protection on grounds of special need. The final declaration of the meeting left unresolved most of the disputes raised. However it was agreed to set up a G.A.T.T. committee on agricultural trade though this decision excluded any commitment to phase out farm export subsidies over the next 2 years. Such a commitment had been sought by the United States and most Third World countries but was strongly resisted by the 10-nation European Economic Community (q.v.) on the grounds that its common agricultural policy would be undermined. Australia dissociated itself from the final declaration, yet symbolised the problem of many nations in seeking free trade for its exports yet succumbing to pressure for the protection of its domestic manufacturing industries. *See* DILLON ROUND; KENNEDY ROUND; TOKYO ROUND.

General equilibrium. Descriptive of a theoretical situation when supply equals demand in all markets in an economy. An economic system is in equilibrium when producers' plans and consumers' plans are consistent, and the forces which bring about changes in prices are in balance.

General equilibrium analysis. Distinguished from partial equilibrium analysis (q.v.) by the assumption that the price of every good is free to vary and that all markets must come into balance, i.e. that all markets must clear. Such analysis usually assumes perfect competition (q.v.) and private ownership of the means of production.

General mortgage bond. A bond (q.v.) which is secured by a blanket mortgage on a company's property.

Generalised system of preferences. (a) *E.E.C.* A system of tariff reductions granted by the European Economic Community (q.v.) to developing countries. The E.E.C. was the first major trading power to introduce generalised preferences in 1971; (b) *U.S.* A system of tariff reductions offered by the United States of America to poorer countries allowing more favoured treatment in trade.

Gentrification. The movement of people into run-down neighbourhoods who invest money in rehabilitating what were once fine houses or apartments; good homes have been created in improving neighbourhoods often at a cost much lower than that of a home in the suburbs or exurbs; gentrification has reversed the earlier wholesale flight from city to suburb. However, gentrification has been criticised for destroying established communities, and making houses too expensive for the lower-income groups.

German Historical School. A school of economists associated with the names Roscher, List, Schmöller, Hildebrand, Bücher, and to some extent Sombart. The school argued that economics was by its very nature incapable of allowing the formulation of abstract and general hypotheses, and that the correct procedure for the study of economic problems was by means of historical investigation. Through such study and the process of induction some 'general laws' might be identified, but they would be specific to certain stages of history. *See* SCHOOLS OF ECONOMICS.

Ghosting. The practice by workers of collecting paypackets for non-existent colleagues; claims by employers with regard to business expenses involving the wages of non-existent employees.

Giffen goods. Commodities of relatively low quality which form an important element in the diet of poor people, e.g. bread and potatoes, the consumption of which has sometimes been known to increase with an increase in price. Sir Robert Giffen is thought to have been the first to draw public attention to the fact that the poor of his time consumed more bread when it was dear than when it was cheap. The explanation probably lay in the fact that a rise in the price of bread caused a fall in real income. Thus after paying for bread, the family was left with less to spend on more expensive things. Thus expenditure on such items as meat and eggs would be reduced. The reduction of these items would, however, leave a nutritional gap which would then be filled by buying more bread. Giffen goods have a very large negative income elasticity; all Giffen goods are technically 'inferior goods' (q.v.) but very few inferior goods are Giffen goods.

Gilt-edged. A high-grade bond (q.v.) issued by a company which has demonstrated its ability to earn a comfortable profit over a period of years and pay its bondholders their interest without interruption.

Gilt-edged stock. Marketable securities, issued by the British Government, whose life may run for many years; known simply as 'gilts'. The Government undertakes to repay the loans according to set terms and to pay interest at a stipulated rate. During their life, gilt-edged stocks can be bought and sold on The London Stock Exchange (q.v.) Bonds can be obtained in two ways:

(a) *Tap.* Bonds are offered for sale at an announced price and yield; if they are not bought on the day of issue, the government sells them later 'drip-by-drip'.

(b) *Tender.* The Bank of England announces the minimum price it will be prepared to accept for a gilt. If the issue is oversubscribed, it will go to the highest bidders; otherwise buyers are allocated their orders at the minimum price, and the rest is sold by tap.

A gilt-edged security is classified as 'short-dated' if it has 5 years or less to run to the final maturity or repayment date; if it has more than 5 years but less than 10 years to run it is classified as 'medium-dated'; if it has 10 years or more to run it is classified as 'long-dated'. *See* CONSOLS.

Gilts. *See* GILT-EDGED STOCK.

Ginne Maes (U.S.). Mortgage-backed certificates issued by the Government National Mortgage Association (q.v.).

Giro system. A mechanism for the transfer of payments operated by the post-office in many European countries and in Japan. Any concern or person may open an account with the 'giro' by paying cash or a cheque into the post office. Transfers from one account to another are made by a written instruction to the post office to debit the 'giro' account of the payer and credit that of the payee. Several payments can be made on a single instruction.

A National Giro was opened in Britain on 18 October 1968. All accounts are held at a single centre at Bootle; payments between account holders can be made by sending transfer instructions to the centre following which both payer and payee are informed that the transfer has been made, a full statement of account being sent to each. Deposits in an account carry no interest and no overdraft facilities are available. Payments in cash are obtainable at any post office by way of withdrawals by an account holder; third parties may also cash Giro cheques. The National Giro offers a simple, cheap and rapid means of transferring money. Deposits are invested in the London money market and elsewhere; the interest earned pays for the many free services offered by the Giro. In 1982, there were over 1.1 million account holders.

Give up. A term with many different meanings in the market place: (a) a member of a stock exchange (q.v.) on the floor may act for a second member by executing an order for him with a third member. The first member advises the third member that he is acting on behalf of the second member and 'gives up' the second member's name rather than his own; (b) The assignment by a floor broker of a floor transaction to another member.

Giving and taking cable. In London means selling and buying U.S. dollars.

Glassco Reports (Can.). The Reports of the Canadian Royal Commission on Government Organisation of 1972–73 which dealt extensively with the area of departmental and central management and control of Government expenditure. Subsequently, there have been changes made in relation to the Treasury Board and its secretariat, and in relation to the Cabinet Committee system including the establishment of a Priorities and Planning Committee.

Glass-Steagall Act (U.S.). An Act passed by Congress in 1933 to improve banking practices in the United States. It denied the right of commercial banks and trust companies to engage in investment banking and established the Federal Deposit Insurance Corporation (q.v.) *See* COMMERCIAL BANK; INVESTMENT BANK.

Global marketing. Marketing in which all markets are served which offer scope for sales, there being no rigid distinction in thought between home and export markets. Global marketing offers an opportunity for a larger volume of production in which lower costs of production per unit of output may be achieved. The prospects of increased profitability in the home market are improved while there are greater opportunities to counter falling demand in one area by increasing demand in others.

'Gnomes of Zurich'. Appellation, not unfriendly, for central European bankers notably members of the Swiss Banking Association.

Going long. In the commodity markets, buying first and selling later. *See* GOING SHORT.

Going private. Description of quoted public companies wishing to revert to private status by purchasing their own shares. There may be a desire for greater control on the part of key shareholders. By this route a company may replace its previously extensive list of public investors with a limited number of selected shareholders. The purpose may be to revert to family control or to reduce the risk of external interference in the operations of the business by speculative investors and financial intermediaries.

Going short. In the commodity markets, selling first and buying later to make delivery. *See* GOING LONG.

Gold bullion standard. *See* GOLD STANDARD.

Gold Exchange Standard. *See* GOLD STANDARD.

Gold Market, London. *See* LONDON GOLD MARKET.

Gold pool. *See* INTERNATIONAL GOLD POOL.

Gold Standard. A monetary system in which each unit of currency is worth a fixed amount of gold. The rules of a gold standard are:

(a) all paper currency must be convertible at its face value into gold;
(b) there must be no restrictions on the import or export of gold;
(c) a gold reserve must be maintained, fully sufficient to meet all demands made upon it.

One of the advantages of a Gold Standard is that it maintains stable exchange rates 'automatically' between countries operating the system. This depends on the 'mint par of exchange' (q.v.). Balance of payments (q.v.) crises do not arise. However, a marked disadvantage is that changes in the stocks of gold cause fluctuations in production and employment. If imports exceed exports, the deficit is met by the export of gold. This reduces the amount of money in the country leading to restriction of credit and falling prices and incomes. As wages generally resist reduction, the effect of deflation is to cause unemployment. A surplus, exports exceeding imports, has an opposite effect. The 'full Gold Standard' described above was operated in Britain until 1914. The gold sovereign, then in circulation, consisted of gold 11/12 fine at £3 17s. 9d. per fine ounce. Between 1925 and 1931, Britain operated a modified system known as the 'Gold Bullion Standard'. Under this modified system, individual bank-notes were no longer convertible into gold on demand; the Bank of England would, however, exchange gold bars of 400 ounces each for an equivalent value in notes.

During the same period, 1925–31, the Scandinavian countries adopted a 'Gold Exchange Standard'. Under this system, the Central Bank would exchange on demand the currency of its country, not for gold, but for the currency of some other country on the Gold Standard. Following the Crisis of 1931, the Gold Standard was generally abandoned, although gold is still used in the settlement of international debts.

Golden avalanche. Descriptive of the flow of gold into the United States of America during the 1930s as a result of an export surplus, high domestic gold prices, and fear of war in other countries. The golden avalanche continued until checked by restrictions imposed during the Second World War.

Golden handshake. Usually a non-negotiable award given to a top executive whose services are being dispensed with; the discretional golden handshake has tended to be displaced by the contractual golden parachute (q.v.).

Golden parachute. A financial compensation package designed and negotiated by top executives prior to any threat of displacement or takeover. If, in adverse circumstances, the top executive is displaced ('let go' is the usual euphemism) or he or she finds it necessary to 'bale-out', the individual descends to earth with the dignity of his golden parachute. Such contracts are usually restricted to the chief executive and the top three to six executives. Ordinary employees are simply dispensed with, subject to any terms negotiated by the relevant trade unions or imposed by national or state legislation. *See* ANTI-TAKEOVER TACTICS.

Good delivery. The delivery of a valid share certificate when selling shares.

Good 'Til Cancelled Order (G.T.C.) or open order. An order to buy or sell securities which remains in effect until it is either executed or cancelled.

Goodhart's law. Coined by Mr. Charles Goodhart, chief monetary adviser at the Bank of England (q.v.), a law which states that any measure of the money supply that is officially controlled promptly loses its meaning.

Gossen's laws. Developed by Hermann Heinrich Gossen (1810–1858): the first law states that the pleasure obtained from each additional amount consumed of the same commodity diminishes until satiety is reached; the second law states that once a person has spent his entire income, he will have maximised his total pleasure from it only if the pleasure or satisfaction gained from the last item of each commodity bought is the same for each commodity; the third law states that a commodity has a subjective value, and the subjective value of each additional unit owned diminishes and eventually reaches zero. It was William Stanley Jevons (1835–1882) who, in the preface to his work *Theory of Political Economy* (1891), admitted that Gossen had 'completely anticipated him as regards the general principles and methods of economics'.

Government Broker. The representative of a firm of stockbrokers which conducted operations in the gilt-edged market on behalf of the Bank of England (q.v.). The Bank does not itself enter the Stock Exchange. Lord Cromwell was appointed Government Broker in January, 1981; he was associated with a 'new model' gilt-edged stock during 1981 in the form of two index-linked issues. The position was abolished in 1984.

Government factories (U.K.). Available in all assisted areas (q.v.) factories provided by the British Government on favourable terms, for rent or sale, new or previously occupied, standard design or custom-built. Rent-free periods may be available.

Government National Mortgage Association. Part of the U.S. Department of Housing and Urban Development, an agency which aids home financing by operating a mortgage-backed programme under which it guarantees securities backed by pools of federally underwritten mortgages.

Government National Mortgage Association Certificates (Ginnie Maes). Certificates which became the basis of an interest-rate financial future launched by the Chicago Board of Trade (q.v.) in 1975. This proved so successful that the International Monetary Market (q.v.) launched another interest-rate contract of its own based on Treasury bills.

Government stock. *See* BRITISH GOVERNMENT STOCK.

Granny bonds. Indexed bonds issued in the United Kingdom which initially were aimed at retired people; the name has stuck even though the bonds are now available to all age groups. While the indexed bonds offered a coupon rate of interest of only 2 per cent, the investor gained through the face value of the bonds being increased in line with inflation. While the coupon rate remained constant it was paid on a steadily increasing principal, so the actual coupon amount also rose over the years.

Granter. The seller of an option (q.v.).

Great Depression (1929–1935), The. A long period of economic and personal distress which followed a crash on the New York Stock Market in October, 1929. The crash was followed by innumerable bankruptcies of banks, factories and mines. The economic distress extended to Europe, Asia, Africa, Australia and South America. About 25 million workers throughout the world were unemployed. Between 1929 and 1932 world wholesale prices fell by about one-third. Cotton was ploughed under in the United States; Canada burned some of her wheat crops; Brazil dumped coffee into the sea. An increased tariff schedule was immediately prescribed by statesmen throughout the world, but the general effect of these tariffs was to hinder international trade and to aggravate the world economic depression. By 1935, only France, Holland, Belgium, Switzerland and Poland remained on the gold standard. Recovery was slow, and not completed by the outbreak of the Second World War.

During 1929–33 the average weekly earnings of American manufacturing workers fell by 33 per cent, and the incomes of American coal miners by almost half. In 1929, more than a quarter of Americans were living on farms; during 1929–33, their farm output held steady but net farm income fell by two-thirds. In consequence of the fall in demand, America's unemployment rose from 1½ million in 1929 to 13 million in 1933.

In Britain, in 1931, there were 21 per cent unemployed among the insured workforce (which was then about two-thirds of the whole labour force). The slump did not bottom out until more than 3 million were unemployed in January, 1933. Many of the jobless were concentrated in the north of England, Scotland and Wales; nearly all the jobs created during the 1920s had been in the Midlands and south of England.

Greenback. The United States dollar.

Green currency. The agricultural unit of account for the European Economic Community (q.v.). An accounting device only, the exchange rates between the national currency and the unit of account are called 'green monies'. The system operated satisfactorily for several years, due to the relative stability of exchange rates of member countries. Problems multiplied, however, in a period of devaluations and transition to general floating of currencies. To overcome temporary difficulties, the Community introduced a system of Monetary Compensation Amounts.

Greenmail. *See* ANTI-TAKEOVER TACTICS.

Green money. A set of special exchange rates used to convert common farm prices into national currencies, in the European Economic Community (q.v.). *See* GREEN CURRENCY; GREEN POUND.

Green pound. A device used by the European Economic Community to calculate prices for Britain's farm and food trade with other community countries. Normally farm support levels are fixed in fictional units of account. Currencies rarely maintain, however, their theoretical value against the unit of account. When a currency floats down, the farmers concerned should receive more from any subsidy fixed in units of account. To keep other members happy, the prices paid to one member may be kept for the time being at the old rate. When Italian prices were kept at the old rate, a 'green lira' was created. Ireland and Britain have had 'green pounds'.

Green stamp plan. A proposal by Professor Kenneth E. Boulding to provide a market mechanism for population control. According to the plan, each human being would receive in adolescence, say, 110 green stamps, 100 of which would enable the owner to have one legal child. A market would then be set up in these instruments so that those who had a strong desire for children could buy stamps from those who did not want to have children. Individual preferences in this matter could thus be expressed while at the same time society could maintain overall social control of the rate of growth of population. There would presumably have to be mild sanctions, argues Professor Boulding, for having illegal children which might entail temporary sterilisation until the illegal children are paid for in green stamps. Professor Boulding has remarked that (not surprisingly) his scheme has met with a good deal of disapproval.

Gregory effect. Named after an Australian National University economist, descriptive of the large swings in Australian terms of trade consequent to the country's status as mainly a primary products exporter In boom periods the international prices of commodities rise more rapidly than the prices of finished goods; the result is a switch of real income to primary producers at the expense of the country's manufacturing industry. However, in an international recession there is a disproportionate fall in commodity prices, and the primary industries find themselves with an excessive cost structure.

Gresham's law. A generalisation embodied in the maxim 'bad money drives out good'; when good and bad money circulate, people hoard good and spend bad. When the value of money depends upon its value as metal, debasement of the coinage by the issuing authority leads to a fall in the value of such money. The British sovereign and half-sovereign when in circulation were worth their face value in terms of the metal they contained and debasement did not occur. Coins today have only token value, their value as metal being much less than their face value; but they are legal tender (q.v.) and their value is determined by other factors.

Named after Sir Thomas Gresham (1519–1579), financial adviser to Queen Elizabeth I.

Gross and net output. The gross output of a firm or industry is the total selling value of production of that firm or industry within a given time-period. Gross output includes the value of materials, fuel and other supplies bought from firms outside the industry. To establish the 'net output', or the value of the contribution made by the industry itself, it is necessary to deduct from the gross output what has been spent on incoming supplies. Net output is therefore the value added by a firm or industry in the productive process in a given time-period. Net output is a useful indicator of an industry's importance in the economy. *See* VALUE-ADDED.

Gross cash flow. Equal to company profit plus depreciation (q.v.); it does not measure the actual flow of funds in an organisation as it does not take account of movements in assets and liabilities or capital raisings. It is important, however, as an indicator of potential cash that may be raised through normal operations.

Gross Domestic Fixed Capital Formation. Investment (q.v.) in fixed assets, e.g. expenditure on buildings, vehicles, plant and machinery for replacing or adding to the stock of existing fixed assets, expenditure on maintenance and repairs being excluded. *See* CAPITAL FORMATION AND DEPRECIATION; DEPRECIATION.

Gross Domestic Product at Constant Prices. The Gross Domestic Product at Factor Cost (q.v.) or the Gross Domestic Product at Market Prices (q.v.) taken over a series of years and adjusted to discount changes in the value of money. Thus the Gross Domestic Product in 1984 may be adjusted to 1977 prices to give a measure of the real change in national income over the 7-year period.

Gross Domestic Product at Factor Cost. The value of goods and services produced within the nation, representing only the sum of the incomes of the factors of production (q.v.). It is equal to the Gross Domestic Product at Market Prices (q.v.), *minus* indirect taxes *plus* subsidies. Valuation at factor cost displays the composition of the gross domestic product in terms of the factors of production employed, the contributions of the factors being measured by the incomes they receive. In 1981, in Britain, the gross domestic product at factor cost was estimated to have been £211,000 million. In real terms this was an increase of 13 per cent over 1971. *See* FACTOR INCOMES; GROSS NATIONAL PRODUCT.

Gross Domestic Product at Market Prices. The value of goods and services produced within the nation, charged at ruling prices. Prices include all taxes on expenditure, subsidies being regarded as negative taxes. In the estimate of gross domestic product only goods for final consumption and investment goods (capital) are included; the values of intermediate goods are implicitly included in the prices of the final goods.

Gross National Product (G.N.P.). A comprehensive measure of a nation's output. It may be measured in two ways: from the demand side as the sum of consumer expenditures, private investment, government purchases, and net exports; and from the supply side as the sum of employee earnings, proprietors' earnings, corporate profit, net interest, rental income, capital consumption allowances and indirect business taxes. The results should be identical as each dollar measures both demand and supply; actual discrepancies are of a statistical and estimating nature. G.N.P. is estimated in both current and constant dollars; a series in constant dollars is a measure of real output (the physical volume of economic activity) over time, and of changes in that output. The measurement of G.N.P. in the United States is undertaken by the Bureau of Economic Analysis in the Department of Commerce, the results being published in the *Survey of Current Business* on a quarterly basis. *See* CONSUMER PRICE INDEX, U.S.; IMPLICIT PRICE DEFLATOR; INDUSTRIAL PRODUCTION INDEX (I.P.I.).

Gross Private Domestic Investment (G.P.D.I.). All private capital formation without any deduction for depreciation in the course of producing the output of the current period; it is composed of fixed investment (both non-residential and residential), the additions to and replacements of private capital, and changes in business inventories. It is the most comprehensive measure of private investment, though a gross, not net, estimate. Though losses due to wear and tear, obsolescence, and accident are difficult to estimate in any time-period, American business makes provision in its accounts for capital replacement; this provides an indirect measure of capital consumption or depreciation.

Group of Eleven. Initially, a group of ten countries consisting of the United States, United Kingdom, Canada, France, West Germany, Sweden, Netherlands, Belgium, Italy and Japan, which agreed to lend if requested to the International Monetary Fund for the purpose of increasing the lending resources of that body. Under the General Arrangements to Borrow, adopted in 1962, the Group of Ten provided the Fund with an additional $6 billion of their currencies. These resources were used to help in a massive rescue operation of the pound in 1964. The Group of Ten agreed on 19 December 1971, on a realignment of currency exchange rates which devalued the U.S. dollar by 7.89 per cent. In January, 1983, Switzerland was admitted to full membership. In the same month, the eleven nations expanded their General Arrangements to Borrow in the International Monetary Fund (q.v.) from $7.1 billion to $19 billion; further the International Monetary Fund could lend this money to developing countries, instead of only to members of the Group of Ten as in the past.

Group of Five. A group of leading industrial countries comprising the United States of America, Britain, West Germany, France and Japan; representatives meet from time to time to discuss issues of mutual concern, e.g. interest rates, problems of large debtor countries, and other financial matters.

Group of Seventy-Seven. A group of less-developed countries (actually over 100) who banded together in 1964 to press for better terms of trade with the richer countries.

Group of Ten. *See* GROUP OF ELEVEN.

Group of Twenty. A group of twenty nations, including the group of eleven (q.v.), which was constituted in late 1972 to negotiate international monetary reform, with special reference to the future of the U.S. dollar as a reserve currency. In June, 1974, the group published its *Outline of Reform* in which it recommended that a new system be based on 'stable but adjustable par values'. However, in the new system of floating exchange rates much of the committee's work has become irrelevant. Even by early 1973 the Smithsonian Agreement (q.v.) had gone beyond repair, and all the great currencies of the world were floating.

Growth. *See* ECONOMIC GROWTH.

Growth recession. A period of slow expansion.

Growth shares. Shares which are expected, as a consequence of higher productivity and increased returns on assets within the companies concerned, to become more valuable. *See* SHARE.

Growth theory. A part of economics which is concerned with analysing the determinants of the rate at which economies grow over time, that is with changes in the major economic aggregates such as national income, capital (q.v.), consumption (q.v.), and employment.

Guarantee fund. A fund maintained by the London Stock Exchange which guarantees members of the public against loss, at the discretion of the Stock Exchange Council, in the event of the failure of a member or members firm. *See* STOCK EXCHANGE.

Guaranteed bond (U.S.). A bond which has interest or principal, or both, guaranteed by a company other than the issuer. Such bonds are usually found in the railway industry when large companies leasing sections of trackage owned by small companies may guarantee the bonds of the smaller companies.

H

Hammer price. A price calculated according to the rules of the Stock Exchange of Great Britain and Ireland (q.v.) which represents the market value of a security at the time of the default of a member firm. *See* COMPENSATION FUND; GUARANTEE FUND.

Hang Seng index. A composite index of prices on the Hong Kong stock market.

Hard-core unemployed. Those whose average term of unemployment is significantly longer than the average, extending to many months and perhaps years with an increasing proportion regarded as unemployable.

Harrod-Domar model. One of the earliest analyses of the process of the growth of an economy, being a synthesis of the independent work of two economists, Sir Roy Harrod (b. 1900) and Evsey D. Domar (1914). The model comprises (a) firms which produce and sell goods, spend on new investment, and pay incomes to households for productive services; and (b) households which spend part of the income they receive on consumption goods and save the rest. The model demonstrates that if the amount saved is equal to the amount invested in every period, then the economy will tend to grow at a rate which is determined by the marginal propensity to save and the incremental capital-output ratio (q.v.).

Hatry Crash, 1929. Crisis on the London Stock Exchange (q.v.) in 1929, precipitated by fraud. Members of the House raised a guarantee fund of £1 million in an attempt to prevent the failure of those members who were actually victims of the fraud. Nevertheless, some members failed and the public lost a good deal of money. This crisis was not the cause of the Great Depression, 1929–35 (q.v.), which ensued in the same year as a consequence of a crash on Wall Street, the New York Stock Exchange. *See* GUARANTEE FUND.

Heckscher-Ohlin law. A principle first put forward by Eli F. Heckscher (1879–1952) in 1919, and subsequently refined by Bertil Ohlin (b. 1899), which states that advantages in international trade arise from the different relative factor endowments of the countries trading; a country will tend to export those commodities which intensively embody the factor with which it is most well-endowed. From this basis theme, Professor Paul A. Samuelson (b. 1915) developed his factor price equalisation theorem. He demonstrated how an increase in the price of a commodity can raise the income of the factor of production which is used most intensively in producing it. The theorem also states the conditions under which, as free trade in commodities narrows differences in commodity prices between countries, the prices (or incomes) of the factors of production also become closer; to some marked degree, therefore, free trade becomes a substitute for the free mobility of the factors of production.

Hedger. One who deals in a physical commodity and who uses futures contracts to manage his price risk.

Hedging. A technique of insurance against fluctuations in the prices of raw materials or goods scheduled for future delivery by dealing in 'futures'. The two basic types of hedge operation are the 'buying hedge' and the 'selling hedge'. *See* FUTURES CONTRACT.

Hidden economy. *See* CASH ECONOMY.

High-powered money. Money consisting of currency (notes and coin) and banks' deposits at the Federal Reserve Bank (q.v.). Part of the currency is held by the public, the remaining currency being held by banks as vault cash. Also called the monetary base; the terms are interchangeable. The manner in which 'the Fed' most often changes the stock of high-powered money is through open-market operations (q.v.). *See* MONETARY BASE.

High technology. More complex and advanced technology relative to the general level in society at any time; thus in its time the steam locomotive would have been high technology. At the present time, the term embraces computer software and hardware; scientific, medical and professional instruments; various kinds of electronic equipment; lasers; robotics; solar energy systems; and biotechnology.

Hire purchase. A procedure for purchasing goods under which the purchaser pays a deposit on receipt of the goods followed by a number of instalments until the debt is cleared. The goods do not become the property of the purchaser until the last instalment has been paid. In the event of the default of the purchaser in respect of the instalments, the firm can resume possession of the goods in question. However this right cannot be enforced without an order of a County Court if more than one-third of the total price has been paid, unless the purchaser wishes to give the goods up. The rate of interest charged is normally higher than that charged for personal loans from banks.

The Consumer Credit Act 1974 gives the consumer much greater protection than before in most credit and hire transactions. It controls the way in which creditors and hirers may seek business, and gives special safeguards to consumers signing agreements. Brokers, owners of hire equipment, debt collectors and others must be licensed. The legislation comes under the surveillance of the Office of Fair Trading.

Hire purchase in industry and commerce works in much the same way as in the retail area. After making an initial down-payment, and paying regular, fixed amounts over an agreed period (covering interest and the balance of the capital cost), a business acquires ownership of the goods. In some instances, a small 'option-to-purchase' fee may be payable as the final step in acquiring the goods. Most short-term contracts are at fixed rates of interest (variable rates are more often charged on longer-term contracts). Interest is charged throughout a contract on the total amount initially advanced.

Hire purchase finance houses. Finance houses concerned with the granting of credit for the purchase of certain classes of goods on the condition that their advances are repaid by regular instalments over a fairly short period of time, together with interest charged on the amount borrowed. Credit is extended to private persons for the purchase of consumer durables, and to industry and agriculture for the purchase of motor vehicles and machinery. *See* HIRE PURCHASE.

Historic costs. The actual monetary cost of raw materials, machinery, products, etc. at the time they were bought or made. Depreciation (q.v.) based upon historic costs will often be insufficient to cover replacement costs, particularly during inflationary periods. *See* CURRENT COST ACCOUNTING.

Hoarding. The act of holding money. If the desire to hoard increases the result will be (assuming that no new money is created) that money incomes will fall. Conversely, if there is a fall in the desire to hold money, incomes will rise. If an increase in the quantity of money circulating brings about a fall in the velocity of circulation or an increase in the volume of trade, then the increased quantity of money need not be accompanied by any rise in the price level. The holding or hoarding of money must be distinguished from money used for investment in capital assets; in the latter case, the money returns to the economic system as income. The term 'hoarding' was used by John Maynard Keynes (1884–1946) to denote liquidity preference (q.v.) as distinct from saving proper.

Holding a call. Buying a call option (q.v.).

Holding a put. Buying a put option (q.v.).

Holding an option. Buying an option (q.v.).

Holding company. A company which holds a majority or the whole of the equity capital of one or more other companies. These other companies are known as subsidiaries, and while they continue to exist their general policy is controlled by the holding company.

A holding company may serve a useful purpose where the optimum size of the financial unit, or the marketing unit is larger than the optimum size of the production unit: the holding company may undertake one or more of these functions, and others, on behalf of the whole group.

On the other hand, the extension of control over the price and output policies of a number of potentially competitive producers may create monopoly conditions not necessarily serving the national interest.

Holding companies (unless specially exempted) are required by the Companies Act of 1948 to publish either separate accounts for all the companies in the group or consolidated accounts for the whole group together.

Home banking service. Launched by the Chemical Bank of New York in September, 1982, and known as the Pronto System, the world's first large scale introduction of computer terminals into customers' homes; the terminals are linked to the bank's central computer. The service offers monetary transfers, bill payments, and balance information.

Pioneered in the United Kingdom by the Nottingham Building Society and the Bank of Scotland. *See* HOMELINK.

Homelink. A joint venture between British Telecom, the Bank of Scotland, and the Nottingham Building Society; the scheme enables customers to operate Nottingham Building Society and Bank of Scotland accounts on their own television screens.

Home trade one. Introduced into Japan in 1984 by the Nikko Investment Bank, the first home brokerage system using a push-button phone to place buy and sell orders.

Homogeneous products. Identical products.

Horizontal integration. The amalgamation of firms engaged in the same stage of production of the same commodity to achieve greater economic strength and profitability. An example is the Bradford Dyers' Association which is a combination of all firms engaged in dyeing. Also known as 'horizontal combination'. *See* VERTICAL INTEGRATION.

Horizontal spread. *See* OPTION SPREAD.

Hot money. Money which is transferred rapidly from one financial centre to another to take advantage of differences in short term interest rates or to escape the financial penalties of devaluation.

Housing Act 1980. An Act which established a charter for public sector tenants in Britain, giving them statutory rights which included security of tenure, provision for succession by a resident relative to the tenancy on death, rights of subletting and taking in lodgers, and, at the landlord's discretion, reimbursement for improvements made by the tenant. In most cases public sector tenants can buy the freehold of their house, or a long lease of their flat, at a discount which depends on the length of occupation.

Hyperinflation. Inflation (q.v.) which has got out of control; runaway inflation. A particularly outstanding example of this occurred in Germany in the 1920s when savings were destroyed in value by an astronomical rise in prices; to the middle classes the effect was disastrous. The problem arose in the financing of the First World War, loss of territory and treasure, and the heavy financial burden imposed on the country after its defeat. Note circulation reached hundreds of trillions of marks. It is reported that the price of an egg reached 80,000 million marks and a newspaper 2,000 million marks. The ratio of the value of the mark to the pre-war value became a million million to one. The currency was finally stabilised. Another outstanding example occurred in Hungary after the Second World War. In 1984, Bolivia had an inflation rate of over 1,000 per cent.

Hypothecation. The pledging of securities as collateral, for example to secure the debit balance in a margin account.

I

Imperfect competition. A market situation in which neither absolute monopoly (q.v.) nor perfect competition (q.v.) prevails; a situation closest to real life in most circumstances. It is characterised by the ability of sellers to influence demand by product differentiation (q.v.), branding and advertising; restriction of entry of competitors into various lines of production either because of the size of the initial investment required or because of restrictive practices; the existence of uncertainty (q.v.) with imperfect knowledge of profits earned in similar or other lines of production; and the absence of price competition in varying degrees.

The theory of imperfect competition was explored by many writers during the inter-war period, notably by Professor Joan Robinson (b. 1903) who published her book, *The Economics of Imperfect Competition*, in 1933. *See* OLIGOPOLY; PRICING.

Implicit costs. Costs in the form of lost opportunities to use resources, including time, in another way, e.g. a major implicit cost of a university education is the foregone opportunity to work and receive an income. *See* EXPLICIT COSTS.

Implicit price deflator. A price index used to deflate the various spending series that comprise the gross national product (q.v.); in effect to remove the effects of inflation and the decline in the purchasing power of the dollar and produce figures in 'constant dollars' over time which can be properly compared. The price index exactly reconciles the current and constant-dollar G.N.P. figures.

Import licence. A Government licence required for all goods imported into Britain. A licence may be an 'open general licence' permitting the unrestricted importation of certain goods in accordance with schedules which are published from time to time. Sometimes an 'individual open licence' may be issued, granting to a particular importer the unrestricted right to import a certain commodity as long as the licence is valid. Frequently a 'specific import licence' is issued to cover shipments up to a certain value only.

Imported inflation. Price rises due to the increased cost of imported raw materials and goods. Imported inflation was a consequence of the 1949 devaluation of the pound and booming raw material prices during the Korean war. World commodity prices also rose rapidly from November, 1972, to early 1974 and, following the Yom Kippur war in October, 1973, oil prices were increased fourfold. Such developments can cause severe cost-push inflation.

In-and-out. The purchase and sale of the same security within a short period; an in-and-out trader is more interested in day-to-day price fluctuations than dividends or long-term growth.

'In the Bank'. A situation existing when the commercial banks are restricting credit and the discount-houses are able to raise cash only by taking bills to the Bank of England for rediscount; the money-market is then described as being 'in the Bank'. *See* LENDER OF LAST RESORT.

Inactive stock. An issue traded on a stock exchange or in the over-the-counter market in which there is a relatively low volume of transactions. On the New York Stock Exchange (q.v.) many inactive stocks are traded in 10-share units rather than the customary 100 shares.

Income. The wealth, measured in money, which is at the disposal of an individual or a community, per year or other unit of time, it may be regarded as a flow of purchasing power which may be expended at once on goods or services or retained for the purposes of capital accumulation.

Income bonds and debentures. Bonds and

debentures or debenture stock, the interest on which is only payable out of profits.

Income effect. The effect which a change in price of a good or service has on a consumer's demand for the good or service, taking into account the change it induces in his real income. An increase in real income due to a fall in the price of a good may lead to a decrease in the amount bought; an exceptional situation in standard demand analysis. *See* GIFFEN GOODS; INFERIOR GOODS; SUBSTITUTION EFFECT.

Income tax, progressive. A system of graded tax payments, individuals with small incomes paying a smaller proportion of their incomes than individuals with large incomes. The system is based on the theory of diminishing marginal utility. In Britain, in June, 1979, the maximum income tax rate was reduced from 83 per cent to 60 per cent, and the basic rate from 33 per cent to 30 per cent. The Chancellor stated that his long-term objective was to reduce the basic rate to 25 per cent.

Incorporated businesses. In Britain, enterprises registered with an official registrar of companies with related obligations, such as those concerning the capital structure of a company, the rights and duties of its directors and members, and the preparation of accounts. Nearly all incorporated businesses are 'limited liability' (q.v.) companies. In 1982, there were about 800,000 corporate enterprises in Britain. *See* PUBLIC LIMITED COMPANY; UNINCORPORATED BUSINESS; PRIVATE LIMITED COMPANY.

Increasing returns, laws of. A generalisation that in many industrial processes a doubling of inputs may result in an output that is more than doubled. This is due to economies that may arise in mechanisation and specialisation, in energy utilisation and avoidance of waste. Increasing returns may characterise a phase of the productive process even when some of the inputs are fixed; however in such situations diminishing returns may soon become apparent. *See* DIMINISHING RETURNS, LAW OF; VARIABLE PROPORTIONS, LAW OF.

Indenture. A written agreement under which bonds and debentures are issued, setting out the maturity date, interest rate and other terms.

Index, Financial Times Industrial Ordinary Share. A geometric index, calculated and published by the *Financial Times* twice daily, at noon and at the close of The London Stock Exchange (q.v.) for the day. Constituents of the index are thirty market leaders, representing a cross-section of British industry.

Index-linked gilt-edged stock. Stock issued by the British Chancellor of the Exchequer initially in 1981, in an attempt to increase the flexibility of the funding programme. The new stock carried a 2 per cent coupon, with both the interest payment and the value of the principal on repayment index-linked.

Index of Consumer Confidence (Aust.). An index created by the Melbourne University Institute of Applied Economics and Social Research and the Roy Morgan Research Centre, Australia; the purpose of the index, based on surveys of about 1,200 consumers, is to measure consumers' willingness to buy. People in the sample are asked about their expectations in relation to personal finance, the national economy, price changes, and market conditions. A changing pessimist/optimist ratio emerges over time.

Index of Leading Indicators. An index maintained by the U.S. Department of Commerce, integrating a wide variety of numerical and financial indicators; widely used in the United States as a guide to future economic trends. The index includes such elements as the prices of raw materials, the average work-week, delivery times from sellers, the money supply, stock prices, new business formation, orders for new plant and equipment, building permits, new orders for consumer goods, and initial claims for unemployment benefits.

Indexation. The automatic adjustment of monetary awards, e.g. wages, salaries, and pensions, with changes in the consumer or retail price index, in order to maintain purchasing power in inflationary conditions.

Indifference analysis. An analysis of consumer demand based on the notion of ordinal utility. The consumer is assumed to possess a given amount of money while being faced with the prices of all the goods that might be consumed; the consumer will then decide on a set or bundle of goods to buy influenced by the money available, the prices, and the tastes of the buyer. The consumer may have considered several alternative sets of goods which could be purchased; they are then ranked in order of preference, i.e. given any two bundles, the consumer can judge whether one is preferred to the other, or whether there is an indifference between them both being regarded as equally desirable. *See* DEMAND, THEORY OF; MARGINAL UTILITY; UTILITY, ORDINAL.

Indifference curve. The locus of all exchanges (or substitutions) of one commodity for another which gives the consumer the same amount of satisfaction. Between all possible combinations the consumer will be indifferent, i.e. he will feel himself no better off, and no worse off, whichever combination he has. *See*

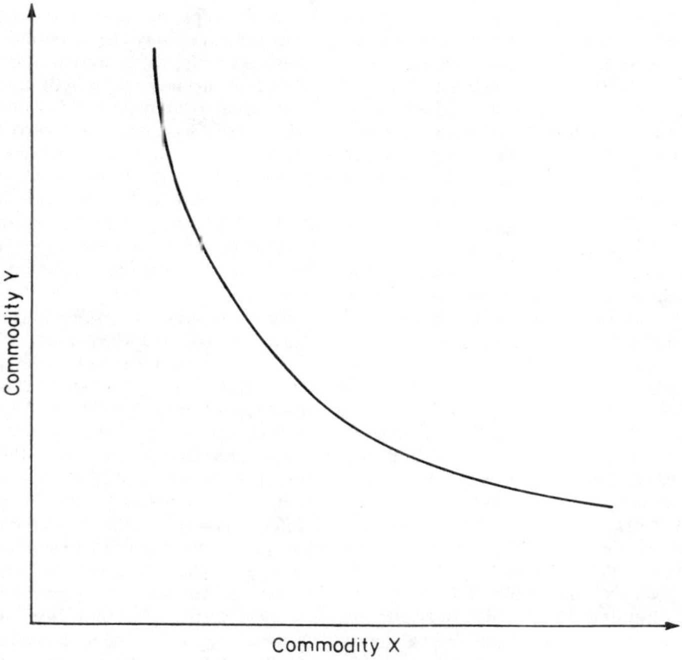

Figure 9 Indifference curve

FIGURE 9. The slope of an indifference curve is negative; as the quantity of X increases, that of Y must decrease.

The curvature of an indifference curve expresses the idea that as one good becomes more plentiful relative to the other, its subjective worth per item becomes smaller in terms of the other. The concept of the indifference curve has been used extensively in the theory of consumer demand, and in welfare economics (q.v.).

Individualism. The name given to a political and economic system that favours the development of the individual rather than that of the state or other association; it is the antithesis of collectivism and socialism. Individualism has found strong advocacy among the English speaking peoples. As a philosophy it rested on the teachings of Adam Smith (1723–1790) and Jeremy Bentham (1748–1832) and was accepted with some modification by John Stuart Mill (1806–1873). Its most extreme exponent was Herbert Spencer (1820–1903). The creed of the individualist is that the best results for mankind can be attained by giving free play to individual energy and initiative, applying this principle both in the sphere of industry and in that of morals, with as little interference by government as possible. Since about 1880, there has been a strong reaction against individualism. *See* LAISSEZ-FAIRE.

Indivisible plant. Plant which must be used on a large-scale, or not at all, if it is to fulfil its functions. The minimum size is determined by technical considerations.

Induction. The act or process of reasoning from particular cases to general conclusions. It is a method by which truths of scientific value are obtained which are not directly deducible from principles already known. The inductive method may be employed to test the findings of economic theory developed by the deductive method. Alfred Marshall expressed the opinion that 'induction and deduction are both needed for scientific thought as the right and left foot are both needed for walking'. There is no one method, therefore, which can be properly called the method of economics. *See* DEDUCTION.

Industrial and Commercial Finance Corporation Ltd. A financial services institution, established in 1945 by the English and

Scottish banks with the approval of the Bank of England and the Government, with the purpose of assisting the business person who requires finance for expansion or development which it is not practicable or convenient to raise by way of banking facilities or a public issue of shares. It assists, therefore, small and medium-sized companies. *See* FINANCE CORPORATION; INVESTORS IN INDUSTRY, P.L.C.

Industrial bank. A bank holding equity stakes in companies as well as making loans; it may function as a finance house (q.v.) providing hire purchase credit. Industrial banks do not normally offer a full range of banking services. Exemplified by the German banks Deutsche, Dresdner, and Kommerz.

Industrial Training Act 1964 (U.K.). An Act to promote the better training of apprentices. The Act requires the Minister of Labour to appoint a Central Training Council to advise him on the exercise of his functions under the Act and on matters concerned with industrial training which he refers to it. It consists of a chairman, employer and trade union members, educationalists, the chairmen of a number of industrial boards and those with a special interest in training. The Act also empowers the Minister to set up Training Boards in industries, after consultation with the employers and trade unions concerned. These Boards comprise equal numbers of trade union and employers' representatives and a smaller number of educational members. The Training Boards undertake a wide range of functions covering all aspects of training.

In 1981, the number of training boards was reduced from 24 to 7; the surviving boards covered clothing, construction, engineering, hotels and catering, road transport, rubber, plastics, and the petroleum industries. The others were abandoned in favour of voluntary arrangements.

Industrial production index (I.P.I.) (U.S.). A measure of the physical volume of output in the nation's manufacturing, mining, and electric and gas utility industries. The I.P.I. is constructed from data on actual product output by individual industries. It is prepared by the Federal Reserve Board and published monthly in the *Federal Reserve Bulletin*. *See* GROSS NATIONAL PRODUCT (G.N.P.).

Industry. In its widest sense all the manifold activities of a country which provide employment, but more narrowly those activities concerned with the production of goods rather than services. Specifically, an industry comprises all those activities which are directed to the production of a given class of goods, e.g. aircraft, ships, machine tools, foodstuffs, etc. An industry may be composed of many business units as in agriculture, or perhaps only one business unit as in the case of coal. An individual firm may make a wide range of dissimilar goods, and thus be participating in the activities of several industries.

Inertia selling. A practice in which goods are sent to householders without having been ordered. The recipient suffers inconvenience in having to return unwanted goods, tending to retain them; later he receives a bill for the merchandise.

Infant industry. A young and growing industry, often considered not quite able to stand on its own feet in the face of foreign competition. Such industries may be afforded the protection of a tariff (q.v.), or granted a subsidy, until strong enough to stand alone. Experience suggests, however, that tariffs and subsidies, once introduced, are not so easily removed. *See* PROTECTION.

Inferior goods. Goods of which less are bought by people in higher-income groups because they can afford to consume more expensive commodities. Inferior goods have negative income elasticities. White-sliced bread is a very good example, less being consumed per head by those who can afford a wider range of more expensive foods. *See* GIFFEN GOODS.

Inflation. A continuously rising price level; a condition in which the volume of purchasing power is constantly running ahead of the output of goods and services, with the result that as incomes and prices rise the value of money falls. Since the Second World War all countries have experienced varying degrees of persistent inflation; some countries such as Hungary and Greece experienced hyper- or runaway-inflations which were quite disastrous. Geoffrey Crowther expressed the view that the term 'inflation' should not be used where rising prices are merely indicating a revival from a depression, the word 'reflation' being more appropriate. Conversely a retreat from inflation may be described as 'disinflation' whenever it falls short of a genuine deflation (q.v.). Both 'disinflation' and 'reflation' signify a movement of credit, prices and wages downwards or upwards to an equilibrium at which consumers' expenditure is no more, and no less, than is sufficient to buy the goods available. John Maynard Keynes thought that only when a 'further increase in the quantity of money produces no further increase in output and entirely spends itself on an increase in the cost unit fully proportionate to the increase in effective demand' could the condition be appropriately designated as one of true inflation. An increase in the volume of purchasing power may be both a cause and an effect of inflation; a cause in so far as it leads to higher prices through increased demand and costs of production, and an effect in that rising prices lead to demands for higher money incomes. Whether an inflation is a 'demand-pull' inflation or a 'cost-push' inflation the total effect is a spiralling of prices and incomes. While any marked inflationary trend may be quite harmful to an economy such as Britain's in which the prices of her exports must be kept competitive, many economists tend to regard a gentle upward trend in prices and incomes as stimulating to the economy. It certainly reduces the burden of fixed interest payments on past debts, although less fair to new lenders who tend to look for higher rates of interest to compensate for the falling value of money.

During the 14 years 1953–67 inflation in the leading industrial countries averaged just over 2 per cent a year. In the United Kingdom it averaged just under 3 per cent per annum. From about 1968 the situation began to deteriorate: during the period 1973–75 inflation averaged 13 per cent per annum for all O.E.C.D. countries, ranging from 22 per cent for the United Kingdom to 7 per cent for West Germany. (*See* FIGURE 10).

In Britain, by 1983, inflation had been reduced to an annual rate of about 5 per cent.

In 1982, the United States inflation rate fell to 3.9 per cent, the lowest in 10 years; in 1979 it had been 13.3 per cent, in 1980 12.4 per cent, and in 1981, 8.9 per cent.

Inflationary spiral. An upward trend of prices, which is partly the result and partly the cause of increases in wages and salaries and other incomes such as profits, dividends, interest and rent. In the year to July, 1975, prices in Britain rose by 26 per cent; in the following twelve months by 13 per cent.

Inflation, cost-push. Inflationary trends initiated by pressure for higher incomes, greater spending not being accompanied by a corresponding increase in goods and services. Cost-push inflation may also arise from increases in the prices of imported raw materials.

Inflation, creeping. Inflation (q.v.) characterised by a slowly rising price level.

Inflation, demand-pull. Excessive demand for goods and services, the symptoms of which are rising prices and scarcities of labour and materials; bidding raises the price of these resources which leads to further increases in the prices of goods and services.

Informal economy. Defined by the Central Statistical Office as 'economic activity generating factor income', that is wages, salaries and gross trading profits arising from the production of goods and services, which cannot be estimated from regular statistical sources used to compile income measures of gross domestic product (G.D.P.) (q.v.). Three activities form the hardcore of the informal economy: the receipt of goods and services greater than the value for tax purposes (e.g. through the receipt of fringe benefits); incorrect tax declarations (e.g. failure to declare income from a second job); and fraud in the production of goods or services in the formal economy (e.g. misappropriation of goods and shoplifting). *See* CASH ECONOMY.

Information agreement. Also known as an open price agreement, or price reporting agreement, an agreement whereby a number of firms undertake to inform each other regularly about past, current and sometimes future prices, and other relevant data such as costs, discounts, rebates, conditions of sale, turnover and often the names of buyers. The information is generally collated and distributed by a central agency, often a trade association. Agreements of this nature fall into two main types; those in which notification is given prior to a change in price ('pre-notification agreement') and those in which notification is only given after a change in price has taken place ('post-notification agreement'). An information agreement serves as a means for coordinating the behaviour of suppliers participating in a given market; it may result in consciously parallel policies with regard to prices, particularly in an oligopoly (q.v.), thus largely paralysing price competition. Information agreements appear to be introduced whenever price-fixing agreements become illegal. In the United Kingdom certain information agreements have been found contrary to the public interest by the Restrictive Practices Court.

Infrastructure. Services regarded as essential for the creation of a modern economy, e.g. power, transport, housing, education and health services.

Initial margin. The deposit which a user of futures markets must make on purchasing or selling a contract; the amount of the deposit represents only a small proportion of the full value of the contract.

Input-output analysis. The quantitative analysis of inter-industry relations. All transactions that involve the sale of products or services within an economy during a given period are

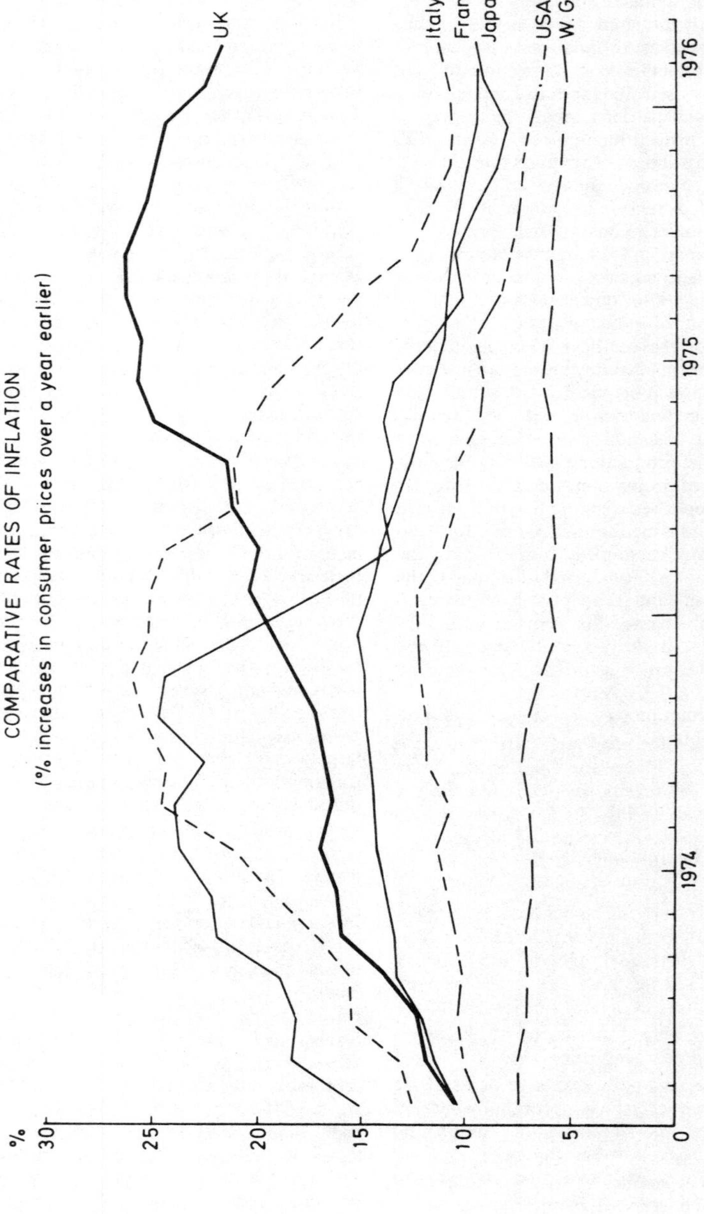

Figure 10 The inflationary surge of 1974–75 (source: O.E.C.D. Main Economic Indicators)

arranged in a square indicating simultaneously the sectors making, and the sectors receiving, delivery. The preparation of input-output tables has significantly added to our knowledge of the industrial economy in past periods. Input-output analysis has been closely associated with the name of Wassily Leontief. *See* NOBEL PRIZE IN ECONOMICS.

Input-output coefficient. A coefficient of proportionality used in input-output analysis (q.v.). Industry j's demand for the output of industry i is proportionate to the total output of industry j. Thus:

$$X_{ij} = a_{ij}X_j$$

where

X_{ij} = output of industry i which is sold to industry j;

a_{ij} = coefficient of proportionality, or input-output coefficient;

X_j = output of industry j.

The value of the coefficient may be zero if industry j does not buy any input from industry i; otherwise it will be positive and is generally assumed to be less than unity.

Inputs. Materials and factor services fed in at one end of the production process and used in the process of production.

Inscribed stock. Securities (q.v.) for which no certificates are issued to the holders; instead a register of stockholders is kept showing the amount of stock held, the names of the stockholders being thus inscribed or registered. Also known as 'registered stock'. Inscribed stocks are issued by government, semi-government authorities and public utilities.

Insider information. Information of commercial value obtained from someone within an organisation, being information not available to the public; such information, if reliable, may ensure an avoidance of loss or the making of a profit.

Institute of International Finance. Located in Washington D.C., an association which grew out of a meeting of international monetary officials and private bankers at Ditchley Park, England, in May, 1982. The Institute had a membership in 1984 of 189 commercial banks; about one-third of the banks were based in the United States, the rest in 38 other countries. The institute gathers detailed information about the financial position of the debtor countries in Latin America, Asia, Africa and elsewhere, and conducts dialogue with them. It works closely with the International Monetary Fund (q.v.). *See* DITCHLEY GROUP.

Institutional economics. A school of economic thought which stresses the importance of non-economic, institutional, political and social factors which may impede, obstruct, or distort normal economic functions. This school of economic thought thrived in the United States in the 1920s. Economists sympathetic to the institutional viewpoint have included Thorstein B. Veblen (1857–1929), Wesley C. Mitchell (1874–1948), and Gunnar K. Myrdal (b. 1898). *See* SCHOOLS OF ECONOMICS.

Institutional investors. A group of investors who have funds to invest as a consequence of the conduct of their businesses. The group includes insurance companies, banks and investment trusts, and industrial companies who administer their own pension schemes or have other funds available.

Insurance. The elimination of risk of loss by the payment of premiums to an insurance company which undertakes to pay for specified losses; the losses of the few are thus met from the premiums of the many. Insurance services fall into the following classes: (a) fire, and other hazards such as riots, explosion, earthquake and hurricane; (b) accident, including motor, third party liability and personal; (c) marine, both hull and cargo; (d) aviation, both hull and cargo; (e) life and endowment; and (f) cover against default by a borrower. This category includes credit insurance, mortgage insurance, and financial guarantees.

Insurance broker. Brokers acting on behalf of the insured; brokers are an essential part of the Lloyd's market and a valuable part of the company market. Many brokers specialise in re-insurance business, acting as intermediaries in the exchange of contracts between companies, both British and overseas, and often acting as London representatives of the latter.

Intangibles. Costs or benefits that either cannot be quantified, or at least cannot be priced, e.g. benefits from highway safety programmes in the form of reduced accidents, or benefits from national parks in the form of scenic beauty.

Interagency Forecasting Committee. A Federal economic forecasting which comprises representatives of the Council of Economic Advisers (q.v.), the Office of Management and Budget (q.v.), and the Departments of Treasury, Commerce, and Labour. Forecasts are presented regularly to the Economic Policy Group which is made up of the President's principal economic advisers.

Inter-American Development Bank (I.D.B.). A bank set up in 1960 by the United States and 19 Latin American countries, with only Cuba opting out. Subsequently, Canada and a number of Caribbean countries joined as regional members. In addition, 16 European countries joined as non-regional members. The bank's basic function has been seen as channelling money from the richer western economies into Latin American development projects. The money has increasingly come from private capital markets. Many agricultural projects have been supported.

Inter-bank money market. A market in sterling funds mainly between banks operating in London, enabling banks to employ balances at rates of interest generally higher than those obtainable on money lent to the discount market. It is closely linked with the foreign exchange and euro-currency markets, and to the other sterling money markets. Money is borrowed and lent overnight and for periods of up to 5 years, though most transactions are for short periods. Lending is normally unsecured.

Interest. The price paid by a borrower to a lender, usually on the basis of X per cent of the capital per annum. The elements of interest are:

(a) a payment for the risk of loss of capital by the lender;
(b) a payment for making the arrangement;
(c) a payment varying with the state of the market in respect of the demand for, and supply of, capital, known as 'net' or 'pure' interest.

Thus the rate of interest tends to equate the supply of money available for borrowing and the demand for loans.

Long-term interest rates are usually higher than short-term rates, due to a greater risk of a change in the rate of yield of securities over a long period. The two rates tend to rise and fall together.

Generally, a low rate of interest and a plentiful supply of capital encourages expansion; a high rate with scarce capital checks it.

In the 'agio' theory, usually associated with Professor von Böhm-Bawerk, it is argued that the fundamental reason for interest lies in the fact that a person prefers present to future satisfactions. Interest may be said to represent the loss in satisfaction experienced by postponing the consumption of goods. It is this surplus of present over future satisfactions that is said to explain the payment of interest. Hence the expression 'interest is the price of time'. John Maynard Keynes (1886–1946) defined interest as 'the price which equilibrates the desire to hold wealth in the form of cash with the available quantity of cash'. *See* LIQUIDITY PREFERENCE.

Interest arbitrage. The drawing on overdraft facilities, not for the purposes for which the facilities were sought but to invest in higher-yielding certificates of deposit or other money market instruments. Also used as a term in foreign exchange markets to describe the taking of opportunity for profit which arises if interest parity theory is not fulfilled.

Interest, classical theory of rate of. A theory that the rate of interest, under the play of market forces, comes to rest at the point where the amount of investment at that rate of interest is equal to the amount of saving at that rate. John Maynard Keynes (1883–1946) argued that the total amount of saving was influenced by many factors, and that the rate of interest merely influenced individual decisions as to what proportion of savings would be invested in industry and how much held as cash. *See* INTEREST; KEYNESIAN REVOLUTION; LIQUIDITY PREFERENCE.

Interest cover. The number of times the fixed interest payments made by a company to service its loan capital are exceeded by earnings; the cover serves as a guide to the ability of a company to meet interest payments out of current income.

Interest, monetary and real theories of. Theories seeking to discriminate between and relate monetary theories of interest and real theories of interest; a contemporary view argues that the market (monetary or nominal) rate of interest is equal to the real rate plus the expected inflation rate. Essentially, monetary theories of interest are short-run theories in which the monetary or nominal rate of interest is the cost of borrowing money and selling securities, and the yield on lending money and purchasing securities. The real rate of interest, on the other hand, is determined by the demand for and supply of real savings. If the monetary rate of interest on investment in securities is 15 per cent per annum, and the rate of inflation is 10 per cent per annum, then the real rate of interest will approximate to 5 per cent per annum.

Interest, productivity theory of. A theory which emphasises the yield from investment as the explanation for the existence of a rate of interest. Eugen von Böhm-Bawerk (1851–1914) adopted this theory as one of his reasons for the existence of a positive interest rate. It was related to his theory of 'round-about' production methods.

Interest rate futures contract. A contract launched initially by the Chicago Mercantile Exchange (q.v.) in 1981; the contract is based on bank-issued debt instruments.

Interest rate peg. The monetary policy followed in the United States from 1942 to 1951 under which the Federal Reserve System (q.v.) adjusted the quantity of money so as to hold the interest rate on Treasury securities constant.

Interest rates, real. Actual interest rates, discounted against inflation to give a real rate; for an actual interest rate of 15 per cent and a rate of inflation of 10 per cent, the real rate of interest may be considered to be about 5 per cent. A current real rate of about 5 per cent is nonetheless high compared with a historical level of between 2 and 3 per cent.

Interest rates, social effects of. The effects of interest rates at various levels on different segments of the population. If interest rates are high those with loanable funds and cash self-evidently benefit, and have an interest in the continuation of such rates. Others may be in a socially neutral position: affluent citizens who do not need to borrow money, or self-financing companies, or those who borrow but are able to pass the full cost along to the public. Those who must borrow money to obtain housing, provide a car, or finance a business, pay the full penalty. High interest rates, even if introduced to ensure the economic health of the country, operate by rewarding the rich and penalising the poor.

Interest, theories of. *See* ABSTINENCE OR AGIO THEORY OF INTEREST; INTEREST, CLASSICAL THEORY OF RATE OF; INTEREST, MONETARY AND REAL THEORIES OF; INTEREST, PRODUCTIVITY THEORY OF; INTEREST, TIME PREFERENCE THEORY OF; LIQUIDITY PREFERENCE THEORY OF INTEREST; LOANABLE FUNDS THEORY OF INTEREST.

Interest, time preference theory of. A theory of the existence of interest rates based on the assumption that an individual prefers consumption now to consumption in the future. It is argued that the individual prefers present consumption for several reasons: (a) the slaking of thirst now takes a natural preference over the contemplation of slaking thirst at some future time; (b) the benefits of deferring consumption may never be enjoyed due to death or incapacity; and (c) the tendency of people to undervalue future benefits. *See* INTEREST; INTEREST, PRODUCTIVITY THEORY OF; INTEREST, THEORIES OF.

Intergovernmental Council of Copper Exporting Countries (C.I.P.E.C.). A council comprising representatives of the world's largest copper-producing and exporting countries. The full members comprise Chile, Indonesia, Peru, Zaire, and Zambia; Australia, Papua New Guinea and Yugoslavia are associate members. The purpose of the council is to keep up the price of copper; however, the efforts of the council were unable to prevent a fall of more than half in the price of copper between 1974 and 1975. By 1984, the price had fallen to the lowest in 50 years. While some members favoured cuts in production, Chile continued to increase production between 1981 and 1984.

Interim dividend. A dividend (q.v.) paid out of profits not yet audited.

Interlocking directorships. An arrangement under which individual directors have seats on the boards of various companies within the same group.

Intermarket spread. A futures trading technique employed, for example, by currency speculators; it involves the simultaneous purchase and sale of futures in different but related instruments in the same month for the purposes of either hedging or speculating. Spread trading is often confined to 'straddle' activity, the simultaneous purchase of futures contracts in the same commodity, but for different delivery months.

Intermarket Trading System (I.T.S.). A communication system which links all U.S. exchanges electronically; it allows orders to be automatically checked against the computer for better prices in another market.

Internal balance. A situation in which full employment and price stability are simultaneously achieved. During the 1970s there was a loss of any semblance of internal balance in many countries, a situation of 'stagflation' with a level of employment below full employment with a continuing marked inflation of money prices. Professor James Meade has argued that an effective combination of full employment with the avoidance of inflation necessarily requires a wage-fixing arrangement which takes as its main criterion the supply-demand conditions in the labour market without undue insistence on the attainment and defence of any particular real wage income. He has suggested the replacement in wage bargaining of the untamed use of monopolistic power through the threat of strikes, lock-outs, and similar industrial action by the acceptance of arbitral awards made by trusted and impartial outside tribunals.

Internal economy. *See* ECONOMIES OF SCALE.

Internal effects. Benefits (or costs) received (or paid) by persons within a particular grouping, usually a decision-making unit, such as a governmental unit or business firm.

Internal inflexibilities. Inflexibilities in organisations arising from ingrained patterns of thought and behaviour, long established procedures and policies, and the tying up of available funds in specific projects; all these factors impede progressive planning. *See* EXTERNAL INFLEXIBILITIES.

Internally generated funds. Trading profits before depreciation and after interest, tax and dividends. Between 1960 and 1980, these contributed about 65 per cent of companies' funds; in 1980 and 1981 it was reduced to about 55 per cent. In most years, internally generated funds have been sufficient to cover investment in fixed assets and stocks.

International Bank for Reconstruction and Development (I.B.R.D.). Bank set up under the Bretton Woods Agreement (q.v.) in December, 1945, for two purposes: to help finance the rebuilding of war-devastated areas and to aid in the advancement of less-developed countries. Nearly one-third of all funds have gone for power projects. Besides lending funds, the Bank provides technical advice to governments or other borrowers on a wide range of development problems. It undertakes general economic surveys for governments wishing to study resources and to plan long-range programmes of development. The Bank has also lent its 'good offices' to help governments solve economic or financial disputes. The Bank's loan funds come in part from member's subscriptions to capital shares. The powers of the Bank are vested in a Board of Governors. It is often referred to as the World Bank (q.v.).

International Banking Act 1978. A U.S. Act to bring foreign banks within the federal regulatory framework; it introduced six major statutory changes:

(a) It limited interstate domestic deposit-taking by foreign banks. Each foreign bank had to elect a 'home state' for the conduct of domestic business; however, existing multi-state networks of foreign banks were allowed to carry on;

(b) It provided the option of federal licensing for foreign bank agencies and branches;

(c) It authorised the Federal Reserve Board (q.v.) to impose reserve requirements on agencies and branches of foreign banks and to limit the maximum rates of interest such offices could pay on time deposits to the same as member banks;

(d) It required federal deposit insurance for those branches engaged in retail deposit taking;

(e) It amended the Edge Act (q.v.) to permit Edge corporations to compete over a broader range of business and permitted foreign banks to set up such corporations;

(f) It subjected foreign banks to the same prohibitions on non-banking business as domestic bank holding corporations; however, once again existing activities were allowed to continue.

International Banking Zones (U.S.). Created in 1981, banking zones which accepted foreign deposits and made foreign loans. These activities were exempt from State income taxes and certain restrictions normally imposed by the Federal Reserve System (q.v.) on such business. The zones represent a relatively free-wheeling international market in money. Zones were centred in New York, San Francisco, Los Angeles, Chicago, Miami, Louisville, and Columbus. The assets in the zones were held in International Banking Facilities (I.B.F.s). Until the free banking zones were established, American and foreign banks had to conduct practically all such business outside the United States.

International Commodities Clearing House Limited (I.C.C.H.). The central British agency for the clearing of commodity transactions and financial futures transactions; it is owned by six major British banks, and in this respect there is a difference from the more common practice in the United States of America of ownership by trading members. Transactions on the London International Financial Futures Exchange (L.I.F.F.E.) (q.v.) are referred to the I.C.C.H.; contracts are checked and matched. Once the 'initial margin' on the transaction is paid, the Clearing House steps between the buyer and seller, becoming a buyer to the seller and a seller to the buyer. Each of the original parties is thereby relieved of any anxiety over the creditworthiness of the other. The financial integrity of the market relies to a large extent on this guarantee by the Clearing House. The Clearing House collects two forms of margin payments; each party pays the 'initial margin' which is in the nature of a good faith deposit. The second margin payment is the 'variation margin' reflecting the daily profit or loss on each contract as its market price changes. In the event of the non-payment of an adverse variation margin, the initial margin provides an element of protection to the Clearing House.

International commodity agreements. Agreements between the producers of primary commodities for the purpose of achieving the stabilisation of prices for the commodity in question, or the raising of prices to consumers; international agreements have been reached at different times and for varying periods in respect of coffee, sugar, wheat, tin, sultanas, olive oil, and petroleum. *See* BUFFER STOCKS; INTERNATIONAL TIN AGREEMENT; ORGANISATION OF PETROLEUM EXPORTING COUNTRIES.

International Development Association (I.D.A.). An affiliate of the International Bank for Reconstruction and Development (q.v.). It was formed in 1960 to help developing nations by extending financial aid on easy terms. I.D.A. finances carefully studied and well prepared projects. It will help countries whose credit standing has not enabled them to borrow from the Bank, and it is prepared to finance a wide variety of projects, e.g. by extending credits for municipal water supply, industrial estates and special training programmes.

International Finance Corporation (I.F.C.). A United Nations agency established in 1956 as an affiliate of the International Bank for Reconstruction and Development (q.v.) to help finance productive private undertakings by investing in them, without government intervention or guarantee. It invests only in the less-developed areas, and in enterprises which are primarily industrial. I.F.C. will not, however, finance more than half of the total cost of an enterprise.

International firm. A firm undertaking operations on an international basis, without the ownership being on an international basis.

International Gold Pool. An organisation established in 1961 by a number of central banks to operate in the London market for the purpose of stabilising the price of gold. The participating countries were the United States of America, Belgium, Italy, Netherlands, Switzerland, Western Germany and the United Kingdom. France was also a member but ceased to take an active part in the pool from July, 1967, onwards. Early in March, 1968, the demand for gold reached a record level, the price pressing against the effective ceiling price of $35 per fine ounce maintained by the gold pool. At the request of the United States authorities the London gold market was closed on Friday, 15 March 1968, and did not re-open until 1 April 1968. During this period an emergency meeting was held in Washington of the governors of the seven central banks still participating in the gold pool arrangement. The outcome was a decision to abandon the gold pool. Gold would continue, however, to be transferred between monetary authorities on the basis of $35 per fine ounce but the authorities undertook no longer to sell, nor necessarily to buy, in the market. In effect a two-tier system for gold would be free to find its own level. On 15 August 1971, the President of the United States announced the temporary suspension of the convertibility of the dollar into gold. Foreign exchange markets in London and several other Western European cities were closed temporarily. A temporary import surcharge of 10 per cent was imposed on dutiable goods imported into the United States.

International liquidity. The ability of countries to meet their international debts and settle their international transactions. Countries keep reserves of gold and foreign currencies and settle their indebtedness to other countries by means of either a transfer of gold or payments in their own or foreign currencies. A country in temporary balance-of-payments difficulties may seek the assistance of the International Monetary Fund (q.v.). *See* BALANCE OF PAYMENTS; BRETTON WOODS AGREEMENT; EURO-DOLLARS; EXCHANGE RATE; FLOATING EXCHANGE RATE; GROUP OF TEN; INTERNATIONAL GOLD POOL; INTERNATIONAL MONETARY FUND; RESERVE CURRENCY; SMITHSONIAN AGREEMENT; SPECIAL DRAWING RIGHTS.

International Monetary Fund. An international financial institution set up in December 1945, as a result of the Bretton Woods Agreement (q.v.) of the previous year. It is an association of governments designed to: (a) promote international monetary co-operation through a permanent institution; (b) facilitate the expansion and balanced growth of international trade; (c) promote exchange stability, maintain orderly exchange arrangements among members, and avoid competitive exchange depreciation; (d) assist in the establishment of a multilateral system of payments in respect of current transactions between members; and (e) provide members with an opportunity to correct maladjustments in their balance of payments (q.v.) without resorting to measures destructive of national and international prosperity. Each member government has been set a quota to be paid into the Fund, payable partly in gold and partly in the member's own currency; the quota determines the member's voting power and the amount of foreign exchange that it may draw from the Fund. A member may purchase foreign exchange, paying its own currency, but the member must 'repurchase' its own currency within 3 or, at the outside, 5 years to maintain the balance in the Fund pool. Currencies drawn from the Fund may be used to relieve a member's balance of payments difficulties; the funds may not be used for military purposes or for programmes of economic development.

In addition, the Fund consults with members on their international financial situation and on specific problems as they arise. On request, the Fund furnishes expert missions to advise and assist governments in working out monetary problems on the spot. In any event, members are kept informed of the latest developments. Policies are laid down by a Board of Governors, representing all members, which normally meets annually. Many of its powers are delegated to a Board of Executive Directors. In recent years, the resources of the Fund have been supplemented by the Group of Eleven (q.v.) agreements. When the I.M.F. opened its doors in 1947 it had only 39 members; by 1967 the number had risen to 106; by 1980 the number reached 140.

By 1983, 11 of the 20 largest Third World borrowers were under I.M.F. programmes as a consequence of the renegotiation of their debts. *See* BRETTON WOODS AGREEMENT; SPECIAL DRAWING RIGHTS.

International Monetary Market (I.M.M.). *See* CHICAGO MERCANTILE EXCHANGE.

International price arbitrage. The mechanism by which domestic prices are influenced by world prices. The producers of domestic goods will tend to raise their prices, if the prices of similar goods imported from the rest of the world also tend to rise. If this happens on a broad front, then the general level of domestic prices will be strongly influenced by the general level of import prices. Imported raw materials will tend to have a similar effect on final prices.

International Sugar Agreement. An agreement between world sugar exporters, aimed at stabilising world sugar prices; the agreement in force between 1977 and 1983 required exporters, at times of excess supply, to put sugar into stocks, and also imposed export quotas as necessary. The agreement also stipulated a price range, but failed on the whole to keep the price within those limits.

International Tin Agreement. An agreement under which seven countries that produce tin and 28 countries that use it, largely in food cans and automobiles, try to limit the rises and falls of the price of tin on the world market. Stocks of tin are released for sale when prices rise and quantities are bought when prices fall. Tin producers and consumers began controlling prices in the 1930s. In 1956 the United Nations set up the International Tin Council. Through the Council new agreements were subsequently made every 5 years. The producer countries are Malaysia, Bolivia, Indonesia, Thailand, Australia, Nigeria and Zaire. The leading consumer countries include the United States of America, the United Kingdom, West Germany and Japan.

International trade or foreign trade. The exchange of goods and services between independent countries or states. *See* BRETTON WOODS AGREEMENT; COMPARATIVE ADVANTAGE, THEORY OF; EUROPEAN ECONOMIC COMMUNITY; FREE TRADE; GENERAL AGREEMENT ON TARIFFS AND TRADE; INTERNATIONAL LIQUIDITY; INTERNATIONAL MONETARY FUND; KENNEDY ROUND; LATIN AMERICAN INTEGRATION ASSOCIATION; SMITHSONIAN AGREEMENT; TOKYO ROUND.

International trade theory. A body of economic theory relating to international trade, including the following: (a) the theory of comparative advantage which states that mutually advantageous trade will always be possible with trade patterns based on relative prices, rather than absolute prices; no one country can have a comparative advantage in all commodities; (b) the Heckscher -Ohlin theory which states that a country will tend to export the commodity that uses relatively more of the factor of production that is relatively abundant in that country. The theory assumes that countries have different quantities of the various factors of production such as land, labour, and capital, but identical production functions; and (c) the factor-price equalisation theory which states that under free international trade, not only the prices of the traded products but also the prices of the factors of production (inputs) such as land, labour, and capital will be equalised among countries. *See* COMPARATIVE ADVANTAGE, THEORY OF; HECKSCHER-OHLIN LAW; PURCHASING POWER PARITY THEORY.

International Wool Secretariat (I.W.S.). Created in 1937, an organisation sponsored by wool producers to promote the demand for wool; it operates today in 44 countries with its headquarters in London, England. Initially, the I.W.S. was set up by Australians and New Zealanders; later South African producers joined it. In 1969, Uruguay became the fourth member. Australia remains the largest contributor to its budget. Wool now accounts for only 5–6 per cent of all fibres used in the world, progressively losing ground to acrylics, polyesters, and nylons, and also to cotton.

√ **Intervention prices.** Price levels for agricultural produce in the common market of the European Economic Community (q.v.) at which national agencies are obliged to buy produce in order to maintain this minimum price level. The intervention price for each commodity is the floor price, always being above the actual costs of production but below the 'target price'. *See* COMMON SUPPORT PRICES.

In-the-money. A put option (q.v.) which has a strike price that is higher than the underlying futures price, or a call option whose strike price is lower than the underlying futures price. For example, if the August 1984 C.O.M.E.X. gold futures contract is trading at $425 an ounce, an August call with a strike price of $400 would be considered in-the-money by $25 an ounce.

Intra-firm and inter-firm comparisons. Comparisons of business efficiency made between firms within the same industry, in order to stimulate improved performance. The members of an industry often collaborate in the regular publication of statistics and organisations are set up to define, collect and compare financial and operating ratios on a confidential basis. The more common ratios used in inter-firm comparisons are:

$$\frac{\text{Net profit}}{\text{Capital employed}}$$

$$\frac{\text{Fixed assets}}{\text{Stocks}}$$

$$\frac{\text{Total capital employed}}{\text{Liquid assets}}$$

$$\frac{\text{Fixed assets}}{\text{Depreciation provision}}$$

$$\frac{\text{Current assets}}{\text{Current liabilities}}$$

$$\frac{\text{Fixed interest capital}}{\text{Equity capital}}$$

Intrinsic value. In respect of share options, the amount by which the market price is above the option's strike price for a call, or below the option's strike price for a put. Options with an intrinsic value are referred to as being in-the-money, while those with no intrinsic value are either at-the-money (if the two are equal) or out-of-the-money. For example, call options with a strike price of $12.60 have an intrinsic value of $1.00 when the share is trading at $13.60. *See* ORDINARY AND TRADED OPTIONS (AUST.).

Inventory. A stock of various goods and raw materials kept on hand by a business firm in order to meet needs promptly as they arise and ensure an uninterrupted operation of the business. Viewed comprehensively, a manufacturer's inventory comprises the raw materials to be used in the product, the goods in process of manufacture, and the stock of finished goods ready for distribution to customers. If sales move ahead of production, the inventory of finished goods declines; if production lags the production inventory will tend to increase. If sales fall and the market remains depressed over a long period, the inventories at all stages will be allowed to decline. An expectation of market recovery may reveal itself initially by a rebuilding of inventories. *See* INVENTORY-LED RECOVERY.

Inventory-led recovery. Descriptive of a recovery from an economic recession which begins with the rebuilding of depleted business stocks or inventories; this will occur if firms anticipate a recovery of demand for goods. In 1982 the inventories of United States firms fell from an average of 100 days of orders to only 50 or 60 days, too low in relation to growing consumer demand in 1983.

Inventory liquidation. A reduction in inventories during a period of recession.

Inverted market. A futures market in which the nearer months are selling at premiums over the more distant months, characteristic of a market in which supplies are currently in short supply.

Investment. Adding to the stock of physical capital; traditionally regarded as a flow of spending on capital goods, e.g. machinery, factory buildings, roads, bridges, houses, and stocks. Companies achieve their optimal capital stocks when the cost of buying an extra unit of capital is equal to the extra profits it will earn, the stream of prospective future profits being discounted by a suitable rate of interest to a present value. If the marginal cost of capital is less than the present discounted value of its future profits, it will pay to buy more capital, i.e. to invest and adjust the stock of capital. In society generally, the term is also loosely applied to the purchase of securities and other financial instruments.

Investment bank. A bank which advises corporations and governments on how to raise capital; guarantees the sale of new bonds and shares, and distributes them to investing institutions and individuals. They do not engage in commercial bank (q.v.) activity such as cashing cheques and granting overdrafts. Investment banks mostly own wholesale distribution facilities in the form of dealing rooms and trading facilities, utilising brokerage houses for the retail end of the business. Under the Glass-Steagall Act (U.S.) (q.v.) investment banks are the only institutions allowed to distribute the full range of corporate as well as government securities.

Investment bankers have also been known

as underwriters, standing between the corporation issuing new securities and the public. It is common practice for one or more investment banks to buy outright from a corporation a new issue of stocks or bonds; this is known as the 'bought deal' (q.v.). This initial sale of new securities is known as a primary distribution or primary offering. The 'big five' or 'special bracket' investment banks in the United States are the First Boston, Goldman Sachs, Merrill Lynch, Morgan Stanley, and Salomon Brothers, underwriting between them over two-thirds of all new issues in the United States. *See* COMMERCIAL BANK.

Investment coefficient. The cost of a unit of capital equipment, e.g. the cost per kilowatt of electricity generating capacity. A concept useful in comparisons between technical units of similar capacity in terms of output, but different in character and efficiency, as in the case of conventional and nuclear generating equipment.

Investment company. A company or trust which uses its capital to invest in other companies. There are two principal types: the closed-end and the open-end. Shares in closed-end investment companies are readily transferable in the open market and are bought and sold like other shares. Open-end funds sell their own new shares to investors and stand ready to buy back their old shares; the shares are not listed on exchanges. Their capitalisation is not fixed and they issue more shares as people want them.

Investment gross and net. Gross investment comprises the total amount of capital goods (q.v.) produced for all purposes. Net investment comprises the net addition to the stock of capital, allowance having been made for the replacement of worn-out equipment. The volume of net investment determines the rate of increase of the capital stock.

Investment trust companies. Companies which invest mainly in equity shares and are often willing to subscribe to, or underwrite new issues of equity capital by industrial and commercial concerns; some investment trusts are also prepared to provide equity finance for private and public unlisted companies and are generally, but not exclusively, looking for companies which have a good track record.

Trusts may be described as equity, property, money market, or cash management trusts, according to the main emphasis of investment; in all cases the aim is to spread the risks. Thus a property trust would hold property in a variety of geographical and urban or rural areas, and these properties would be of various classes and kinds.

Investors in Industry, plc. Successor to Finance for Industry (q.v.), a body formed in 1983 to continue support of British industry; it is owned by nine London and Scottish banks and the Bank of England. Only one part of the group retained its former name of Industrial and Commercial Finance Corporation Ltd. What used to be Technical Development Capital Ltd. (q.v.) became Investors in Industry, Ventures Division. Between 1945 and 1983, the group provided over 7,000 companies with long-term and permanent capital.

Invisible earnings (U.K.). An element in the balance of payments (q.v.) which includes: (a) services in the field of commerce and finance; and (b) earnings of British holdings of property and enterprises abroad. As invisible exports tend to exceed in value the services rendered by overseas countries to Britain and the earnings of foreign capital invested in Britain, the net earnings contribute to offsetting deficits in visible trade. Government military and non-military spending overseas and contributions to international organisations represent invisible imports. The net receipts of U.K. shipping companies while a large item in the overseas accounts make only a small contribution to net earnings. Civil aviation also yields little or no net earnings. Travel represents a deficit as more Britons travel abroad than overseas residents visit Britain. However, financial and allied services; underwriting and other insurance; interest, profits and dividends from overseas investments, all yield a substantial net surplus.

In 1981, there was a surplus of over £3,000 million on Britain's invisible earnings, mainly as a result of a return to a substantial surplus on interest, profits and dividends.

Invisible hand. The influence of market forces through which self-interest often benefits the community as a whole. A term used by Adam Smith (1723–1790) in his *Enquiry into the Nature and Causes of the Wealth of Nations* (1776). In this work he states: 'The uniform constant, and uninterrupted effort of every man to better his condition, the principle from which public and national, as well as private opulence is originally derived, is frequently powerful enough to maintain the natural progress of things towards improvement, in spite of both the extravagance of government and the greatest errors of administration. Like the unknown principle of animal life, it frequently restores health and vigour to the constitution, in spite not only of the disease, but of the absurd prescriptions of the doctor'. The individual intends only his own gain and he is led 'by an invisible hand to promote an end which was no part of his intention'.

Invoice discounting. A means of generating cash by selling to a factoring company or finance house, at a discount, either a selection of invoices on a firm's larger debtors or an entire sales ledger. The client agrees his requirements with the discounting company and which debtors' obligations are to be discounted. Then the client assigns invoices to the discounting company in respect of all turnover with those approved debtors as and when he decides he wishes to raise cash. He then receives immediately an agreed proportion (up to 75 per cent) of the gross amount due on the assigned invoices. As and when received, customers' payments in respect of assigned invoices are forwarded to the discounting company. Finally, at the end of each month, the discounting company pays the balance of the purchase price, less charges on the assigned invoices settled during the month.

Irredeemable debenture. A debenture (q.v.) containing no provision for the repayment of the principal in normal circumstances. If the company goes into liquidation, however, the debenture has a prior claim to repayment.

Irredeemable security. A security issued with no date of redemption laid down. *See* SECURITIES.

I.S.–L.M. model. A simplified but useful model of the economy that places particular stress on the channels through which monetary and fiscal policies affect the economy; as a model it stands at the core of modern macro-economics (q.v.). It comprises two equations:

> Investment (I) = Saving (S), representing goods market equilibrium; and
>
> Money Demand (L) = Money Supply (M), representing money market equilibrium.

The I.S. curve is the schedule of combinations of the interest rate and level of income, such that the goods market is in equilibrium. The I.S. curve is negatively sloped because an increase in the interest rate reduces planned investment and thereby reduces aggregate demand and the equilibrium level of income. The L.M. curve is the schedule of combinations of the interest rate and the level of income, such that the money market is in equilibrium. *See* FIGURE 11.

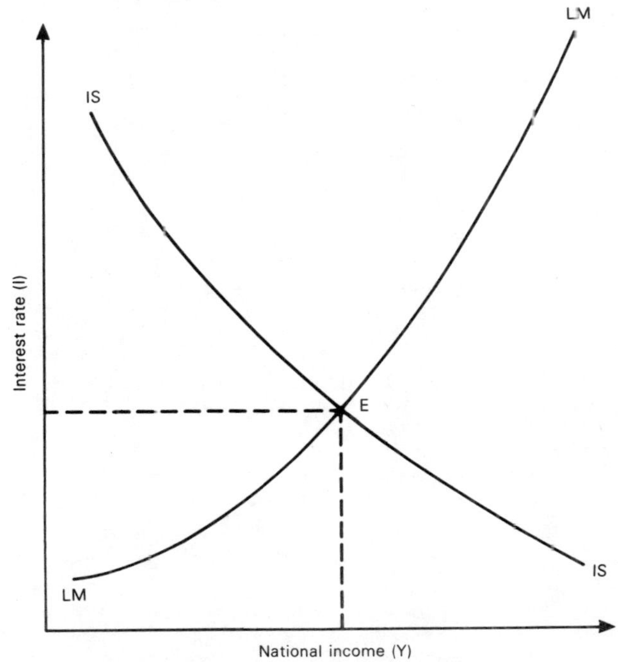

Figure 11 The I.S.–L.M. model

Issue. Any of a company's securities; or the act of distributing such securities.

Issue price. In respect of public issues and offers for sale of equities (q.v.), the prospectus price of the shares. In placings it is the price of the shares to clients; in offers for sale by tender it is the price determined by the tendering. *See* PLACING; OFFER FOR SALE; OFFER FOR SALE BY TENDER; PUBLIC ISSUE.

Issued capital. That part of the authorised capital of a company which has been subscribed. Such capital may be fully-paid-up, or partly-paid up.

Issuing house (U.K.). Financial firm specialising in the issuing or floating of new securities for governments, municipalities and companies. The issuing house undertakes that the whole of a new issue of securities will be sold and makes all necessary arrangements such as advertising the prospectus, etc.; arrangements are made with underwriters to take such part of the issue as is not subscribed to by the public, paying the underwriter a fee of so much per cent. *See* ISSUING HOUSES ASSOCIATION.

Issuing Houses Association. An Association, formed in 1945, to promote the common interests of Issuing Houses. *See* ISSUING HOUSE.

Italian banking system. A banking system consisting of a central government bank (the Banca d'Italia), together with six 'public law' banks, three banks of 'national interest', and over 100 'ordinary credit banks'. The 'public law' and 'national interest' banks have branches throughout the country; the extent of public ownership in these banks is substantial. The 'ordinary credit banks' are much more localised, but undertake a considerable volume of commercial banking. In addition, there are co-operative banks and savings banks. Reserve requirements are met either by interest-bearing accounts at the central bank or in holdings of specified government securities or both.

J

Jawbone (U.S.). Descriptive of verbal appeals as an aspect of the voluntary approach to the implementation of monetary policy. During periods when restraint in bank lending is desirable, the Federal Reserve Board and Reserve Banks may appeal to the commercial banks to scrutinise loan applications particularly carefully giving priority to loans which will add to productive capacity. *See* MORAL SUASION.

Jenkins Committee (U.K.). A Committee charged with the task of reviewing the Companies Act 1948. The most immediate of the Committee's proposals was that companies should give full and up-to-date information on the real value of assets, turnover, profits, reserves, etc. Such information was already supplied by the more progressive companies to their shareholders. *See* COMPANIES ACTS 1948 TO 1985.

Job splitting. A practice where two people share the same job for one wage.

Jobber's turn. *See* STOCKJOBBER.

Jobbers. *See* STOCKJOBBER.

Jobbing. Trading in and out of positions on the same day on futures exchanges. *See* POSITION.

Jobcentres. A concept in employment offices which provide self-service facilities; freed from the task of distributing unemployment benefit, a network of 800 jobcentres has been created in Britain. The first jobcentre was opened in Reading in May, 1973.

Jobless growth. Increases in production made possible by more and better use of machinery and innovations, without an increase in employment.

Joint costs. Costs which are incurred in the production of two or more products and which cannot be attributed to any one of them; an allocation of costs may prove a wholly arbitrary business.

Joint demand. A situation which exists when the satisfaction of a want involves two or more separate commodities being used in conjunction with each other, e.g. knives and forks, petrol and motor-cars, pens and ink, records and record players.

Joint Industrial Councils (U.K.) or Whitley Councils. Permanent joint bodies of employers and employees whose function is to consider matters affecting the progress and well-being of the trade concerned from the point of view of all those engaged in it, so far as is consistent with the general interests of the community.

Joint profits. The profits earned by a small group of rival firms; firms in a small group may be motivated towards a set of policies which will maximise the combined profits of the group, i.e. the group will behave as a single firm acting as a monopolist, or conversely each firm may behave in a way which seeks a larger share of smaller joint profits. The actions of rival firms thus affect the size of the joint profits, as well as the division among them. *See* OLIGOPOLY.

Joint-stock banks. Deposit banks whose business is mainly or exclusively in the United Kingdom, e.g. the clearing banks, the Scottish banks the Northern Irish banks and other domestic banks which are members of the British Bankers' Association.

Joint supply. A situation in which the supply of one commodity inevitably involves the supply of another, e.g. beef and hides. An increase in the supply of beef involves an increase in the supply of hides; an increased demand for one may be accompanied by reduced prices for the other.

Juglar Cycle. Business cycles (q.v.) of between 9 and 11 years' duration identified by Clement Juglar of France; he has been credited with being the first to speak of business cycles. Juglar divided business cycles into three phases: prosperity, crisis, and liquidation. He argued that the sole cause of the crisis was the prosperity phase that preceded it, and that depression always followed the crisis; the excesses and maladjustments of the prosperity phase made the crisis and depression inevitable. Standard business cycle theory has been mainly concerned with explanations of the Juglar cycle. These theories have been classified by Gottfried Haberler as: purely monetary theories, monetary overinvestment theories, nonmonetary overinvestment theories, underconsumption theories, and psychological theories. Most modern theories are based on time lags occurring in necessary adjustments between production and demand, investment and interest rates, and so on.

Junk bonds. The bonds of companies that rating agencies classify as 'speculative' with respect to their capacity to meet their obligations, e.g. rated BB or B by Standard and Poor. The market for junk bonds has grown dramatically in the United States, as investors realised that the risk of default by lower-rated companies was compensated for by higher yields. The market has enabled highly geared companies to reduce their dependence on bank finance.

K

Kabutocho. Tokyo's equivalent of Wall Street (q.v.).
Kaffirs. South African mining shares.
Kansas City Board of Trade (K.C.B.T.). One of the oldest of U.S. commodity exchanges, evolving from a local commercial organisation in 1856; it is now the largest cash wheat trading centre and the largest hard winter wheat futures market in the world. The exchange also offers stock futures contracts based on the Value Line Average Stock Index (q.v.). The exchange has some 220 members representing 85 firms engaged in all branches of the grain and grain products industry; membership comprises public and private elevator operators, grain commission merchants, flour and feed manufacturers, exporters, futures traders, brokerage firms, and co-operative marketing associations.
Kennedy Round. A description used for negotiations which led to an extensive and substantial reduction of tariffs. The U.S. Trade Expansion Act 1962, empowered the U.S. President (then President John F. Kennedy) to cut tariffs by up to 50 per cent on a wide range of goods, subject to reciprocity. Ministers of G.A.T.T. member countries met in 1963 to decide the broad lines that the negotiations should take and agreed that negotiations should begin on 4 May 1964 in Geneva. After 3 years of Kennedy Round negotiations it was decided on 15 May 1967, that tariff reductions of up to 50 per cent on industrial commodities would become effective by 1972 between the participating countries. These extensive tariff reductions mean that tariffs are no longer a formidable barrier to trade and the result should be an accelerated expansion of world trade. Other non-tariff barriers, such as quotas, remain however, while primary producing countries did not fare well in the Kennedy Round negotiations. *See* GENERAL AGREEMENT ON TARIFFS AND TRADE (G.A.T.T.).
Kerb market, South Korean. An unofficial money-lending market in the Republic of Korea, where interest rates charged are sometimes more than twice the official lending rates. The market attracts borrowers because the official banking system is unable to meet demand.
Kerb trading. (a) Inter-office telephone trading on the London Gold Futures Market (q.v.) permitted outside official market hours enabling the market to operate 24 hours a day; all such deals must be subsequently registered with the international commodities clearing house: (b) The trading which takes place in some commodity exchanges around 20 minutes after the official market has ended; the kerb market enables a ring member to complete business interrupted by the bell in the official sessions. Originally kerb trading took place on the actual kerb outside the exchanges. *See* CURB EXCHANGE (U.S.).
Keynesian Revolution. Appellation for the profound changes in fundamental economic thinking brought about by the challenging contributions of John Maynard Keynes (1883–1946). In 1936 appeared Keynes' most famous work *The General Theory of Employment, Interest and Money*. The General Theory is basically an analysis in terms of fundamental economic principles of the causes of unemployment, that is, unemployment over and above 'frictional' unemployment arising from people changing jobs. In it he argued that there were fundamental errors in the premises underlying classical and neo-classical economic theory and that the automatic self-righting qualities that had been attributed to the economic system were fictitious. For example, traditional theory held that in the case of the labour market, as in that of other markets, the price of labour tended to be adjusted to a level at which all labour would find employment. According to this theory,

therefore, labour had only to lower its price for full employment to be restored. The *General Theory* analyses the possibility of stable equilibrium with high unemployment with no natural forces tending to redress it, irrespective of the price of labour. Employment, Keynes argued, was determined by total effective demand which depended upon the propensity to consume and the propensity to invest. Keynes' *General Theory* evoked a storm of controversy, although in the following 10 years many became converted to his way of thinking. Indeed, the White Paper on *Employment Policy* (Cmd. 6527) published in 1944 marked official recognition of the victory of the Keynesian Revolution—the Government now accepts responsibility for the maintenance of a 'high and stable level of employment', despite the difficulties of achieving this in recent years. *See* BRETTON WOODS AGREEMENT; LIQUIDITY PREFERENCE; PROPENSITIES TO CONSUME AND SAVE; MULTIPLIER; SAVINGS EQUAL INVESTMENT.

Keynesian School. A school of economists which in whole or substantial part supports the following tenets: (a) Fiscal policy is a greater influence in the economy than monetary policy, i.e. money supply is considered to have a negligible effect on output and prices—'money does not matter'; (b) an incomes policy is important in helping to achieve an inflation rate limitation; (c) it is possible to achieve a more stable macroeconomic environment if policy instruments are used in a discretionary manner by the authorities rather than being set according to some simple rules; (d) exchange rates are an important policy instrument in achieving a balance-of-payments target; (e) tax rates (and to a lesser extent government expenditure) may be adjusted in order to keep unemployment at a reasonable level, ensure low inflation, and achieve a balance-of-payments equilibrium.

An extreme Keynesian view would be that money wage restraint is all that matters. Once that is achieved, everything else, and especially a non-inflationary money supply, will come into line. In contrast to the Monetarist School (q.v.) the money wage is regarded as an exogenous variable, and the money supply as an endogenous variable. *See* AUTOMATIC STABILISERS; BUSINESS CYCLES; CAMBRIDGE SCHOOL; CLASSICAL SCHOOL; CONSUMPTION FUNCTION; ECONOMICS; FISCAL POLICY; FULL EMPLOYMENT; INTEREST; LAISSER-FAIRE; MACRO-ECONOMICS; MARSHALLIAN ECONOMICS; MULTIPLIER; NEO-CLASSICAL ECONOMICS; PROPENSITIES TO CONSUME AND SAVE; SCHOOLS OF ECONOMICS.

Killing the bond. Stripping a bond (q.v.) of its interest coupons to become a zero coupon bond; such bonds are often considered 'better dead than alive'. *See* ZERO COUPON BONDS.

Kinked demand curve. A demand curve that may be characteristic of firms in certain oligopolistic industries; it occurs when a firm judges that if it cuts its prices, other firms will cut theirs too; but that if it raises its prices, other firms may be content to leave theirs unchanged (in this event a potential loss of market is involved). Thus the demand curve is relatively inelastic below the going price, and relatively elastic above the going price. *See* FIGURE 12.

Kitchin Cycle. A notion developed by the British statistician, Joseph Kitchin, that business fluctuations could be divided into two categories: major cycles and minor cycles, the major cycles being aggregates of two or perhaps three minor cycles each minor cycle averaging some 40 months in length. Kitchin based his findings on commodity prices, bank clearings, and interest rates in the United States and Great Britain for the period 1890 to 1922. Kitchin did not attempt a serious theoretical explanation of the observed phenomenon suggesting only rhythmical movements due to psychological causes and variations in crops. *See* BUSINESS CYCLES.

Kite. A bill, often called an 'accommodation bill' (q.v.), drawn on a person who has received nothing in return. It is an expedient for obtaining credit for a short period.

Kondratieff Cycle. Identified by the Russian economist Nikolai D. Kondratieff, the longest cycles or waves found in economic history. An analysis of economic time series for England, France, Germany and the United States, by Kondratieff suggested that there existed a cycle of an average duration of some 54 years. The hypothesis has been subjected to a great deal of criticism; some students have found different patterns when using different techniques, others that Kondratieff's position was supported by price level series and interest rates but not by production and consumption data. *See* BUSINESS CYCLES.

Krugerrand. A legal coin struck by the South African Mint in 1967, and minted each year since as part of a public policy to encourage private gold-holding. The coin is made of 22-carat gold and weighs 33.93 grams.

Kuwait Fund for Arab Economic Development. Established in 1961, under the auspices of the Kuwait Government, a fund initially intended to assist Arab countries. The fund now offers

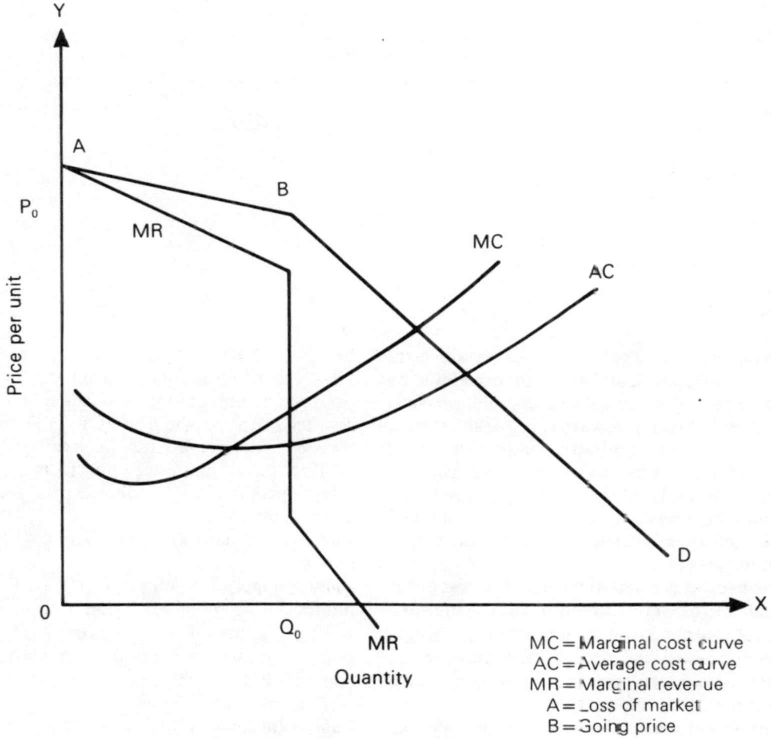

Figure 12 Kinked demand curve under oligopoly

aid to all less-developed countries. Algeria, Egypt, Jordan, Lebanon, Morocco, Sudan and Tunisia have all been granted loans.

Kuznets Cycle. Identified by Simon S. Kuznets after extensive studies, particularly of American economic development, long swings in economic growth rates exhibiting a duration of some 15–20 or more years; the swings were most marked in the building construction industry. Kuznets identified peaks in 1873, 1892, and 1913 with troughs in 1878 and 1896. Kuznets (and others) also argued that these growth rate swings could be found in the 1920s and 1930s. *See* BUSINESS CYCLES.

L

Labour. One of the 'factors of production' (q.v.); the combination of all exertions by individuals, whether they be manual, physical or mental, directed towards the production of wealth (q.v.). Labour is quantitative, involving both effort and time; it is also qualitative, both intelligence and skill determining its efficiency. Labour may be regarded as a flow of services generated by a heterogenous stock of human capital.

Labour-costs per unit of output. The cost of the labour in real terms involved in making each unit of output from a factory. High wages associated with high productivity may mean a lower labour cost per unit than low wages associated with low productivity.

Labour, division of. *See* DIVISION OF LABOUR.

Labour force. The proportion of a population entering the labour market; employed plus unemployed.

Labour-intensive industry. Industry in which the ratio of labour input to capital input is higher than the average ratio for industry as a whole. The capital input may be measured by the depreciation costs of plant and equipment. Examples of labour-intensive industries are the textile, leather products, furniture industries and service industries. The U.S. Postal Service is about 85 per cent labour-intensive. *See* CAPITAL-INTENSIVE INDUSTRY.

Labour, mobility of. The ease of movement of labour between areas and occupations. Movement from one area to another is known as geographic or lateral mobility. Occupational movement is described as vertical mobility.

Labour, productive and non-productive. Productive labour is all effort, by hand and brain which contributes to the supply of goods and services which command a price. The definition thus embraces the work of bricklayers, machinists, labourers, engineers, solicitors, teachers, civil servants and nurses. Adam Smith (1723–1790) adopted a more narrow view, regarding labour as productive or non-productive according to whether or not it resulted in the production of tangible material objects. Today even labour involved in the production of material objects is not considered productive if the objects produced have no exchange value.

Labour, specialisation of. *See* DIVISION OF LABOUR.

Labour supply. Or supply of effort, the total number of hours of work that a population is willing to supply. It is a function of: (a) size of population; (b) proportion of population able and willing to work; and (c) number of hours worked by each individual.

Labour turnover. The number of workers who leave, or are replaced, in a given period expressed as a percentage of the average number of workers employed during the period.

Labour unit. A term used by John Maynard Keynes (1883–1946) in the sense of a unit of ordinary labour; labour that was paid, for example, twice as high as ordinary labour being counted as two labour units. Labour could be made homogeneous by this device.

Laffer curve. A curve showing the relationship between taxation and incentives; associated with the name of Professor Art Laffer of the United States of America, the principle of the curve has been a tradition in economic thought since the time of A. J. E. J. Dupuit (1804–1866). The curve reveals that tax revenue will be zero both when tax rates are zero and when they are 100 per cent; in the former case, zero because the government does not wish to collect tax while in the latter case, with a tax rate of 100 per cent, there would be no incentive to produce and work. In the lower lefthand reaches of the curve, revenue rises when tax rates are raised; the effect is not such as to provide a positive disincentive to work and promote the substitution of leisure. Indeed, there might be some slight incentive to greater effort; certainly the tax base expands and revenue rises. The income effect at this stage dominates the substitution effect. With increasing tax rates, a disincentive element begins to appear, but revenue will continue to rise as long as the marginal percentage reduction in the taxable base is less than the marginal percentage increase in the tax rate. At the peak of the curve, the percentage reduction in the taxable base is exactly equal to the percentage increase in the tax rate. To the right of the peak revenue begins to fall, since higher tax rates generate a marked percentage reduction in the taxable base (through disincentive effects) that is greater than the percentage increase in tax rates. While it should be possible to calculate from the Laffer Curve the implicit trade-off between disincentive effects and tax revenue, controversy continues about the shape of the curve. *See* FIGURE 13.

Lag, decision-making. Time-lag between the receipt of information by a decision-maker and the taking of action on it; this is partly because there is a minimum time in which a thoughtful and wise decision can be made, and partly because there is often institutional inflexibility about decision-making, e.g. the need for decisions to be embodied in an annual Budget.

Lagged relationship. Between x and y, a relationship in which the value of y at any point in time depends on the value of x at a previous point in time, e.g. what is produced now (y) is not determined so much by present prices but, as production takes time, by prices (x) prevailing at some previous time when production plans were made.

Laissez-faire. A policy of non-interference by the State in economic affairs. The underlying philosophy is that man is moved predominantly by self-interest and that there exist certain immutable laws which produce a natural harmony. It is argued that if everyone is left alone to pursue his own interests (to produce, buy and sell, borrow and lend) without outside interference, then the result will be to the

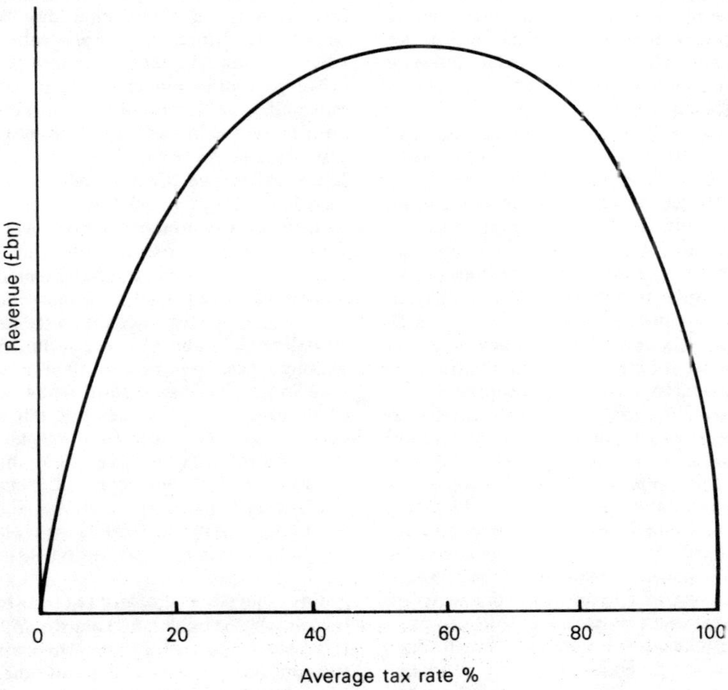

Figure 13 Possible Laffer curve for the United Kingdom

mutual benefit of all. The laws of supply and demand will ensure the best deployment of capital and labour; the function of government is, therefore, to act as umpire and not to take part in the game.

Historically, laissez-faire was the expression of the new individualism as applied to industry; it constituted a revolt against all ecclesiastical and government interference in the affairs of commerce and industry. Its evolution can be traced back to the 15th century. By the early 19th century most economists and the governing classes in Britain had come to believe in laissez-faire. The policy found its advocates in Adam Smith (1723–1790), David Ricardo (1772–1823), Thomas Robert Malthus (1766–1834), John Stuart Mill (1806–1873) and John Locke (1623–1704). The practical expression of the philosophy did much to ensure the development of commerce and industry. The system did not produce all the good results that were expected, and the reaction to its failings found expression in factory and health legislation, trade unionism and socialism. In western countries today state intervention in the economic sphere is widespread and increasing; in communist countries it is all embracing. As Sir Hubert Henderson remarked, 'A considerable departure from laissez-faire is necessary in order to realise the theoretical results of laissez-faire'.

Land. One of the factors of production (q.v.). It is virtually fixed in quantity, although the supply of useful land may be increased by the use of fertilisers, irrigation and machinery, and it can be contracted rapidly on a large scale by neglecting the principles of soil conservation. Land, in the economic sense, includes natural resources such as coal, oil and water; natural resources are neither inexhaustible nor rigidly limited. It has no cost of production, and in this respect differs fundamentally from the other two factors, labour and capital.

Land use. The deployment of the services of land for a variety of uses, e.g. agriculture, industry and commerce, housing, and recreation. Land use planning has as its object the spatial co-ordination of such activities on a national, regional and local level. Through zoning, performance specifications and building codes, governments can not only specify the uses to which land can be put but also place restrictions on those uses. Controls can prevent the establishment of industries with a high air pollution potential in poorly ventilated basins and valleys, and the establishment of noisy or odorous processes near residential districts. The land use implications of proposed transport developments may be properly taken into account at all levels of planning.

Landrum-Griffin Act 1959 (U.S.). Legislation which defines rules for union behaviour. Since the Act was passed, many individuals in unions have been indicted or charged with crimes with many convictions.

Laspeyres' index. A type of index often used for measuring changes, e.g. in prices. It is relatively easy to construct and uses base-period weights. The index utilises the following method:

$$\frac{\Sigma P_n q_o}{\Sigma P_o q_o}$$

where, P_o = price in the base-year; q_o = quantity in the base-year; and p_n = price in the year being considered. In times of rising prices, the index tends to over-estimate price increases. The reason for this is that no account is taken of the possible fall in the consumption of those goods whose prices have grown fastest, or of the possible increase in consumption of those goods whose prices have fallen, relatively speaking. *See* PAASCHE INDEX.

Last trading day. The final day under a commodity futures exchange's rules during which trading may take place in a particular delivery futures month. Futures contracts outstanding at the end of the last trading day must be settled by delivery of physicals or by cash settlement.

Latin American Free Trade Association (L.A.F.T.A.). An association formed in 1960 to develop a common market based on the European Economic Community (q.v.) model. Initially seven countries participated being Argentina, Brazil, Chile, Mexico, Paraguay, Peru, and Uruguay; later they were joined by Ecuador, Colombia, Venezuela and Bolivia, making eleven members in all. While reductions in internal import tariffs were achieved, little progress was made in establishing a common external tariff. In 1969, Chile and Peru joined with Bolivia, Colombia, and Ecuador to form a new economic group under the Andean Pact (q.v.). L.A.F.T.A. was wound up in August, 1980, being replaced by the Latin American Integration Association (L.A.I.A.) (q.v.).

Latin American Integration Association (L.A.I.A.). Founded in August, 1980, as a successor to the Latin American Free Trade Association (q.v.) by a treaty signed in Montevideo by eleven countries to establish a common market; the countries were

Argentina, Bolivia, Brazil, Chile, Colombia, Ecuador, Mexico, Paraguay, Peru, Uruguay and Venezuela.

Laundered money. The conversion of dirty money (that is, money unlawfully obtained) into clean money by passing it through the hands of an intermediary, e.g. casino, trust, or friend, in such a manner that its route cannot be traced; also money passed through alternative routes so as to minimise tax liability in a legal or illegal manner.

Lausanne School. School of economists based in Lausanne, Switzerland, associated most prominently with the names of Leon Walras (1834–1910) and Vilfredo Pareto (1848–1923); the school was noted for the development of general equilibrium theory, the theory of consumer behaviour and exchange, and the application of mathematics to economic theory. Walras occupied the newly created chair of economics at Lausanne from 1870 to 1892, being succeeded by Pareto who held the chair from 1892 to 1907. Walras is regarded as the founder of mathematical economics (q.v.). *See* SCHOOLS OF ECONOMICS.

Layfield Committee (U.K.). A committee of inquiry into local government finance set up in 1974 under the chairmanship of Mr. (later Sir) Frank Layfield; it reported in 1976. The Committee found that there was a lack of financial accountability in local government, partly because of a confusion of responsibilities between the central government and local authorities.

Le Second Marché. Established in 1983 in Paris, a new stock market for small and medium-sized firms replacing the 5-year-old intermediary market.

Lease. An arrangement whereby the use of land, buildings, or equipment is granted by a landlord or owner (lessor) to a tenant or customer (lessee) for a specified term at an agreed rental. *See* BUSINESS FINANCE; EQUITY LEASING; FINANCE LEASE; LEASE BACK AGREEMENT; LEASE LENDING; LEASING ARRANGEMENT, CUSTOMER-SPECIFIC; LEASING COMPANIES; LEVERAGED LEASING; OPERATING LEASE; TAX BASED LEASES.

Lease-back agreement. An arrangement whereby the owner of a property sells that property to a person or organisation, and then leases it back again for an agreed period and rental; a lease-back arrangement releases the funds of the seller for other purposes reducing the amount tied up in buildings or equipment.

Lease lending. A form of lending which developed rapidly in the late 1970s; e.g. a bank buys an asset (such as an aircraft) and rents it out to the borrower (for whom this often has tax and cash flow advantages). Citibank, New York, has become one of the largest dealers in secondhand aircraft in the world.

Leasing arrangement, customer-specific. A leasing arrangement under which the leasing company purchases plant, equipment, or vehicles to the firm's requirements, and then leases them to the firm for an agreed period at an agreed charge. The leasing company sometimes provides servicing and maintenance. Leasing is of particular advantage to companies currently paying little or no tax, and which may not therefore be able themselves to receive the full benefit of 100 per cent first-year tax allowances available for investment in plant and machinery. A leasing company may be able to use the full tax allowances, so that their clients are able to benefit indirectly by way of reduced leasing payments.

Leasing companies. Companies which buy and own plant and equipment needed by other businesses, leasing it at agreed rentals. This form of finance has grown quickly in importance in recent years. *See* FINANCE; LEASE LENDING; LEVERAGED LEASING.

Legal tender. Money which a person is obliged by law to accept in payment of a debt.

Lender of last resort. A traditional role of the Bank of England (q.v.); it is the one bank which will never refuse assistance to discount houses, if it is asked for. The Bank will rediscount acceptable bills of exchange or Treasury bills tendered by the discount houses; or more commonly the discount houses will be lent money against 'eligible paper' such as bills of exchange, Treasury bills or short-term government securities, for a minimum period of 7 days. The discount houses may become short of money by the calling in of loans by the commercial banks (q.v.). As they borrow for very short periods and lend for somewhat longer periods, this right to borrow from the Bank of England is essential for their operations. *See* DISCOUNT HOUSE.

Lending. On a commodities exchange, selling a commodity on a nearby date and simultaneously buying forward, thereby extending a long position. *See* LONG.

Letter of credit. (a) An order in writing from a banker to his agent abroad, or to a banker abroad, to authorise the payment of a sum of money to the person named in the letter. (b) An arrangement facilitating early payment for goods despatched overseas. An overseas seller will stipulate in his contract with the buyer concerned that the buyer shall establish a letter of credit in the seller's favour. This provides that, as soon as the seller has the documents, such as Bills of lading showing that the goods are in course of shipment, he can present them to a bank for payment.

Letter of hypothecation. A letter from an exporter to his bank authorising it, in the event of the importer failing to accept or pay a bill of exchange (q.v.), to sell the goods exported and remit the proceeds less expenses. If the bank makes an advance to the exporter such a letter enables it to recover the loan by selling the goods, if the importer does not pay.

Letter of regret. A letter conveying regret sent to an applicant who has applied for new shares in response to an offer for sale but has been unsuccessful. *See* ALLOTMENT LETTER.

Letter of renunciation. Method by which a shareholder may assign part or all of his rights to subscribe to a 'rights issue' (q.v.) to someone else.

Leverage.

(a) The control of investments much larger than the funds actually available for investment. For example, an investor buys bonds and then sells or lends them back to the dealer, while agreeing to repurchase the bonds later at a specific price; this kind of repurchase agreement allows an investor to control large quantities of bonds with relatively small funds. In the extreme, if interest rates are falling, an investor can buy bonds and then sell them again without ever putting up any money, but simply by closing out a position and taking a profit;

(b) The effect on the per-share earnings of the common stock of a company when large sums must be paid for bond interest or preferred stock dividends, or both, before the common stock is entitled to share in earnings. Leverage may be advantageous for the common stock when earnings are good, but may work against the common stock when earnings decline.

(c) In the commodities markets, the buying or selling of futures contracts on margin; the putting up of a deposit in order to trade a contract. The margin necessary to trade may represent only about 5–10 per cent of the full value of the contract. If a trader buys $100,000 worth of a commodity by depositing $10,000 in cash, an increase in the price of the commodity of 10 per cent means that the trader has doubled his money. If the price falls by 10 per cent then the trader is 'wiped out'.

Leveraged buy-outs. Business acquisition in which the managers of the business successfully bid and take control, in a transaction financed largely by borrowing; the debt is ultimately paid either out of the earnings of the business, or from the sale of its assets. Bank loans may provide more than 85 per cent of the funds required, with a floating interest rate. Such enterprises are vulnerable if interest rates rise, or the earnings stream falls off.

Leveraged investment. Descriptive of an arrangement when only a percentage of the value of a contract has to be put down to acquire, say, an option or futures contract.

Leveraged leasing. A popular form of business financing, the three parties being: the lessor who promotes the purchase of the equipment providing a substantial portion of funds (some in the form of equity); the lender, who provides the balance of the finance enabling much larger items of equipment to be leased and over longer periods; and the lessee, who pays a lease rental for the use of the equipment. Leveraged leasing differs from conventional leasing in being appropriate for very expensive assets (such as drilling rigs, aircraft, mining equipment, sugar ships, supply vessels, and dump trucks) with very long terms ranging up to 20 years.

Lewis model. Developed by Sir W. Arthur Lewis (b. 1915), the model describes how the transition from an agrarian to an industralised economy depends more on a healthy, growing and cheap workforce than on conventional capital.

Libor. The London inter-bank offered rate; this is the interest rate paid by banks in London for borrowing dollars from other banks in London. Its significance is that the interest rate on many variable rate securities is tied to Libor.

Licensed dealer (U.K.). A dealer in securities (q.v.) licensed by the Department of Trade and Industry under the Prevention of Fraud (Investments) Act 1958, but not a member of the London Stock Exchange (q.v.).

Licensed deposit-taking institutions (U.K.). In the United Kingdom, institutions authorised to accept deposits within the terms of the Banking Act 1979 (q.v.). In 1984, there were 308 licensed deposit-taking institutions. During that year, the Bank of England (q.v.) revoked the licences of seven deposit-taking companies. The Bank considered that all had conducted their business without the care and prudence required of a deposit-taking business. Some had suffered considerable losses and had been unable to achieve prudent levels of capital and liquidity; in some cases business was excessively concentrated in loans to associates; some had failed to keep proper records and had been consistently late in filing the quarterly returns with the Bank; and some had misled the Bank about material aspects of their business.

Lien. A claim against property: a bond is usually secured by a lien against specified property of the company.

Lifeboat. A special committee of the Bank of England (q.v.) and the London and Scottish clearing banks which meets from time to time to consider joint support operations in respect of ailing companies; however, in 1983 only one active company was still receiving support under these arrangements.

Lifetime Employment System (Japan). An employment philosophy in Japan which ensures that full-time employees of big companies are guaranteed complete job security until they reach the compulsory retirement age of 55. The philosophy developed after the First World War when rapid development meant competition for a skilled labour. However, retirement at 50 or 55 on an inadequate pension seriously circumscribes the concept of 'life-long'.

Limit, at. *See* AT LIMIT.

Limit losses, let profits run. An essential criterion for trading success in stock and commodity markets; in practice there is always a tendency to take profits early, and hence limit profits, while failing to get out of losing situations early enough, for this means admitting error. It is easy to take a profit, and difficult to accept a loss.

Limited liability (U.K.). An arrangement, authorised by statute since 1855, under which a shareholder in a business cannot lose more than the amount he has paid for his shares (i.e. the fully paid amount). The introduction of the principle of limited liability has been one of the most important developments in modern industrial organisation. With limited liability investors are more willing to lend money and it provides a means of financing large-scale production or projects. To the investor, it opens up an opportunity for spreading risks by holding shares in a large number of different companies. Without limited liability, every person sharing the ownership of a business is jointly responsible for the debts of his firm to the full extent of his private resources. British bankruptcy law is extremely exacting; a bankrupt may be left with only the clothes he wears, his bedding and the tools of his trade. Limited liability companies are of two types, private limited companies (q.v.) and public limited companies (q.v.).

Limited order. Instruction to a stockbroker (q.v.) to buy or sell shares at specified prices only. *See* MARKET ORDER.

Limited recourse finance. A form of business finance which has gained increasing prominence as a preferred method for the financing of large natural resource projects involving very large capital investment; because comparatively few companies can afford to bear all the risks associated with projects of these dimensions, the sponsors of a project may take up a one-third interest; the balance of funding would be provided by lenders. Project sponsors are increasingly using limited recourse finance; the financial liabilities of a project's equity sponsors are restricted in comparison with those that normally result from project borrowings.

Line of credit. The extending of short-term loans to a business by a commercial bank; the bank assures its customer that it will provide short-term funds up to some specified limit, with the interest rate set at some spread over the bank's prime rate; the interest rate thus floats with the prime rate.

Liquid assets. Assets either in the form of money, or which can be quickly converted into money. The liquid assets of a commercial bank are coin, notes, and balances at the Bank of England; money at call or short notice; and discounted bills.

Liquid market. A market where the selling and buying can be accomplished with ease, due to the presence of a large number of interested buyers and sellers.

Liquid, to be. To hold cash.

Liquidation.

(a) The conversion of assets (q.v.) into cash, when they are not already in that form. In terminating or winding-up a business, 'going into liquidation' means not only converting assets into cash but also the paying of all business debts and the distribution of the balance of cash, if any, among the owners of the business. In 1981, some 8,000 British firms went into liquidation; in 1982, some 12,000 or twice as many as in 1975. However, as many new businesses were started as old ones passed into liquidation; in 1981, new businesses outnumbered those going into liquidation.

(b) The sale of a futures contract (q.v.) to offset a previous purchase, or the purchase of a contract to offset a previously made short sale. The term 'liquidation' is loosely used on the exchanges for any operation that cancels a previously existing position.

Liquidity. The availability of cash, and of assets readily convertible into cash (called liquid assets), to meet immediate obligations; a volume of reserves plus credit facilities, reflected in an ability to meet current financial liabilities in cash.

Liquidity, corporate.

(a) The availability of cash and or liquid assets to meet the immediate needs of a business, e.g. its maturing cash obligations. A likely failure to meet cash obligations may compel a firm to seek additional financing in circumstances which are unfavourable to it; in the extreme there may be a need to liquidate assets under pressure at distress prices. The alternative may be insolvency leading to bankruptcy and liquidation. Hence the importance of corporate liquidity management policies to ensure that needs are met in the most efficient and productive manner.

(b) The ability of the market in a particular security to absorb a reasonable amount of buying and selling at reasonable price changes. Liquidity is one of the most important characteristics of a good market.

Liquidity preference. The degree of preference for holding money instead of securities (q.v.). If the 'liquidity-preference' of the community increases, this means that the demand for money increases, while the demand for securities falls. Lord Keynes defined three motives for the holding of money:

(a) the transactions motive, i.e. the need for cash to meet current requirements;

(b) the precautionary motive, i.e. to have something in hand to meet unforeseen contingencies;

(c) the speculative motive, arising from uncertainty regarding the future rate of interest.

Expressed mathematically, the quantity of money which the public will hold when the rate of interest is given is $M = L(r)$, where M is the quantity of money, L the function of liquidity-preference and r the rate of interest.

Liquidity, preference theory of interest. A Keynesian theory which attributes the rate of interest to the demand for and supply of money and money substitutes, with demand being determined by liquidity preference (q.v.) and the supply by banking policy. Liquidity preference is held to vary inversely with the rate of interest, and vice versa. Thus when interest rates are high little cash is demanded by the economy because liquidity preference is weak. Conversely, when interest rates are low, more cash is demanded as liquidity preference is strong. *See* INTEREST; INTEREST, THEORIES OF; LOANABLE FUNDS THEORY OF INTEREST.

Liquidity trap. A hypothetical situation in which the public is prepared, at a given interest rate, to hold whatever amount of money is supplied; in such circumstances monetary policy is powerless to influence the interest rate. A liquidity trap exists at zero interest rates, for at zero interest rate the public would not want to hold any bonds; money attracts no interest and has an advantage over bonds in being usable in transactions. During the 1940s and 1950s it was believed that there was a liquidity trap at low positive interest rates. Belief in the existence of a liquidity trap was the basis of the Keynesian belief that monetary policy has no effect on the economy. However, there has never been strong empirical evidence of a trap at any level of interest rates.

Listed company or quoted company. A company which has signed the listing agreement of a stock exchange. Companies listed on a stock exchange undertake to provide far more information about themselves than company law alone demands, e.g. any large acquisitions or disposals made by the company. A listed company on The London Stock Exchange (q.v.) is also bound by the 'Rules of The Panel on Takeovers and Mergers'. Listing gives a company the advantage of a regulated market in its securities.

Liverpool Cotton Exchange. A highly organised market for cotton. Cotton is graded by the Liverpool Cotton Association, which consists of merchants, brokers and spinners. The prices quoted on the market are for immediate delivery i.e. 'spot' (q.v.) and for future delivery, i.e. 'futures' (q.v.). Thus cotton may be sold before it arrives at port, and indeed even before the crop has been harvested.

Listed stock. The stock of a company which is traded on a stock exchange (q.v.); the various stock exchanges have different standards for listing. The New York Stock Exchange (q.v.) requires for an original listing a national interest in the company, and a minimum of 1 million shares publicly held among not less than 2,000 round-lot stockholders; a minimum aggregate market value is also prescribed.

Lloyd's. The Corporation of Lloyd's, a City of London institution which pioneered marine insurance, brought a greater measure of safety to shipping, and built up a complicated information service throughout the world. Insurance has not been confined to marine risks, however, and it is now possible to insure at Lloyd's against almost any kind of risk. Anyone wishing to accept insurance business at Lloyd's must satisfy the governing committee that he or she is a person of wealth and reliability. Those admitted as members of the society carry on insurance business through appointed representatives known as underwriters. Between 1972 and 1982, the membership of Lloyd's increased four times to 21,000. Each full member has to show assets of £100,000. In January, 1983, a new 17-member council was appointed, while the following month a first chief executive was appointed.

Lloyd's Register of Shipping. A society of underwriters, shippers and merchants. The society not only compiles a complete list of all ships in the world over 100 tons: it has laid down definite ship-building standards, and through over one thousand surveyors, stationed at the principal ports at home and abroad, sees that these standards are put into effect. 'A1 at Lloyd's' means first class in Lloyd's Register of Shipping: the first in a series describing the condition of a vessel, the letter referring to the state of the hull and the figure to the condition of the stores and equipment. A first class guarantee to Lloyd's (q.v.) for marine insurance purposes.

Load. The portion of the offering price of shares of open-end investment companies in excess of the value of the underlying assets which cover sales commissions and all other costs of distribution. The load is usually incurred only on purchase, there being, in most cases, no charge when the shares are sold (i.e. redeemed).

Loanable funds theory of interest. A theory that interest rates are determined by the supply of, and the demand for, funds available for lending. The supply of such funds is determined mainly by: (a) the extent of savings, and (b) the net increase in deposit currency. The demand for such funds is determined mainly by: (a) the opportunities for new capital formation, and (b) the desire to increase cash balances. The theory has much in common with the liquidity preference theory of interest. *See* INTEREST; INTEREST, THEORIES OF; LIQUIDITY PREFERENCE THEORY OF INTEREST.

Loan-back fund. Defined in Australia as a superannuation fund which has more than 10 per cent of its assets loaned back to the employer.

Location, theory of. A branch of the theory of the firm to embrace an analysis of locational decisions; a body of theory which attempts to explain and predict the locational decisions of firms, and the spatial pattern of industry, commerce, and agriculture which results from the sums of individual decisions. Early work in the area of agriculture was undertaken by Johann Heinrich von Thünen (1783–1850), and in the area of industry by Max Weber (1864–1920).

Locked in. Descriptive of an investor when he has gained a profit on a security he owns but does not sell because his profit would immediately become subject to capital gains tax.

Locked-in loss. Describes a situation in which an investor in a commodity or stock exchange finds himself in a losing position, and attempts to offset the potential loss by engaging in a spread or straddle. *See* SPREAD TRADING.

Lomé Convention. A Convention signed at Lomé, Togo, in 1975 by members of the European Economic Community (q.v.) and 46 developing countries in Africa, the Caribbean, and the Pacific. Under the Convention, all industrial exports and most agricultural exports from these 46 countries to the Community became free of duty. Financial and technical aid was also agreed upon, and the European Development Fund was set up by the Community to administer and channel aid funds to developing Lomé countries. Negotiations for a third Lomé Conventiontion were concluded in 1984, the second Lomé Convention expiring in January, 1985. Developing nation demands for greater funds were matched by an E.E.C. emphasis on the need for better management of funds.

London Baltic Exchange or simply 'The Baltic'. A London market founded in the early 18th century devoted to shipping services and cargoes; it is international in scope and the largest market of its kind in the world. As a commodity exchange (q.v.) it specialises in the grain trade with a well-established futures market, e.g. in E.E.C. wheat and barley, U.K. potatoes, and soya bean meal. Almost any business connected with ships, cargoes, and air freight is transacted. The exchange has some 2,500 elected members representing some 750 company members invariably working in one of two capacities, either representing the owners of ships and aircraft, or the users of ships and aircraft. Most of the world's bulk cargo chartering is negotiated at some stage by a member of the Baltic Exchange; the Exchange is high on the list of Britain's invisible export earners.

London clearing banks. *See* CLEARING BANKS, LONDON.

London Commodity Exchange. A commodity exchange (q.v.) emerging from the London Rubber Exchange which was founded in 1932 by the rubber trade association. During the Second World War, the rubber exchange was joined by members of the London Commercial Sale Rooms. In 1954, a review resulted in the formation of a new company comprising rubber and sale room members; the title of the London Commodity Exchange was adopted. The exchange, one of the most important of its kind, has assumed the character of a futures market.

London discount market or money market. A market the principal function of which is to match the needs of the borrowers of money for short periods of time with the funds available from the lenders of such money. The money market comprises the eleven discount houses of the City of London, the commercial banks (q.v.), the accepting houses, and the Bank of England. In 1981, the Bank of England (q.v.) no longer undertook to announce continuously the rate at which it would supply cash to the London discount market. *See* ACCEPTING HOUSE; DISCOUNT HOUSE; LONDON DISCOUNT MARKET ASSOCIATION; MONEY MARKET.

London Discount Market Association. An association of discount houses of the City of London, England. The members enjoy discount window facilities at the Bank of England (q.v.); these facilities are in fact confined to this body. *See* DISCOUNT WINDOW LENDING.

London Docklands Development Corporation. Established by the British Government in 1981, a statutory body charged with the task of rehabilitating some 2,000 hectares (5,000 acres) of derelict dockland in London's working-class East End. Of the 50,000 residents, over 90 per cent were housed in council-owned houses, distinctly downmarket in character; some 20 per cent of the labour force was unemployed. The area had little industry, poor public transport, and bad roads.

London Foreign Exchange Market. A market operating by telephone within the City of London, and by telephone, telex and cable with overseas financial centres. There are nearly 260 dealers, comprising the banks authorised as foreign exchange dealers by the Bank of England (q.v.) under the Exchange Control Act 1947. There are about 10 firms of foreign exchange brokers, who act as intermediaries between the banks.

London gold fixing. The single price for gold distilled twice a day by five London bullion dealers from buy and sell orders from all over the world. This price provides a standard of gold value for traders in Zurich, Paris, Hong Kong, Singapore, Tokyo, New York, Chicago, and throughout the world. In 1982, it was estimated that gold bullion worth more than $10 billion changed hands through the London gold market (q.v.).

London Gold Futures Market (L.G.F.M.). Established in 1982, a market and exchange in the City of London for trading and dealing in gold contracts for future delivery; the market is owned by the London Gold Market (q.v.) and the London Metal Exchange (q.v.) jointly. Membership comprises floor members and non-floor members; non-floor members may issue market contracts but may not attend the floor of the market. The floor membership is made up of 38 member companies. All transactions carried out are registered, cleared and guaranteed by the International Commodities Clearing House. The members buy and sell contracts promising delivery of gold in lots of 100 troy ounces for the current month and five specified future months, on behalf of clients throughout the world. The prices arrived at on the floor reflect the international supply and demand position. To enter into a gold futures contract the buyer or seller puts up an initial margin (q.v.). The L.G.F.M. is the only gold futures market in the European time zone; the official market hours overlap the trading hours of the gold market in the United States of America and the Far East.

London Gold Market. A major free market for gold bullion. The market was closed between September, 1939, and March, 1954. It was closed again briefly between 15 March and 1 April 1968, as a result of a crisis in gold. Since 29 December 1958, all currently earned sterling in the hands of non-residents has been freely convertible into gold. The gold market is served by five firms dealing in gold bullion; representatives of the firms meet each working day to fix the official London gold price, but prices may vary considerably during the course of a day. The London gold price is quoted in dollars. *See* INTERNATIONAL GOLD POOL.

London International Commodities Clearing House. A clearing house owned by six large British banks which provides for transactions in the futures markets and commodities markets. One of the tasks of the clearing house is to hold the margin all exchange members are required to maintain every day. This is calculated daily in the light of their open trading positions; it is meant to reduce the risk of loss through default.

London International Financial Futures Exchange (L.I.F.F.E., pronounced 'life'). A financial futures market which opened in London in September, 1982, it was housed in the Royal Exchange building near the Bank of England. Initially, only two contracts were traded: a 3-month Euro-dollar contract and a sterling/dollar currency contract; others were rapidly added. *See* TABLE 3 AND FIGURE 14.

London Metal Exchange (L.M.E.). Formally established in 1877 in Lombard Court, London (and now at Plantation House) a physical market where metals can be bought and sold at any time. The market provides facilities for hedging, both buying hedges and selling hedges. By registering daily price quotations, the market indicates world trends in both the supply and demand for metals. The

TABLE 3

THE LONDON INTERNATIONAL FINANCIAL FUTURES EXCHANGE (L.I.F.F.E.)
SUMMARY OF CONTRACTS

Contract	*Unit of trading*	*Contract standard*	*Delivery months*
Twenty year gilt interest rate	£50.000	Any Gilt Stock with a life of between 15–25 years, as listed by L.I.F.F.E.	March June September December
Three month sterling interest rate	£250,000 (£500,000 from March 1985 delivery month onwards)	A 3-month £ deposit facility at a designated bank in London, or cash settlement (at buyer's option)	March June September December
U.S. treasury bond	U.S. $100,000	Any U.S. treasury bond with a life of at least 15 years	March June September December
Three month Eurodollar interest rate	U.S.$1,000,000	A 3-month Eurodollar deposit facility at a designated bank in London, or cash settlement (at buyer's option)	March June September December
Sterling currency	£25,000	Delivery of the designated currency	March June September December
Deutsche mark	D.M.125,000	Delivery of the designated currency	March June September December
Swiss franc	S.Fr.125,000	Delivery of the designated currency	March June September December
Japanese yen	Yen 12,500,000	Delivery of the designated currency	March June September December
F.T.-S.E.100	Valued at £25 per full index point (e.g. value £25,000 at 1000.0)	Cash settlement	March June September December

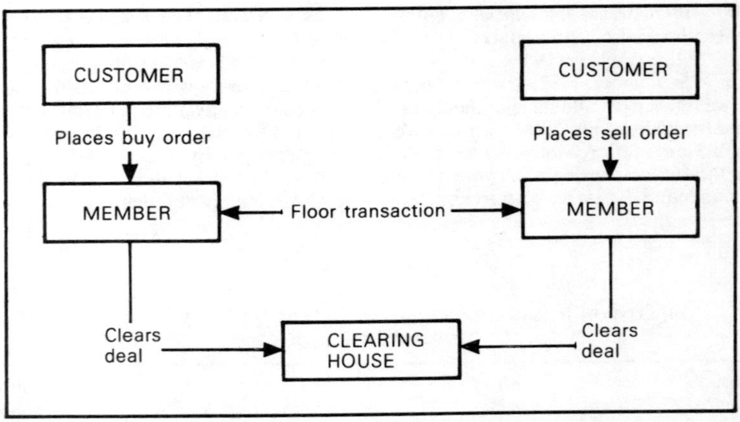

Figure 14 The pattern of events from the customer, through the London International Financial Futures Exchange (L.I.F.F.E.) (q.v.) to the International Commodities Clearing House Limited (I.C.C.H.) (q.v.).

exchange has 21 delivery points in the U.K. and continental Europe. There are 36 seats at the exchange; over half the seats are owned by overseas companies. The exchange is managed by a board of directors and a committee of subscribers. Dealings take place in prescribed minimum quantities for copper, lead, zinc, aluminium, nickel, tin, and silver; trading is restricted however to brands of metal which have been listed by the committee.

London Stock Exchange, The. A single stock exchange formed in 1973 from the seven exchanges in the British Isles. The governing body, the Council of the Stock Exchange, has 46 members elected by the members of the exchange.

In 1983, revised rules were adopted to allow outsiders on the Stock Exchange Council, and establishing an appeals committee for those refused membership. The aim was to eliminate restrictive practices and encourage competition. In 1984, The London Stock Exchange abolished fixed commissions, and the previously mandatory distinction between brokers (agents) and jobbers (dealers). In addition, all stock exchange members became entitled to act as broker/dealers. This is known as dual-capacity. Broker/dealers prepared to quote two-way prices in specific stocks must register as market-makers in order to receive privileges such as reduced stamp duty; market-makers must broadcast their prices to all member firms via a stock exchange automated quotation system; and broker/dealers and market-makers must time stamp their dealing slips. *See* SINGLE CAPACITY; STOCKBROKERS; STOCKJOBBERS.

Long.

(a) A description of a buyer or holder of securities (q.v.) who has more of a particular security than he has contracted to deliver; the 'longs' are usually those who have bought expecting a rise in prices. *See* SHORT.

(b) Signifies ownership of securities: 'I am long 100 U.S. Steel' means the speaker owns 100 shares.

(c) The market position of a futures contract buyer whose purchase obligates him to accept delivery unless he liquidates his contract with an offsetting sale.

Long- and short-period. As defined by Alfred Marshall (1842–1924), the long-period is one in which there is time for the supply of those things which are used in producing a commodity to adapt themselves to demand whereas the short-period does not allow such a movement. Depending on the case in mind, therefore, the short-period could vary from an hour to several months or even years.

Long gilts or longs, gilt-edged securities (q.v.) without a redemption date within 15 years.

Long hedge. The purchase of futures contracts for hedging purposes.

Long liquidation. The sale of a previously held long position (q.v.).

Long-run marginal costs. *See* MARGINAL COSTS, LONG-RUN.

Lorenz curve. In measuring the income distribution of a community, a curve showing what percentage of families receive what percentage of the community's family income; the curve indicates the degree of inequality in income distribution. The Lorenz curve has other uses, e.g. the measurement of concentration (q.v.) in industry.

Loss leader. A good sold by a retailer below normal price, not for the purpose of making a profit on the sale of the good, but for the purpose of attracting customers likely to purchase other goods at his shop. Under the Resale Prices Act 1964, it is lawful for a supplier to withhold goods from a retailer who has been using goods of the same description as loss leaders.

M

M0. (M-nought). *See* MONEY SUPPLY.
M1. *See* MONEY SUPPLY.
M1-B. A United States money supply concept which consists of currency plus demand deposits; currency consists of notes and coin in circulation, while demand deposits are deposits against which cheques can be written in commercial banks and thrift institutions. Prior to the 1980 changes in definitions only demand deposits at commercial banks were included in what was then designated M1. M1-A corresponds closely but not exactly to the old M1. *See* MONEY SUPPLY.
M3. *See* MONEY SUPPLY.
Macro-distribution. The distribution of national income into such broad aggregates as wages, rent, interest and profits.
Macro-dynamics. An area of economic study examining the determinants of the rate of increase (or decrease) of the main categories of demand for capital goods, consumer goods, exports, and so on.
Macro-economic policy. Public policy concerned with the ways in which certain policy instruments such as government expenditure, the money supply, and rates of interest, may be used to achieve certain desirable targets such as full employment, balance-of-payments equilibrium, and a low rate of inflation. A characteristic of the 1970s and the 1980s has been the failure of many industrial nations, despite the use of macro-economic policies, to achieve these targets.
Macro-economics. A branch of economics (q.v.) concerned with the analysis of the economy in the large, i.e. with such large aggregates as the volume of employment, saving and investment, the national income, and so on. More specifically, it is concerned with the economy's total output of goods and services, the growth of that output, the price level and rates of inflation, unemployment, the balance of payments, exchange rates, booms and recessions. It embraces the study of economic policies and policy variables that affect national economic performance, monetary and fiscal policies, money stock and interest rates, the public debt, and federal and central government budgets. In sum, macro-economics is vitally concerned with the interactions among the goods, labour, and assets markets of the national economy. *See* MICRO-ECONOMICS.
Malthusian theory of population. A theory of population developed by Thomas Malthus (1766–1834) and published in *An Essay on the Principle of Population* in 1798. The essence of the theory may be summarised as follows:

(a) that population would soon out-strip the means of feeding it, if it were not kept down by vice, misery or self-restraint;
(b) that in a state of society where self-restraint does not act at all, or only acts so little that we need not think of it, population will augment until the poorest class of the community have only just enough to support life;
(c) that in a community where self-restraint acts effectually, each class of the community will augment until it reaches the point at which it begins to exercise that restraint.

Population, Malthus declared, tended to increase in a geometrical progression, whereas the means of subsistence increased in only arithmetical progression. In his first edition, Malthus places emphasis on the positive checks that tend to increase the death-rate: pestilence, famine and war. The *Essay* was recast in a second edition in 1803; in this the author somewhat modifies his gloomy forbodings, hoping that personal restraint might prove an effective factor in the check to an increasing population. *See* CLASSICAL SCHOOL.
Managed currency. A currency system which is

not based on a metallic standard such as the 'gold standard' (q.v.) which was regarded, in its pure form, as a more or less automatic system, but is one in which the quantity of money in the country is regulated by the monetary authorities.

Management ratios. A method of providing management with information in which the levels of various activities in a business are measured one against another. For example:

$$\frac{\text{Production Costs}}{\text{Production}}$$

$$\frac{\text{Production Overheads}}{\text{Production}}$$

$$\frac{\text{General and Administration Costs}}{\text{Production}}$$

$$\frac{\text{Production}}{\text{Assets employed}}$$

Manchester School. A group of men, active during the period 1820–50, who advocated free trade and opposed most encroachments into laissez-faire (q.v.) in economic and social matters. Bright and Cobden were prominent leaders of the group. *See* SCHOOLS OF ECONOMICS.

Manpower Services Commission (M.S.C.). A statutory body established in Britain in 1973 composed of government, business and trade union representatives. The M.S.C. pays the operating costs of the industrial training boards; it also operates through the Youth Opportunity Programme (q.v.). *See* INDUSTRIAL TRAINING ACT 1964.

Margin. Money put up by a client in part payment of the purchase of a stock under a forward contract.

Margin call. A demand upon an investor to put up money or securities with his broker; the call is made when a purchase is made or when a customer's equity in a margin account declines below a minimum standard set by the Exchange or by the firm.

Margin requirements (U.S.). The percentage of cash down-payment that the Board of Governors of the Federal Reserve System (q.v.) requires purchasers of securities to make when they borrow to buy specified securities. An increase in margin requirements tends to discourage speculation on borrowed credit, while a decrease tends to encourage security purchases. Separate regulations have covered these activities: Regulation T has covered credit extended by brokers and dealers, Regulation U has governed loans made by commercial banks, while Regulation G has applied to credit granted by others.

Marginal analysis. A tool of analysis found in all branches of economic theory, marginal analysis is concerned with the relationships between marginal changes in related economic variables; marginal changes being very small increments or decrements in the total quantity of a variable. The search for optimum values, maximands and minimands, involves the definition and analysis of marginal concepts. *See* SCHOOLS OF ECONOMICS.

Marginal cost. The change in the total cost of production which results when output is varied by one unit; the cost of producing M+1 units minus the cost of producing M units. *See* MARGINAL COSTS, LONG-RUN; MARGINAL COSTS, SHORT-RUN.

Marginal cost pricing. A concept in which selling prices are brought into equality with the marginal costs of production, through variations in output; a situation which arises automatically under equilibrium conditions with perfect competition, and which some economists have thought could well be introduced as a general pricing policy, to achieve optimum public benefits. Clearly, the nationalised industries represent an area in which the principle could be most readily adopted. Under conditions of imperfect competition (q.v.) however, marginal cost pricing is not profit maximising, and price is not perfectly cost-related. Only when marginal cost equals marginal revenue is profit maximised (or losses minimised) and a perfect relationship achieved between revenue and costs. A maldistribution of resources could arise if the public sector adopted a policy which does not accord with prevailing practice in the private sector. Application of the principle is also complicated by the existence of marginal taxation on the prices of some goods. The measurement of marginal cost also presents difficulties. The aim of marginal cost pricing, to reduce prices to the public and produce more, could well be self-defeating and does not seem to have retained much support.

I. M. D. Little in his *Critique of Welfare Economics* discusses the debate on output and price policy in public enterprise and concludes that no single answer is forthcoming to the questions of optimum output level and the pricing policy for arriving at the desired output level. *See* PRICING.

Marginal costs, long-run. The costs of supplying on a continuous basis those services and products which can be costed separately; they include provision for replacement of fixed assets needed for the continued provision of services, together with a satisfactory rate of return on capital employed.

Marginal costs, short-run. The increase in total costs which results from an increase in production when not all the inputs used by the firm can be varied; the additional costs of increasing output within existing capacity. In electricity generation, the main element of cost in short-run marginal costs consists of fuel. *See* FIGURE 15.

Marginal efficiency of capital. The earning power of the last increment of capital invested: or, as defined by Keynes in his *General Theory of Employment, Interest and Money* (1936), 'the relation between the prospective yield of one more unit of a type of capital and the cost of producing that unit'.

Marginal firm. A firm which is the last to enter, or the first to leave, a particular line of production. It is not necessarily the least efficient firm and may, indeed, be the most efficient.

Marginal land. Land which is the last to be brought into, or the first to be taken out of, a particular line of production. This will not necessarily be land which is just worth cultivating.

Marginal producer. A producer who would be just induced to produce a certain commodity at the prevailing level of profits being obtained from it, but if profits fell slightly would withdraw from production.

Marginal product. The amount added to the total product by the addition of one more unit of capital-and-labour. George J. Stigler in his *Theory of Price* makes five propositions regarding the marginal product: (a) the sum of the first n marginal units is equal to the total product of n units of capital-and-labour; (b)

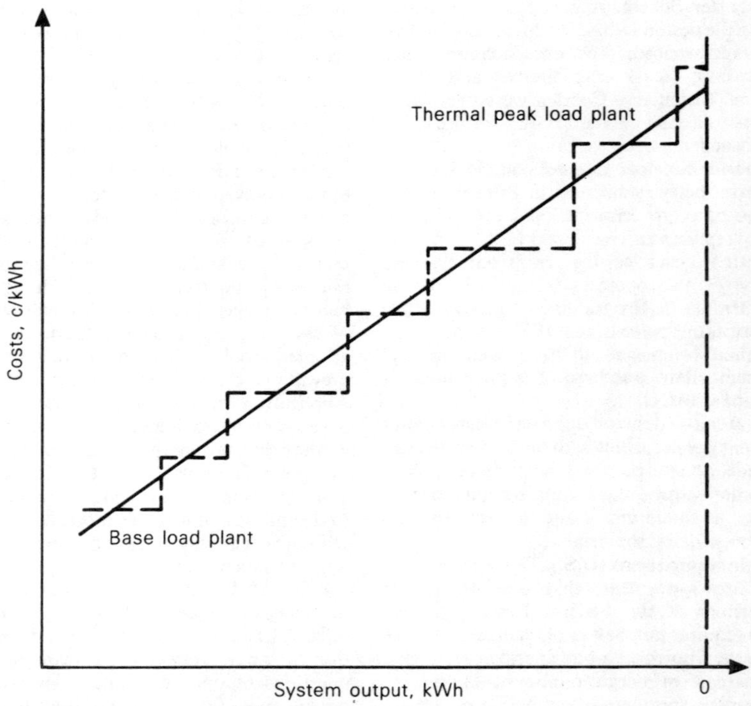

Figure 15 The short-run marginal cost curve (within system capacity) for a system up to output O. The horizontal short-run marginal cost curves of individual generating sets are shown by a broken stepped line. In a real system, the short-run marginal cost curve for the system may take a form departing from the linear, but always conforming to the same characteristics of increasing marginal running costs per kWh with increasing system output.

when the average product is increasing, the marginal product is greater than the average product, but it does not follow that the marginal product increases when the average product increases; (c) when the average product is decreasing, the marginal product is less than the average product; (d) when the average product is at a maximum, the marginal product equals the average product; and (e) the addition or subtraction of a fixed sum from all of the total products will have no effect on the marginal product.

Marginal revenue. The change in total revenue resulting from varying the output sold by one unit; it equals the total revenue from N units minus the total revenue from N – 1 units. Under conditions of perfect competition the marginal revenue is constant and is equal to average revenue or price. This is not the case in respect of imperfect or monopolistic competition in which the output of each supplier influences price. To sell an additional unit in these conditions requires a lowering of the price of the marginal and all other units of the supply. The marginal revenue is thus less than the price of the product. The magnitude of marginal revenue depends upon the price necessary to ensure the extra unit of sales. The latter is dependent on the elasticity of demand. If a considerable reduction of price is required to obtain the extra sale, the marginal revenue may be zero, or negative. The marginal revenue may also be calculated:

$P(1+1/E)$ if elasticity is treated as negative, and

$P-P/E$ if elasticity is treated as positive where P is price and E is elasticity.

'Marginal' revolution. A description accorded to the contributions of William Stanley Jevons (1835–1882), Carl Menger (1840–1921) and Leon Walras (1834–1910), who solved the apparent conflict between value and utility by recognising that it was the specific utility depending on the last available or marginal unit of a commodity, and not the generic utility, which determined its value. Jevons did not employ the adjective 'marginal', using the term 'final utility' instead. He published his *Theory of Political Economy*, embodying this new theory, in 1871. In the same year Menger produced a similar work in Vienna which is considered the best non-mathematical statement of the principle of marginal utility. Walras' work appeared 3 years later in Switzerland. The 'marginal' approach to the theory of value opened a new period in the history of economic thought. *See* SCHOOLS OF ECONOMICS.

Marginal significance. *See* MARGINAL UTILITY.

Marginal social and private net products. Concepts associated with the name of A. C. Pigou, the marginal social net product is the total net product of physical things, or objective services, due to the marginal increment of resources in any given use or place, no matter to whom any part of this product may accrue; the marginal private net product is that part of the total net product of physical things, or objective services, due to the marginal increment of resources in any given use or place which accrues in the first instance, i.e. prior to sale, to the person responsible for investing resources there. Pigou's thesis was that, in general, industrialists are interested not in the social, but only in the private, net product of their operations. Self-interest will tend to bring about equality in the values of the marginal private net products of resources invested in different ways; but it will not tend to bring about equality in the values of the marginal social net products, except when marginal private net product and marginal social net product are identical. When there is a divergence between these two sorts of marginal net product, self-interest will not, therefore, tend to make the national dividend a maximum. Such divergences between the social and private net product are likely to occur even under conditions of simple competition. Pigou's view stands in sharp relief to the opinions of the Classical School (q.v.). For example, David Ricardo said, 'Where there is free competition the interests of the individual and that of the community are never at variance.'

Marginal utility. The increase or decrease in the total utility of consumption of a good which results from increasing or decreasing the quantity of the good consumed by one unit. A good may have a very low marginal utility, but a very high total utility, e.g. water. *See* PARADOX OF VALUE.

Marginal utility, law of diminishing. A proposition that the marginal utility (q.v.) of a commodity to anyone, other things being equal, diminishes after some point with every increase in his supply of it. Alfred Marshall stressed an implicit condition in this law—that we do not suppose time to be allowed for any alteration in the character or tastes of the person concerned. The law explains why most demand curves slope downward to the right, indicating that more goods will be bought at any price than at a higher price. Purchasers tend to equate marginal, not total, utilities.

In translating the law of diminishing marginal utility 'into terms of price', Alfred Marshall (1842–1924) wrote in his *Principles*: 'The larger the amount of a thing which a person has the less, other things being equal (i.e. the purchasing power of money, and the amount of money at his command being equal), will be the price which he will pay for a little more of it: or in other words his marginal demand price for it diminishes.' *See* FIGURE 16.

Marginal utility of money. The increase or decrease in total utility (q.v.) resulting from the addition or subtraction of one unit of currency to or from the total supply of money of a consumer.

It is generally held that the marginal utility of money diminishes as the quantity of money possessed by an individual increases.

Mark. A price given in the official list of The London Stock Exchange under the heading 'Business Done'.

Mark to market. The daily adjustment of an account on a commodity exchange to reflect profits and losses on open contracts, based on closing market prices at the end of the day.

Marker price. In respect of crude oil, a listed price; in 1982, the Saudi Arabian marker price for crude oil was $U.S. 34 a barrel, a price which was regarded as a benchmark for a large segment of the international oil trade.

Market. An area, however large or small, where buyers and sellers are in sufficiently close contact with each other to ensure that the price of a commodity tends to be the same in all parts of the market, allowance being made for transportation costs, tariff barriers, and other obstacles.

There are markets for all kinds of goods, services, raw materials, foodstuffs, manufactured goods, labour, currency, and so on. A market may be confined to a village or town, or be international in scope. *See* PERFECT MARKET; PRICING; SPOT MARKET.

Market clearing. Descriptive of a situation in

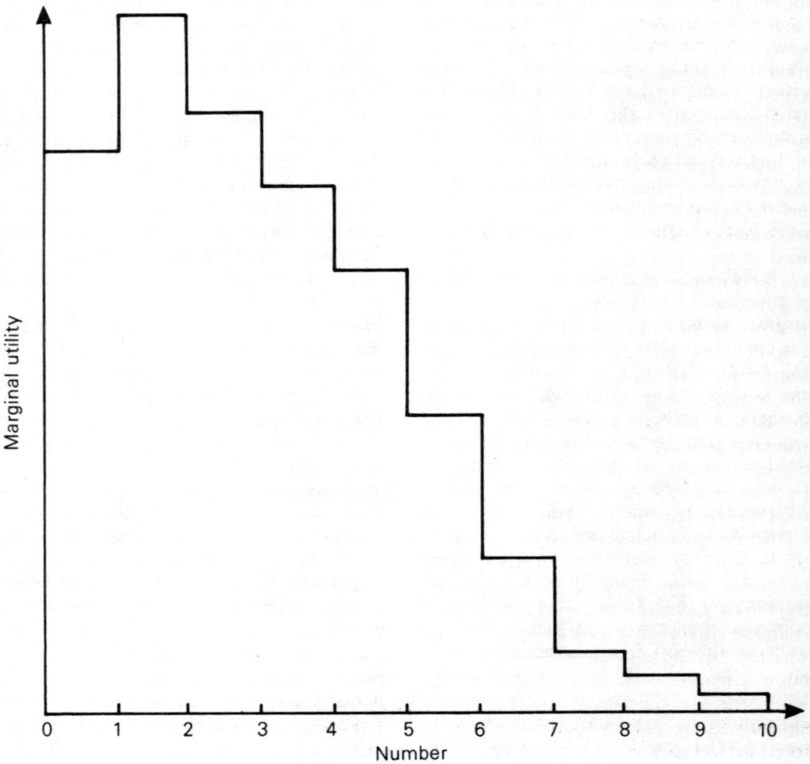

Figure 16 Diminishing marginal utility.

which the forces of supply and demand are so in balance that all the goods are sold, i.e. the market has cleared.

Market economy. An economy in which the crucial economic decisions and choices are made in a decentralised manner by numerous private individuals and firms, operating through a free price-and-market mechanism. Equilibrium prices and quantities are determined in a market economy through the laws of supply and demand; consumer preferences expressed through the price mechanism influence the kinds of goods and services produced.

Professor John Kenneth Galbraith, in his *Economics and the Public Purpose*, 1974, has described the model as 'not implausible as a description of a society that once existed. Nor is it entirely unsatisfactory as a picture of that part of the economy called the market system . . . The market system, in its admixture of monopoly and competition, does conform in broad outline to the neoclassical model. The latter model is a rough description of half the economy; it has lost touch with the other and in many ways decisive half' (p. 27). *See* PRICING.

Market if touched order. A market order executed when a transaction occurs at, or better than, a specified price after the order is transmitted. Unlike a stop order (q.v.) used to limit losses, the market if touched order is placed above the existing market if a sell, and below the market if a buy.

Market maker. A broker or specialist who is obliged to assist in the maintenance of a fair and orderly market on a stock exchange (q.v.). This function complements the normal activities of the specialist (q.v.) by adding increased depth to the market when buying and selling for his own account.

The term is also used more widely. From 1986, British banks (merchant banks and clearing banks alike) have been able to engage in market making, distributing both equities and government 'gilt-edged' bonds.

Market order. Instruction to a stockbroker (q.v.) to buy or sell shares at the best offer price or the best bid price prevailing at the time the instruction is given. *See* LIMITED ORDER.

Market overt. Generally a market held on such days and in such a place as may be prescribed by charter, custom or statute. In the City of London, a market overt means every shop in which goods are exposed for sale, for such things only as are usually sold in the shop.

Market, perfect. *See* PERFECT MARKET.

Market performance. The performance of a firm or industry in a market measured against specified criteria. These criteria or goals may include: (a) the efficient employment of scarce factors of production to yield the greatest possible real income; (b) the full employment of the factors of production; (c) growth and progressiveness in enlarging and improving the flow of goods and services; and (d) equity in the distribution of income.

Market research. A management aid which involves the systematic collecting, recording and analysing of data about problems relating to the marketing of goods and services. Industrial marketing research is confined to industrial markets, marketing activities and inter-industry relationships, whereas consumer marketing research is concerned with the needs and demands of ordinary people. A sub-division of marketing research is 'sales analysis' which involves an analysis of data obtained from the internal sales records of a firm.

Market socialism. The joining of the social ownership of the means of production with a free market system to guide the allocation of resources in the economy; markets assist the allocation of resources at the micro level, while social ownership and a planning mechanism are used to achieve macro-economic objectives.

Market structure. The economically significant features of a market (q.v.) which affect the behaviour of firms in the industry supplying that market. The main elements of market structure are: (a) concentration (q.v.) and concentration ratio (q.v.); (b) product differentiation (q.v.); (c) barriers to the entry of new firms; (d) growth rate of market demand; (e) price elasticity of market demand; (f) ratio of fixed to variable costs in the short run.

Marketable securities. Securities which may be readily sold on the exchanges or secondary markets; they include certain categories of Treasury securities (q.v.), government agency securities, bankers' acceptances (q.v.), commercial paper (q.v.), repurchase agreements (q.v.), certificates of deposit (q.v.), and bonds (q.v.), stocks and shares (q.v.).

Marketable treasury securities. Treasury securities (q.v.) which may be sold in secondary markets prior to maturity; about 60 per cent of Treasury securities are marketable. U.S. government agencies hold large amounts of non-marketable Treasury securities.

Marshallian economics. The neo-classical economics (q.v.) associated with Alfred Marshall (1842–1924) and his followers. Marshall founded the early Cambridge School of economics, though the later school was associated with John Maynard Keynes and his followers and the neo-Keynesian school.

Marshall was Professor of Political Economy at Cambridge between 1885 and 1908. As a result of his efforts a separate School and Tripos in Economics and associated branches of Political Science was established at Cambridge in 1903. Marshall's famous work *Principles of Economics* (1890) and other works placed him in line with the Classical School (q.v.), particularly Adam Smith and John Stuart Mill. The more striking contributions to economic science made in his *Principles of Economics* were:

(a) The clarification of the respective roles played by demand and by costs of production in the determination of value;
(b) The general theory of economic equilibrium in which all the elements of the economic world are kept in their places by mutual counterpoise and interaction, a theory strengthened by two subsidiary concepts—the 'margin' and 'substitution';
(c) The explicit introduction of the element of time as a factor in economic analysis, with the concepts of the 'short' and 'long' period;
(d) The distinction between 'external' and 'internal' economies;
(e) The doctrine of 'normal profit' (q.v.) assisted by the concepts of 'quasi-rent' (q.v.) and the 'representative firm'.
(f) The concept of consumer's surplus (q.v.);
(g) The introduction of the idea of elasticity;
(h) Proof that laissez-faire (q.v.), regarded as a principle of maximum social advantage, breaks down in certain conditions, theoretically and not merely practically; and
(i) An examination of the effects of monopoly.

Marshall's successor was A. C. Pigou (1877–1959). *See* SCHOOLS OF ECONOMICS.

Marshall–Lerner criterion. In its simplest form, a rule which states that the price elasticities of demand for imports and exports must sum to greater than unity for an improvement to be effected in the balance of trade through a change in a country's exchange rate. If the price elasticity of exports plus the price elasticity of imports is less than unity, then an increase in the cost of imports following a devaluation of the domestic currency will outweigh the value of the growth of exports. Abba P. Lerner (b. 1903) developed the argument in his book *Economics of Control*, using the elasticity concepts of Alfred Marshall (1842–1924).

Marxist socialism. A creed developed by Karl Marx (1818–1883) which had its origin in the conditions created by the Industrial Revolution.

Marx attempted to show that the capitalist system could not by its very nature survive, that it would in the course of time be replaced by socialism, and that the class which would effect the revolution would be the new industrial working-class or 'proletariat'. He formulated the 'materialist interpretation of history', viewing society as something undergoing constant change with one event linked to another by a cause and effect relationship. He argued that social classes take shape in response to their share in, and control of, wealth production; thus at any time the class which has the greatest economic power has the greatest political power. He saw the history of all hitherto existing society as the history of class struggles—to quote the *Communist Manifesto*, 'Freeman and slave, patrician and plebian, lord and serf, guild-master and journeyman, in a word, oppressor and oppressed stood in constant opposition to one another, carried on an uninterrupted, now hidden, now open fight, a fight that each time ended, either in a revolutionary reconstitution of society at large, or in the common ruin of the contending classes'. In a capitalist system the 'bourgeoisie' and the government are one. Marx drew attention to what he called a 'contradiction' in the capitalist system, that although production was increasing by leaps and bounds, the workers had not the power to demand a greater share in the new wealth. Marx's argument ran that, in the light of the spectacle of great wealth on the one hand and poverty on the other, the working people would eventually rise and seize power from the ruling classes. Having won, the workers 'by hand and brain' could then go forward to the building of socialism—a state of society in which all the means of production, distribution and exchange, are owned in common. Yet even at the time Marx wrote, the facts were not quite as he stated them. The poor were growing rather better off, and the falling mortality rate for children pointed to a real rise in living standards. He did not foresee the growing influence of trade unions, the impact of democracy, or the possibility of progress through evolution. *See* CLASSICAL SCHOOL; ECONOMIC

INTERPRETATION OF HISTORY; SCHOOLS OF ECONOMICS.

Matched and lost (U.S.). Descriptive of the situation when two bids to buy the same stock are made on the floor of the stock exchange simultaneously, and each bid is equal to or larger than the amount of stock offered; both bids are deemed to be on an equal basis so the two bidders spin a coin to decide who buys the stock. Also applies to offers to sell.

Matched sale-purchase transactions. Sales of securities to dealers in the money market (q.v.) by the Federal Reserve System (q.v.) with a concurrent commitment to repurchase securities at a future date.

Mathematical economics. The application of the techniques of mathematical analysis to economic variables, with the object of discovering relationships between those variables. The relationship between variable numbers is symbolised by the term 'function'. Thus demand is a function of price, price being taken as the independent variable. Instances of variable numbers or quantities in economics are prices, incomes, costs of production, amounts of goods bought or sold on a market, and the amount of factors of production employed by a firm or industry. These can all be converted into numbers of units; some into physical units, others into money or 'value' units. Economic relationships are expressible, therefore, by means of mathematical functions. There is a curve corresponding to each function to interpret a relationship between two economic variables, e.g. demand and supply curve. Diagrams of this sort may be used to throw into prominence arguments which are being advanced. The application of mathematical techniques in economics is discussed in Professor R. G. D. Allen's well-known book *Mathematical Analysis for Economists.* Professor P. Samuelson has expressed the view that 'knowledge of mathematics is needed only for certain branches of higher economic theory. Logical thought is the key to understanding basic economic principles; and the shrewed use of evidence is the key to success in their application.' Further, that 'economics uses the deductive method of logic and geometry, and the inductive method of statistical and empirical inference'. Much valuable work is being carried on today at Cambridge and London in the Development of mathematical models to take account of all the variables of the nation's economy. *See* ECONOMETRIC MODELS; MATHEMATICAL SCHOOL.

Mathematical model. *See* ECONOMETRIC MODEL.

Mathematical school. A school of economists who have adopted a mathematical approach to economic problems. The English economist William Stanley Jevons (1835–1882) belonged to both the Mathematical and Final Utility Schools. In 1862, he presented a paper to the British Association entitled 'The General Mathematical Theory of Political Economy.' A full exposition of mathematical economics was contained in a work by Leon Walras (1834–1910) of the University of Lausanne entitled *Eléments d'Economie politique pure,* which appeared in 1874. He applied mathematical analysis to a régime of perfectly free competition. Some economists today consider mathematics of limited use in economics; others regard it as an indispensable tool in the study of the workings of the economic system and perhaps the principal way in which applied economics can hope to effectively contribute to national economic forecasting. *See* SCHOOLS OF ECONOMICS.

Maturity. (a) The date on which a loan or bond or debenture becomes due and is to be paid off, i.e. the capital refunded; (b) when applied to a futures contract (q.v.), the period within which a contract may be satisfied by delivery, i.e. the period from the first notice day (q.v.) to the last trading day (q.v.) of a futures contract.

Maximum price fluctuation. The maximum amount a contract price can change, up or down, during one trading session as fixed by a commodity exchange (q.v.). Once the upper or lower price limits are reached on a particular contract further trading in that contract will not be permitted for a stated period.

Mayday. A commemorative term for 1 May 1975, when fixed commissions for brokerage were eliminated in the United States in favour of negotiated rates. The effect was a general fall in commission charges.

'Mazel'. Short for 'mazel und bracha', meaning 'luck and blessing', a word used to conclude deals in the ruby market, West 47th Street, New York. All deals are concluded with 'mazel', a word that binds both buyer and seller more firmly than any written contract.

Meade Committee on Direct Taxation. A committee chaired by Professor J. E. Meade for the Institute for Fiscal Studies which sat 1975–77; the report was entitled *The Structure and Reform of Direct Taxation* (London: Allen and Unwin, 1978). The Committee recommended: (a) the replacement of individual income tax and capital gains tax by an expenditure tax system; (b) a special new tax on housing; (c) far-reaching changes in the system of corporation tax; (d) mainly flat rate social security benefits financed solely from taxation, and many other changes.

Medium gilts or medium, gilt-edged securities (q.v.) with a redemption date between 5 and 15 years ahead.

Medium-term financial strategy. A financial strategy introduced by the British Government for the 1980s to control the growth of money supply (broadly defined as M3) and the growth of the public sector borrowing requirement (q.v.); money supply targets were set at 7–11 per cent for 1979–80 to fall to 4–8 per cent in 1983–84. However, wages escalated and within a year the inflation rate jumped from 10–22 per cent, and the money supply was not reduced. It was not until 1984 that the inflation rate moderated to 4–5 per cent.

Member bank reserves. Currency held by banks who are members of the Federal Reserve System (q.v.), plus their deposits at Federal Reserve Banks.

Memorandum of association (U.K.). A document to be submitted to the Registrar of Companies when seeking registration of a company. The memorandum sets out the name of the company, the objects of the company and the amount and sub-division of its authorised (or nominal) share capital. The precise requirements are specified in the Companies Act 1985. *See* ARTICLES OF ASSOCIATION; COMPANIES ACTS 1948 TO 1985.

Mercantilism. A political and economic policy, well-established in England during the 17th and early 18th centuries, aimed at increasing national wealth and power; by means of regulations and endeavour it was hoped to make England supreme among other commercial nations. Mercantilism rested upon five principles:

(a) The state had the duty to foster national welfare by adopting the appropriate economic and power policies, though this involved the exploitation of neighbours and colonies;

(b) the health of the national economy depended partly upon an increase of population; and partly upon

(c) an increase in the mass of precious metals in the country;

(d) foreign trade must be stimulated, for only through a favourable balance of trade could the quantity of precious metals be increased—'the most important of the means which make a kingdom without mines abound in gold and silver';

(e) commerce and industry were of greater importance as branches of the national economy than agriculture.

These ideas no doubt served their purpose; indeed Mercantilism was perhaps the only practicable policy at the time. The phase passed and the views of the Classical School (q.v.) began to take the stage. *See* SCHOOLS OF ECONOMICS.

Merchant bank. Historically, a specialised bank which helped to give London an international reputation as a world financial centre for short-term and long-term borrowing; the merchant banks are of two kinds known as (a) accepting houses, engaged in the work of acceptance credit and (b) issuing houses, engaged in transactions involving the sponsoring of capital issues on behalf of their customers. They also engaged in the work of the gold and foreign exchange markets and have many other functions in connection with the financing of trade, investment management and insurance. *See* ACCEPTING HOUSE; ISSUING HOUSE.

Merchanting. A type of trade which consists of buying goods in one overseas country and selling them in another. Many of these transactions are negotiated in the London Commodity Exchange and other centres.

Merchanting facility account. A new method of financing merchanting trade in foreign currencies, introduced by British banks to meet exchange control requirements introduced in November, 1976. The trade had previously been extensively financed in sterling.

Merger. A union of two or more firms in a transaction by which one absorbs the other(s), or a new firm is created utilising the assets of the absorbed firms. Under the British Fair Trading Act (q.v.), mergers are defined as occurring when two enterprises are brought under common ownership or common control; control is defined so as to include the ability materially to influence a company's policy e.g. through partial shareholding.

Merger, conglomerate. *See* CONGLOMERATE MERGER.

Merit goods and services. Goods and services which the state believes individuals should consume in greater quantities than they otherwise would, e.g. hospital services, education, personal social services, employment services, and the arts. Such goods and services may be provided free or at greatly reduced prices, by means of subsidies. *See* PUBLIC GOODS AND SERVICES.

Micro-dynamics. An area of economic study examining the forces governing the rates of increase (or of decrease) of demand for particular commodities, or those governing the rates of increase or decrease in the prospects of particular firms or industries.

Micro-economics. Or economics (q.v.) 'in the small'; a branch of economics concerned with the analysis of the behaviour of individual consumers and producers, particularly with the optimising behaviour of individual units such as households and firms. It examines the determination of prices in particular markets, and the effects of monopoly in such markets. This branch of theory is used in many areas of applied economics (q.v.). *See* MACRO-ECONOMICS.

Mid-America Commodity Exchange. Incorporated initially as the Chicago Open Board of Trade, a federally designated commodity futures exchange which became the Mid-America Commodity Exchange in 1973; membership exceeds 1,200 with 30 clearing member firms. The Mid-America specialises in 'minicontracts' or small size contracts in grains, livestock, metals, foreign currencies and financial futures including U.S. Treasury Bill and Bond Futures. The exchange trades some 3 million futures contracts a year; it also operates a clearing house through which all fugures contracts are settled in cash.

Middle price. In Britain, the price half-way between the two prices shown in *The Stock Exchange Daily Official List* under 'quotations', or the average of both buying and selling prices offered by a stockjobber (q.v.). The prices found in newspapers worldwide are normally their estimate of the middle price.

Military-industrial complex. Term coined by President Eisenhower to describe the complex relationships between the United States defence establishment and the private business firms who are its suppliers; these firms often take on the character of submanagement units in the public sector. The normal characteristics of the market economy almost cease to exist; furthermore it is often feared that these firms might also wield undue influence on the policies of government.

Minimum Lending Rate. A 'last resort' lending rate adopted by the Bank of England (q.v.) in preference to the bank rate (q.v.) in October, 1972. The minimum lending rate was considered a more flexible instrument which could change more frequently in accordance with circumstances, without attracting undue attention. In 1981, the Bank of England abolished the minimum lending rate; its aim became to conduct its money market operations by reference to an unpublished band of very short term interest rates. The new arrangement allowed the influence of market forces on the structure of interest rates to be as large as possible. The minimum lending rate was briefly restored in 1985.

Minimum wage legislation. Protective legislation to establish minimum wages for workers in certain industries. The need for such legislation has usually arisen because the trade unions in the industries concerned have been either non-existent or too weak to negotiate wage rates for their members. The U.K. Trade Board Acts of 1909, 1913 and 1918 set up Trade Boards for this purpose. The Wages Councils Act of 1945 repealed earlier legislation and set up Wages Councils with powers to propose regulations fixing remuneration and holiday conditions. The former Trade Boards became Wages Councils. These Councils fix the remuneration of over one million employees. Legislation was consolidated in the Wages Councils Act of 1959. Other legislation has been introduced to deal with particular cases, e.g. the Agricultural Wages Act and the Catering Wages Act. In 1985, Britain had 26 wage councils setting the minimum wage levels for low wage earners such as part-time women employees.

Minneapolis Grain Exchange. Founded in 1881, a United States grain terminal market which has evolved from a relatively isolated and provincial market to one integrated with other U.S. and world exchanges; the aim is to facilitate the marketing of agricultural produce from the Upper Mid-West. Futures contracts are traded in hard red spring wheat, durum wheat and sunflower seeds. However, the exchange is best recognised as the world's largest cash grain market, in which traders buy and sell the actual grain on the basis of samples brought to the trading floor. Some one million bushels of grain are traded in the cash market every day.

Mint par of exchange. Under a Gold Standard (q.v.), the relative value of the coins of different countries. The rate of exchange between two countries on the Gold Standard will only vary from this by the cost of the transport of gold between the two centres.

Mixed credit schemes (U.K.). Government schemes involving normal commercial credit financing and government assistance on a non-commercial basis; it describes proposals in which government aid is added to a commercial bid to secure contracts for the supply of capital goods or services to a developing country. The practice tends to distort competition among industralised countries through the introduction of another form of subsidy, and also tends to distort development priorities in the recipient developing countries.

Mixed economy. An economy in which resources are allocated partly through the decisions of private individuals and privately-owned business enterprises and partly through the decisions of the Government and state-owned enterprises. The two sectors are known as the private and public sectors, respectively.

Monetarist equilibrium. A concept of long-term equilibrium in the economy in which flexible wages and prices ensure a level of aggregate output at which full employment is maintained. Further, this long-run equilibrium in output and employment will be determined not by monetary or fiscal policy acting on aggregate demand, but solely by the profit maximising decisions of the suppliers of goods.

Monetarist school. A school of economic thought named after Professor Milton Friedman of the University of Chicago, which argues that postwar Keynesianism has led to excessively erratic management of the economy. The monetarists believe that it would be best for government to concentrate on allowing each year a 'fixed throttle' increase in the money supply, perhaps around 4 or 5 per cent a year. Indeed, any increase in the money supply much in excess of the increase in productive capacity will lead to inflation. If the money supply is kept under control, it is argued, employers will either be unable to pay higher wages or, if they do, some will go out of business and unemployment will rise. One of the difficulties with high rates of inflation is that a sudden reversion to slow growth in the money supply could precipitate a slump.

Monetarists believe that economies have a natural tendency towards full employment; however, it is conceded that this can take several years to achieve because prices and wages adjust only slowly. Nevertheless, monetarists are convinced that any contrived boosts to demand (whether monetary or fiscal) will have lasting effects only on prices, since it is considered that the long-run aggregate supply curve is vertical. They see no point in trying to fine-tune demand, advocating instead a stable and slow rate of monetary growth. An extreme monetarist position would be that control of the money supply is all that matters: once this is achieved, everything else, and especially the full employment wage rate, will come into line. Money supply is regarded an exogenous or control variable, and the money wage as an endogenous variable. *See* SCHOOLS OF ECONOMICS.

Monetarists. Those who believe that monetary policy (q.v.) is the most important means available to a government for influencing the level of economic activity. *See* CHICAGO SCHOOL; MONETARIST SCHOOL.

Monetary Accord of 1951. An agreement between the U.S. Treasury and the Federal Reserve System (q.v.) which ended the interest rate peg (q.v.), permitting monetary policy (q.v.) to respond to other objectives.

Monetary base. Descriptive of paper currency and coin issued by the government and the liabilities of the central bank to the commercial banks; also known as high-powered money. The money supply held by the public is some multiple of the monetary base, so that an increase in the base provided by the government and the central bank will cause the money supply to increase by more than the increase in the base. In 1980, in the United States, a $1 increase in the monetary base resulted in an increase of about $2.40 in M-1A (demand deposits and currency), though it is clear that this multiplier is not constant. *See* MONEY SUPPLY.

Monetary Compensatory Amounts (M.C.A.s). A technique used in the European Economic Community (q.v.) as an aspect of Common Agricultural Policy (q.v.) to bridge the gap between green rates and real rates in respect of agricultural produce crossing national frontiers; monetary compensatory amounts may be positive or negative. If a real currency increases in value, the national government may wish to keep its farm prices stable; in this instance a positive M.C.A. is imposed. If a real currency falls and the green rate is to be kept steady, a negative M.C.A. is applied.

Monetary Control Act 1981 (U.S.). *See* DEPOSITORY INSTITUTIONS DEREGULATION AND MONETARY CONTROL ACT 1981.

Monetary multiplier. A number giving the expected change in income, per unit change in the money supply (q.v.).

Monetary policy. The use of changes in the money supply and the cost and availability of credit, to serve national economic goals.

In the United States, monetary policy is controlled by the Federal Reserve System (q.v.) (through changes in the stock of money, in interest and discount rates, and through control of the banking system); while fiscal policy (q.v.) is under the control of Congress (through the regulation of tax rates and government spending). America's monetary policy is essentially implemented by the open-market committee; the purchase of bonds from the 'open-market' has been the basic tool of monetary control.

Monetary rule. A rule advocated by members of the Monetarist School (q.v.) that governments should allow the money supply to grow at a constant rate which permits the growth of real output, but is not so excessive as to generate inflation.

Monetary sector. Introduced by the Bank of England (q.v.) in November, 1981, in place of the previously defined 'banking sector' (q.v.), a category of institutions made up of all recognised banks, including discount houses and licensed deposit-taking institutions, the trustee savings banks, the National Girobank, the Banking Department of the Bank of England, and certain institutions in the Channel Islands and the Isle of Man. The effect of the change of definition was to add about 10 per cent to sterling M3 (q.v.) largely attributable to the trustee savings banks. Each of the 96 banks in the monetary sector has to keep $\frac{1}{2}$ per cent of its eligible liabilities in a non-interest-bearing account at the Bank of England (q.v.). This new cash ratio replaced the two requirements hitherto placed on the clearing banks alone—a cash ratio of $1\frac{1}{2}$ per cent and a reserve asset ratio (q.v.) of 10 per cent.

Money. Any generally accepted medium of exchange; something that will be accepted by most people in exchange for goods and services and for the payment of debts, e.g. bank notes, coin and bank deposits. In some societies stones, shells, tobacco and feathers have been generally accepted. Gold, silver and copper have been popular as they do not deteriorate with time or wear out quickly; they have a high value per unit of weight and are divisible into fairly small units. Money confers complete liquidity (q.v.) on its holder. *See* MONEY, FUNCTIONS OF; MONEY SUPPLY.

Money at call and short notice. Day-to-day loans to the money market (q.v.) which earn relatively low rates of interest and may be called in at short notice.

Money, functions of. The ways in which money serves as: (a) a medium of exchange, permitting the separation of exchange into the two distinct acts of buying and selling; (b) a measure of value, in serving as a unit in terms of which the relative values of different commodities and services can be expressed; (c) a standard for deferred payments, permitting the calculation of payments due at some future date; and (d) as a store of value, permitting saving. This last function is seriously impaired in conditions of severe inflation (q.v.); in this context the value of money is perishable

Furthermore, many investors have come to regard currencies not as a medium of exchange but as commodities whose worth depends on the expectation of their resale value rather than any underlying economic trend.

Money funds. Schemes which pool monies for investment in the wholesale and other short-term money markets and thus can offer a higher rate of interest than conventional deposit accounts. There are two types of scheme. The first is operated by a deposit taking institution which accepts monies in its own name so that they are a liability of the company. The second type of scheme is operated by a managing institution which accepts monies under a trust agreement and holds them outside its own balance sheet. In the United Kingdom, these off-balance sheet money funds customarily take the form of a unit trust (q.v.) in which investors participate in a common fund.

Money illusion. An illusion sometimes created that changes in money income represent a change in real income, although the changes may merely reflect changes in the cost of living and the purchasing power of the currency; an atmosphere of prosperity may surround a rising personal income and encourage the purchase of luxuries, although in reality aggregate purchasing power in the market may not have changed at all, the costs of luxuries and necessities rising pro rata. Newspaper reports may sometimes make comparisons of money income or revenue between periods to illustrate or imply massive growth, e.g. 'the income from tourism has doubled in the last 5 years'; measured in terms of real income taking full account of changes in the cost of living, income from tourism may have increased somewhat, or even significantly, but not by 100 per cent, while an actual decline cannot be precluded.

Money market. A national market comprising institutions and arrangements through which the demand for, and the supply of, short-term funds are brought together. These funds are usually short-term financial assets which are close substitutes for money and known as money market instruments; they can be quickly converted into money without the risk of undue losses. Only prime quality borrowers such as government and government agencies, large commercial banks and other financial institutions, and high-rated non-financial corporations have ready access to the money market as a source of funds. Money markets are located in major centres such as New York and London (the largest), Paris and Tokyo. Dealers are in constant touch with each other and with major borrowers and investors, though trading takes place mainly by telephone and telex. Arbitrage (q.v.) tends to keep prices uniform.

Money market fund (U.S.). A mutual fund whose investments are in high-yield money market instruments such as federal securities, certificates of deposit, and commercial paper. Its intent is to make such instruments, normally purchased in large denominations by institutions available indirectly to individuals.

Money market instruments. Short-term financial assets with minimum money and credit risk; close substitutes for money. Short-term assets are generally those maturing in 1 year, or less. Risk is minimal since the short-term nature of money market instruments limits the volatility of their prices when interest rates change. Some banks are large-scale dealers in money market instruments, e.g. the Federal Reserve System (q.v.) and the Bank of England (q.v.) in their capacity of conducting monetary policy. While differing from country to country, financial instruments typically include treasury bills, certificates of deposit, commercial paper, bankers' acceptances, federal funds, and inter-bank deposits.

Money market mutual funds. An avenue for small savers in America to gain access to the major money markets; the funds gather small savings and invest these in lumps in the large money markets, by-passing most American restrictions that limit the rate of interest available to small savers on short-term deposits.

Money market trust. *See* UNIT TRUST.

Money supply. A supply of purchasing power comprising several streams. In Britain, definitions of the money stock vary with the degree of liquidity, starting with the most liquid:

M0 (M-nought) = The monetary liabilities of the monetary authorities; it is made up of notes and coin and the deposits which the banks voluntarily keep at the Bank of England (q.v.) (as distinct from statutory cash ratio deposits). It is regarded as the monetary base (q.v.).

M1 = Notes and coins in circulation, plus sterling current accounts held by the British private sector.

M2 = M1 plus deposit accounts with the deposit banks and discount houses; M2 has ceased to be used in official U.K. money statistics. Sterling M3 = M1, plus sterling deposit accounts held by all British residents.

M3 = Sterling M3, plus bank deposits in foreign currencies held by British residents.

PSL1 (private sector liquidity) = the private sector's share of sterling M3 (which is nearly all of Sterling M3), plus the private sector's holdings of other money-market instruments (e.g. treasury bills, deposits with local authorities), plus certificates of tax deposit (which companies buy to set aside for future tax liabilities).

PSL2 = the first two components of PSL1, plus the private sector's savings, deposits and securities (e.g. in building societies and trustee savings banks), plus certificates of tax deposits (as in PSL1, but excluding building societies' holdings of certificates of tax deposits).

Four measures of the United States money stock are prepared on a regular basis:

M-1A comprising private demand deposits in commercial banks and currency in circulation (excluding deposits due to foreign commercial banks and official institutions).

M-1B M-1A plus other check account deposits (i.e. negotiable-order-of-withdrawal accounts, accounts subject to automatic transfer service, credit union share draft balances, and demand deposits at mutual savings banks).

M-2 M-1B plus savings and small denomination time deposits at all depository institutions, shares in money market mutual funds, overnight repurchase agreements issued by commercial banks, and overnight Eurodollar deposits held by U.S. residents at Caribbean branches of U.S. banks.

M-3 M-2 plus large time deposits at all depository institutions and term repurchase agreements issued by commercial banks and savings and loan associations.

In recent years, great attention has been given in economic analysis and monetary policy to the effect of money supply on overall economic activity. These measures are provided by the Federal Reserve Board and published in the *Federal Reserve Bulletin*.

Money transmission. All the ways by which the ownership of money may be transferred from one person to another in the course of making payments. After cash, the most common form of payment in Britain and the United States is the cheque. In the United States some 48 billion cheques were written in 1982. In several European countries, the role of the cheque has been taken over by 'giro' systems run by banks or post offices. Giros allow account holders to transfer money between themselves by means of written paper instructions. Giro systems dominate in West Germany, Holland, Sweden and Switzerland. Beside the cheque and giro, standing orders on banks may be used for making regular payments. Direct debiting of regular but variable amounts has also come into vogue. To people on the move, travellers' cheques are of considerable use; American Express is by far the largest in this business. Plastic cards have come into widespread use also for making payments, obtaining credit, making debits, and guaranteeing cheques. It was said in 1981 that the average American family had 2.0 children and 7.3 plastic cards.

Monopolies and Mergers Commission. In Britain, a Commission first set up in 1949 as the Monopolies and Restrictive Practices Commission under an Act of the previous year. It was reconstituted in 1956 as the Monopolies Commission under the Restrictive Trade Practices Act of that year. The Commission consisted initially of not less than 4 nor more than 10 persons appointed by the President of the Board of Trade. It is an independent statutory body, with its own officers and staff, whose function is to inquire into the existence and effect on the public interest of monopolies in the supply, processing and export of goods, and of certain restrictive practices not dealt with by the Restrictive Practices Court (q.v.) which is a separate body. For the purposes of the Commission, the term 'monopoly' was defined as a condition where one supplier or a group of interconnected bodies corporate, or a number of concerns which act together in such a way as to restrict competition, control at least one-third of the supply of specific goods, either in the United Kingdom as a whole, or in some specified area of the United Kingdom. The Commission's recommendations led to the abandonment of various types of restrictive practices in the industries surveyed usually after agreement between the Board of Trade and the industry concerned without resort to powers of compulsion. The Monopolies and Mergers Act 1965 strengthened and extended the legislation on monopolies. It reorganised and enlarged the Monopolies Commission; provided for the investigation of services as well as goods and of proposed or recently completed mergers; made special provision for newspaper mergers; and strengthened the ability of the Government to take action on the basis of Monopolies Commission reports to prohibit mergers and break up undesirable monopolies and mergers. The functions of the Commission now derive from the Fair Trading Act 1973 (q.v.) and the Competition Act 1980 (q.v.). Broadly these are to investigate and report on various aspects of competition in commerce and industry—monopolistic and oligopolistic market structures, mergers, particular practices which may restrict competition, and the efficiency of public bodies—and to recommend remedial action in the event of findings against the public interest.

Monopolistic competition. A market situation in which competition exists between each of two or more (perhaps numerous) sellers whose products are close, but not perfect, substitutes for one another. Products are differentiated by means of distinctive brand names, variations in preparation and presentation, and by skilful advertising. Monopolistic competition is descriptive of imperfect competition (q.v.) in general, and includes oligopoly (q.v.). Edward H. Chamberlin (1899–1967) introduced the term in his *Theory of Monopolistic Competition* (1933). Chamberlin recognised that to many the very term 'monopolistic competition' would seem self-contradictory. He argued that, adopting his definitions, neither element excluded the other. His view was that once a product became differentiated, each particular firm had an absolute monopoly of its own special brand. However, there could still be many suppliers of similar but not homogeneous products. A great number of firms producing close substitutes presented a market situation of monopolistic competition.

Monopoly. A market structure (q.v.) with a single seller of a commodity or service dealing with a large number of buyers; the seller has complete control over the quantities of goods offered for sale and the price at which the goods are sold; further, the goods have no close substitutes and entry to the industry may present formidable obstacles. The monopolist seeks to maximise profits, which may involve higher prices and more limited supplies than a competitive or ologopolistic situation would permit. *See* OLIGOPOLY.

Monopoly, discriminating. A monopoly which charges different prices to different customers for the same commodity. By breaking up the market into various parts in this way, and by charging in each part of the market that price which will maximise profits, the monopolist may hope to increase his total profit. Much depends, of course, on the extent to which a market may be effectively broken up. The basic principle is one of equating marginal revenue with marginal cost in each of the markets or sub-markets.

Monopoly profit. Profit greater than normal profit (q.v.).

Monopsony. A single buyer in the market; a buyer's monopoly. For example, a nationalised industry may be the sole or main purchaser of certain classes of equipment. In 1975, 87 per cent of the output of the four main suppliers of post office equipment in Britain went to the Post Office. The Central Electricity Generating Board is virtually the sole purchaser of larger electricity generating equipment and nuclear power plant.

Moonlight economy. *See* CASH ECONOMY.

Moonlighting. The practice of having a second full or part-time job.

Moral suasion. One of the instruments used by the Bank of England in controlling the activities of the commercial banks (q.v.); it comprises the making of recommendations to the commercial banks who may prefer to act on these rather than wait for action to be forced on them through the use of open-market operations (q.v.) or the issue of a directive. *See* JAWBONE (U.S.); TREASURY DIRECTIVE.

Mortgage. The conveyance of property by a debtor (mortgagor) to a creditor (mortgagee) as security for a debt, with a condition that the property shall be reconveyed on payment of the debt.

Mortgage-backed housing bonds. Or secondary mortgage securities, an arrangement to increase the amount of funds available to financial institutions for home-finance by tapping funds held by large institutions who seek long-term secure investments; the usual procedure is for an official agency backed by government and banks to market housing bonds backed by mortgages over real estate. The housing bonds are negotiable fixed interest investments. In effect the agency acts as a middleman selling securities to investors while passing the proceeds back to mortgagees.

Mortgage banks. Banks which specialise in borrowing short-term deposits to make longer-term loans for house purchase. While deposits may be for as little as 7 days, mortgages may run for up to 30 years.

Mortgage bonds. Similar to bonds issued by industrial corporations, carrying a specified maturity date and rate of interest; the essential difference is that they are issued for buying houses rather than factories. Mortgage banks (q.v.) arrange the issue, and then lend the money raised to house buyers.

Mortgage insurance. Insurance cover against default on mortgage repayments to building societies, banks, credit unions, pension funds, and private lenders. *See* INSURANCE.

Mortgage loans. Loans for which specific assets in land and buildings are used as security. They are usually for at least 20 years and exceptionally for as long as 35 years. About 75 per cent of the lender's independent valuation of the property or land is the maximum usually lent.

Mortgage protection schemes. Schemes guaranteeing mortgage repayments if a home-builder is retrenched; in Australia, towards the end of 1982, two major home builders announced that under an insurance agreement with Lloyds of London wage-earners who were breadwinners in their homes bought after that time would automatically have mortgage repayments made up for them if they were retrenched or made redundant; repayments would be covered for up to 2 years.

Multilateral Development Banks (M.D.B.s). Banks providing financial assistance across a broad spectrum of countries. Four major multilateral banks are the World Bank (q.v.), the Inter-American Development Bank (I.D.B.), the Asian Development Bank (A.D.B.) (q.v.), and the African Development Bank (A.D.B.) (q.v.). In the first two, the United States is by far the largest shareholder. Furthermore, the World Bank does more than three-quarters of all M.D.B. lending.

Multinational corporation. A corporation or company operating in a number of countries with production or service facilities outside the country of its origin; the principal decisions of the company are taken in a global context. Also called international companies.

The United States has gradually lost some of its dominance of multinational business; its share of international investment in new and existing companies fell from 52 per cent to 43 per cent between 1960 and 1980. Over the same period, Britain's share shrank from 17 per cent to 12 per cent. Japanese investment increased from 1 per cent to 7 per cent; West German investment from 1 per cent to 8 per cent; and Swiss investment from 3 per cent to 7 per cent.

Multiplier. A ratio indicating the effect on total employment or on total income of a specified amount of a real capital investment. This important economic concept shows how fluctuations in the amount of investment (q.v.), although small in relation to the national income, are capable of generating fluctuations of much greater magnitude in total employment and income; in other words, putting one man out of employment due to a cutting back of investment leads to more than one man's loss of employment and earnings. The multiplier applies equally to the expansion of employment as well as to contraction. In Britain in 1938, it is thought that the multiplier was about two, i.e. the setting to work of one of those who were then unemployed would have led to an average employment and wages for one other man. Modern estimates are closer to 1.5.

The reasons for this amplification are as follows. Let us visualise a situation in which the country's resources are not fully utilised. The Government, eager to provide useful work and to tackle social problems, launches a large-scale slum clearance and re-housing programme. To carry out this task it is necessary to employ more workers in the building industry and in all the ancillary industries, e.g. brickmaking, cement manufacture, prefabrication, etc. All this activity is covered by the amount of initial investment which covers the cost of labour and all the materials required. Incomes of all kinds will increase by the amount of the additional investment. As earnings increase so will expenditure (although not by as much). The spending of those who have benefited directly will create secondary employment in other industries—food, clothing, entertainment, etc. The recipients in these industries will, in turn, have more to spend, creating tertiary employment. The increase in income to which the original investment gave rise will be multiplied as prosperity spreads.

The concept of the 'multiplier' was first introduced into economic theory by Richard F. Kahn in an article 'The Relation of Home Investment to Unemployment' (*Economic Journal*, June, 1931). He laid down general principles by which to estimate the actual quantitative relationship between an increment of net investment and the increment of aggregate employment which will be associated with it. The concept was incorporated into John Maynard Keynes' *General Theory of Employment, Interest and Money*. As the multiplier is the ratio between employment or income and investment, it is thus the reciprocal of the ratio of savings to income, i.e. the reciprocal of the marginal propensity to save.

The concept of the multiplier is often used to refer only to the multiplier effects of an increase in investment; in fact the concept is of general application and applies just as well to government expenditure and taxation, and to changes in export demand. It remains a crucial concept in Keynesian economics.

Municipal bonds. Bonds issued by a state, county, city, or town. *See* STATE AND LOCAL GOVERNMENT BONDS.

Mutual funds and trusts. Investment-type financial institutions. Mutual funds own securities and issue shares of stock the value of which is dependent upon the value of the securities owned by the mutual fund. Traditionally, mutual funds have been committed to common stock or bonds, in varying proportions. In more recent years, it has become possible for mutual funds to hold tax-exempt securities, while some have been specially formed to hold money-market securities of a short-term nature. Trusts include both personal trusts and investment-trusts; many shopping centres and other types of investment have used a trust form, with investors owning beneficial interests in the trust.

N

Naked options. A discouraged practice in which operators sell options on shares and securities they do not possess. *See* OPTION TRADING; SHARE OPTIONS.

Name day. *See* TICKET OR NAME DAY.

National Association of Securities Dealers Automated Quotation System (N.A.S.D.A.Q.). An automated quotation system through which the shares of over 4,000 companies are traded in the United States over-the-counter market (q.v.). It provides the world's largest stock market after the New York and Tokyo stock exchanges.

National Association of Securities Dealers Inc. A body which effectively runs the official United States over-the-counter securities markets, and operates N.A.S.D.A.Q., the National Association of Securities Dealers Automatic Quotation System (q.v.). It is a non-profit, self-regulatory organisation; it sets standards for the listing of securities and for the broker-dealers who make markets in them, providing surveillance of trading activities. In 1984, some 4,000 broker-dealer firms belonged to the Association; while more than 250,000 registered representatives were subject to N.A.S.D. regulations. Some 4,700 securities were traded. It was the second largest stock market in the United States, and the third in the World (after the Tokyo stock exchange). The N.A.S.D. was established under the authority granted by the 1938 Maloney Act amendments to the Securities Exchange Act 1934.

National Association of Securities Dealers and Investment Managers (U.K.) (N.A.S.D.I.M.). A self-regulatory agency formed in 1979 recognised by the Secretary of State for Trade and Industry; members of N.A.S.D.I.M. are exempted from the need to become individually licensed dealers in securities under the supervision of the Department of Trade and Industry (q.v.). N.A.S.D.I.M. has a seat on the Council for the Securities Industry. N.A.S.D.I.M. has the power to create and administer its own rules and to discipline its members. It was originally known as the Association of Licensed Dealers in Securities.

National Board for Prices and Incomes (U.K.). A Board set up by the Government in 1965 to keep prices and incomes under review. Its terms of reference were outlined in the White Paper *Prices and Incomes Policy* (Cmnd. 2639). The Board comprised an independent chairman, a number of independent members, a businessman and a trade unionist. The Board was not a statutory body. Persuasion and pressure of public opinion were relied upon to ensure that the findings and recommendations of the new body were accepted by the parties concerned. The Prices and Incomes Act 1967 could be invoked to delay increases in prices and incomes for up to several months. The Board was wound-up in November, 1970.

National Bus Company (U.K.). An authority set up under the Transport Act, 1968, which assumed responsibility for the bus interests of the Transport Holding Company in England and Wales, taking over most of the main network of local bus services outside the municipalities. The Company operates through subsidiary companies. The national bus company operates some 15,000 buses and coaches. It was proposed in 1984 to re-organise these into separate companies.

National Coal Board (U.K.). A body created by the Coal Mines Nationalisation Act of 1946 to take control of most of the coal mines in England, Wales, and Scotland. The Board's statutory duty is to develop the industry efficiently and provide coal in such quantities and at such prices as to further the public interest. By the end of 1982 there were 198 N.C.B. collieries in operation with a total annual output of 127 million tonnes. The industry remained the largest in Western

Europe and one of the world's most technologically advanced.

National Companies and Securities Commission, Australian. A statutory authority which is responsible to the Australian Ministerial Council for Companies and Securities for the development of policy and the uniform administration of laws relating to companies and the regulation of the securities industry.

National debt. The debts of the British Government, accumulated largely through borrowing from the British people over many years. The Debt comprises:

(a) Funded Debt—consols, War loans, etc., which have no contractual repayment date;

(b) Unfunded Debt—floating debt (mainly short-term borrowing against Treasury bills); other internal debts such as 'dated' securities, National Savings Certificates, Defence Bonds, Premium Bonds, National Development Bonds, etc.; and external debt.

The National Debt rose from £650 million in 1914 to £7,435 million in 1918. From £7,131 million in 1939 it rose to £23,647 million in 1946. In 1973 it was £36,910 million of which £1,615 million was repayable in currencies other than sterling, mainly to the United States and Canadian Governments. Another £3,727 million was short-term debt mainly in the form of 91-day Treasury bills; the remainder comprised long-term loans including a variety of stocks, bonds, loans and certificates carrying fixed rates of interest and with fixed or indeterminate dates of repayment.

At the end of March, 1982, the national debt amounted to some £118,000 million, of which £2,000 million was in currencies other than sterling. Of the £116,000 million sterling debt some £91,000 million consisted of gilt-edged stock; the remainder was made up mainly of national savings certificates, certificates of tax deposits, Treasury bills, and ways and means advances.

Until 1968, the national debt was transacted through the Consolidated Fund, but it now appears in the accounts of the National Loans Fund (q.v.).

In the United States, at the end of 1979, the national debt was about $650 billion, or over $3,000 for every person in the United States.

National Economic Development Council ('NEDDY'). A Council set up by the Government in 1961 with the following objects:

(a) to examine the economic performance of the nation with particular concern for plans for the future in both the private and public sectors of industry;

(b) to consider together what are the obstacles to quicker growth, what can be done to improve efficiency and whether the best use is being made of our resources;

(c) to seek agreement upon ways of improving economic performance, competitive power and efficiency; in other words, to increase the rate of sound growth.

The Council is responsible for indicative planning only, responsibility for final decisions on matters of national policy remaining with the Government.

In 1975, some 37 working parties covering 60 per cent of British manufacturing industry were set up to report on the supply constraints in their own particular industrial sectors. Their reports contained over 300 recommendations for action. *See* ECONOMIC DEVELOPMENT COMMITTEES.

National economic goals. Generally, a high and stable level of employment, a satisfactory growth rate, reasonable price stability, and equilibrium in the international balance of payments. In the early 1980s, the American economy suffered a serious malfunction in respect of achieving these objectives.

National Economic Summit (Aust.). A summit meeting convened by the Hawke Labour Government in April, 1983, comprising representatives of the trade unions, employers, farmers, self-employed professions, the six state governments, the northern territory, and the Federal Government; the purpose of the meeting was to review the deepening recession in Australia and examine ways-and-means of reversing the adverse trend in unemployment. The bringing together of traditional adversaries was a signal achievement, and led to a better understanding of national economic problems and the prospects of achieving improvements for all sections of the community through a national strategy based on consensus.

National Enterprise Board (U.K.). A statutory board created by the Industry Act 1975 to generally promote enterprise and employment, particularly in the assisted areas. The Act requires the Board to seek government approval before acquiring a shareholding in a company of 30 per cent or more, or costing over £10 million; where the Board's investment is unwelcome government approval must be sought where the shareholding will exceed

10 per cent. The Board may be directed to assist ailing industries. It has controlled the financial targets, budgets and cash requirements of Rolls-Royce, British Leyland and Alfred Herbert the machine-tool manufacturers.

National Freight Corporation (U.K.). Originally a publicly-owned authority, established under the Transport Act 1968, responsible for all freight services provided by the public sector of the transport industry which originated by road. Operating from 1 January 1969, the Corporation had the duty of providing integrated road and rail freight services in Great Britain, using road and rail transport to the best advantage. The Corporation took over from British Rail commercial responsibility for the freightliner service, and all the road haulage and shipping activities formerly undertaken by the Transport Holding Company. The National Freight Corporation was sold to its employees, managers, and bankers, for just over £50 million in 1981.

National Futures Association (N.F.A.). Created in 1982, an industry self-regulating agency with about 1,000 members; it is based in Chicago. While the Commodity Futures Trading Commission (C.F.T.C.) (q.v.) retains regulation of the exchanges, floor traders, floor brokers, registered representatives of brokerage houses, and oversees the National Futures Association itself, nevertheless the N.F.A. has superseded the C.F.T.C. in the auditing of brokerage firms, and the registration and surveillance of brokerage firms, commodity pool operators, commodity trading advisers, and introducing brokers affiliated with commodity brokerage firms.

National Incomes Policy (U.K.). A policy of restraint in relation to increases in personal incomes with the object of slowing down inflationary trends. The object is to keep increases in personal incomes broadly in line with increases in productivity in industry. Restraint in wage claims has been called for by the British Government several times since the Second World War. In 1948, the Government issued a White Paper on Personal Incomes, Costs and Prices which had a limited effect in checking wage increases, partly due to some support elicited from the Trades Union Congress and partly due to increased resistance by some employers to wage demands. The effect was, however, short-lived. A later appeal by Mr. Macmillan in 1956 elicited little response. In the 1960s Mr. Selwyn Lloyd introduced a 'guiding light' for permissible movements in incomes of about 2½ per cent per annum, being broadly in accord with increases in productivity at that time. His appeal was pushed with energy, but soon crumbled in the face of economic forces.

In 1965, a new 'norm' for increases in all money incomes was established, this being an annual average increase of 3–3½ per cent; the implication being that if some got more, others would get less. Subsequently a ceiling of 3½ per cent per annum was adopted, not as a 'norm' but as an 'absolute maximum'. However, an acceptable productivity agreement might permit a pay increase above the maximum. In 1971, the Confederation of British Industry (q.v.) asked its member firms to forgo price increases where possible and to limit unavoidable increases to a maximum of 5 per cent in the 12-month period to 31 July 1972. A commitment was obtained from 176 large member companies and from over 700 smaller ones; the nationalised industries gave a similar undertaking.

The 'Social Contract' was an agreement reached between the trade unions and the British Labour Party in 1973 in respect of a voluntary incomes policy. Labour promised social and industrial policies sought by the unions, such as higher pensions and more taxes on the rich, while the unions promised to moderate their wage claims according to certain guidelines. The main objective of wage deals was to ensure that real incomes were maintained, while all major rises were to be kept 12 months apart. Productivity deals and pay structure reforms, together with deals for the lower-paid workers, were excluded from the agreement. However, the guidelines were not observed and the contract failed. Wages rose by 32 per cent, an all-time record. Agreement was reached in mid-summer 1975 between the British Government and the Trades Union Congress (q.v.) on an anti-inflation policy which was far more specific and simple than the previous 'Social Contract'. Some changes were made in controls on prices and profit margins, but the more important aspect was a restriction on incomes, which the previous 'Social Contract' policy had failed to achieve.

For the year 1978–79, the Government announced a norm for increases of 5 per cent; the policy collapsed in the face of a revolt by the unions. Mrs. Shirley Williams, Minister responsible for prices and consumer protection 1974–76 said later that this 'winter of discontent' effectively destroyed the Labour Government and brought Mrs. Thatcher to power.

National Insurance Scheme (U.K.). Britain's social security system based on contributions by employers, employees, and the self-employed, and calculated as a percentage of annual earnings up to a ceiling (in 1981, £10,400 a year). National insurance charges raised about 15 per cent of all current revenue in 1981–82.

In 1983, employers paid approximately 12 per cent on earnings for most employees, while most employees paid 9 per cent on earnings; there was a reduced rate contribution for some married women and widows. Special contributions were retained for the self-employed.

National Investment and Loans Office (U.K.). Set up in 1980 as a result of a merger of the Public Works Loan Board and the National Debt Office. *See* NATIONAL LOANS FUND.

National Labour Relations Act 1935 or Wagner Act. United States legislation which guaranteed employees the right to organise, to form labour unions, and to bargain collectively with management.

National Loans Fund. A British Government account opened in 1968 to provide for the domestic lending of the Government and all the transactions relating to the national debt (q.v.). Payments from the Fund include the interest and expenses of the national debt; any deficit on the Consolidated Fund (q.v.); and loans to the nationalised industries and public corporations, local authorities, and the private sector. The receipts of the fund include interest on loans; profits of the Issue Department of the Bank of England (q.v.); interest service transfer from the Consolidated Fund and borrowings.

National Research and Development Corporation (N.R.D.C.). Established in 1949 by the then president of the British Board of Trade, Mr. Harold Wilson; initially N.R.D.C. had the right of first refusal on virtually all inventions emerging from government-financed laboratories, and was able to direct funds into joint ventures for new technology. Commercially, the body was not too successful. In 1981, it was merged with the National Enterprise Board (q.v.).

National Savings Bank. The network of over 20,000 post offices in Britain through which depositors may hold savings accounts; in 1982, there were about 20 million accounts.

National Savings Income Bonds. Introduced in Britain in 1982 by the Department of National Savings, a bond designed to provide savers with a regular monthly income.

National Savings Securities. Non-marketable U.K. government securities sold to the personal sector. These include national savings certificates, national savings income bonds, premium savings bonds, and Save-As-You-Earn contracts. These schemes represent a major source of funds for financing the public sector borrowing requirement (q.v.).

National Savings Stock Register. A register maintained by the British national savings department at a separate bonds and stock office; the bonds and stock office offers a service for the purchase and sale of British government stock (q.v.) by post as an alternative to buying through a stockbroker (q.v.).

National Securities Trading System (N.S.T.S.). Sponsored by the Cincinnati Stock Exchange in 1978, a fully automated, electronic trading system which links exchanges and 'upstairs' market makers in physically dispersed locations. *See* INTERMARKET TRADING SYSTEM.

Nationalisation. State ownership and control of any of the means of production, distribution or exchange. Nationalisation was for many years an important item in the policies of the British Labour Party and the objective of the common ownership of the means of production distribution and exchange remains enshrined in Clause Four of the Party's Constitution. In practice, the Party has limited its aims to the nationalisation of certain basic industries—coal, gas, electricity, transport, iron and steel, and water. The Conservative Party has also engaged in limited schemes of national ownership. These concerns falling within state ownership in Britain have included the:

(a) Post Office (1657);
(b) Central Electricity Board (1926);
(c) British Broadcasting Corporation (1927);
(d) London Passenger Transport Board (1933);
(e) British Sugar Beet Corporation (1937);
(f) British Overseas Airways Corporation and British European Airways (1939 and 1946 respectively), later merged to form British Airways;
(g) Bank of England (1946);
(h) Coal Mining Industry (1947);
(i) Cable and Wireless (1947) (now denationalised);
(j) Inland Transport (1948);
(k) Electricity Supply Industry (1948);
(l) Gas Industry (1949);
(m) Iron and Steel Industry (1951 and 1967);
(n) Rolls-Royce Ltd. (1971);
(o) British Nuclear Fuels Ltd. (1971);

(p) Radiochemical Centre Ltd. (1971);
(q) British Leyland (1975);
(r) British Shipbuilders (1977).

In the mid 1980s a process of selling-off segments of nationalised industry was set in train. *See* PRIVATISATION.

The nationalised industries have been used at various times to 'defeat inflation' by keeping prices down; to help with government funding by restraining investment; to provide an extension to the social services in sustaining uneconomic activity; and to assist British industry by purchasing in the home market rather than taking a 'best buy' from overseas.

Natural protection. Protection derived without special measures from bulky or non-durable products, implying relatively high transport costs and the need to be physically close to the market; in consequence it is costly for potential competitors to enter that market with supplies from another region.

Natural rate of unemployment. A level of unemployment in a country considered 'normal' as it embraces those changing jobs, including seasonal workers, and allows for a certain amount of restructuring of industries. In 1982, it was argued that the natural rate of unemployment in the United States had risen from the traditional 4 per cent to 6.5 per cent because of the greater number of women and young people in the labour force; the latter were considered more likely to move into and out of jobs. In October, 1982, 10.4 per cent, or nearly 12 million Americans were out of work, apart from those too discouraged to look for it.

Near money. Assets readily convertible into money (q.v.), e.g. deposit accounts, deposits with savings banks and building societies, and certain short-term government securities. In the United States of America 'near money' comprises time and savings deposits in commercial banks, deposits at mutual savings banks, savings and loan shares, U.S. Savings Bonds and U.S. Securities due in less than 1 year.

Nearby month. The nearest active trading month of a financial or commodity futures market.

Negative gearing. A situation which arises when, for example, the interest payments due on the borrowing for an investment exceed the net revenue from the investment. Under some taxation systems, the loss may attract tax relief against other income.

Negative income tax. A government payment to individuals whose income falls below prescribed levels; the opposite of an income tax. *See* INCOME TAX, PROGRESSIVE.

Negative real growth. A contraction in the value of economic activity, taking inflation into account.

Negative real interest rate. An interest rate which is lower than the rate of inflation, e.g. when money is lent at a return of say 7 per cent per annum while money is losing value at the rate of 15 per cent per annum. Despite the interest earned the lender is worse off in real terms at the end of each year than at the beginning. In this situation, characteristic of Britain in the mid 1970s, borrowers are favoured at the expense of lenders.

Negotiable. With reference to a security, the ability to transfer title by delivery.

Negotiable Certificates of Deposit (N.C.D.). Documents or certificates providing evidence of money on deposit at interest in a commercial bank in amounts in excess of $100,000; they are negotiable and payable to the bearer, and may be sold by an individual if funds are desired before maturity of the certificate. The secondary market for negotiable certificates which developed in Wall Street is now nationwide. However, many banks still issue non-negotiable certificates.

Negotiable instrument. A claim, the title to which passes by delivery. Examples of such claims are bills of exchange, cheques, promissory notes, share warrants, dividend warrants, and debentures payable to bearer. Transfer is by delivery only. A bill of exchange (q.v.) payable to a certain person 'only' is not a negotiable instrument. Neither is a cheque with 'not negotiable' written on it. Bills of lading, dock warrants, share certificates and postal orders are not negotiable. A creditor is not bound to take a negotiable instrument in payment of a debt; he may insist on payment in legal tender (q.v.).

Negotiable Order of Withdrawal (N.O.W.). Introduced into the United States in 1981, accounts which transfer money from a time deposit to a demand deposit automatically as and when needed; the effect is similar to offering interest on demand deposits.

Negotiable Time Certificates of Deposit (N.T.C.D.). Short-term notes issued to the money market (q.v.) by large commercial banks for the purposes of borrowing when additional funds are required by the banks for lending purposes of their own. Denominations are for $100,000 or more, with maturities typically ranging from 60–120 days.

Neo-classical economics. Descriptive of economic science as it evolved from the work of the classical school (q.v.) during the last quarter of the 19th century; the addition of marginal analysis by Austrian, British, and American economists led eventually to the substitution of the new term. Neo-classical economics has undergone much refinement since then. *See* SCHOOLS OF ECONOMICS.

Neo-classical equilibrium. A concept of neo-classical economics (q.v.) in which the equilibrium between production and purchasing power was established at a level where all willing and useful workers were employed. Thus, if workers were unemployed, wages would fall in consequence of the competition for jobs; it would then be profitable for producers to hire more men. It was conceded that as a consequence of lower wages, demand and prices would also fall; however, as wages did not represent the whole of production costs they would fall further. The fall in real wages would be the decisive factor in expanding employment; expansion would continue until all were employed. The theory depended upon an assumption that wages would fall faster than demand and prices (which may not happen) and that trade unions would be prepared to accept lower money-wages for their members (an unlikely and rare event).

Neo-classical model. A view of the economy held in whole or substantial part by the neo-classical economists; the essentials of the system appeared to be as follows. Individuals use income in the main derived from their own productive activities in the purchase of various goods and services available in the market; their tendency is to so distribute their income that the satisfaction derived from the last unit of expenditure for any particular purposes is equal to that derived from expenditure for any other purpose. At this point satisfaction (and occasionally, happiness) is maximised. The patterns of expenditure convey important messages to producers.

The producer is motivated by the prospect of profit; this, over an unspecified period of time, he seeks to maximise. In response to price change signals, producers expand or contract production, and enter or leave markets. Production is deemed to be at the command of the consumer. Changes in the technical conditions of production which reduce costs will tend to increase profits; production will be increased and prices will fall. The benefits of reduced costs of production flow to the consumer. The shift in prices, influences the conduct of consumers.

Basic to the neo-classical model was a view that the economy will always tend towards an equilibrium at which resources, including the workforce, will be fully employed or very nearly so. A combination of fiscal and monetary policies would ensure a comparative stability of prices. Any tendency towards inflation could be curbed by curtailing demand. *See* NEO-CLASSICAL EQUILIBRIUM.

Neo-Marxian School. *See* CAMBRIDGE SCHOOL.

Neo-Ricardian School. *See* CAMBRIDGE SCHOOL.

New Cambridge School. A school of economists associated with certain members of the Cambridge Economic Policy Group at the Department of Applied Economics, University of Cambridge. Since the 1970s, the school has made a number of distinct analytical contributions concerned with the long-run behaviour of the economy. *See* CAMBRIDGE SCHOOL; SCHOOLS OF ECONOMICS.

New Classical School. A school of economics associated with the names of Lucas, Sargent, and Minford. The school believes that (1) expectations are rational; and (2) markets clear very quickly when wages and prices are flexible, up and down. Thus, willing buyers and willing sellers strike bargains which satisfy reasonably all parties. Involuntary unemployment can happen only when wages are inflexible, or are fixed at infrequent intervals with workers being temporarily priced out of employment. In a flexible system, unemployment tends to be at its 'natural rate'; it exists because some people choose to be unemployed (on account of generous social security benefits, or while changing jobs). If the system is flexible, it is argued, governments cannot use a fiscal and/or monetary boost to increase output and employment. *See* SCHOOLS OF ECONOMICS.

'New Economic Policy'. (1) The policy introduced by Lenin into the Soviet Union shortly after the end of the First World War, temporarily restoring free markets and financial incentives in some sectors of the economy in order to stimulate more rapid reconstruction. (2) The policy introduced by the Nixon Administration in 1971, imposing an initial freeze of wages and prices, followed by various phases of wage-price controls and a number of international measures including a 10 per cent surtax on imports and the complete severing of the dollar from gold.

'New Economics'. Descriptive of the analytical and philosophical approach to economic policy-making used by the Kennedy and Johnson administrations in the 1960s. The New Economics emphasized the goal of re-attaining full employment and to move towards a full utilisation of resources. It emphasized economic growth in order to achieve full employment and potential output.

New issue. A stock or bond sold by a corporation for the first time; the proceeds may be used for new plant and equipment, for additional working capital, or to retire outstanding securities of the company.

New Keynesian School. A school of economics associated with the names of Klein, Tobin, Hicks, and Meade. In common with monetarists, its adherents believed that economies tend towards a full-employment equilibrium; however, they also believed that this may take many years to reach unless governments take steps to boost demand during a recession. It is argued that a boosting of demand and output will be effective because, in the short- as distinct from the long-term, the aggregate supply curve slopes up from left to right. Originally, the argument between Keynesians and monetarists was about the proper respective roles for monetary and fiscal policies; Keynesians favoured fiscal policies (taxes and government spending) as the correct course, while monetarists preferred monetary policy (interest rates and money supply). Most monetarists today believe that demand-management can affect output and employment only briefly, while Keynesians argue that the effects may last long enough to be worthwhile. *See* SCHOOLS OF ECONOMICS.

New Socialism. A concept advanced by Professor John Kenneth Galbraith in his *Economics and the Public Purpose* (1974) as a remedy for unequal development, unequal income, unequal and bizarre distributions of public expenditures, enviromental damage, discriminatory and ineffective stabilisation policies. He envisaged three reforms as necessary for the New Socialism: (a) the need to enhance radically the power and competence of the market system, and enhance affirmatively its development in relation to that of the planning system (q.v.) and so reduce the systematic inequality in development between the two systems; (b) redefining the purposes of the planning system to make these serve the public interest, restricting resources use in areas of overdevelopment, asserting the higher purposes of the environment, and devoting technology to public purposes; and (c) the management of the economy as one entity, instead of the present two—one that is subject to the market and one that is planned by its constituent firms.

New York Clearing House. A voluntary association of banks located in the City of New York. The Constitution of this association states as its object 'the effecting at one place of the daily exchanges between the members thereof and the settlement of the balances resulting from such exchanges, the promoting of the interests of the members, and the maintenance of conservative banking through wise and intelligent co-operation.' The New York Clearing House was formed in 1853, the first institution of its kind in the United States. There were some 57 banks in New York at that time. The amount of cheques exchanged on Tuesday, 11 October 1853, was $22.6 million. The amount for the second Tuesday in October, 1980, amounted to $192.7 billion. In April, 1970, the Clearing House Interbank Payments System (C.H.I.P.S.) was brought into operation enabling large sums of money to be transferred between member banks electronically, eliminating the use of official cheques.

New York Commodity Exchange (COMEX). Established in 1933, today the world's largest commodity futures exchange in metals, notably gold, silver, copper, and aluminium; financial futures are also traded. Established at the World Trade Centre, it has 138 member firms. In 1983, the number of contracts traded exceeded 20 million, about one-half being in gold. The COMEX Clearing Association is the Exchange's clearing house for transactions.

New York Futures Exchange (N.Y.F.E., pronounced 'knife'). A subsidiary of the New York Stock Exchange (q.v.), established in 1980; it has over 1,800 members including independent floor brokers, brokerage firms, futures commission merchants, clearing house firms and specialists. It also has 54 clearing house members. The exchange trades futures contracts based on the New York Stock Exchange composite stock index and on three sub-indices: financial, industrials and utilities.

New York Mercantile Exchange. Founded in 1872, a commodity market serving the agricultural, industrial, marketing and investment communities; some of the 400 individual members are associated with brokerage houses, others represent businesses with interests in particular commodities, while a few trade on their own behalf. The exchange is controlled by a Board of Governors. NYMEX currently conducts future trading in round white potatoes, imported lean beef, platinum, palladium, No. 2 heating oil, and No. 6 industrial fuel oil. At the World Trade Centre in New York, the exchange shares a trading floor with three other New York commodity exchanges; the Commodity Exchange Inc., the Coffee, Sugar, and Cocoa Exchange Inc., and the New York Cotton Exchange. *See* TABLE 4.

New York Stock Exchange. The principal

TABLE 4

NEW YORK MERCANTILE EXCHANGE COMMODITY SUMMARY

Commodity	Contract unit	Minimum fluctuation: Per unit quoted	Minimum fluctuation: Per contract unit	Maximum fluctuation*: Per unit quoted	Maximum fluctuation*: Per contract unit	Delivery months†
Round white potatoes	50,000 lb.	1¢ per 100 lb.	$5.00	$.50 per 100 lb.	$250	Nov., Mar., Apr., May
Imported lean beef	36,000 lb.	2¢ per 100 lb.	$7.20	$1.50 per 100 lb.	$540	Jan., Mar., May, Jul., Sep., Nov.
Platinum	50 troy oz.	10¢ per oz.	$5.00	$20.00 per oz.	$1000	All months
Palladium	100 troy oz.	5¢ per oz.	$5.00	$6.00 per oz.	$600	All months
No. 2 heating oil	42,000 gallons	$.0001 per gallon	$4.20	$.02 per gallon	$840	All months
No. 6 industrial oil	42,000 gallons	$.0001 per gallon	$4.20	$.02 per gallon	$840	All months

†Board of Governors may approve other delivery months.
*Subject to expanded limit rules and special rules governing delivery months and last trading days. See individual Exchange publications.

security market in the United States of America, whose beginnings may be traced back to 1792. Trading is conducted by brokers and specialists, each specialist firm being responsible for a certain number of stocks. Their function is to maintain an orderly market in those stocks. The trading floor itself has several trading posts for particular stocks. when the broker receives an order from his client he goes to the appropriate post. In the presence of other brokers and specialists an auction takes place at which the broker trades the stock on the best terms he can get. If the client has set price limits which the broker is unable to meet he passes the order on to the specialist for execution at the earliest moment. For this service the specialist receives brokerage commission. In 1980, there were 377 member firms of the New York Stock Exchange doing business with the public, rising from 364 in 1977.

New York Stock Exchange Stock Index. A price index that closely reflects changes in the weighted average of all the 1,500 common stocks traded on the New York Stock Exchange (q.v.).

Nil paid. A new issue of shares, usually as a result of a rights issue (q.v.) on which no payment to the company has yet been made.

Nobel Prize in Economics. First awarded in 1969, a 'prize in economics to the memory of Alfred Nobel'. The 1969 joint-award went to Jan Tinbergen of the Netherlands School of Economics in Rotterdam and Ragnar Frisck of the University of Oslo; they were cited 'for having developed and applied dynamic models for the analysis of economic processes'. Both had pioneered in econometrics and mathematical economics. The 1970 award went to Paul A. Samuelson for his many contributions in raising the level of scientific analysis in economic theory. The 1971 prize went to Simon S. Kuznets for his '. . . empirically founded interpretation of economic growth which has led to new and deepened insight into the economic and social structure and process of development'. Sir John R. Hicks and Kenneth J. Arrow shared the 1972 prize for 'erudite and fundamental theories' about economic events. The 1973 winner was Wassily Leontief from Harvard University. Leontief was described as 'the sole and unchallenged creator of the input-output technique', a method for studying specific interdependencies within an economy as well as for predicting major trends and the effects of significant events. By 1973, the technique had been used in 50 countries to study and predict economic trends. The 1974 award was shared jointly by Professor Gunnar Myrdal of Sweden and Professor Friedrich von Hayek of Austria. The award was made for their pioneering work in the theory of money and economic fluctuations and for their 'penetrating analysis of the interdependence of economic, social and institutional phenomena'. The 1975 prize was shared by Leonid V. Kantorovich of the Soviet Institute of Economic Management and Tjalling C. Koopmans of Yale University. The two men were chosen 'for their contributions to the theory of optimum allocation of resources', a matter of fundamental importance to both collective and free-enterprise economic systems.

Milton Friedman (b. 1912) won the 1976 prize for economics, being described by the Royal Swedish Academy of Sciences as a pioneer in the well-founded reaction to the earlier post-Keynesian one-sidedness. The Academy referred to 'his achievements in the fields of consumption analysis, monetary history and theory, and for his demonstration of the complexity of stabilization policy'. Friedman had revived respect for the market as an allocator of resources and promotor of economic efficiency.

The 1977 prize in economics was shared by Bertil Ohlin (b. 1899) and James Meade (b. 1907), for major treatises in international trade published in the 1930s and the 1950s. The Academy noted that 'the breadth and importance of Ohlin's and Meade's contributions have . . . not become obvious until the '60s and '70s in conjunction with the growing internationalization of the economic system'.

In 1978, Herbert A. Simon (b. 1916) received the award. Attention was drawn to his early publications on structure and decision-making within economic organisations, a relatively new area of economic research. The research demonstrated that individual executives work in discrete areas and make decisions on the basis of limited information. Their goals may be either short-term or restricted to a single aspect of corporate activity. Executives and hence corporations engage in fragmented 'satisficing' behaviour, a far cry from undistracted profit maximisation. Simon rejected the concept of the corporate firm as an omniscient, rational, profit-maximising, entrepreneurial activity; replacing this concept by one of a number of co-operating decision-makers, whose capacity for rational action is limited both by lack of knowledge about the total consequences of decisions and by personal and social ties. Individual firms strive not to maximise profits but to find acceptable solutions to acute problems; this might mean that a number of partly contradictory goals need to be reached at the same time.

In 1979, the joint winners were Sir W. Arthur Lewis (b. 1915) and Theodore W. Schultz (b. 1902), for creative and practical contributions particularly in relation to the economic policies of developing countries. *See* LEWIS MODEL.

The 1980 prize went to Lawrence Klein (b. 1920) who had spent his career teaching econometrics, mainly at the University of Pennsylvania, and building elaborate (and broadly Keynesian) forecasting models. He had played a leading part in Project Link, an attempt to integrate the forecasts of individual economies into a world-wide whole.

In 1981, the prize was won by James Tobin, a Keynesian, for work that illuminated the practical financial behaviour of investors, consumers, and corporations providing a basis for understanding how subjects actually behave when they acquire different assets and incur debts. *See* NEW KEYNESIAN SCHOOL; PORTFOLIO THEORY; Q-RATIO.

George Stigler (b. 1911) was the winner of the 1982 economics prize. A close associate of Milton Friedman at the University of Chicago, Stigler has been a free market economist. His main work has been in micro-economics: the theory of price, market operations, and how information blockages and government regulations affect markets.

In 1983, the prize was awarded to Professor Gerard Debreu for his application of mathematical theory to economics, development of new analytical methods, and reformulation of the theory of general equilibrium.

The 1984 prize went to Sir Richard Stone of Cambridge University, England, for pioneering work in the development of systems for keeping track of any country's national finances.

Noble. A coin made from platinum (or white gold as it is known because of its colour). It is legal tender (q.v.) in the Isle of Man, an off-shore British tax haven.

No liability. A legal situation in which shareholders cannot be sued by a company for the non-payment of calls (q.v.); in the event of failure to pay, the shares are forfeited. The Australian Companies Act permits the registration of mining companies as 'no liability' companies.

Nominal Gross National Product. The measure of the value of output in the national economy in a given period at the market prices of that period, i.e. in current dollars or pounds. The 1982 nominal G.N.P. measures the value of the goods produced in 1982 at the market prices prevailing in that year. *See* GROSS NATIONAL PRODUCT; REAL GROSS NATIONAL PRODUCT.

Nominal income. The monetary value of income; changes in nominal income may be due to either changes in real income (q.v.) or changes in the level of prices.

Nominal stock. Stock at face value; the actual value on the market may be higher or lower than the nominal value.

Nominal value. The value given to shares when they are created. For example, the £1 nominal shares of a company may now stand in the region of £3 or £4, which is known as the market price.

Nominee shareholder. A bank, firm of stock-brokers or other institution, which holds shares on behalf of clients.

Non-cumulative preferred stock. A preferred stock (q.v.) on which unpaid dividends do not accrue. *See* CUMULATIVE PREFERRED STOCK.

Non-Oil Developing Countries (N.O.D.C.s). Developing countries which sustained economic shock as a result of the oil price increases of 1973 and 1979, incurring large deficits which had to be met by commercial borrowing or assistance from international agencies.

Non-performing loans (U.S.). Loans in respect of which the borrower has defaulted in respect of payment of interest or repayment of capital. In 1983, State chartered banks in the United States were allowed to extend from 60–90 days the permitted period of grace before loans in arrears could be categorised as non-performing for regulatory purposes, to come generally into line with federally-chartered banks.

Non-price competition. Competition in product quality, labelling, advertising, delivery services, and so on.

Non-recourse finance. (a) Finance (q.v.) provided by a specialist finance company which, for a commission, assumes financial responsibilities on behalf of an exporter. The company passes on to the exporter any down-payments credited from the overseas buyer and most of the amount remaining due within 15 days of shipment, this being without recourse once the goods have been accepted by the buyer.

(b) A loan, the repayment of which is conditional upon the project making a profit; no profit, no repayment. Such a high-risk loan implies a high potential return to the lender.

Non-renounceable issue. *See* ENTITLEMENT ISSUE.

Non-voting shares. Shares which do not entitle the holder to vote at the General Meetings of the company. The purpose of issuing these shares is to raise additional capital from the public while control is retained by the holders of the voting shares. It has often been argued that the issue of non-voting shares should be prohibited by law.

'No par value' shares (U.S.). Shares which have no nominal value (q.v.). This type of share is illegal in Britain.

Normal price. The long-run price of a commodity, defined by Alfred Marshall as the 'value which economic forces would bring about if the general conditions of life were stationary for a run of time long enough to enable them all to work out their full effect'.

Normal profit. The average rate of reward per unit of output in an industry or sector of the economy over a period of time. Normal profit is the minimum rate of profit necessary to ensure that a sufficient number of people will be prepared to invest, undertake risks and organise production. The rate differs from industry to industry, according to the degree of risk and difficulty involved. Industries in which the rate of reward is above normal will tend to expand; those in which rewards are below normal will tend to contract. This may in some instances be a slow and erratic process; in others fairly rapid. Costs of production, in an economic sense, include an allowance for normal profit.

Normative economics. Economic studies consisting of statements on what individual business or public policy ought to be, the statements being based upon the value-judgments of the economist concerned. *See* POSITIVE ECONOMICS.

North-South dialogue. Descriptive of discussions between the developed and developing countries, e.g. as took place at the Conference on International Economic Co-operation in 1976 at which a prospective New World Economic Order was debated. The essence of the dialogue is whether and to what extent there should be a permanent transfer of resources from developed to developing countries. *See* BRANDT COMMISSION; UNITED NATIONS CONFERENCE ON TRADE AND DEVELOPMENT (U.N.C.T.A.D.).

Norwegian-E.E.C. Free Trade Agreement. An agreement signed in 1973 which gave Norway access to the European Economic Community (q.v.) free trade area of 270 million people. In 1982, about 70 per cent of Norwegian exports went into the E.E.C. compared with 47 per cent in 1974.

Norwegian Referendum 1972. A referendum held in Norway on 26 September 1972, in respect of prospective membership of the European Economic Community (q.v.). The outcome of the vote was 47 per cent in favour, and 53 per cent against. All parties seemed to accept the result as final.

Novation. In the commodity markets, the substitution of a new contracting party for an existing contracting party; such a facility gives individuals complete flexibility to enter or leave the market by arrangement.

N.O.W. Account. *See* NEGOTIABLE ORDER OF WITHDRAWAL (N.O.W.).

NYMEX. *See* NEW YORK MERCANTILE EXCHANGE.

N.Y.S.E. common stock index. A composite index covering price movements of all common stocks listed on the New York Stock Exchange (q.v.). The index is computed continuously and printed on the ticker tape each half hour. Point changes in the index are converted to dollars and cents so as to provide a meaningful measure of changes in the average price of listed stocks. The composite index is supplemented by separate indexes for four industry groups: industrial, transportation, utility and finance.

O

Odd lot. An amount of stock less than the established 100-share unit or 10-share unit of trading: from 1–99 shares for the great majority of issues, or 1–9 for so-called inactive stocks.

Odd-lot broker (U.S.). A broker who caters for odd-lot customers, i.e. customers who wish to sell or buy shares or stock in lots of less than 100, the usual minimum number for trading on the stock exchange. In making up round lots of 100 the odd-lot broker is able to engage in selling and buying. His purchase of round lots may be split between customers.

Off-board. Over-the-counter transactions in unlisted securities, or a transaction in listed shares that is not executed on a national securities exchange.

Offer. The price at which a person is ready to sell; as opposed to bid, the price at which one is ready to buy.

Offer for sale (U.K.). The offer of new securities to the public, not on behalf of the company itself, but by one or more holders to whom they have already been issued. Normally the holder is an issuing house (q.v.) which has bought the new issue from the company concerned and is now offering them to the public at a slightly higher price, the difference covering the expenses of the offer. A prospectus must be published, which includes particulars of the underwriting arrangements. In Britain in 1980, the minimum value of the shares offered had to be in excess of £500,000 and not more than 10 per cent of these could be reserved for preferential applicants, such as employees of the company. *See* OFFER FOR SALE BY TENDER; PLACING; PUBLIC ISSUE; RIGHTS ISSUE.

Offer for sale by tender (U.K.). An exceptional method of making a new issue of equities (q.v.). As in the case of an offer for sale (q.v.) an issuing house (q.v.) purchases the shares from the company prior to issue. On the basis of a prospectus, tenders are invited from the public for the shares; however the prospectus only states a minimum price and tenders are to be made above this price. After the tenders have been received, the issuing house then fixes a price at which the shares are to be sold. The company receives the full price of the shares, less the remuneration of the issuing house. *See* PLACING; OFFER FOR SALE; RIGHTS ISSUE; STOCK EXCHANGE INTRODUCTION.

Office of Fair Trading (U.K.). Set up under the British Fair Trading Act 1973 to strengthen earlier legislation on monopolies and mergers and to keep a close watch on consumer interests. It is under the control of the Director General of Fair Trading.

Office of Federal Procurement Policy (O.F.P.P.). A specialised office established within the Office of Management and Budget (O.M.B.) (q.v.) in 1974; its administrator, appointed by the President with the consent of the Senate, provides overall direction of procurement policies, regulations and procedures for executive agencies. The Federal Acquisition Institute was added to O.F.P.P. in 1977 to provide leadership and assistance in improving the quality, efficiency, and performance of acquisition and procurement personnel.

Office of Management and Budget (O.M.B.). Established in 1970, replacing the former Bureau of the Budget (q.v.); the Office has continued to perform the Bureau's function of assisting the President of the United States in the preparation and execution of the Federal budget, a function strengthened by a greater emphasis on fiscal and program analysis. The Office operates under the Budget and Accounting Act of 1921. More specifically, the functions of O.M.B. are to prepare the budget and formulate the Government's fiscal programme; supervise and control the administration of the budget; evaluate the performance of

Federal programmes; provide overall direction for procurement policies, regulations and procedures administered by executive agencies; and to review organisational structures and management procedures.

Offsetting contract. A futures contract (q.v.) which offsets or closes out an earlier obligation to deliver or take delivery of the commodity in question. For example, the buyer of a March wheat contract can sell a March wheat contract before March. The difference between the price when the trade was initiated and the price when it was offset is the gain or loss on the trade.

Offshore. A marketing area beyond the regulation of the home country, e.g. the Eurodollar market is off-shore to the United States, that is it cannot be regulated by the Securities and Exchange Commission.

Oil facility loan scheme. A loan scheme set up by the International Monetary Fund (q.v.) in 1973, following the dramatic increase in the price of oil, to assist consuming countries with severe balance-of-payments problems; in 1974 a total of $8,000 million was allocated for the facility, mostly financed by borrowings from Organization of Petroleum Exporting Countries (O.P.E.C.) (q.v.). Italy borrowed about $1,700 million, while the United Kingdom borrowed $1,200 million. The scheme was terminated in 1976.

Okun's law. A relationship between real economic growth and changes in the rate of unemployment. The law states that for every 2½ percentage points growth in real gross national product, above the trend rate that is sustained for a year, the unemployment rate declines by 1 percentage point. The law is simply a rule-of-thumb for assessing the implications of real growth for unemployment. The U.S. economist Arthur M. Okun (1928–1980) was a firm advocate of Keynesian economic theories, believing that fiscal policy was a better means of controlling the economy than federal monetary policy. Okun was president of the Council of Economic Advisers (q.v.) before joining the Brookings Institution in 1969.

Oligopoly. A situation in which a market, or a large part of a market, is supplied by a small number of firms each of which possesses a significant degree of economic influence. Each firm is strong enough to influence the market but not strong enough to disregard the reactions of competitors. There is a tendency in such markets for competition to shift from price to non-price matters such as quality, service and advertising.

During the 1930s, oligopoly came to be recognised as an emerging form of market organisation. Influential works of that period were Edward H. Chamberlin's *The Theory of Monopolistic Competition* (1933) and Joan Robinson's *The Economics of Imperfect Competition* (1933). A conventional public view emerged that firms with monopoly or near-monopoly power were likely to be unprogressive in attitude, and to use their market power to discourage potential competitors and suppress invention. In 1942, Joesph A. Schumpeter in his *Capitalism, Socialism and Democracy* held that oligopoly and monopoly were technically more progressive than competitive enterprise; indeed, because of monopoly profits they could spend more on technical development.

Oligopsony. The equivalent of oligopoly (q.v.) on the buyers' side of the market; only a few buyers in the market.

One-stop banking. Universal banking in which customers can obtain every financial service in one branch. One-stop banking encourages cross-subsidisation, that is the offering of loss leaders in the hope of more than making up for them once a customer is booked into the total range of services.

One-way callable stock. Stock which cannot be redeemed by the holder, but which can be redeemed at the sole discretion of the issuing authority.

Ontario Securities Commission (O.S.C.). The supervisory body in Ontario, Canada, in respect of the securities markets. In 1982, the Commission decided to allow trading in stock index futures in contracts on the Stock Exchange, for an experimental period of 3 years. This period would determine whether the market would be dominated by hedgers or speculators.

Open contracts. In a commodity market (q.v.), contracts which have been bought or sold without the transaction having been completed by subsequent sale or purchase, or by making or taking actual delivery of the financial instrument or physical commodity. *See* POSITION.

Open interest. The total number of futures contracts, whether purchased or sold, recorded on the books of a commodity exchange (q.v.) which are not offset by the opposite transactions or by physical delivery of the commodity.

Open market operations. The purchase or sale of securities by a central bank (q.v.) designed to influence credit conditions, money supply, or interest rates. While in the United Kingdom, open market operations involve the sale of bonds to (or purchase from) the non-bank private sector to reduce or increase the money supply, in the United States it involves the sale of Treasury bills to (or purchase from) banks to reduce or increase deposits with the Federal Reserve System (q.v.).

Purchases or sales are made by the Federal Open Market Committee (q.v.); purchases increase reserves through payments to member banks, while sales reduce reserves since the Federal Reserve System collects by charging the reserve account of the purchasing bank.

In the United States, operations may be dynamic or defensive. Dynamic operations are those undertaken to increase or decrease the volume of reserves in order to ease or tighten credit. Defensive operations are those taken to offset the effects of other factors influencing reserves. For example, the Federal Reserve System may sell securities to offset increases in reserves resulting from an inflow of cash into commercial banks from other sources. *See* RESERVE REQUIREMENTS.

Open outcry. Open transactions as conducted in commodity exchanges and financial futures exchanges, as opposed to dealing by private treaty. In established futures markets, members stand around a stepped pit quoting prices verbally and, in a busy market, by hand signals. In this way a deal can be struck for an agreed number of contracts at an agreed price between a willing buyer and seller; everyone in the market has an equal chance to fulfil all or part of each offer or bid. *See* INTERNATIONAL COMMODITIES CLEARING HOUSE LIMITED; LONDON INTERNATIONAL FINANCIAL FUTURES EXCHANGE.

Open position. The total number of futures contracts entered into a particular delivery month which have not been liquidated by an offsetting futures transaction or by actual delivery.

Opening prices. The prices at which business first commences on the floor of the Stock Exchange (q.v.) at the official opening time.

Operating cost ratio (U.S.). Operating costs expressed as a proportion of the value of net sales.

Operating lease. A lease (q.v.) under which goods are leased for only part of their estimated life, and so the rental covers only part of their capital costs. *See* FINANCE LEASE.

Operating profit (U.S.). The value of net sales minus total operating costs.

Operating ratios. Ratios indicating the operating efficiency of a business. Examples of operating ratios are:

$$\frac{\text{Cost of Sales}}{\text{Stock (including stores and work in progress)}}$$

$$\frac{\text{Stock of Finished Goods}}{\text{Production costs for period}}$$

$$\frac{\text{Trade Creditors}}{\text{Purchasers}}$$

Opportunity cost. The real cost of satisfying a want, expressed in terms of the cost of the sacrifice of alternative activities. For example, if capital funds could earn 15 per cent elsewhere, then that is their cost in present use.

If machinery has no alternative use whatsoever, the opportunity cost is zero; historical cost in this instance is irrelevant. The opportunity cost of factors currently obtained from outside the firm is measured by the price currently paid for their services. In the case of factors already owned by the firm, it is measured by the amount for which factors could be hired out or sold to another firm. If a government chooses to build more schools and finds it must cut down on its road construction programme, then the cost of the schools programme can be represented as so many miles of road.

Optimisation. A key concept in micro-economics (q.v.): the consumer is assumed to maximise utility or satisfaction, subject to the constraints of income; while the producer is assumed to maximise profit and minimise costs, subject to the technological and legal constraints within which it operates.

Optimum firm. A firm in which the costs of production per unit of output are at a minimum, having regard to the existing state of technical knowledge and managerial ability. Expansion up to this size is accompanied by falling average costs as a result of economies of scale (q.v.); beyond this point costs begin to rise due to the diseconomies arising from the increasing scarcity of the factors of production (q.v.), increasing selling costs or managerial difficulties. The optimum is not a fixed point, but changes with every development in techniques and machinery, movements in the rate of interest, or improvements in facilities for buying, selling or research. Furthermore, the optimum firm is not a simple concept; there is an optimum size for technical production, for finance, for marketing, for management and for risk. All these optima have to be reconciled as far as possible to the best advantage. For the multi-product firm, there is an optimum output for each of the firm's product lines;

hence the view is sometimes taken that there is no real limit to the size of the firm as a co-ordinating organisation, providing that the managerial organisation can be suitably adapted.

It is only under conditions of perfect competition, however, that the optimum output will coincide with the earning of maximum profits. Maximum profits are made when output has expanded to a point where marginal revenue equals marginal cost. In the circumstances of imperfect competition (q.v.) or monopoly (q.v.) the optimum size may not necessarily be reached, or it may be exceeded. However, in a competitive world the firm with the lowest average costs per unit of output in the long, as well as in the short, term is most likely to survive and to retain the support of investors. Firms therefore *tend* to optimise output.

Option. The right to buy or sell shares or property within a stated period at a predetermined price. The right to buy is known as a call option, and the right to sell a put option. Individuals may write (sell) as well as purchase options, and are obliged to deliver or buy the stock at the specified price. There are options markets on the Chicago Board Options Exchange, and the American, Midwest, Pacific and others. These differ from the over-the-counter market in that trading is limited to selected issues, expiration of contracts is standardised at four dates during the year, exercise prices are set at multiples of 5 below 50 and multiples of 10 above 50, and option prices are determined continuously through an auction market system.

Option spread. The simultaneous purchase and sale of share options (q.v.) within the same class of option; basically used by the investor to reduce risks associated with a long or short position. The options may be either at the same exercise price with the same or different expiry months, or at different exercise prices with the same or different expiry months. The spread, expressed in cents or pence per share, is the difference between the buying and selling premiums. A calendar spread is the simultaneous purchase and sale of options within the same class with different expiry dates; such spreads are also referred to as time or horizontal spreads. Another common spread is the price or vertical spread; the simultaneous purchase and sale of options within the same class with the same expiration date but with different exercise prices. A diagonal spread is a combination of calendar and price spreads.

Option trading. The buying and selling of share options (q.v.) as conducted for example on the Chicago Board Options Exchange, and known as 'the hottest game in town'.

Optional term stock. Debenture stock offered at a fixed rate of interest for a maximum term, but giving the option to redeem the investment earlier if required; for example, such a stock may be offered at 15 per cent per annum for 2 years, but after 12 months the investment may be redeemed in whole or part giving 30 days' notice.

Options, four components of. (1) *Expiry date*—the date on which all unexercised options in the particular series expire; (2) *Exercise price*—the price at which the buyer can purchase or sell the shares during the currency of the option; (3) *Number of shares*—a contract may consist of 1,000 shares; (4) *Premium*—the final element of the option and the only variable; it is the price paid to acquire the right to buy or sell, but not the obligation to exercise. *See* OPTION.

Ordinal utility. *See* UTILITY, ORDINAL.

Ordinary and traded options (Aust.). The two broad categories of share options available on the Australian stock exchanges; ordinary options can be negotiated for all securities listed while traded options are available only in the shares of 11 listed companies. With ordinary options the strike price (q.v.) is variable as it is set at the ruling market price of the share (the strike price for a put option is set at the bid price and for a call option, at the offer price). Option premiums vary with the strike price, the option period, and the volatility of the share's market price. The option period is variable though most commonly for the duration of 3 months. No standard contract size applies. There is however no secondary market in ordinary options (that is, they cannot be resold); the right to buy or sell at the strike price must be exercised to make a profit or minimise a loss. In respect of traded options a fixed strike price applies; option periods are also fixed. Contracts consist normally of 1,000 shares. They can however be readily sold in the secondary market for such options.

Ordinary shares (U.K.). The equities of a limited company. They carry the right to the residue of a company's assets after it has paid all its creditors and preference shareholders, and share in the distribution of profits, if any, after the prior claims of the preference-share holders and debenture holders have been met. Whatever the amount of profit, it is rare for all of it to be handed out in dividends to shareholders. Prudent directors of companies put part of the profits into the reserve fund. This fund may then be used to expand the business, instead of relying solely on additional borrowed capital. *See* EQUITIES; NON-VOTING SHARES.

Organisation for Economic Co-operation and Development (O.E.C.D.). An organisation which came into being on 30 September 1961, succeeding the Organisation for European Economic Co-operation (O.E.E.C.). The O.E.C.D. was set up under a convention signed in Paris on the 14 December 1960, by the Member countries of the O.E.E.C. and by Canada and the United States. This convention provides that the O.E.C.D. shall promote policies designed: (a) to achieve the highest sustainable economic growth and employment and a rising standard of living in member countries, while maintaining financial stability, and thus to contribute to the development of the world economy; (b) to contribute to sound economic expansion in member as well as non-member countries in the process of economic development; (c) to contribute to the expansion of world trade on a multilateral, non-discriminatory basis in accordance with international obligations. The members of O.E.C.D. are Australia, Austria, Belgium, Canada, Denmark, Finland, France, the Federal Republic of Germany, Greece, Iceland, Ireland, Italy, Japan, Luxembourg, the Netherlands, Norway, Portugal, Spain, Sweden, Switzerland, Turkey, the United Kingdom and the United States.

Organisation for European Economic Co-operation (O.E.E.C.). An organisation established in 1948 to allocate aid received under the European Recovery Programme among the participating countries, subject to the approval of the Economic Co-operation Administration in Washington, and to generally stimulate intra-European trade. It was superseded in 1961 by the Organisation for Economic Co-operation and Development (q.v.).

Organisation of Petroleum Exporting Countries (O.P.E.C.). An association of countries formed in 1960 for the purpose of promoting the interests of the oil-exporting countries. The countries comprised Algeria, Bahrain, Brunei, Ecuador, Gabon, Indonesia, Iran, Iraq, Kuwait, Libya, Nigeria, Oman, Qatar, Saudi Arabia, Trinidad and Tobago, the United Arab Emirates, and Venezuela. Until the Arab–Israeli Yom Kippur war in October 1973 the aim of O.P.E.C. was essentially defensive; oil was more of a buyers' market and resources were effectively in the hands of the international oil companies. O.P.E.C. imposed oil sanctions against countries friendly to Israel, and in any event the market began to develop into a sellers' market. From $U.S.2 a barrel in mid-1973, the price of oil rose to $U.S.10 a barrel in 1974. It created an oil crisis, and a balance-of-payments crisis for many countries, and helped precipitate the worst post-war recession. A unitary pricing system was adopted by O.P.E.C., although in the late 1970s this developed into a two-tier pricing arrangement. In June 1979 Saudi Arabian light crude was offered at $U.S.18 a barrel, while other prices ranged between $U.S.20 and $U.S.23.50 a barrel. In 1979 the members of O.P.E.C. held about 80 per cent of the non-communist world's proven oil reserves and more than two-thirds of total world reserves. They supplied about 30 million barrels of oil daily, being 63 per cent of the supply of crude oil to non-communist countries. About 75 per cent of this came from the six member countries on the Persian Gulf: Saudi Arabia, Iran, Iraq, Kuwait, the United Arab Emirates and Qatar. Saudi Arabia is by far the largest exporter. In December 1978 political unrest caused a total halt to Iran's crude oil output; this had only partly recovered by mid-1979. About 30 per cent of the supplies to Europe come from O.P.E.C. countries. However, the United States is the largest single petroleum importer, the second largest being Japan.

In the early 1980s, the cartel became much less effective due to substitution and conservation in consumer countries and the development of alternative sources coupled with general economic recession. *See* PETRODOLLAR RECYCLING.

Ortoli facility. Named after its founder, a special financial facility set up by the European Economic Community (q.v.) for investment projects; it is run by the European Commission (q.v.). Borrowers send their projects to the Commission for approval, in accordance with Council guidelines. A special loan of 1 billion ecus was made after the Italian earthquake in November, 1980.

'Other things being equal'. *See* CETERIS PARIBUS.

Out-of-the-money. A put option whose strike price is lower than the underlying futures price, or a call option whose strike price is higher than the underlying futures price.

Output response function. A hypothesis that if the aggregate effective demand for goods and services within an economic system steadily increases output will increase, but ultimately at a diminishing rate of response. This relationship will be the net result of several factors: (a) reduced unemployment associated with increasing scarcity of suitable labour; (b) longer hours of work, but not longer than acceptable to the labour force; (c) attraction of married women and other 'marginal' workers into the labour force, but with a subsequent 'drying-up' of this source of additional labour; (d) increased productivity with more effective utilisation of capacity, associated with increasing difficulty in securing further improvement; and (e) increasing scarcity of raw materials in relation to increasing requirements.

Outside shareholders. Parties holding an interest in subsidiaries that are not fully-owned by a company; also referred to as a minority interest.

Overbought and oversold. Terms descriptive of opinions as to price levels; if a security has enjoyed a sharp rise in price after a period of vigorous buying, some may consider that it has been 'overbought' and that the price is artificially high; conversely after a period of heavy selling the price of a security may show a marked fall and some may consider that the price has fallen too low as a result of 'overselling'.

Overdraft. *See* BANK OVERDRAFT.

Overheads. Costs not directly chargeable to any unit produced. They include rent of premises, salaries of salesmen and research, salaries of directors, etc. and all other general expenses, as opposed to costs of raw materials, wages, etc., the proportion of which that goes into each unit can be determined.

Overheating. A concept applied to a situation of excessive demand for real resources in conditions of full employment.

Overmanning. A situation in which the number of operators employed to operate a plant or production line, or the number of workers in a team, is higher than that thought necessary as a result of work-study assessment or through comparisons with other factories at home or overseas; in consequence output per employee is below standard. Overmanning may arise for a number of reasons including demarcation considerations between trades, deficiencies in the general work arrangements, or the result of agreements between employers and trade unions.

Overseas Projects Fund (O.P.F.). A fund set up in 1973 to help United Kingdon companies in their pursuit of major overseas projects; financial assistance was available towards pre-contractual expenses of large package and turnkey projects, and also towards the costs of feasibility and consultancy studies likely to lead to such projects.

Over-subscription. A situation in which the value of the applications for a new issue of securities (q.v.) exceeds the value of the securities offered. *See* ALLOTMENT LETTER; LETTER OF REGRET.

Over-the-counter market (O.T.C.M.). A market operated by security dealers for stocks not listed on the stock exchanges. A British market developed in the early 1970s in response to demands from both industrial companies and institutional investors for a better mechanism for trading in the shares of small and medium-sized companies; through this arrangement a company has all the normal advantages of listed shares including liquidity for shareholders and access to additional capital. In 1984, some 26 companies were operating in the British O.T.C. market. In the 1920s an O.T.C. market in securities evolved in the United States providing facilities for transactions in securities mainly of smaller companies looking for external finance. A multi-locational market of leading investment banks and stockbrokers has operated outside the trading floor of stock exchanges. For every ten U.S. companies for whose securities there is a market, some nine are now traded O.T.C. with only one listed on the stock exchange. *See* NATIONAL ASSOCIATION OF SECURITIES DEALERS INC.

Overtrading. A situation in which a firm has little working capital.

Own something, owe something. Euphemisms for going long and going short.

Oxford Group. A group of economists at the University of Oxford during the late 19th and early 20th centuries; it placed a much greater emphasis on historical evidence, adopted an inductive method which emphasized the relative character of theorising, and encouraged professional engagement with practical economic and social issues. However, the group did not establish a reputation comparable with the Cambridge School (q.v.) or the London School of Economics. Names associated with the Oxford Group were W. J. Ashley, Edwin Cannan, M. E. Sadler, H. Llewellyn Smith, L. L. Price, and W. A. S. Hewins. *See* SCHOOLS OF ECONOMICS.

P

Paasche index. A type of index for measuring changes, e.g. in prices. It utilises current period weights, but since current-year weights are seldom known, the index is difficult to construct. The index utilises the following method:

$$\frac{\Sigma P_n q_n}{\Sigma P_o q_n}$$

where P_o = price in the base-year; P_n = price in the year under consideration; and q_n = quantity in the year under consideration. The index has the disadvantage that in times of generally rising prices it tends to underestimate price increases. *See* LASPEYRES' INDEX.

Paid-up capital. That part of the issued capital (q.v.) which is paid up by the shareholders.

Pan ticket. A document that accompanies a grain sample of a commodity that is to be sold in the cash market; it lists official grade, test weight, moisture content, point of origin and other relevant information.

Paper entrepreneur. A business organiser who applies the skills of the entrepreneur (q.v.) to the task of achieving short-term profits for the firm, not through new productive investment but through strategies involving simply the rearrangement of assets and the clever manipulation of rules and numbers, shrewd manoeuvring, the transfer of losses from the firm to the public through a successful plea for public subsidies or tax concessions, threats of legal actions and takeovers, and the finessing of accounts and taxation returns. Such enterprise does not add to collective wealth, but successfully undertaken, re-assigns the allocation of wealth. The pursuit of profits through these avenues has diverted attention and resources away from the difficult task of transforming the productive base of many industries; in the end it contributes positively to the decline of national economic health.

Paper gold. *See* SPECIAL DRAWING RIGHTS (S.D.R.S).

Paper profit. An unrealised money increase in the value of an asset; an individual will have made a paper profit on a house if it is worth more in monetary terms than when it was bought. A paper profit may be realised on sale, for more or less than the amount estimated. However, a paper profit may not prove to be a real profit once inflation (q.v.) is taken into account.

Par. On futures exchanges, a reference to the standard delivery point or points or to the quality of the commodity represented in a contract that is deliverable at contract price.

Par exchange rate. *See* PAR VALUE.

Par value or par exchange rate. (1) The price of one country's currency in terms of another. The value of each currency is expressed in terms of gold; from these valuations the rates are obtained. The initial par value of the pound sterling, established with the International Monetary Fund (q.v.) in December, 1946, was 3.58134 grammes of fine gold per pound sterling, or 403.000 U.S. cents per pound sterling. In September, 1949, the par value of the pound was changed to 2.48828 grammes of fine gold, or 280.000 U.S. cents per pound. In November, 1967, the par value of the pound sterling was changed to 2.13281 grammes of fine gold, or 240.000 U.S. cents per pound.

(2) The nominal or face value of a security as determined by the company or issuing body; it often has no relationship with the market price of the share.

Paradox of thrift. A paradox that in certain economic circumstances the more frugal and thrifty are individuals and households, the lower will be the level of national income and factor employment; and the more prodigal and spendthrift are individuals and households, the higher the level of national income and factor employment. The latter statement implies some unemployment of resources, otherwise spending may simply result in inflation.

Situations arise in which what is 'good' for the individual and household may be 'bad' for the nation.

Paradox of value. A paradox in which an essential to life, such as water is normally little valued, but a luxury, such as diamonds, carries a high price. The explanation lies in the fact that the amount of water available is normally so great that its marginal utility (q.v.) is zero. In respect of diamonds, the stock is small and the demand great; the marginal utility is high. It was William Stanley Jevons (1835–1882), Carl Menger (1840–1921) and Léon Walras (1834–1910) who resolved the apparent conflict between value and utility by recognising that it was the specific utility depending on the last available, or marginal unit of a commodity, and not generic utility, which determined its value.

Pareto criterion of allocative efficiency. A test of allocative efficiency which requires that it must not be possible to change the existing resource allocation in the economy in such a way that somebody is made better off, and no one worse off, for if this is possible the existing resource allocation must be sub-optimal and involve 'welfare waste'. Hence a policy is socially beneficial if someone is made better off and no one is made worse off; there is an increase in total welfare. *See* LAUSANNE SCHOOL; COMPENSATION PRINCIPLE.

Pareto improvements. Generally, changes which would make at least one member of society better off without making anyone worse off. A society in which no one can be made better off without making someone else worse off is said to be in a Pareto optimal state. The Pareto criterion for improvement does not allow comparisons between social states when one or more persons gain at the expense of others; and it does not identify the best or optimal social state. The 'compensation principle' was devised in an attempt to meet the former of these shortcomings. *See* COMPENSATION PRINCIPLE.

Pareto optimality. Any of a number of efficient states of economic affairs, from which it is impossible to deviate so as to make one person or group better off without making some other person or group worse off. The Paretian criterion, as usually conceived, does not concern itself with the distribution of income; a result may be Pareto optimal even if the distribution it represents is totally unacceptable.

Pareto's Law. An empirical relationship describing the number of persons whose income is x in a given population, advanced by Vilfredo Pareto (1848–1923), Italian economist and sociologist. Pareto concluded from his studies that national income had an inevitable tendency to be distributed in the same way regardless of social and political institutions and systems of taxation. Subsequent studies have refuted both the universality and inevitability of Pareto's Law.

Pari passu. Equal in every respect; term used to describe new issues of shares in relation to shares already in issue.

Paris Bourse. The French equivalent of the London Stock Exchange. *See* BOURSE; STOCK EXCHANGE.

Paris Club. *See* GROUP OF ELEVEN.

Partial equilibrium analysis. Economic analysis of a small sector of an economy such as the market for a particular commodity, in which the prices of several or all other commodities are held fixed relative to one another, and spillovers between markets are largely ignored.

Participating preference share. Preference share (q.v.) which also entitles the holder to a limited share in residual profits.

Participating preferred stock (U.S.). Preferred stock (q.v.) which under certain conditions, shares in earnings beyond the normal stated dividend.

Participation rate. The proportion of a population, of working age, in the labour force, whether employed or unemployed. The proportion tends to fall during an economic downturn as 'discouraged workers' opt out of the employment market when employment opportunities diminish; hence official unemployment figures in such circumstances tend to understate the problem.

Partnership, limited (U.K.). A partnership which includes limited partners whose financial obligations to the firm are limited to the amount of capital they have invested. This arrangement is permissible under the Limited Partnership Act 1907. A limited partner is debarred, however, from taking an active share in the management of the firm. There are not many partnerships of this type in Britain. Canadian law also permits this form of business unit. *See* PARTNERSHIP, THE.

Partnership, the (U.K.). An association of persons carrying on a business in common with a view to profit. It may comprise any number of people from 2 to 20 (10 in the case of a bank). The liability undertaken by partners is unlimited—each partner is personally liable for debts incurred by the firm to the full extent of his private fortune. Sole proprietors (q.v.) often turn their businesses into partnerships. It is a way of obtaining additional capital and sharing both risks and management functions. It is easy to form and dissolve a partnership. *See* PARTNERSHIP, LIMITED.

Pass a dividend. Fail to pay a dividend (q.v.).

Patent. A grant from a government to a person or persons conferring for a specified time the exclusive privilege of making, using or selling a new invention. Thus an inventor gains the right to exclude all others from duplicating his invention for use or sale. Patents seek to encourage more inventive activity but restrict competition, furthering monopoly in various ways.

Pay-back method. A method of comparing the profitability of alternative projects; the object is to determine over what period the net cash generated by an investment will repay the cost of the project:

$$\text{Pay-back period} = \frac{\text{Cost of Project}}{\text{Annual Increase in Income (after tax)}}$$

The most serious drawback of the pay-back method is that it takes no account of the life of the investment, and ignores the timing of proceeds.

Pay board. A statutory body established by the British Government on 30 March 1973, to ensure that the provisions of the Price and Pay Code relating to remuneration were observed. The general principles of the Code were to limit the rate of increase of incomes in money terms to a level more in line with the growth of national output, so as to progressively reduce the rate of cost and price inflation; to apply the limit fairly; and to leave decisions on the amount, form and distribution of increases within the limits to those who normally determine pay. The Pay Board was scrapped by the Labour Government when it came to power in 1974.

Pay day. *See* ACCOUNT DAY.

Payroll tax. A tax imposed by a Government on the wages-bill of a business. In the United States a payroll tax was authorised by the Social Security Act 1935, to provide for unemployment insurance and, in certain cases, for workmen's compensation. In Australia, a payroll tax is levied on employers by State Governments generally. With inflationary trends in incomes, the system guarantees an automatic growth in State revenues. It has been argued that a payroll tax is inequitable as it has no regard to company profitability, and the tax bears most heavily on labour intensive industries. In Britain, a payroll tax was introduced in 1966 under the description of 'selective employment tax', though abolished in 1971. Some economists hold the view that such a tax discourages firms from 'hoarding' labour which they may not really need at a particular time, but are afraid to lose

Pecuniary culture. A social system in which the accumulation of physical wealth is both acceptable to that society, and valued highly by that society.

Pecuniary effects. Effects arising from changes in relative prices which only redistribute goods and services among people without affecting total production of consumption opportunities. Such effects involve improvements in the economic position of some persons but correspondingly impaired positions for others.

'Penal' terms. Severe terms or conditions imposed by the Bank of England (q.v.) in respect of loans to discount houses, made in the Bank's capacity as 'lender of last resort' (q.v.). Although the Bank of England will never refuse to lend at last resort to the discount houses which form the London Discount Market Association, the Bank dictates the terms on which it will lend particularly in respect of the rate of interest payable on money so borrowed and the period for which cash may be borrowed; as a matter of policy it always makes these terms 'penal' and thus borrowing is kept to a minimum. Loans are usually for a minimum period of 7 days and a minimum lending rate: A penal rate has never been charged on discount-window lending to banks that need extra reserves; indeed the discount rate has been regularly kept two or three percentage points below comparable market rates.

Penn Square bank crash. The failure of the Penn Square Bank of Oklahoma City in July, 1982, considered by many the costliest bank failure in the history of the United States. The failure appeared due to the recession in the oil and gas industries, which resulted in many non-performing loans (q.v.); it was accompanied by allegations of fraud and criticisms of the poor quality of the bank's loans. The bank was closed by the U.S. Federal Deposit Insurance Corporation (q.v.) and liquidated.

Penny line, the. Descriptive of people waiting at the entrance of a work-site to ascertain whether there is any work for them; characteristic of the Great Depression (q.v.) generally, and of specific industries offering casual or day work, such as the port and building industries. *See* DECASUALISATION.

Penny stocks. Low-priced issues of often highly speculative stocks. Penny stocks or shares may also emerge as a result of a recession; sometimes these low-price penny shares offer good opportunities for profit in the stockmarket in the event of recovery.

Perfect competition. A concept used in economic analysis, for the purpose of exposing the basic forces common to all markets. On the supply side it implies (a) *many firms*, competing with each other, but each supplying so small a proportion of the total output as to be unable to exert a perceptible influence on the market price by changes in output; each firm is a 'price-taker', and not a 'price-maker'; (b) *a perfectly elastic supply of the factors of production*, each firm being able to increase output without driving up the level of wages, interest or rent; (c) *mobility*, firms being completely free to enter or leave the industry without artificial hindrances; (d) *complete knowledge*, each firm being fully informed about the activities of other firms in the industry and, in particular, their profitability. On the demand side, the concept implies (a) *many purchasers*, no single buyer being able to perceptibly influence the market price by varying the size of his purchases; (b) *complete knowledge*, each buyer knowing what price is being asked for a particular commodity in every part of the market; (c) *absence of transport difficulties or costs*, which might prevent or impede a purchaser from taking full advantage of slight differences in prices for the same commodity in various parts of the market; (d) *homogeneity of product*, the product of any firm being accepted by the purchaser as an exact substitute for the product of any other firm. The concept of perfect competition is as much removed from reality as the concept of absolute monopoly, imperfect competition being a better general description for a modern economy based on free enterprise. *See* IMPERFECT COMPETITION; PRICING.

Perfect market. A concept sometimes used in economic theory for the purpose of studying certain effects, in which it is assumed that there are no transfer costs of goods from place to place so that uniform prices would be established everywhere, and that every seller is in contact with every buyer and every buyer in contact with every seller. *See* IMPERFECT MARKET.

Perfect marketing transparency. The objective of price information agreements; a market is perfectly transparent for the sellers if all sellers know exactly the prices asked and obtained by their competitors, the terms of sale, the quality of their competitors' products and the names of their customers. The result may be conscious parallelism (q.v.) with regard to prices, particularly in an oligopoly (q.v.), paralysing price competition. *See* INFORMATION AGREEMENT.

Permanent income. The average income expected to be received over a period of years.

Permanent income hypothesis. A hypothesis that household consumption expenditures are related to permanent income (q.v.) and not affected by deviations from this amount.

Permanent-income theory of consumption. A theory, developed by Milton Friedman (b. 1912), that people gear their consumption behaviour to their permanent or long-term consumption opportunities, and not to their current level of income. In its simplest form this hypothesis of consumption behaviour may be expressed:

$$C = cY^p$$

where: Y^p is permanent disposable income, and C is consumption. Thus consumption varies in the same proportion as permanent income; a 10 per cent increase in permanent income raises consumption by 10 per cent. To the individual some increases in income appear of a permanent nature and influence the pattern of consumption, while other increases are transitory and do not change the long-term pattern. The permanent-income hypothesis pays careful attention to the ways in which individuals form their expectations about their future incomes.

Petrodollar recycling. The use of the massive earnings of the members of the Organization of Petroleum Exporting Countries (q.v.) to support by way of loans the economies of countries shaken by the dramatic increases in oil prices. The quadrupling of the price of oil in 1973–74 and the major price rises of 1979 created vast surpluses for the O.P.E.C. countries which reached an annual peak of about $120 billion by 1980. Many countries which had been paying $2.60 a barrel of oil before 1973, had to pay $12.00 a barrel initially and more later; this created serious balance of payments problems. The leading world banks which had accepted the deposits of the O.P.E.C. countries were then able to provide funds to the countries that had no oil. The banks acted as a turntable, recycling petrodollars. However, 1983 witnessed a dramatic fall in oil surpluses due to falling demand and a moderation of prices. The switch in Britain from cheap foreign oil to dearer North Sea oil was detrimental to the standard of living but strengthened Britain's balance-of-payments position enormously, compared even with 1973. In 1980, the United States spent $74 billion on imported oil while Britain spent nothing.

Petty's Law. A statement of the tendency for the proportion of the working population engaged in service industry to increase with economic development. Sir William Petty (1623–1687) was the pioneer of numerical economics, his main interest being in public finance. He made important contributions in respect of monetary theory and fiscal policy; his best-known work *Political Arithmetic* was published in 1691.

Phantom competition. The quotation by customers of other suppliers' prices at lower levels than the true ones.

Philadelphia Stock Exchange. Also known as the PHLX, the first stock exchange (q.v.) in the United States being founded officially in 1790. It was preceded by an unofficial exchange founded in 1746. In 1984, the exchange listed the stock of over 1,200 major corporations. It also offered over 75 stock options. Foreign currency options included the British pound, German mark, Japanese yen, Swiss franc, and the Canadian dollar. The proximity of the exchange to the New York Stock Exchange (q.v.) places it in a highly competitive situation.

Phillips curve. Developed by Professor A. W. Phillips of the London School of Economics, a graphical curve which plots annual price changes (%) against unemployment rate (%). The curve suggests that as unemployment declines, wages and prices must rise; conversely as unemployment rises, wage and price increases tend to diminish. It is recognised that education, training of the unskilled, employment for hard-core unemployed, and facilitating the movement of people in search of jobs to where jobs are available, has the effect of 'shifting' the Phillips curve in the direction of more employment with less inflation. Figure 17 illustrates an early Phillips curve for the United States for the years 1960–68.

On the other hand, a commonly held view among economists is that, as inflation reaches a certain level, businessmen, wage-earners, and consumers anticipate further inflation and take it into account when setting prices, demanding wage-increases or timing purchases. The effect is that the level of inflation accompanying any given level of unemployment tends to rise over time, i.e. the Phillips curve shifts upwards and outwards. *See* FIGURE 18.

The Monetarist School (q.v.) in analysing the determination of the level of employment has produced what is called the 'price expectations augmented Phillips Curve'. This more complex analysis concludes that the trade-off between a lower level of employment and a higher rate of inflation occurs only in the short-term, when inflation is unanticipated. In the long-run when wage and price changes are

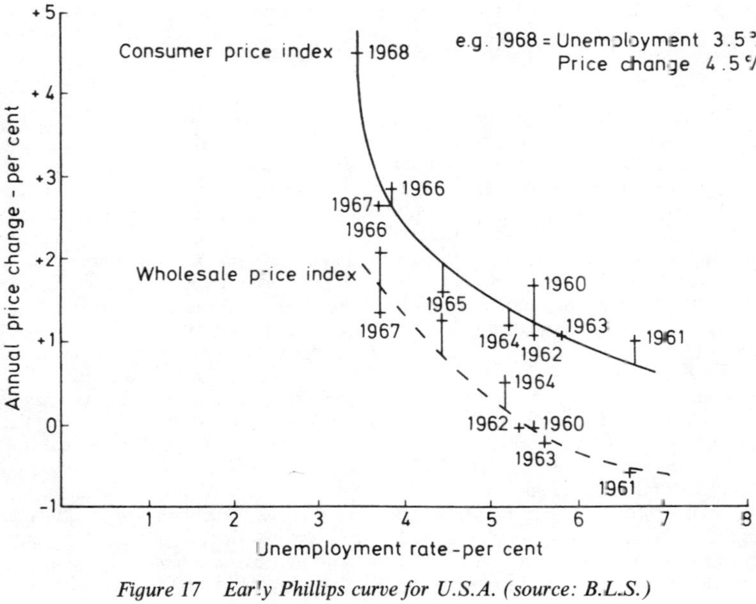

Figure 17 Early Phillips curve for U.S.A. (source: B.L.S.)

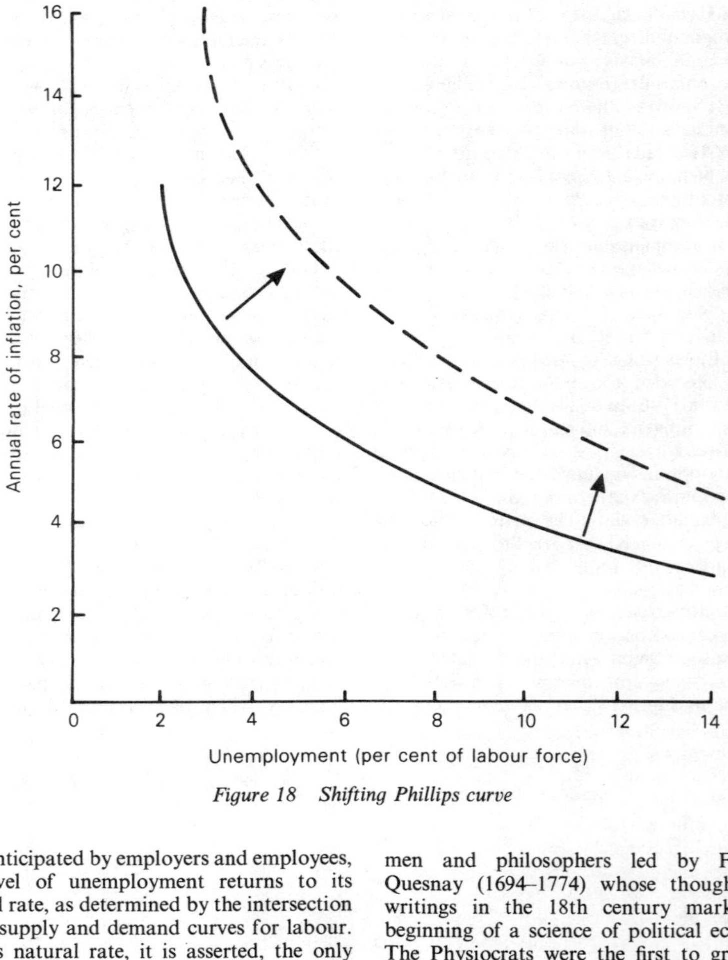

Figure 18 Shifting Phillips curve

fully anticipated by employers and employees, the level of unemployment returns to its natural rate, as determined by the intersection of the supply and demand curves for labour. At this natural rate, it is asserted, the only people who are unemployed are those that, at the going real wage rate, do not wish to work and those that are undertaking voluntary job changes (in this context the monetarist views the natural rate of unemployment as 'full employment').

Professor Phillips (1914–1975) was born in New Zealand; he became Tooke professor of economic science and statistics at London University (1958–67) and professor at the Australian National University (1967–70). The Phillips Curve has become less relevant with the advent of 'stagflation' (q.v.), that is the positive association of high inflation with high unemployment rates.

Physiocratic School. A group of French statesmen and philosophers led by Francois Quesnay (1694–1774) whose thoughts and writings in the 18th century marked the beginning of a science of political economy. The Physiocrats were the first to grasp the conception of a unified science of society. Their studies brought them to believe in a 'natural order' based upon property, security and liberty. It was the essence of that natural order that in a free system the particular interest of the individual can never be separated from the common interest of all; therefore restriction is artificial and liberty natural. The Government's duty lay in upholding the rights of private property and individual liberty by removing all artificial barriers and punishing those who threatened the existence of any of these rights. They believed in the concept of free competition, a process resulting in the establishment of the *bon prix*, which is the most advantageous price for both parties. From this it followed that both labour and trade must be free. Quesnay argued that 'to secure the greatest amount of pleasure with the least possible outlay should be the aim of all economic effort'. This is what the natural order aimed at. Alfred Marshall in his *Principles of Economics* (1890) commented that the chief motive of the Physiocrats was not to increase the riches of merchants and fill the exchequers of kings; it was to diminish the suffering and degradation which was caused by extreme poverty—'They thus gave to economics its modern aim of seeking after such knowledge as may help to raise the quality of human life.'

Physiocratic doctrine was a reaction to mercantilism (q.v.) and tended to place a single-minded emphasis on agriculture as the only source of income and wealth. Despite this, its contribution remains distinctive. Quesnay devised the famous Tableau Économique when attempting to trace the flow of production and wealth through a nation's economy. *See* SCHOOLS OF ECONOMICS.

Pig on pork (U.K.). A bill of exchange (q.v.), the drawer and the drawee (acceptor) being of the same family, e.g. when a subsidiary company draws a bill on its parent.

Pigou effect or real balance effect. A change in expenditure caused by a change in the value of money holdings that occurs as a consequence of changes in prices. Named after A. C. Pigou (1877–1959) a view that consumption is not solely a function of income; thus consumption might rise with respect to a given income when prices are falling, and consumption might rise and exceed income if people are able to draw on money savings during any period (past savings may be used up and debts incurred). As the price level falls the real value of the community's money balances increases and consumption may well increase. Thus aggregate demand may increase with falling prices. The economy thus contains a countervailing influence tending to sustain demand and restore equilibrium at a level at which resources are fully employed.

Pit. An octagonal area on the floor of an exchange, surrounded by a tier of steps, in which dealings in certain designated futures contracts take place by means of open outcry (q.v.).

Pit broker. An exchange member who executes orders in the pit (q.v.) for other members who have a presence on the floor but choose not to carry out their own floor transactions.

Pit trading. The principal method of trading used on exchanges such as the Chicago Mercantile Exchange (q.v.) in which traders buy or sell futures contracts in octagonal pits located on the exchange floor. When two brokers agree on a price, after announcing their bids and offers by open-outcry (q.v.) as well as the delivery month and the number of contracts (commonly referred to as cars or lots) involved, a contract is completed. The price at which the trade has been made is quickly disseminated via the exchange's computerised ticker system. Exchange pit clerks who record the information on cards are known as 'pit observers'.

Placing. A method of issuing securities to raise new capital. By this method a firm of stockbrokers, acting on behalf of the company concerned, sells shares or stock to large institutions or other investors. A proportion of the shares must be made available to the public through the medium of The London Stock Exchange (q.v.). This method is normally only used in the case of smaller companies. *See* OFFER FOR SALE; PUBLIC ISSUE; RIGHTS ISSUE; STOCK EXCHANGE INTRODUCTION.

Planning system. A term used by Professor John Kenneth Galbraith in his *Economics and the Public Purpose* (1974) to describe that part of the national economy planned by its constituent firms; the concept must be distinguished carefully from that of State planning systems, the more common use. The planning system is considered the dominant part of the economy to which the market system is subordinate; it supplies power, fuel, machinery, equipment, materials, transportation and communications—a large share of the goods and services that firms in the market system must purchase. The planning system has power over its prices, and increases in wages costs can be readily passed on to the public so that profits may be kept at the former level. In the planning system, need is not only well-served but extensively created. But the system is inherently unstable, in the absence of state intervention.

Plant mix. The proportions of different types of plant in a system, or contemplated for the future. In respect of electricity generating plant, the different types are usually classified as coal, oil, natural gas, nuclear, hydro, pumped storage and gas turbine. The first four are simply labelled by the fuels they use and are all steam-electric plants. Hydro plant implies hydro-electric plant, in which the water used for electricity generation flows entirely via dams from natural catchment areas. In pumped storage schemes water is pumped from a lower reservoir to a higher reservoir, base-load electricity at off-peak times being used, and released from the upper reservoir to generate electricity at peak times. Gas turbine plant is used for peak-load generation purposes.

Plc. Public limited company (q.v.). *See* COMPANIES ACTS 1948 TO 1985.

Point. (a) Variations in the fourth figure after the decimal point in a rate of exchange (q.v.). If a currency is quoted at 7.1453 to another unit of currency, and then drops to 7.1458, it is said to have weakened by five points. The term may also be used to describe the minimum units by which bids and offers on an exchange may vary.

(b) In the United States, in the case of stock, a point means $1; if ABC shares rise three points, each share has risen $3. In the case of bonds, a point means $10, since a bond is quoted as a percentage of $1,000; a bond which rises three points gains 3 per cent of $1,000, or $30 in value. An advance from 87 to 90 means an advance in dollar value from $870 to $900. In the case of market averages, a point is simply a step in a scale; if, for example, the Dow-Jones industrial average rises from 870.25 to 871.25, it has risen by one point.

(c) The minimum price fluctuation permitted in a commodity traded on a futures exchange, e.g. in trade steers, is one point or 0.1 cent per kilogram. This is not to be confused with an index point in the share price index contract where one index point equals 10 points.

Poison pill. *See* ANTI-TAKEOVER TACTICS.

Political business cycle. Movements in trade and industry, employment and investment, induced by political leaders through short-term pre-election policies; the aim is to boost election prospects while being aware that the consequences of ill-considered policies will be borne by the community in a post-election environment. Deflation may be necessary to eliminate the problems caused by the pre-election boom (usually inflation).

Political economy. Originally economic thought regarded as a branch of statecraft; as the older name for economics it became discarded. More recently, however, the term has reappeared in relation to economics regarded as a study in which moral judgments are made on particular issues. It stands in contrast to positive economics in which every effort is made to exclude personal value-judgments.

The term 'political economy' has a long history. It appears in the title *Traité de l'Économie politique* written by Antoyne de Montchrétien, a French mercantilist, in 1616. In 1767 it appeared in Sir James Steuart's *Principles of Political Economy*. It came into more general use during the 19th century, and was used by Jevons and Walras.

Economus was an ancient classical Greek term descriptive of the principles of housekeeping; within this context the adoption of the term 'political economy' may have been an adaptation of the word to social or public housekeeping. There seems to have been no significant difference between the use of the term 'political economy' and the later and today more usual term 'economics'.

Politico-economic models. Models which facilitate the study of how the state of the economy affects the polity, and how political behaviour affects the economy.

'Polluter pays' principle. A principle which equates the price charged for the use of environmental resources with the cost of damage inflicted on society by using them. The price charged may be levied directly, e.g. as taxes on the process which generates pollution or as the purchase price of licences which entitle the holder to generate specific quantities of pollutants. If the producer or consumer can avoid the additional expense, he will attempt to do so; there is, therefore, an incentive to refrain from using the polluting item or to change consumption patterns or production processes in ways which mitigate pollution. Alternatively, in a reversal of principle, measures may take the form of direct payments from the public purse to polluters not to pollute. The difficulty with either procedure is to decide the 'right' price to charge, or the 'right' subsidy to pay; both involve an assessment of the monetary value of a clean and unimpaired environment. For this reason, non-market techniques of pollution control are frequently preferred; under the 'polluter pays' principle, non-market measures encompass the promulgation of regulations governing in various ways the emission or effects of pollution. Regulations eliminate some of the uncertainty which is inherent in market approaches. The 'polluter pays' principle was affirmed at the United Nations Conference on the Human Environment held in Stockholm in 1972. However, an examination of the practices of members of the Organisation for Economic Co-operation and Development reveals that a majority provide some incentive to industry to install pollution control equipment.

Pork barrelling. The use of government funds as a source of political benefit; for example the channelling of funds into major public works such as water supply projects, where they will be of most political benefit to those determining the priorities.

Portfolio. The list of securities held by a person or Institution.

Portfolio management. The arrangement of investments so as to achieve a balance of risks and rewards acceptable to the investor. At one extreme, the investor may prefer virtually riskless, highly liquid short-term securities, issued by stable governments; at the other the investor may prefer high risk/high return ventures. Whatever the preference, or the mixture of preferences, portfolio management involves a careful assessment of investment characteristics: The ability to sell a security before maturity, and at a good figure; the terms on which a recovered principal could be reinvested to further long-term financial targets; the likely effects of an economic recession on particular assets; the effect of inflation on the value of assets, by way of enhanced earnings and appreciation or the reverse; the possible effects of changes in government policies, e.g. in respect of protection (q.v.); the vulnerability to political risks; the vulnerability of the investment to the vagaries of the weather (drought, fire and flood); the possible effects of technological change, or structural change; the possible effects of prolonged industrial unrest; and short- and long-run likely performance, as situations change. Risks may be reduced by diversification of investment into several contrasting streams, streams in which an adverse event while detrimental to one may be favourable to another; and rewards may be enhanced by constant review of the investments with a view to more effective groupings.

Portfolio theory. Devised by Professor James Tobin (1981 Nobel Memorial prize in economics), a guide to the management of a portfolio; it was based on his studies of how subjects actually behave when they acquire different assets and incur debts. The theory suggests that investors do not, and should not, seek only the highest average rate of return they can get from an investment portfolio. Rather, in order to avoid taking undue risks, investors both do and should pay attention to the 'variance' or instability of the stocks or bonds or other assets held.

Position. An interest in a commodity market (q.v.), either long or short, in the form of open contracts which have not been liquidated.

Positional goods. A term used by Professor Fred Hirsch to emphasise the socially-influenced values attaching to the utility stemming from a given flow of goods and services. Many things valued in society have hierarchical significance and personal satisfaction is often derived from being top of the tree in one respect or another, or in enjoying a high status. To many people position in the hierarchy matters very much, and goods and services associated with well-regarded positions become more highly valued as basic necessities are met. A general rise in real incomes can cause dissatisfaction among those whose progress has been less rapid than that of others; indeed some will feel worse off than before. Hirsch has sought to explain why economic growth can yield less satisfaction than might be expected and why problems of distribution equity can loom large.

Positive economics. Economic studies concerned with what is, not what ought to be; in principle independent of any value-judgment of the economist concerned. The task of positive economics is to provide a system of generalisations which may be used in making predictions about the consequences of changes in policy or circumstance. *See* NORMATIVE ECONOMICS.

Potential real gross national product or potential output. An estimate of the level at which the gross national product (q.v.) would be if there were full employment of labour; the difference between potential G.N.P. and actual G.N.P. is called the G.N.P. gap; this serves as a measure of economic slack and of the waste of productive resources due to insufficiently high levels of employment.

Preference, cardinality of. The view of utility (q.v.), held by many economists before the 1930s, that the amount of utility is related to the quantity of commodities already possessed and that changes in utility arising from changes in the quantities possessed can be measured. During the inter-war years, attention shifted to the ordinal aspect of utility; the opinion developed that it was unnecessary to assume that utility was measurable and that a more satisfactory theory of consumer behaviour could be constructed simply on the assumption that the utility from different combinations of commodities could be ranked in order of preference by consumers. *See* INDIFFERENCE ANALYSIS; INDIFFERENCE CURVE.

Preference share. A share which gives the holder a prior claim over the holders of ordinary shares, both in respect of the payment of dividend and in respect of return of capital if the company goes into liquidation; preference shares carry a fixed rate of interest (e.g. 5 per cent on the par value of the share). *See* PARTICIPATING PREFERENCE SHARE.

Preferred ordinary share. A share which carries a right to a fixed dividend, after the payment of dividend to preference shareholders. *See* DEFERRED ORDINARY SHARE.

Preferred stock (U.S.). Shares representing ownership of a business, but the owners of preferred stock have a prior claim on distributed earnings over any claim by common stockholders, and a prior claim on the company's assets if the business is dissolved. Preferred stock has a stated dividend rate; however this dividend must be declared by the company's Board of Directors each time it is due. Dividends are therefore not as certain as in the case of bond interest payments, and a higher rate of return compensates for the higher risk; on the other hand earnings are generally less than for common stock. *See* BOND; CALLABLE PREFERRED STOCK; COMMON STOCK; CONVERTIBLE PREFERRED STOCK; CUMULATIVE PREFERRED STOCK; NON-CUMULATIVE PREFERRED STOCK; PARTICIPATING PREFERRED STOCK.

Premium. (a) The difference between the price at which a security was issued and the price at which it now stands, if the latter is the higher; (b) The excess of one futures contract price over that of another; (c) The difference by which one spot commodity sells over another grade of the same or another spot commodity.

Present worth. The capital sum, which, if invested at the time of the commissioning of a plant, would together with the interest earned suffice to pay the annual capital charges on the plant as they occur year by year.

If it is necessary to calculate an average annual cost over the whole life of the plant, the total present worth may be converted to an 'equivalent average annual cost' by multiplying by the appropriate annuity rate. Present worth factors and annuity rates may be found from *Inwood's Tables*, Archers *Tables of Repayments*, etc.

For a 12 per cent interest rate, the present worth factor is given by:

$$\frac{1}{1.12^{m}}$$

where m = years of life of the plant (assumed for depreciation purposes).

The present worth method offers a general and systematic approach to the problem of allocating a series of irregular costs to the units of a continuous output.

Price. The value of a commodity or service in terms of money; an exchange ratio, e.g. thirty pence a pound. The term 'price' is used in relation to the exchange value of goods and some services; in respect of human services the equivalent terms 'wage', 'salary', 'commission' or 'fee' are used. Again the price of borrowing money is called 'interest' and the price of hiring land or equipment 'rent'.

Price Commission. A statutory body established by the British Government in April, 1973, to ensure that the provisions of the Price and Pay Code relating to prices were carried out. The purpose of the Code was to limit the extent to which prices may be increased on account of increased costs and to secure reductions as a result of reduced costs; to reinforce the control of prices by a control on profit margins, while safeguarding investment; and to reinforce the effects of competition and to secure its full benefits in the general level of prices. Abolished in 1974.

Price discovery. Descriptive of a process whereby prices are established on exchanges through a continuous auction process. *See* CHICAGO BOARD OF TRADE; NEW YORK MERCANTILE EXCHANGE.

Price discrimination. The charging of different prices to different groups of individuals for the same goods or services for reasons not associated with difference in costs. This may occur when there is a geographical separation of markets, the structure of demand in each market being different. It may also occur in respect of railway freight charges. It has also been practised by medical practitioners in communities of wide disparity of wealth. The conditions for discrimination are: (a) The seller can control the amount of a product that is offered to a particular buyer; and (b) the seller can either legally prevent the resale of the commodity by one buyer to another, or such resale would be costly or physically impossible for buyers to arrange. The results of price discrimination appear to be mixed promoting greater output and consumption in some instances and proving restrictive and anti-social in others. *See* 'CHARGING WHAT THE TRAFFIC WILL BEAR'; PRICING; ROBINSON-PATMAN ACT (U.S.).

Price/earnings ratio. A ratio which enables investors to consider stocks on a basis of price against earnings. The total earnings of the company (after taxes and provisions for preference dividends, if any) in a recent year are divided by the total number of ordinary shares; this gives the earnings for each ordinary share. The earnings per share are then compared with the latest price per share. Many advisers suggest that, as a general rule, investors should look for stocks that have a price of between 10 and 15 times the earnings per share.

Price expectations augmented Phillips curve. *See* PHILLIPS CURVE.

Price leadership. A form of conscious parallelism (q.v.) with regard to prices whereby the price policy of one firm, the price leader is deliberately followed by others. The price may be set by the dominant firm in the industry, or it may be set by a firm which habitually leads in price changes though not necessarily the largest. In what is called barometric price leadership, the price leader changes the price when he judges that the climate is right. *See* PRICING.

Price limits. A form of protection which operates for most contracts on the London International Financial Futures Exchange (L.I.F.F.E.) (q.v.); a certain variation is set above and below the previous day's closing or settlement price; if either the upper or lower limit is reached then trading ceases for a period. The practice varies in different parts of the market as to whether the pause in trading is for a limited period, such as an hour, or for the rest of the day. In either case, the pause provides a calming influence which prevents a news item or rumour from causing undue volatility in the market. On re-opening, the market will have decided whether there were good underlying reasons for the rise or fall in prices and if the reasons were justified then the market will start trading again at new levels reflecting changed prices in the underlying cash markets. *See* INTERNATIONAL COMMODITIES CLEARING HOUSE LIMITED.

Price mechanism. System used in a competitive society for the distribution of scarce resources through the agency of price. If too little of commodity A and too much of commodity B is being produced, the demand price for A rises, and that for B falls. The signal is thus given to the productive system to make the necessary adjustments. If competition were perfect these adjustments would continue until marginal cost and price were equal. The prices of all goods and services form an inter-related system; what we are prepared to pay for A depends on the terms which we can obtain for B, C, D, etc. In other words all prices are mutually determined. Price tends to equate the amount sellers are prepared to offer for sale and the amount which buyers wish to buy.

The market system theoretically leads to a point of maximum efficiency through the marginal equivalence of costs and prices. Producers seek to minimise their costs while consumers maximise their satisfaction. At the point of maximum efficiency, a redistribution of output could not increase the satisfaction of anybody without reducing that of someone else.

One of Alfred Marshall's greatest contributions to economics was the discovery that pricing problems should be treated primarily from the view point of time. He distinguished three fundamental time periods in pricing:

(a) market price—the price of a commodity during a period in which its supply is fixed;

(b) short-run normal price—the price of a commodity during a (longer) period in which the rate of production (per unit of time) is variable but in which there exists a fixed amount of plant;

(c) long-run normal price—the price of a commodity during the period in which the rate of production is completely variable.

He recognised the roles of supply and demand in the determination of price, but also the long-term influence of costs of production on supply and hence on price.

However, the market system only works perfectly when all the preconditions for perfect competition (q.v.) exist. Even in conditions of imperfect competition (q.v.) a market system may perform better than any conceivable alternative in respect of the range of goods and services considered.

The price mechanism is defective in that it does not necessarily succeed in regulating supply as required; in that it does not necessarily operate without inflation; and in that it does not automatically adjust social and private marginal net products. There are areas in which the price mechanism not only fails, but could not operate. In these instances, the state often finds it necessary to produce goods which cannot be provided by the market, e.g. low-income and welfare housing. In addition, in world commodity markets price has proved a singularly ineffective weapon for achieving reductions in output. Small diminutions in price or demand have produced gluts of astonishing proportions. This has been largely due to the efforts of the small peasant who, faced with a reduction in price, increases his output in order to maintain his income. During the Great Depression, 1929–35 the world stock of foodstuffs and raw materials increased two- or three-fold while prices declined some 50 per cent or more. Remedies have included proposals for 'buffer stocks' (q.v.) and for Government controlled quota arrangements. *See* DEMAND; MARGINAL SOCIAL AND PRIVATE NET PRODUCTS; PRICING.

Price shading. The practice of selling below published prices.
Price-specie-flow mechanism. The mechanism by which balance-of-payments disequilibria are corrected under the gold standard (q.v.). If country A is importing more than it exports, it will pay for the extra imports in gold. This flow of gold will reduce the money supply in Country A and increase the money supply of its creditors. The change in money supply will lower the price level in Country A and raise the price levels in the creditor countries. These price changes will tend to correct the initial disequilibrium by making it cheaper to buy from Country A and more expensive to buy from its creditors.
Price spread. *See* OPTION SPREAD.
Price theory or micro-economic theory. Theory concerned with how the price system handles the problem of allocating scarce resources in a market economy; price theory is concerned with how relative prices are determined, not with how the general price level is determined. Price theory may be divided into five sub-sections: (a) the theory of demand and consumer behaviour; (b) the theory of the business firm; (c) the theory of market organisation; (d) the theory of distribution; and (e) the theory of general equilibrium and welfare economics. *See* PRICING.
Prices Surveillance Authority (Aust.). A regulatory body created by the Australian Government in 1983 to investigate applications for price rises and initiate investigations into financial institutions, charges imposed by government authorities, and fees charged by professional people. The term 'price' was to include a charge of any description and any pecuniary benefit arising from the supply of goods or services. The Authority's predecessor was the Prices Justification Tribunal.
Pricing. *See* ADMINISTERED PRICING; ANTICIPATORY PRICING; ARBITRAGE; 'CHARGING WHAT THE TRAFFIC WILL BEAR'; COMMODITY EXCHANGE; COST OF SERVICE PRINCIPLE; EQUILIBRIUM PRICE; FLOATING EXCHANGE RATE; FULL COST PRICING; IMPERFECT COMPETITION; INTERVENTION PRICES; MARGINAL COST PRICING; MARKET; MICRO-ECONOMICS; PERFECT COMPETITION; PRICE DISCRIMINATION; PRICE MECHANISM; PRICE, THEORY OF; RESALE PRICE MAINTENANCE; STOCK EXCHANGE; SUPPLY AND DEMAND, LAWS OF; TARGET RETURN PRICING; VALUE-ADDED TAX.
Primary dealer (U.S.). *See* REGULATED PRIMARY DEALER (U.S.).
Primary industry. A term sometimes used in a wide sense to include not only all types of rural industry but all types of mining and quarrying activities; often the term is restricted to rural industries only. In this latter sense, the term embraces the production of goods from agriculture, forestry and fishing. *See* SECONDARY INDUSTRY; TERTIARY INDUSTRY.
Primary market. The principal underlying market for a financial instrument or physical commodity. *See* COMMODITY EXCHANGE.
Prime credits. Large financially strong corporations of excellent credit standing and able to sell commercial paper (q.v.) in the money markets.
Prime rate (U.S.). The lowest interest rate payable by borrowers having the highest credit rating.
Private limited company. In Britain, an incorporated business enjoying limited liability (q.v.) but which cannot invite the public to subscribe for any of its shares or debentures; it must restrict the right to transfer its shares. It must comply with the requirements of the Companies Acts. At the end of 1981, there were some 792,000 private companies in Britain. *See* COMPANIES ACTS 1948 TO 1985; COMPANY, LEGAL FORMATION OF; INCORPORATED BUSINESSES; UNINCORPORATED BUSINESSES.
Private placing. The provision of business capital by a finance company, not by way of an ordinary loan but by the purchase of a new issue of debentures or shares.
Private sector. The 'private sector' of the economy is the combination of elements in the economy which are not organs or agencies of central or local government and therefore includes the company sector and the personal sector.
Privately placed bonds. Newly issued bonds placed with a small number of purchasers through private negotiations; purchasers in this kind of sale are typically large financial institutions such as life insurance companies. *See* BOND; PUBLICLY ISSUED BONDS.
Privatisation. The selling back to the private sector of government assets, such as nationalised industries, share stakes owned in private companies, testing stations, research centres, publicly-owned shopping centres and bus services. During the early 1980s, both the British and Australian Governments pursued vigorous policies of selling their assets. The Thatcher Government in Britain reduced its share in or sold British Aerospace, Ferranti, Fairey, British Sugar, Cable and Wireless, Britoil, Jaguar, British Telecom, British

Airways, British Petroleum, and several others. Later proposals included British Gas. By 1985, twelve major sales had involved the transfer of 400,000 workers to the private sector.

Probate price. The price used in the United Kingdom in valuing shares for taxation purposes. It is calculated on the 'quarter up' principle: that is, instead of taking the middle price in the official list, the difference between the two prices given under 'quotation' is divided by four and this amount is added to the lower one.

Producer goods. Goods made for the purpose of producing consumer goods and other capital goods, e.g. machinery of all kinds. Synonymous with 'capital goods'.

Producer Price Indexes (P.P.I.). Measures of the monthly changes in prices received by commodity producers. There are three U.S. Indexes relating to: commodity groupings (farm products and industrial commodities); output of selected industries; and processing stages (raw materials, intermediate materials, and finished goods). The finished goods component in the processing stages series is often regarded as the key overall indicator of inflation in primary markets. The P.P.I.s are compiled by the U.S. Bureau of Labor Statistics and published in the *Monthly Labor Review*.

Producer sovereignty. The dominance of large producers within the economy and their ability to manage the demand for major public goods. Professor John Kenneth Galbraith describes the mechanism of sovereignty in his book *Economics and the Public Purpose* (1974); the intelligence which justifies research and development comes through the public bureaucracy to which the technostructures of the weapons firms are symbiotically related. Military secrecy can be invoked to exclude public and legislative intrusion into the relevant decisions. These decisions are made by and within the organisations that have most to gain from the investment in innovation. The use of technical innovation in the management of demand of major public goods is the ultimate achievement of producer sovereignty.

Producers' surplus. The excess of the total earnings of a supplier of a good or service over the payment actually necessary to just induce him to continue to supply the amount involved. It is the excess of revenue over the total avoidable costs (q.v.) of supply. The term was invented by Alfred Marshall (1842–1924) although the concept had been well developed by A. J. E. J. Dupuit (1804–1866). The magnitude of the surplus depends on production costs, the elasticity of the supply curve, price and market conditions.

Product differentiation. Attempts to create differences between products of a similar nature, e.g. breakfast cereals, by introducing distinct brand names, variations in preparation and presentation, and by skilful advertising. The object is to ensure that the product of any one firm is not regarded as a perfect substitute, in the mind of the buyer, for the product of any other firm. If a product establishes itself in the public mind, it may then command a price somewhat higher than another product of similar qualities.

Product market. The market in which goods and services are bought and sold in a private economy; the main sellers are privately-owned and publicly-owned business firms and the main buyers are private consumers or householders. To be distinguished from the factor market (q.v.).

Production. Activities resulting in a supply of useful goods and services. These activities include mineral extraction, manufacturing, agriculture, transport and communication, wholesale and retail distribution, and the work of civil servants and local government employees.

Production coefficient. The quantity of productive services necessary to produce one unit of a commodity, e.g. if it requires 15 cwts. of coke to produce one ton of pig-iron, then the production coefficient is 3/4. The concept is useful for studying trends. Some production coefficients appear to be fixed or partially so, while others are variable; in the long-run, however, probably all coefficients are variable.

Production costs. *See* COSTS OF PRODUCTION.

Production function. The relationship between input of production services and output of product, per unit of time. Production functions are descriptive of techniques or systems of organisation of production services. The problem of production consists in selecting the most appropriate production function and then determining the input which will minimise costs. The micro-production function is the production function of the firm, while the macro- or aggregate-production function is the production function of an industry, a sector of the economy, or the economy as a whole.

Production-possibility curve. A graphical presentation showing the alternative productive possibilities of a given supply of factors of production (q.v.). A production-possibility curve is a 'maximal' concept plotting all those combinations of goods which can be produced if all resources are fully employed; any point within the curve corresponds to possible combinations of products using resources at less than full employment. Figure 19 shows the relative quantities of consumer goods and capital goods which may be produced from given amounts of labour and materials. The slope of the curve measures the rate at which one commodity can be transformed into another; or the marginal (opportunity) cost of producing an extra unit of any one commodity in terms of the unit(s) of the other commodity sacrificed. The slope of the curve is often referred to as the marginal rate of transformation. With economic growth and continuously improving productivity (q.v.), the transformation or production-possibility curve will tend to move outwards, offering varying combinations of increasing quantities of goods. *See* FIGURE 20.

Production, theory of. A branch of economics (q.v.) concerned with the study of alternative production methods and the consequences of decisions taken in respect of production methods; also with the analysis of the determinants of a firm's choice of quantities of inputs, given its production function (q.v.), the prices of the inputs, and the level of output desired. Theory is based on the hypothesis that the firm will wish to use that production function and set of quantities of the inputs which will minimise the overall costs of production for a given output. By varying the output, it is then possible to construct the output-cost relationships which are the basis for much of the theory of the firm. Analysis in production theory forms the basis for the theory of

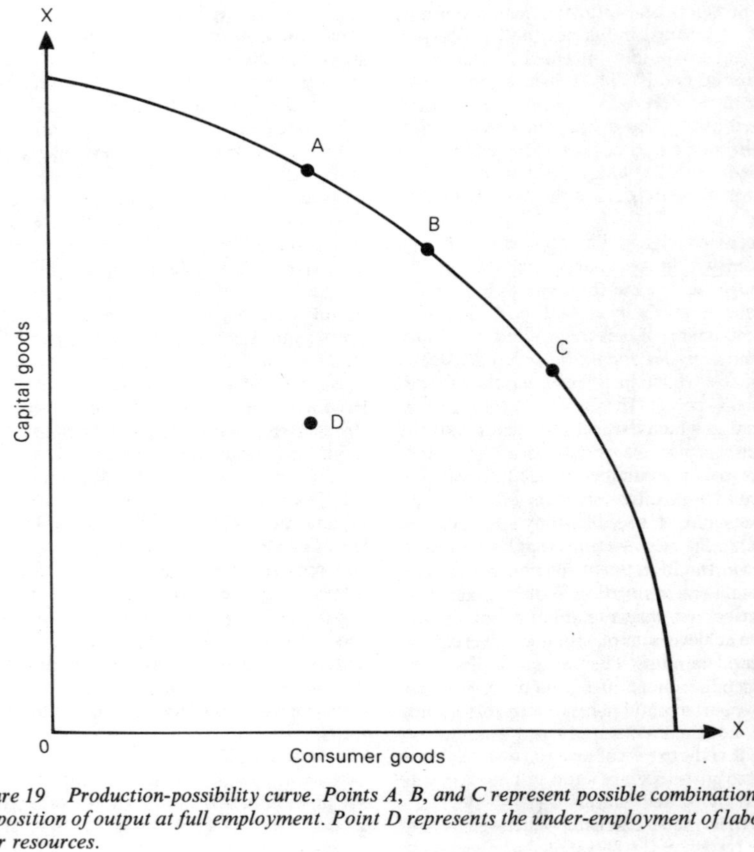

Figure 19 Production-possibility curve. Points A, B, and C represent possible combinations of the composition of output at full employment. Point D represents the under-employment of labour and other resources.

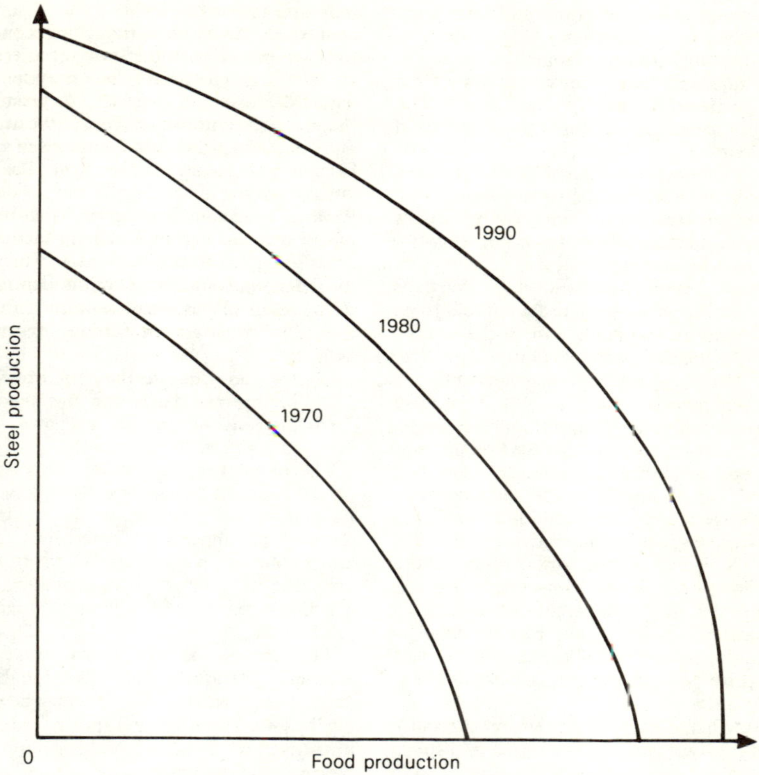

Figure 20 Outward shifts of the production-possibility curve.

marginal productivity, and the determination of factor prices. *See* CAPITAL EMPLOYED, RETURN ON; DIMINISHING RETURNS, LAW OF; ECONOMIES OF SCALE; FACTORS OF PRODUCTION; INCREASING RETURNS, LAW OF; MARGINAL PRODUCT; OPTIMUM FIRM; PRODUCTION COEFFICIENT; PRODUCTION FUNCTION; PRODUCTIVITY; VARIABLE PROPORTIONS, LAW OF.

Production, time structure of. The time interval between a decision to undertake production and the beginning of the outflow of the product; the more capitalistic or 'capital intensive' the method of production, the longer will be the time interval. In respect of a power station some 5/6 years may elapse between a decision to build and the initial flow of electricity into the Grid.

Productivity. The efficiency with which productive resources, i.e. labour, capital and land, are used; the motive for increasing productivity is to produce more goods at a lower cost per unit of output while maintaining quality. It is not easy to measure changes in productivity, but the relationship of output to man-hours expended is often adopted as a rough guide; this criterion relates to input of labour only, without reference to capital or land, and in certain circumstances may give a misleading picture. The increasing total annual production in Britain has been due partly to an increase in population, but mainly to increasing productivity per man-hour. The rate of improvement in total output and productivity has yet to achieve the targets set by the National Economic Development Council (q.v.) as within Britain's capacity. The main factors contributing to high industrial productivity are:

(a) adequate buildings, plant and equipment intensively used and kept up to date by replacement;
(b) suitably trained labour;
(c) adequate and steady supplies of raw materials;
(d) efficient services, e.g. power, transport, etc.;
(e) the best managerial skills and technical know-how applied to the organisation of production and the lowering of costs;
(f) markets capable of absorbing the whole of the output;
(g) good employee/employer relationships;
(h) an industrial climate favourable to expansion and confidence in the future;
(i) the abandonment of restrictive practices (q.v.) by both management and employees.

Profit maximisation. A traditional assumption in the theory of the firm that the firm attempts to maximise returns or profits. It has been argued that subject to the constraints of knowledge, energy, and ambition, the firm in the market system, competitive or monopolistic, does in fact attempt to maximise profits in the short- or long-run. However, it has been suggested in recent years that the single aim of maximising profits cannot be considered an adequate description of the driving force of enterprise. Security of earnings may also be an important aim.

Growth may provide the element of security sought; hence profit maximisation as a single-minded goal may be traded off against growth, growth being pursued from time-to-time at the expense of profits. With growth goes increasing power in markets, over community attitudes, and in relation to government. A growing firm is better able often to control its technology, its costs and prices; its long-term profitability may or may not be improved, but earnings are more secure and survival progressively insured against the threats of takeover or bankruptcy. Hence the great corporation tends to become larger.

The changing structure of the firm has also influenced objectives. Shareholders, the recipients of profits and the owners of the firm, tend no longer to participate actively or effectively in the running of their firms, accepting a reasonable level of dividend. Control passes to management which sees satisfactions and rewards as much linked with size as with profits; hence management may attempt to maximise the rate of growth of the firm while attempting to achieve only a reasonable profit level.

Indeed, more recent theory suggests that firms do not seek to maximise anything, but only aim to reach satisfactory levels of sales, profits, growth and security. The participants today in business include managers, workers, shareholders, customers, and suppliers, each with their own set of goods; the results are therefore a compromise between competing and conflicting interests. This is known as the behavioural theory of the firm. *See* FIRM, THEORY OF THE.

Profits. In accountancy terms, what remains out of business earnings after paying current expenses (costs of production) and providing for the maintenance intact of the money value of the assets of the business. In the case of an individual employer two further items may be deducted:

(a) the salary due to the employer himself for his own work, and
(b) interest on any of his own capital invested in the business.

The remainder may be regarded as 'pure profit' which is the reward for taking risks. Pure profits are more clearly distinguished in the case of 'impersonal' enterprises (private and public companies largely) where all salaries due and interest on all capital employed are taken account of fully in the costs of production.

The term 'normal profits' appears in economic literature. This term can be best defined as the least sum which must be paid to the business person (or firm) to induce the investment of capital in any particular process. Normal profit or expectation is equal to what could be obtained if it was employed in some other way, allowing for different degrees of risk and for any 'non-monetary' advantages or disadvantages. Economists regard normal profit as a necessary cost of production—a cost necessary to call forth a sufficient supply of that special kind of labour, enterprise. Profit may include an element of rent or quasi-rent. High profits may be earned in some industries as a consequence of monopoly power, rather than a high degree of uncertainty. Such profits are not a necessary cost, but an economic rent (q.v.) exacted at the expense of the community. In a perfectly competitive economy, profit as defined by the economist (as a surplus above 'normal profit') is zero in the long-run.

Project financing. A form of lending increasingly used for natural resource developments, where more emphasis is placed on the borrower's future cash flow for repayments, rather than an immediate asset.

Promissory note. Simply a promise to pay a certain sum at a stated time, in documentary form. Depending upon its credit standing such a note is negotiable. Promissory notes were introduced to the Australian money market in January, 1977, in denominations of not less than $100,000. The time to maturity when payment becomes due ranges from 10 to 180 days. These promissory notes, issued by large business houses, are covered by the Bills of Exchange Acts 1909–73. They may be sold on a discount basis to mature at the principle amount. Sale and transfer does not require endorsement as in the case of a bill of exchange (q.v.). However, the avoidance of this commitment restricts the use of these notes to such bodies as trading banks, insurance companies, and superannuation funds.

Pronto system. *See* HOME BANKING SERVICE.

Propensities to consume and save. Concepts developed by John Maynard Keynes (1883–1946) which represent the fractions of the total proceeds or income derived from employment which are, respectively, consumed and invested. The amount which a community spends on consumption depends (a) partly on the amount of its income; (b) partly on the other attendant circumstances; (c) partly on the subjective needs and the psychological propensities and habits of the individuals composing it; and (d) the principles on which the income is divided between them. Keynes defined the principal objective factors which influence the propensity to consume as (a) a change in the wage-unit, i.e. a change in real income; (b) a change in the difference between income and net income; (c) windfall changes in capital values not allowed for in calculating net income; (d) changes in the rate of time-discounting, i.e. in the ratio of exchange between present goods and future goods; (e) changes in fiscal policy, e.g. rate of income tax, tax on 'unearned' income taxes on capital gains, death duties, etc.; (f) changes in the expectation of the relation between the present and future levels of income. Keynes also defined the subjective factors—the motives or objects of subjective character—which lead individuals to refrain from spending out of their incomes. These motives are (a) to build up a reserve against unforseen contingencies; (b) to provide for future needs—old-age, family education, etc.; (c) to enjoy interest and appreciation, because a larger real consumption at a later date is preferred to a smaller immediate consumption; (d) to enjoy a gradually increasing expenditure; (e) to enjoy a sense of independence and power to do things; (f) to secure a *masse de manoeuvre* to carry out speculative or business projects; (g) to bequeath a fortune; and (h) to satisfy pure miserliness. Keynes described these eight subjective motives to save as the motives of Precaution, Foresight, Calculation, Improvement, Independence, Enterprise, Pride and Avarice. Apart from the savings of individuals, Keynes also defined the motives for saving by central and local government, by institutions and by business corporations. These are (a) to secure resources to carry out further capital investment; (b) to secure liquid resources to meet emergencies, difficulties and depressions; (c) to secure a gradually increasing income; (d) financial prudence and the anxiety to be 'on the right side'.

Property trust. *See* UNIT TRUST.

Prospectus. A document issued by a company or person wishing to raise capital by public subscription; the minimum contents of a prospectus are defined in the Companies Act 1985. The requirements of the Stock Exchange Council must also be complied with if it is intended to apply to the Council for a quotation. In the United States such securities must be registered with the Securities and Exchange Commission (q.v.). The prospectus discloses such information as the issuer's property and business, the nature of the security offered, the use of the proceeds, the issuer's prospects, and the company's history. A preliminary version of a prospectus is called a red herring.

Protection. The adoption by the State of special measures to protect an industry from competition. Three types of argument have been used in support of protection:

(a) It may be considered desirable to forgo the economic advantages flowing from the international division of labour for the purpose of making a country self-sufficient in respect of certain commodities, or in respect of all commodities;

(b) It may be thought expedient to impose *tarif de combats* (q.v.) in order to induce other countries to lower their tariff barriers in respect of one or more commodities. This exception to free trade policy was recognised as permissible by Adam Smith.

(c) It may be thought desirable to give temporary protection to a young and growing industry. This is known as the 'infant industry' argument. It is to be found in John Stuart Mill's *Principles of Political Economy*

(d) To improve the terms of trade, or combat the threat of unemployment.

See CLASSICAL SCHOOL; COMPARATIVE ADVANTAGE, THEORY OF; CUSTOMS DUTY; EXCISE DUTY; INFANT INDUSTRY; INTERNATIONAL TRADE; TARIFF.

Proxy. A written authorisation given by a shareholder to another person to vote on his behalf at a company meeting.

Proxy variable. The taking of unemployment or some other variable as a 'proxy' for demand, instead of directly measuring demand forces.

P.S.B.R. *See* PUBLIC SECTOR BORROWING REQUIREMENT.

PSL1. *See* MONEY SUPPLY.

PSL2. *See* MONEY SUPPLY.

Pty. Abbreviations for 'Proprietary' used as part of the names of private limited companies in Australia. *See* LIMITED LIABILITY.

Public cognisance. A term used by Professor John Kenneth Galbraith in his *Economics and the Public Purpose*, 1974 to describe the political recognition by the public of the basic divergence between the goals pursued by the planning system (q.v.) and the public interest. He described the subordination of the State to individual purposes which makes producer interest and public interest appear identical as a 'disguising myth'. He described the underlying conflict as general, and not confined to a few specific cases. *See* NEW SOCIALISM.

Public corporation. A corporate body created by public authority, with defined powers and functions, and financially independent. It is administered by a Board. Its capital structure and financial operations are similar to those of a public company, but the stockholders (if any) have no equity interests and no voting rights or power to appoint Board members. The first public corporation to meet this definition was the Central Electricity Board set up in 1926 to promote and control the bulk generation of electricity and to construct and maintain the bulk transmission lines. The British Broadcasting Corporation was established shortly afterwards under a Royal Charter.

Public debt ratio. The ratio of public money debt in a nation expressed as a ratio of gross national product (G.N.P.) (q.v.). O.E.C.D. studies reveal that the public debt/G.N.P. ratio is around 40 per cent in the United States of America, Japan, West Germany, and Australia. In Britain, the ratio has been just over 50 per cent. The rapid growth in public debts relative to G.N.P. since the early 1970s has caused concern in many countries. Apart from increasing debt interest payments, such growth may lead to an upward pressure on interest rates and fears of future inflation.

Public goods and services. Goods and services distributed by the state free to its citizens, being indivisible benefits shared by everyone equally. No private entrepreneur could provide and sell such goods and services efficiently on an individual basis. Examples are external defence, police, maintenance of law and order, regulation of industry, overseas representation, tax collection, civil defence. *See* MERIT GOODS AND SERVICES.

Public issue. A method of issuing equities (q.v.) to raise new business funds for capital investment. The company fixes a price for the shares to be issued, and the public are invited through the newspapers to apply for stated amounts of the shares at the specified prices. The company does not sell the shares first to an issuing house, although an issuing house may be retained as adviser. *See* ISSUING HOUSE; PLACING; OFFER FOR SALE; OFFER FOR SALE BY TENDER; RIGHTS ISSUE; STOCK EXCHANGE INTRODUCTION.

Public limited company. In Britain, an incorporated business which can invite the general public to subscribe for its shares and debentures and whose shares may be quoted on the stock exchanges; the company must comply with the requirements of the Companies Acts, and carry the words 'public limited company' or 'plc' after its name. At the end of 1981, there were some 8,000 public limited companies in Britain, in contrast to some 792,000 private companies, and some 2 million unincorporated businesses. *See* COMPANIES ACTS 1948 TO 1985; COMPANY, LEGAL FORMATION OF; LIMITED LIABILITY; INCORPORATED BUSINESS; UNINCORPORATED BUSINESS.

Public sector. The 'public sector' of the economy usually denotes the combination of the central Government, the local authorities and the nationalised industries and other public corporations.

Public Sector Borrowing Requirement (P.S.B.R.). The needs of the public sector (q.v.) for finance to support spending and lending in excess of its revenues; a measure of the creation of new government debt. For the financial year 1983–84, the P.S.B.R. in Britain amounted to 3 per cent of the gross national product (q.v.). The P.S.B.R. is financed through the sale of securities to the non-bank private sector; sales of foreign exchange; sales of gilt-edged securities to overseas holders; national savings; special sales of assets; and increased bank and monetary sector lending to the public sector. The containment of the size of the P.S.B.R. has been a constant problem for the British Government.

Publicly issued bonds. Bonds offered for sale publicly to a large number of potential purchasers, in contrast to privately placed bonds (q.v.); pension funds, private and public institutions, and many private individuals dominate this market. *See* BOND.

Punting. Speculating, the essence of life in the world's finance markets, including the share, stock, commodity, and futures markets.

Purchasing power parity theory. A theory which asserts that, left to the free play of market forces, the rates of exchange between currencies depend upon the relative purchasing power of the currencies in the country concerned. Thus changes in exchange rates will tend to reflect the changes in the relative price levels in the different countries. A rise in the price level in one country will tend to be offset by a fall of the exchange rate so that the price of the country's export and import commodities will remain the same in world markets. The theory has much validity in the long run.

Pure competition. A large number of small firms selling a homogeneous product. *See* PERFECT COMPETITION.

Pure monopoly. A situation in which a single seller offers a product which has no close substitutes. *See* MONOPOLY.

Put option. The Buyer (taker) acquires the right to sell a futures contract at a basis (or strike) price agreed at the time of concluding the contract.

Put through. A special dealing procedure applying usually to very large orders on The London Stock Exchange, by which the stockbroker (q.v.) finds both a seller and a buyer, and the stockjobber (q.v.) 'puts the shares through' the market for a very small turn (q.v.).

Put, to. To sell.

Puts. A holder's option to sell.

Putsefoot. A put option (q.v.) on The London Stock Exchange Index.

Pyramid selling. A selling technique which involves a company selling the right to sell a product, or the right to sell the right to sell a product. A pyramid company offers earnings to buyers of rights through the very act of selling more and more distributorships or franchises, and by charging participants for a place higher up the pyramid. Higher earnings are offered for selling franchises than for selling the product. The typical recruitment pattern involves each participant recruiting one person a week. The impracticability of this has resulted in many people losing heavily. The pyramid company has been outlawed in many American States, France, Canada, and several other countries.

Pyramid sub-contracting. A system in which a sub-contractor agrees to do a given job for a fixed cash sum; this is then parcelled out in agreed cash amounts among 'self-employed' workers recruited to do the job. *See* CASH ECONOMY.

Pyramiding. (a) When a tax is imposed at an early stage of production, the effect on the final price when a percentage increase is made at each successive stage of manufacture. (b) The purchasing of the same security on a rising market. (c) The concentration of control over joint-stock companies by a series of controlling interests in holding companies. (d) A technique of adding to an initial investment or 'position' in a commodity market by adding more contracts to that position; it is often considered imprudent to avoid adding more contracts at any one time than the number of contracts in the original or 'base' commitment. Generally it is advised that additions should be on a progressively small scale; hence the description 'pyramiding'. *See* ADDING TO A POSITION.

Q

Q-ratio. Devised by Professor James Tobin (1981 Nobel Memorial prize in economics), a ratio, derived empirically, which measures the relationship of the market value of physical capital (such as existing plant or other corporate asset) to its replacement cost. When the Q-ratio is low, corporations tend to acquire existing assets rather than build new plant and equipment. High interest rates may make existing assets look cheap and expensive to replace.

Quality of life. In current usage, a phrase which appears to cover a miscellany of desirable things not necessarily recognised, or adequately recognised, in the market place. Some qualities of the life of a community which cannot readily be valued or measured include such matters as civil liberties, compassion, justice, freedom and fair play. Then there are the important matters of the material standard of living, health and education, community relationships, employment opportunities and security of employment, job satisfaction, housing conditions, travelling time, nutrition and general stress, personal and family relationships. Environment protection is an important element in the quality of life of all communities at all stages of development.

Quangos. Quasi-autonomous non-government organisations, created by governments for the purposes of delegating or avoiding responsibility. Quangos include boards, commissions, authorities, and agencies which operate outside the normal departmental structure of government. Some are very large comprising nationalised industries or municipal organisations, while many are small being concerned with the supervision, regulation or control of limited activities. Governments may take credit for the achievements of their quangos when things go well, but are able to turn on and denigrate appropriate quangos when things go wrong.

Quantity Theory of Money. A theory developed by the American economist Irving Fisher (1867–1947), the essentials of which are contained in the equation:

$$MV = PT$$

where M = the amount of money (bank notes, etc. plus bank deposits); V = the velocity of circulation; P = a price index covering all transactions; and T = total volume of transactions per unit of time.

From this equation it may be deduced that with V and T constant an increase in M must result in an increase in P. With V and P constant, an increase in M could be offset by an increase in T. With both P and T constant, a decrease in M could be offset by an increase in V. If T is constant, an increase in P must be due to an increase in M or V, or both. The equation is useful in indicating the relationship between the four parameters. This suggests that inflation (q.v.) can be controlled by the monetary authorities through the regulation of the quantity of money in existence. If a certain growth in real income is anticipated, this can be achieved without inflation by allowing the quantity of money in the economy to increase at the same rate.

Efforts to control the quantity of money in the economy may be hindered through the existence of quasi- or near-money and because of the operations of non-bank financial intermediaries in developing and extending forms of credit; it has been argued that variations in the money value of total expenditures need not, because of these factors, bear any stable relationship with variations in the quantity of money. This argument shifts attention to the determinants of total expenditure and to the total liquidity in the economy, and to the possible need for fiscal as well as monetary policy in attempting to control the economy. The significant differences between the monetarist and Keynesian approaches, and the nature of their respective recommendations, derive from the relative emphasis given to the practical importance of the money supply (q.v.). The controversy has been of very great importance in Western economies.

The New Quantity Theory is presented:

$$MV=Y$$

where Y = money income.

In the older Quantity Theory, more money could affect either P, T, or V. In the new version, only Y or V can be affected. Milton Friedman (b. 1912) regards V as a function solely of a set of variables, none of which can depend on the money supply; the direct impact of changes in the money supply is, after a time lag, not at all on V but entirely on Y. There is direct causation from M to Y.

Quarter up. *See* PROBATE PRICE.

Quasi-rent. Payment made for a commodity or service for the time being in limited supply. In such circumstances more is paid for a particular commodity or service than would really be necessary to maintain the existing supply. Where quasi-rent exists there is a true surplus, or 'economic rent' (q.v.). The quasi-rent may be eliminated either by an increase in supply, if this is practicable, or a fall in demand. The concept of this differential payment or quasi-rent was developed by Marshall.

Quaternary employment. Employment in educational establishments, research and development centres, and in providing consultant and specialist services, meeting the needs of the primary, secondary and tertiary sectors of the economy.

Queueing, theory of. Theory concerned with the rates at which productive facilities and services should be provided in order to achieve optimum efficiency, i.e. to minimise 'queues' or bottlenecks and synchronise better the supply of facilities or services with the demand for them. In management science, queueing theory attempts to describe how customers arrive for a service, how that service meets their requirements in terms of average and variations in service time, how long a customer may have to wait and how long a service unit may be idle. Also known as 'waiting line theory'.

Quick assets (U.S.). Current assets which can be quickly converted into cash.

Quick assets ratio (U.S.). Quick assets (q.v.) divided by current liabilities.

Quoted or listed company. A company whose shares are traded on The London Stock Exchange (q.v.).

R

Radcliffe Committee (U.K.). A Committee appointed by Treasury Minute dated 3 May 1957, 'to inquire into the working of the monetary and credit system, and to make recommendations'. The Committee's Report was presented to Parliament in August, 1959. The Committee concluded that the monetary mechanism could not, as operated through changes in the bank rate (q.v.), be relied on to control the economy but should be supplemented by increasing use of physical and other controls, and that there should be more central control over the banking system.

Rally. A brisk rise following a decline in the general price level of a security market, or of an individual stock or share.

Range. The difference between the highest and the lowest price at which a given futures contract has traded during a particular period of time, e.g. the opening period of the market, the closing period of the market, or any day, week, or month.

Ratchet theory of pricing. A view that manufacturers tend to raise prices when costs rise, but do not reduce them when costs fall.

Rate support grant (U.K.). The main channel of Exchequer (q.v.) aid to local authorities, replacing the general grant and the rate-deficiency grant.

At the beginning of each year, the local authorities assess their anticipated expenditure, except for housing which attracts separate subsidies. The Government agrees to meet a percentage of this expenditure and to distribute grants according to a formula which has three elements:

(a) a needs element which reflects the services an authority provides;
(b) a resources element paid to authorities with a relatively low rateable value per head;
(c) a domestic element, a direct subsidy to householders to prevent rates rising faster than incomes.

In 1981–82, the rate support grant in England and Wales took the form of a single block grant together with prescribed ceilings for the level of total local authority capital expenditure.

Rational expectations school. A group of economists who, disenchanted with the failures of macro-economic policies in the 1970s, have reconsidered the basic premises of modern macro-economics; this reconsideration has placed great emphasis on expectations in the community, on the credibility of policies, and on the limited scope available for discretionary stabilisation policies. The group recognises the role of expectations in influencing outcomes, e.g. the expectation of inflation has a strong influence in respect of present wage negotiations and price-setting.

The rational expectations school argues that there need be no involuntary unemployment, for anyone can find work by asking for it at a wage below the existing wage. The aim is that markets should clear and that economic agents should set wages and prices so as to achieve full employment, maximise profits, and maximise economic welfare. In this way, the prime responsibility for managing the economy moves from government to the employer, employee, trade union, and consumer; in the realm of government, the group sees the need for a permanently lower growth rate of nominal money. The expectations of a high inflation rate should be removed from the system, even though this may aggravate the immediate unemployment problem. In the longer term, the group does not accept that the level of output can be affected by changes in monetary policy, and indeed that only unexpected changes in the stock of money could affect the level of output. The group concedes no role for monetary policy in the long-term in systematically influencing output or unemployment. Any systematic policy such as monetary expansion in a time of recession is immediately known and wages and prices are set accordingly. The rational expectations approach is used by several schools of economics (q.v.), especially the New Keynesians. *See* NEW CLASSICAL SCHOOL; NEW KEYNESIAN SCHOOL.

Real Estate Investment Trust. An organisation similar to an investment company (q.v.) in some respects but concentrating its holdings in real estate investments.

Real gross national product. The value of the output of the national economy measured in the prices of some base year, permitting a true measure of the change in actual economic physical output. *See* GROSS NATIONAL PRODUCT; NOMINAL GROSS NATIONAL PRODUCT.

Real income. The value of goods and services produced within a given time period; changes in real income over or between time periods are computed by adjusting changes in nominal income (q.v.) arising from changes in the level of prices alone.

Real interest rate. An interest rate calculated by deflating nominal interest rates by the rate of inflation. If the inflation rate is higher than interest rates, investors are left with a negative real return; if yields exceed the rate of increase in the consumer price index, the return is positive.

In Britain, in the mid-1970s, real interest rates were negative for long periods; notwithstanding this, the personal savings ratio rose. In the 1980s, by contrast, real rates were positive and high, while the savings ratio fell. This highlights the importance of inflation as an independent influence on savings and consumption.

Real money balances. The quantity of goods and services which can be purchased from a given stock of money held by individuals. Changes in real-money balances are computed by adjusting changes in the quantity of money held to take account of changes in the level of prices.

Real wage resistance. Description used by Sir John Hicks (b. 1904) to describe the reluctance of workers to accept a cut in their standard of living. An increase in prices consequently leads to a price-induced rise in wages in order to maintain the standard of living

Recession. A significant reduction in employment and production, trade and investment; defined by Arthur M. Okun (1928–1980) as two consecutive quarters of negative growth in the gross national product (q.v.).

Recognised bank. *See* BANKING ACT, 1979.

Recognition lag. The period that elapses between the time an economic disturbance occurs and the time policy-makers and governments recognise that action is required. The recognition lag may be negative, if a problem is foreseen and appropriate policy actions adopted before the event. Most lags are positive due partly to the difficulties of collecting appropriate data and partly because it is never certain what the consequences of a disturbance will be.

Red herring. *See* PROSPECTUS.

Redeemable preference share. A share which a company may repay out of its reserve funds. This class of share may be issued by a company only if authorised by its articles of association.

Redemption price. The price at which a bond may be redeemed before maturity, at the option of the issuing company; also the price the company must pay to call in certain types of preferred stock. *See* CALLABLE.

Refinancing or refunding. The sale of new securities by a company the money being used to retire existing securities perhaps to save interest costs or extend the maturity of the loan.

Reflection effect or full-circle effect. When for example an extension of aid overseas leads indirectly to an increase of exports as well. Suppose that out of £1 million aid to a country, half is spent on third-country products; if part of this expenditure on third country products is reflected back to the donor country as third country imports, allowance should be made in assessing the cost of aid for this reflection effect.

Regional assistance (U.K.). Assistance by the British Government to regions with special problems; Britain is divided into special development areas, development areas (jointly known as the assisted areas) and enterprise zones (q.v.). Qualifying investments attract government grants of between 15 and 22 per cent of the capital involved. From 1979, the amount of cash available and the size of the assisted areas have been reduced. In 1981–82, some £500 million was allocated for regional aid.

Regional policy (E.E.C.). A programme of assistance by the European Economic Community (q.v.) to its depressed regions; cheap loans and grants supplement national spending. A regional fund was established in 1975; funds are allocated between the member states according to pre-fixed quotas. While the poorer countries receive most, all member states receive something. West Germany has a quota of almost 5 per cent, mainly for the Saar.

Registered bond. A bond which is registered on the books of the issuing company in the name of the owner: it can be transferred only when endorsed by the registered owner. *See* BEARER STOCKS OR BONDS.

Registered provident societies. A variety of institutions registered under the Friendly Society Acts, Industrial Assurance Acts, and other Acts. Societies include friendly societies, industrial assurance societies, industrial and provident societies, building societies, trade unions, certified loan societies, railway savings banks, superannuation and other trust funds. These societies are important as media for saving and investment and bestow many timely benefits on their contributors and dependents.

Registered unsecured notes. Issued by some companies, notes which give the holder the option or right to purchase, at a definite future time, a certain number of ordinary shares in the company. Notes yield a fixed rate of interest. These options are in effect rights in the unissued stock of a company.

Registrar of companies. *See* COMPANY, LEGAL FORMATION OF.

Registration of securities (U.S.). The registration of new securities under the Securities Act 1933 before a public offering may be made. Before a security may be admitted to dealings on a stock exchange, it must be registered under the Securities Exchange Act 1934.

Regular way delivery. A description of procedures on the New York Stock Exchange (q.v.) when securities, unless otherwise specified, are to be delivered to the buying broker by the selling broker, and payment made to the selling broker by the buying broker on the fifth business day after the transaction. Regular way delivery for bonds is the following business day.

Regulated primary dealer (U.S.). A member of the network of banks, brokerage-houses, and bond dealers that transact United States government securities. In 1984, the average turnover was some $60 billion a day. Primary dealers are those permitted to bid directly for new issues of government debt. The New York Federal Reserve Bank imposes a capital-adequacy test for such dealers. Since 1982, the primary dealers have had to make daily reports to the New York Fed on the value and volume of their business.

Regulation Q. Of the U.S. Federal Reserve System; a Regulation which sets limits on the rates of interest that U.S. commercial banks may pay on deposits. The limits, which are altered from time to time, vary according to the term and size of the deposits. The original purpose of the Regulation was to ensure prudent banking, but more recently it has been used as a weapon of monetary control. Easier monetary conditions in the U.S.A. led to the partial suspension of Regulation Q (on deposits of 30 to 89 days) in June, 1970. Regulation Q accelerated the growth of the Euro-dollar and Euro-currency markets, since Europeans were prepared to pay higher interest rates. In the early 1980s, the United States began to phase out interest-rate ceilings.

Renounceable documents. In the United Kingdom, temporary evidence of ownership, of which there are four main types. When a company offers shares to the public it sends an *allotment letter* (q.v.) to successful applicants. If it has a rights issue (q.v.), it sends a *provisional allotment letter* to its shareholders, or in the case of a capitalisation issue, a *renounceable certificate*. Any of these may be replaced, in the initial dealing period, by a *split receipt*, which takes the place of the original letter or renounceable certificate. All of these are, in effect, bearer securities, and are valuable. Each includes full instructions on what the holder should do if he wishes to have the newly issued shares registered in his own name, or if he wishes to *renounce them* in favour of somebody else.

Rent restrictions. Statutory control of the rents of privately owned dwellings. Legislation controlling rents was introduced into Britain during the First World War; rents were gradually decontrolled between the wars, but full rent control was re-introduced on the outbreak of the Second World War. The Rent Act 1957 allowed the gradual decontrol of rents, but the process was halted by the Labour Government in 1965. The Rent Act 1965 extended rent control to all privately owned rented properties of a rateable value of up to £400 in London and £200 elsewhere, and prevented eviction without a court order from premises of any value. In disputes between landlords and tenants, a local rent officer attempts to negotiate a 'fair' rent; if either party refuses to accept his decision the case may then be referred to a Rent Assessment Committee whose verdict is binding. The legislation was consolidated in the 1968 Rent Act. The Rent Act 1974 extended security of tenure to tenants of furnished property. In 1947 about 60 per cent of households lived in privately rented accommodation; by 1977 only 17 per cent; and by 1982 only 12 per cent (2.6

million). Tenancies continue to be regulated, a 'fair rent' being fixed by independent rent officers and, in some cases, by a rent tribunal. Tenants have a wide degree of security of tenure and may not be evicted without a court order.

Rent, Ricardo's theory of. A proposition that the rent of a piece of land is the excess of the yield of that piece of land over that of the worst land in cultivation. Ricardo considered that land at the margin of cultivation yielded no rent; indeed if rent was charged the land would not be cultivated. Farmers would have to pay more for the use of more fertile land, and the excess yield over that of 'no-rent' land would be its rent. Thus, the net return to farmers on a unit of land of any given fertility would tend to be the same. Ricardo regarded the rent of land as a surplus, or economic rent (q.v.). The ready conclusion that may be drawn from this theory is that as the world's population increases so landlords will receive ever-growing sums of unearned economic rent. This may be ultimately true, and is true in certain areas. But only a fraction of the land of the world suitable for agriculture and building has yet been brought into use. Ricardo's theory arose out of the condition of his time in which land was demanded mainly for corn; he did not foresee the growing demand for land for alternative uses such as building which would introduce another element into agricultural rents—a payment to keep land out of an alternative use.

Repos. *See* REPURCHASE AGREEMENTS.

Reproduction costs. Costs involved to achieve a sustained level of production; such costs might be involved in conserving the natural environment or providing a training programme for recruits to the industry. Such costs, such as those incurred in a major re-afforestation programme may yield no return in the short- or medium-term. *See* EXTERNAL EFFECTS.

Repurchase agreements. A method of financing in which a borrower sells U.S. government securities to a lender for a very short period of time, usually 1 day, and at the time of sale agrees to repurchase the securities at a stated price. The lender then knows the exact interest to be earned, and is in a secured position in the event of a default by the borrower. The securities are usually held by a bank trust department as trustee or by the Federal Reserve Bank for the region; in a case of default, the securities are delivered to the lender, these being in bearer form. Repurchase agreements are widely used by U.S. government bond dealers to finance their inventories of securities at as low a cost as possible. Such lending is popular with both banks and non-finance firms because the loans are fully secured. Repurchase agreements are now widely used by the Bank of England (q.v.). Usually called REPOs.

Resale price maintenance. A trade practice binding shopkeepers and dealers to sell goods at prices laid down by the manufacturer or other supplier. The principal effect of resale price maintenance is that it eliminates price competition between distributors of price-maintained goods. Formerly, in Britain, a manufacturer could refuse to supply a trader who failed to comply with his prescribed prices. In addition, the collective enforcement of resale prices by trade associations was widespread; if a trader reduced the price of one line of one manufacturer, his name might be placed on a 'stop list' and as a consequence he might be unable to obtain supplies of a wide range of goods made by other manufacturers.

In 1947, the Lloyd Jacob Committee reviewed the question of resale price maintenance. It was recommended that no action be taken which would deprive an individual producer of the power to prescribe and enforce resale prices for goods bearing his brand, but that collective sanctions should be made illegal. In 1956, the Restrictive Trade Practices Act prohibited the collective enforcement of resale price maintenance. At the same time the Act strengthened the power of the individual manufacturer to enforce resale prices set by him.

In 1964 the practice of resale price maintenance was again reviewed by Parliament and on this occasion it was decided to abolish all resale price maintenance save in those instances where a manufacturer could demonstrate that its retention for his goods was in the public interest. The result was the Resale Prices Act 1964 (q.v.). *See* PRICING.

Resale Prices Act 1964. Described as 'an Act to restrict the maintenance by contractual and other means of minimum resale prices in respect of goods supplied for resale in the United Kingdom.' The Act states that 'any term or condition of a contract for the sale of goods by a supplier to a dealer, or of any arrangement between a supplier and a dealer relating to such a sale, shall be void in so far as it purports to establish or provide for the establishment of minimum prices to be charged on the resale of goods in the United Kingdom'. The Act does not preclude a supplier from publishing recommended prices for his goods, but it is unlawful for dealers to withhold supplies from a dealer because he has sold such goods below the recommended price. It is however legal for a supplier to withhold goods which have been sold as 'loss leaders' (*see* LOSS LEADER). The Restrictive Practices Court may rule that any good or class of good is exempted for the purposes of the Act, but in every case it must be established that the resulting detriment to the public as consumers or users of the goods in question arising from the Act would outweigh any detriment to them resulting from the maintenance of minimum resale prices of goods. By 1971, nearly 500 classes of goods had been refused exemption; exemptions were granted only in respect of two classes (books and maps and medicaments).

The Resale Prices Act 1976 (which consolidated earlier legislation) imposed a general ban on the maintenance of minimum resale prices. The Act does not prevent manufacturers or suppliers from fixing maximum resale prices; neither does it prevent them from recommending or suggesting the price at which their goods should be resold. The Restrictive Practices Court (q.v.) may exempt goods from the ban on resale price maintenance (in 1983, only books and certain pharmaceutical products were exempted).

Reserve asset ratio. The ratio which United Kingdom banks had to maintain between eligible reserve assets and total sterling deposits, or eligible liabilities (q.v.). With effect from 5 January 1981, the reserve asset ratio was reduced from its traditional 12½ per cent to 10 per cent; for short periods during that year it was reduced from 10 per cent to 8 per cent. On 20 August 1981, the reserve asset ratio was abolished.

Reserve-deposit ratio. The ratio of reserves which are to be held with the Federal Reserve Bank (q.v.) by the commercial banks and the deposits held by the banks. The reserve-deposit ratio is determined in two ways: first, the banking system is subject to Federal Reserve Bank regulation in the form of minimum reserve requirements (these reserve requirements vary by type of deposit and also by bank size and location); and second, banks may wish to hold excess reserves beyond the level of required reserves. However, between 1970 and 1980 excess reserves have been less than 1 per cent of total reserves.

Reserve requirements. The volume of reserves that member banks must hold with a central bank, such as the Federal Reserve System (q.v.), as a percentage against existing deposits. A reduction in the reserve requirement increases excess reserves and tends to stimulate the economy, while an increase tends to have the opposite effect.

Reserve tranche. Formerly known as the gold tranche, a credit line extended by the International Monetary Fund (q.v.); the reserve tranche is 25 per cent of a country's quota and may be borrowed automatically. In addition to the reserve tranche, there are three credit tranches (each being 25 per cent of the quota) carrying progressively tougher terms.

Resource rent tax. A tax based on profits in excess of a level necessary for the commencement or continuation of a project. It may combine the functions of royalties and income taxes, but it could also be superimposed on an existing system of taxes and royalties. From 1984, a special tax was imposed by the Australian Government on new minerals and energy projects; however a threshold rate equal to the long term bond rate plus 15 per cent was considered adequate to ensure continued incentives for exploration. Only above this threshold would the full rate of 40 per cent tax on profits apply.

Restrictive practice. (a) Any inefficient working method or system which is difficult to alter, due to opposition from the management, the workers, or both. The practice may be perhaps unnecessary overtime working, for which the management is primarily responsible; or it may be a set of traditional working practices for which the unions are primarily responsible.

(b) A practice in restraint of trade or production. Among firms such practices as common prices, collusive tendering, allotment of sales or ouput quotas, division of markets, exclusive dealing and loyalty rebates to customers may be employed.

Restrictive Practices Court. A British Court set up in 1956 by the Restrictive Trade Practices Act of that year. The Restrictive Trade Practices Acts of 1956 and 1968 govern the registration and judicial examination of restrictive agreements. They require the registration of a wide range of restrictive agreements among producers and traders, and established the principle that price fixing and other restrictive arrangements are contrary to the public interest, unless the contrary is proved. Thus producers and traders wishing to operate such restrictions have to show that what is proposed is *positively* in the public interest. The Court examines and passes judgment on cases brought before it by the Registrar of Restrictive Practices. The Restrictive Trade Practices Act of 1956 was also important for prohibiting the collective enforcement of resale price maintenance (q.v.). Under the Fair

Trading Act 1973 (q.v.), the Director-General of Fair Trading became responsible for the enforcement of the Restrictive Trade Practices Act, a function carried out previously by the Registrar of Restrictive Trading Agreements.

Restrictive Trade Practices Act 1976 (U.K.). An Act which consolidates earlier legislation providing for the registration and subsequent judicial examination of agreements between two or more persons carrying on business in the U.K. in the supply of goods or commercial services under which certain kinds of restrictions are accepted. The legislation (which previously applied only for goods agreements) was applied to services by the Restrictive Trade Practices (Services) Order 1976.

Restructuring. The reforming of the administrative and management structure of a company, or the revising of its share capital structure; sometimes the term is a euphemism for the dismissal of workers without any serious restructuring being involved.

Reswitching of techniques. Descriptive of the possibility that a given manufacturing technique may be the most profitable one for business firms to adopt at two different rates of profit, while being unprofitable at rates between the two. For this reason, it is not possible in general to draw a negatively inclined demand curve for capital as a function of the rate of profit or rate of return on capital.

Retail banks. *See* WHOLESALE BANKS.

Retender. A situation in which holders of futures contracts who have received a delivery notice through the clearing house may under certain conditions sell a futures contract, submitting the notice to the clearing house in satisfaction of the short position.

Retention ratio. The percentage of the available disposable income (i.e. earnings after tax and after fixed interest and dividend obligations have been met) retained within the firm.

Revealed Preference Theory (R.P.T.). First formulated by Professor Paul A. Samuelson (b. 1915), a theory of consumer behaviour based solely on an analysis of choices actually made by the consumer in various price-income situations. A given income level and set of prices enables the consumer to select 'bundles' of goods he could purchase; the bundle selected is the revealed preference to all the other bundles that might have been purchased instead. Another income-price situation could reveal another bundle of goods as the revealed preference.

Revolving credit agreement. A written contractual agreement between a commercial bank and a customer for the bank to provide short-term funds up to a specified limit for a stipulated period of time at an interest rate generally tied to the prime rate (q.v.). Customers often pay a commitment fee for this type of credit arrangement in addition to compensating deposit balances.

Rights issue. The offer of new shares by a company to existing shareholders. Each shareholder has the right to subscribe to the new shares up to a given proportion of the shares he already holds, on the basis of, say, 1 for 1, 3 for 5, etc. The shareholder may either accept the offer himself, or may assign part or all of his 'rights' to someone else by means of a 'letter of renunciation'. Such 'rights' are valuable as the new shares are offered to shareholders at a price below the current market price. The making of a 'rights' issue by a company is a cheap and convenient way of raising additional capital (q.v.), particularly if the amount required is moderate in relation to the amount already issued. *See* OFFER FOR SALE; PLACING; PUBLIC ISSUE.

Ring (U.S.). A circular platform on the trading floor of an exchange, consisting of steps upon which traders and brokers stand while executing future trades. *See* COMMODITY EXCHANGES; PIT.

Ring trading. Auction sales in which traders form a ring around a caller.

Risk. Chance of injury or loss. There are two types of risk:

(a) insurable risk, e.g. fire, burglary, etc.;
(b) non-insurable risk or uncertainty, e.g. the risk of loss through changes in the future demand for goods. This type of risk or uncertainty may be reduced by, inter alia, hedging (q.v.). *See* UNCERTAINTY.

Risk capital. Capital subject to considerable risk. Also called 'venture capital.' *See* SECURITY CAPITAL.

Risk management. The process of identification, classification, measurement, and appropriate control of risks that threaten assets, both people and property, and the prospective earnings of a business or other enterprise; the costs of control and management of risks need to be weighed against the cost of insuring against risk, both elements being needed in most instances.

Robinson Patman Act 1936 (U.S.). An Act introduced to strengthen the Clayton Act 1914 (q.v.); it prohibited price discrimination (q.v.) in the sale of commodities of like grade and quality, where the effect of such discrimination was substantially to lessen competition, unless such discrimination was justified by savings arising in the manufacture or sale of the commodity in question.

Roll-over. Describes: (1) A special straddle trading procedure involving the shift of 1 month of a straddle into another future month, while holding the other contract month. The shift can take place in either the long or short straddle month; *see* STRADDLE. (2) A category of renewable bank deposit, e.g. a 5 year deposit rolled over every 3 months. (3) Renewing credit i.e. to roll-over debts by borrowing to pay them; and (4) borrowing to pay interest (if interest on a loan is rolled over for 3 years, it means you may borrow to pay the first 3 years' worth).

Roll-up shares. Share issues in which all the income is re-invested, after expenses, and added to capital values; in Britain such values have been taxed as a capital gain rather than income.

Rort (Aust.). Any trick, act of deception, or scheme for cheating; fraudulent tax evasion. *See* TAX-RORT ACCOUNT.

Rotation group bias. Identified in United States and Canadian labour market studies, the tendency for people to be more inclined to describe themselves as being unemployed and looking for work, when first interviewed, than when re-interviewed in later months. The explanation offered for rotation group bias is that people become more honest at repeat survey interviews, particularly if faced with the same interviewer in whom they can develop confidence.

Round lot. (a) Usually one hundred shares or more, being the normal unit of trading on a stock exchange (q.v.); (b) One standard contract of a specific commodity traded in the futures market (q.v.), e.g. 5,000 bushels of wheat, 36,000 pounds of pork bellies.

Round tripping. The movement of funds to profit by slight margins of gain; interest-rate arbitrage.

Round turn. The execution for the same principal of a purchase transaction and a sales transaction which offset each other.

Royal Commission on the Depression of Trade and Industry. A Royal Commission which reported in 1886; the report outlined the reasons why British firms were failing to keep pace with foreign competitors, especially the Germans and Americans: under-investment; small-scale and ramshackle plant; a lack of scientific training in managers; a failure to exploit new inventions; poor labour relations; salesmen without knowledge of foreign languages and overseas market conditions; and cultural norms which down-graded the engineer and tradesman while revering the life-style of the classically-educated English gentleman.

Royal Economic Society. A Society which has for its object the general advancement of economic knowledge. It was founded, under the name of the British Economic Association, at a meeting held at University College, London, on 29 November 1890. Its formation was the outcome of a circular, prepared by the Cambridge economist Alfred Marshall in consultation with others, entitled *Proposal to form an English Economic Association.* The Society became incorporated by Royal Charter in 1902. The Royal Economic Society's official publication, the *Economic Journal*, published quarterly, is intended to reflect the various shades of economic opinion, and to be the organ, not of one school of economists, but of all. The *Journal* numbers among its contributors leading economists of all countries.

S

Sales and leaseback. *See* LEASE-BACK AGREEMENT.

Samurai bonds. Bonds denominated in yen, issued in Japan by a foreign borrower.

Sandilands Committee. A Committee into inflation accounting, under the chairmanship of Sir Francis Sandilands, which reported to the British Government in 1976. The Committee concluded that the existing accounting conventions did not adequately allow for changes in costs and prices, recommending a new system of current cost accounting. *See* CURRENT COST ACCOUNTING; HISTORIC COSTS.

Satisficing. An alternative theory of economic behaviour advanced by Herbert Simon in 1957. It is a view that individuals and organisations are not concerned with achieving the best possible or optimal results at all times, but only in maintaining certain satisfactory positions. As long as results occur above certain points then anything will do, and there will be no motivation to improve the situation further. A decision-making body is studied not on the assumption that it seeks optimal results but on the assumption that it is a 'satisficing' organism; instead of continuously striving for the best it reacts when and only when the considerations which affect its welfare have fallen to levels unsatisfactory to it.

Saving. That part of income not consumed; the withholding of money from expenditure on goods and services. The amount saved out of any given income depends upon the Propensities to Consume and Save (q.v.), and out of any addition to income on the marginal propensities to consume and save. In discussing the national economy, however, economists frequently use the term 'saving' for expenditure of a special kind—the employment of income in the creation of new capital. Thus saving is identified with investment in real assets, and not with the 'hoarding' (q.v.) of money which is simply the non-expenditure of money held. Adopting this definition the savings and investment of a community can never diverge.

Savings banks. Institutions aiming at encouraging and facilitating the small saver. Often supported by central or state government, they have become particularly popular in continental Europe. In 1981, in West Germany, Austria and Spain, they accounted for over 35 per cent of total deposits.

Savings equal investment. A maxim of Lord Keynes (1884–1946) who defined savings and expenditure on capital goods or investment (q.v.) as being of necessity equal to one another. The logic of his argument was as follows:

Income = Expenditure on consumption goods and savings.

Output = Output of consumption goods and investment.

Since Total Income = Value of Total Output; and

Expenditure on consumption goods = Output of consumption goods.

Savings = Investment.

This is the simplified (closed economy, no government) form of the basic Keynesian relationship. It really amounts to Injections = Withdrawals. This is both an identity and an equilibrium condition. In Keynesian theory, the relationship is used to calculate the equilibrium level of income.

Savings, point of zero. A level of disposable income at which it is all consumed. Above this point, out of each additional unit of income a varying percentage will be devoted to consumption and the remainder saved; below that point dissaving will occur, i.e. past savings will be used up and debts incurred.

Say's law of markets. A law formulated by the French economist J. B. Say stating that every increase in the supply of goods is a corresponding increase in the demand for goods so long as producers have directed their production in accordance with each other's wants. Hence, it was argued, a general over-production of goods cannot occur. For a barter economy, this is a truism. Under modern conditions, however, the exchange of products takes place in two stages—first of all the exchange of a producer's product for money, and, subsequently, the exchanging of money for another producer's product. The second part of this operation may be postponed. If a sufficient number of buying decisions are postponed, the demand for goods may become temporarily restricted without necessarily curtailing the volume of production. In the long run, a reduction in the velocity of circulation of money would have a serious effect on demand, prices and production. Say formulated his law of the market in 1803. His view was generally accepted by the Classical School (q.v.) and it was not seriously questioned until the Great Depression, 1929–35 (q.v.) when John Maynard Keynes (1883–1946) effectively challenged its validity under modern conditions. *See* KEYNESIAN REVOLUTION.

Scale down. To buy at regular price intervals in a declining market; to scale up means to sell at regular price intervals as the market advances.

Scale order. An order to buy (or sell) a security which specifies the total amount to be bought (or sold) and the amount to be bought (or sold) at specified price variations.

Scalpers. Mainly floor brokers on commodity and stock exchanges who are in and out of the market the same day, trading and attempting to profit on moves of fractions of a cent or penny.

Schools of economics. *See* ACTIVISTS; AUSTRIAN SCHOOL; CAMBRIDGE SCHOOL (POST-KEYNESIAN); CHICAGO SCHOOL: CLASSICAL SCHOOL; GERMAN HISTORICAL SCHOOL; INSTITUTIONAL ECONOMICS; KEYNESIAN REVOLUTION; KEYNESIAN SCHOOL; LAUSANNE SCHOOL; 'MARGINAL' REVOLUTION; MARSHALLIAN ECONOMICS (NEO-CLASSICAL SCHOOL); MATHEMATICAL SCHOOL; MERCANTILISM; MONETARIST SCHOOL; NEO-CLASSICAL ECONOMICS; NEW CAMBRIDGE SCHOOL; NEW CLASSICAL SCHOOL; NEW KEYNESIAN SCHOOL; NEW SOCIALISM; OXFORD GROUP; PHYSIOCRATIC SCHOOL; RATIONAL EXPECTATIONS SCHOOL.

Scorched earth tactics. *See* ANTI-TAKEOVER TACTICS.

Scrip. A document which states that a person is the registered holder of a number of securities; the most common form of scrip is a share certificate (q.v.).

Scrip certificate. A provisional certificate for shares or debentures in a company, or for Government bonds. The scrip certificate is issued when the allotment money is paid; in due course it is exchanged for the share certificate (q.v.) or bond when all the instalments have been paid. *See* SCRIP; SCRIP DIVIDEND.

Scrip covered option. An option in which the seller (known as the writer) owns the security concerned (known as the underlying security); as opposed to a cash covered option, where the option is written against cash or other liquid asset. *See* SHARE OPTIONS.

Scrip dividend. The distribution by way of dividend of shares or debentures. The power to issue 'scrip dividends' must be contained in the articles of association (q.v.) of the company concerned.

Scrip or bonus issue of shares. The issue of additional shares free of charge to shareholders in proportion to the shares they already hold. This may be done when a company increases its capital by using some of its profits for this purpose and feels that the previously issued share capital does not give a true picture of the amount of capital actually employed by the firm. Indeed the gap between the nominal and market value of its shares may have become misleadingly large, with dividends expressed as a high percentage of nominal capital.

If a company makes a scrip or bonus issue to shareholders of one new £1 share for every £1 they hold and at the same time announces that there will be no change in the amount available for dividend payments, all that happens is that a shareholder who previously held one £1 share worth, say, £3.50 on the market now holds two £1 shares worth £1.75 each. The dividend, expressed as a percentage of nominal capital, would be halved in these circumstances. Thus a scrip or bonus issue does not add to the capital available to the business concerned and may be regarded as a bookkeeping transaction.

Scripophily. A term coined in the mid-1970s to describe the hobby of collecting antique bonds, stocks, and other financial instruments.

Second best, theory of. Essentially, a theory first advanced by R. G. Lipsey and K. Lancaster that if some part of the economy does not fulfil the Pareto optimal criterion it need not be optimal for any other sector of the economy to be expected to attain that position. In other words, optimality may require that other sectors of the economy assume positions which diverge from the perfectly competitive one. The theory brings into question the soundness of such recommendations as marginal cost pricing (q.v.) for the nationalised industries. *See* PARETO CRITERION OF ALLOCATIVE EFFICIENCY; PARETO OPTIMALITY.

Secondary banks. Institutions which sprouted in Britain during the mid-1960s to provide finance to the property market. They offered higher interest rates to depositors than the clearing banks could pay. These funds were used to finance property development which offered lucrative returns. In consequence overbuilding occured in London, while at the same time fewer businesses could afford high rents. In the recession of 1974, some secondary banks collapsed.

Secondary distribution. Also known as a secondary offering, the redistribution of a block of stock some time after it has been sold by the issuing company. Usually the block is a large one such as might be involved in the settlement of an estate.

Secondary industry or manufacturing industry. The processing of raw materials into finished products, including such activities as building and construction, and the supply of electricity and gas. *See* PRIMARY INDUSTRY; TERTIARY INDUSTRY.

Secondary market. A market for the purchase or resale of securities or other titles to property or commodities outside the organised exchanges and primary markets. In the United States, the secondary mortgage market enables holders of mortgages who need funds to dispose of their holdings before maturity. The secondary stock market deals in unquoted securities, private placings and dealings among brokers, merchant bankers and other institutions and individuals. *See* OVER-THE-COUNTER MARKET; UNLISTED SECURITIES MARKET.

Secondary mortgage market. *See* MORTGAGE-BACKED HOUSING BONDS.

Securities. Stocks, shares or bonds. They are in two main forms:

(a) bonds; fully-paid stock, shares, stock units; and unnumbered shares; and

(b) partly-paid stock or shares.

See CUMULATIVE PREFERENCE SHARE; DEBENTURE; DEFERRED FOUNDERS' OR MANAGEMENT SHARES; DEFERRED ORDINARY SHARE; NON-VOTING SHARE; ORDINARY SHARE; PREFERENCE SHARE; PREFERRED ORDINARY SHARE; REDEEMABLE PREFERENCE SHARE; SHARE; STOCKS AND SHARES.

Securities Act 1933 (U.S.). An Act of Congress which governs the issuance of stocks, providing for full disclosure of all relevant information regarding the stock being offered. A 'registration statement' must be made to the Securities and Exchange Commission (q.v.). If the S.E.C. considers the information inadequate or misleading, the issue may be stopped or delayed.

Securities and Exchange Commission (U.S.). Established by congress to help protect investors, a Commission which administers the Securities Act 1933, the Securities Exchange Act 1934, and other legislation relating to trusts, investments and public utilities. The Securities Act 1933 seeks to ensure that investors have enough information in relation to new security issues to allow rational decision-taking. The Commission was actually created by the Securities Exchange Act 1934. The Act requires brokers and dealers to register with the Commission; gives the Commission broad supervisory authority over the stock exchanges and requires continuous disclosure by publicly quoted companies of relevant facts. It outlaws manipulation and fraud and empowers the Federal Reserve Board to limit the use of credit in security speculation. The Act has been progressively broadened and strengthened. The Commission has five members, not more than three of whom may be members of the same political party. The setting up of the Commission was a direct outcome of the Great Depression (1929–35) (q.v.).

In 1983, the Commission issued a ruling that any foreign company wanting to have its shares traded on the official over-the-counter market would need to be registered with the Commission, save for those foreign companies—already listed—on the National Association of Securities Dealers (q.v.) automatic quotation system (N.A.S.D.A.Q.).

Securities and Investments Board (U.K.). A body created in 1985 to co-ordinate self-regulation in the investment markets.

Securities Investor Protection Corporation. A non-profit membership corporation created by the U.S. Congress which provides funds for use, if necessary, to protect customers' cash and securities which may be on deposit with a S.P.I.C. member firm should that firm fail and be liquidated.

Security capital. Capital subject to a minimum amount of risk, as opposed to risk or venture capital. *See* RISK CAPITAL.

Security deposit, initial. Synonymous with the term margin (q.v.), a cash amount that must be deposited with the broker for each contract as a guarantee of fulfilment of the futures contract (q.v.). If the amount falls below a certain level, the broker may issue a call for an amount of money which will restore the customer's equity in the account to the original margin level; this is known as a security deposit (maintenance).

Self-financing ratio. The amount of capital required for new investment by an organisation obtained from its own earnings (i.e. from depreciation funds, profits and surpluses) expressed as a percentage of total capital requirements. The British electricity supply industry provides about half of its capital needs from internal resources; the balance required comes from external borrowings by the Electricity Council.

Self-liquidating advances. Bank advances to customers which are for the purpose of tiding over a temporary shortage of funds only, e.g. when the farmer is faced with a heavy outlay of wages during the 'seed-time to harvest' period, the loan being repaid when the crop is sold.

Sell stop. *See* STOP ORDER.

Seller's option. A special transaction on the New York Stock Exchange (q.v.) which gives the seller the right to deliver the stock or bond at any time within a specified period, ranging from not less than 6 business days to not more than 60 days.

Seller's put or wild card option. An option exercised by traders who have sold futures short at a time when bond cash and futures prices are falling. Just before the expiration of a contract, with prices declining, the trader buys the cheapest Treasury Bonds in the cash market and delivers or 'puts' them to holders of long futures, thus settling contractual obligations. However, the expectation of falling prices may be disappointed at the time when a purchase becomes imperative, hence the wild element.

Selling hedge or short hedge. Selling futures contracts to provide protection against a possible decline in the prices of commodities.

Serpell Report. The report of a committee set up in May, 1982, under the chairmanship of Sir David Serpell, to study ideas on how British Rail might reduce its dependence on subsidies, then being about £1 billion a year. The report was published in January, 1983, and considered the next 20 years. A central conclusion was that a commercially viable British Rail would have to reduce its track from 18,000 kilometres to about 2,600 kilometres, a core network serving only London and a handful of major towns. British Rail had emphasised that its losses were not very large, if lines covered by its Public Service Obligation Agreement with the Government were ignored. Under that Agreement large numbers of unprofitable lines were to be kept open, the subsidy for these in 1981 alone being £810 million.

Service. In economic science, a useful function fulfilled by a person, or organisation, and for the benefits of which consumers are prepared to pay a price. Payment, like service itself, may be direct or indirect. The basic economic magnitude was regarded by F. H. Knight as service, not good. Hence one may refer to the service of a dwelling to its owner (shelter or rental value), the service of a piano (music) and the service of food (nourishment).

Settlement. The conclusion of a securities transaction in which a customer pays a debit balance he owes a broker or receives from the broker the proceeds from a sale; the term also applies to continuous daily clearing or 'netting out' of transactions among brokerage houses, usually through a centralised securities clearing corporation. *See* ACCOUNT DAY.

Settlement price. The price determined by the clearing house (q.v.) on a commodity exchange at the close of each trading session to be the single reference point in determining losses and profits, margin requirements, and the next day's price limits.

Shadow price. A price or value imputed to unpriced social benefits or losses or to resources which are not satisfactorily priced in commercial markets. The concept is much used in cost-benefit analysis (q.v.). In evaluating any project, the economist may adjust a number of market prices and attribute prices to unpriced gains and losses likely to arise.

Share. The individual portion of a company's capital owned by a shareholder. Shares are divided into different classes according to their terms of issue. Shares are bought and sold in multiples according to their price; for a low price share a marketable parcel may be 1,000 shares, while for a very high price share a marketable parcel may be as low as one share.

In 1963, pension funds, insurance companies, investment trusts and unit trusts owned a quarter of all British listed ordinary shares; by 1978, this proportion had risen to half. *See* COMMON STOCK (U.S. AND CAN.); CUMULATIVE PREFERENCE SHARE; DEFERRED, FOUNDERS' OR MANAGEMENT SHARES; DEFERRED ORDINARY SHARES; NON-VOTING SHARES; ORDINARY SHARE; PARTICIPATING PREFERENCE SHARE; PREFERENCE SHARE; PREFERRED ORDINARY SHARE; PREFERRED STOCK (U.S.); REDEEMABLE PREFERENCE SHARE.

Share certificate. A certificate which is evidence of a person's ownership of shares. As soon as it is issued the seller's certificate is cancelled by the company concerned. Should the seller have disposed of only part of his holding he receives a new certificate for the balance.

Share incentive scheme. Schemes by which managers in industry acquire a stake in their companies, through the acquisition of shares; most schemes only benefit managers who stay for a number of years. Schemes may provide for interest-free loans. A high proportion of public companies in the United States of America appear to have such schemes, but only a small proportion in the United Kingdom. The incentive element usually derives simply from the need to keep up share prices by good company performance.

Share index futures. Futures contracts providing a means by which portfolio managers, underwriters, and others can reduce the risks of price fluctuations in the sharemarket; such futures were first traded in the United States in 1982. Share price index futures provide a means of achieving a change in portfolio exposure quickly, efficiently and at low cost, without buying or selling a single share.

Share Indices, The Times. Share indices designed to provide a yard-stick for the performance of an average portfolio of shares held by an average investor and invested in an average selection of shares. They also show what happens to some of the major elements of a general portfolio, e.g. those shares of companies making capital goods or consumer goods.

Share options. A contractual right, acquired at a cost and valid for a specified period, which entitles the holder to either buy or sell a share (or, in some cases, do both these things) at a pre-determined price. Options provide three significant potential benefits: leverage, the cost of an option representing a relatively small percentage of the price of the underlying share; limited liability, in that an option buyer's loss can never exceed the amount originally paid for the option; and the only way an investor can profit from a decline in share prices.

Share price index futures. A futures contract (q.v.) which enables portfolio managers, share underwriters and others to reduce the risks of price fluctuations in the sharemarket. On the Sydney Futures Exchange (q.v.), the contract unit is a sum of money equal to the All Ordinaries Share Index, multiplied by 100 and expressed as dollars. So if the index is 761.5, the contract value will be $76,150. Share price index futures are unusual in that they contain no provision for delivery of any commodity. Contracts which are still open on the last day of trading are automatically closed out by an offsetting transaction.

Share raid. A take-over bid or method of acquiring control of a company; an outside organisation may offer to buy a proportion (say 55 per cent) of the company shares at an attractive price on a 'first come, first served' basis.

Share-farming agreement. Agreement by which the owner or leaseholder normally provides the land and some capital inputs, and the share-farmer provides the labour and remaining inputs. The proceeds are divided between the two parties, say upon a 50:50 basis. In Australia, sample surveys by the Bureau of Agricultural Economics have revealed proportions of share-farming of about 13 per cent in dairying and 20 per cent in wheat-growing, although the proportions clearly fluctuate from year to year.

Shareholders' funds. Capital, accumulated profits and reserves generated by a company; shareholders' funds are the liability of a company due to shareholders. Ordinary shareholders funds are those attributable to ordinary shareholders, i.e. excluding amounts owing to preference shareholders and to outside shareholders in subsidiary companies. *See* OUTSIDE SHAREHOLDERS.

Shares, method of issuing. *See* OFFER FOR SALE; OFFER FOR SALE BY TENDER; PLACING; PUBLIC ISSUE; RIGHTS ISSUE.

Shelf registration. An arrangement approved by the U.S. Securities and Exchange Commission in 1982, through rule 415, which allows corporations to pre-register a new issue of bonds or shares, without the assistance of an underwriter or investment bank (q.v.), placing the new issue 'on the shelf' for up to 2 years. When market conditions appear favourable, the issuer simply invites bids from investment banks to buy the issue as a whole, or in large blocks, which they then resell. The introduction of rule 415 speeded up the trend towards the bought deal (q.v.).

Sherman Antitrust Act 1890 (U.S.). An Act introduced as a major deterrent to the abuse of economic power by corporations and trusts. It declares to be illegal every contract, combination or conspiracy in restraint of trade or commerce among the States. It also condemns any attempt to monopolise any part of this trade, and provides that injured parties may bring civil suits to recover triple the amount of damage they have suffered. The effectiveness of the Act was strengthened by additional legislation. *See* CLAYTON ACT 1914; FEDERAL TRADE COMMISSION (U.S.).

Shipping conferences. Associations of ship-owners the purpose of which is to fix rates to be charged, and often the capacity allowable on each trade route. These cartel (q.v.) arrangements are frequently threatened by non-conference outsiders who seek a larger share of the trade. According to Lloyd's *Shipping Economist*, ship-owners in the Far Eastern Freight Conference (a closed conference which limits both capacity and rates) had slipped from carrying almost 85 per cent of trade between northern Europe and the Far East in 1975 to less than 70 per cent in 1982. In another example, ship-owners in the North Atlantic Conference (an open conference limiting only rates) had dropped from carrying almost 60 per cent of their trade in 1975, to about 45 per cent in 1982. Outsiders tend to steal away the high-margin cargoes, such as electrical goods.

Shop stewards. In the early days of single-employer bargaining in Britain, an elected representative of the shop floor charged with conducting negotiations. By 1982, practically every unionised plant in Britain had adopted the shop steward system. Many companies have formalised their relations with the shop stewards, by recognising their position and holding regular meetings with them. The average shop steward is responsible for about 30–50 workers. Shop stewards wield considerable authority when bargaining is carried out at plant or company level; union officials play a much larger role when national agreements are at stake, or the bargaining is at multi-employer level. Where the plant is part of a larger company, shop stewards tend to form combines. Full-time shop stewards now outnumber union officials.

Short. A description of an investor in securities (q.v.) who has contracted to deliver at some future time more of a particular stock than he holds; the 'shorts' are usually those who have sold in anticipation of a drop in prices, hoping to be able to buy at a lower price in time for delivery. Selling short can also occur in commodity markets. During 1976 in the United States large quantities of potatoes were sold short, in the hope that prices would fall below the contract price by the time deliveries became due. However, a shortage of potatoes and a sharp rise in potato prices caught speculators by surprise. Brokers could neither find enough to buy nor pay the market price for them. This caused the largest default in contracts in United States commodity trading history. Somewhat differently expressed, a short is someone who has sold one or more futures contracts to establish a market position and who has not yet closed out this position through an offsetting purchase; the opposite of long (q.v.).

Short banking. The practice of not paying all monies received in business activities into the company's bank account.

Short covering. Buying stock to return stock previously borrowed to make delivery on a short sale.

Short end of the Treasury security market. A reference to short-term Treasury bills and notes with a duration of 90 days, 6 months, and up to 1 year, compared with notes and bonds with a duration in maturity of up to 30 years.

Short gilts or shorts. Gilt-edged securities (q.v.) with a redemption date within 5 years.

Short hedge. The sale of a futures contract for hedging purposes.

Short position. Stocks sold short and not covered as of a particular date. *See* SHORT.

Short-run. Usually a year or less in the analysis of a business situation; it may also indicate a period too short for (a) a firm to alter its plant capacity and infrastructure, and (b) allow other firms to enter or leave the particular industry. By contrast, in the long-run all costs are variable costs and entry into or departure from a particular industry has time to take place.

Short-run marginal costs. *See* MARGINAL COSTS, SHORT-RUN.

Short sale. *See* SHORT.

Short-term financial assets. *See* BANKER'S ACCEPTANCES; COMMERCIAL PAPER; MONEY MARKET; MONEY MARKET INSTRUMENTS; NEGOTIABLE TIME CERTIFICATES OF DEPOSIT; U.S. TREASURY BILLS.

Short-term money market. A market in which large borrowers and lenders of money and large buyers and sellers of securities come together to transact their daily business dealings; deals range from a minimum amount of $50,000 to many millions of dollars, there being no absolute maximum, with periods of loan ranging from overnight to as long as 6 months. The short-term money market is used daily by governments, banks, public authorities, large corporations, pension and superannuation funds, and wealthy individuals either to maximise the income of short-term surplus funds, or to minimise the cost of short-term working finance requirements.

Singapore International Monetary Exchange (SIMEX). An offspring of the old Gold Exchange in Singapore, an international financial futures exchange trading in gold and foreign currencies. The exchange is linked with the Chicago Mercantile Exchange (q.v.) to provide a 14-hour continuous trading facility. Traders are able to buy and sell futures contracts under a 'mutual offset' arrangement between the two exchanges. The exchange is backed by the Monetary Authority of Singapore. The link-up came into effect in 1984.

Single capacity. A strict separation between the functions of stockjobber (q.v.) and stockbroker (q.v.) on the London Stock Exchange (q.v.). Jobbers are market makers, dealing in securities as principals for their own account. They normally deal only with brokers, who act as agents for the buyer or seller; brokers channel all their business through jobbers. The single-capacity system came to an end in 1986, being replaced by a dual-capacity broker-jobber arrangement. Firms can now, if they wish, operate in a dual or single capacity, with the emphasis being on dual capacity. *See* LONDON STOCK EXCHANGE.

Single-premium deferred annuities. Annuities which are purchased with a single payment to an insurance company; interest from this type of investment often accumulates tax-free until the investor makes withdrawals, usually after retirement.

Sinking fund. A fund built up by equal periodic instalments in order to accumulate a certain sum by a given date for some specific purpose, e.g. the replacement of a physical asset. The interest is itself periodically reinvested and allowed to accumulate with the periodic contribution of principal. The sinking fund instalment, consisting of an annual payment, is equal to the original capital cost of the asset multiplied by a sinking fund factor equal to:

$$\frac{i}{(1+i)^n - 1}$$

where i is the rate of interest, and n the plant life expressed in years. *See* DEPRECIATION; DEPRECIATION FUND METHOD.

Sinners' taxes. Taxes on alcohol, tobacco and betting.

Site value rating. The levying of local rates on owners of land rather than occupiers. It is claimed that site value rating would encourage owners to make their land available for development, that it might often prove unprofitable for landowners to hold on to land for speculative reasons, and that it might tend to retard the rise in land values. It is argued, however, that if the principle was introduced in Britain considerable difficulties of valuation would arise because of the complicated system of land tenure, the artificial restrictions imposed by contract or by statute, the imprecise nature of development plans and the lack of reliable evidence upon which valuations can be based. The principle is, however, applied in other countries.

Slutzkins, dry and wet. Tax minimisation or avoidance schemes developed in Australia. In February, 1977, litigants by the name of Slutzkin won the approval of the High Court of Australia for the conversion of company income, on which tax had been paid, into a capital gain which could then be distributed to shareholders in tax-free amounts. The procedure is for a promoter to buy a company at a discount and then 'strip' the dividends; the company is then sold to someone else at a capital loss which can then be used by the promoter to offset profits elsewhere. This is the dry Slutzkin, considered legal. A wet Slutzkin is a situation in which a company has a company tax liability; however the company is sold without payment of tax to a promoter who strips the assets and quickly passes the company to sham directors; the company records are meticulously destroyed. The company disappears with no tax paid, and without records. The procedure is wet in the sense that the company is destined for the 'bottom-of-the-harbour'. *See* BOTTOM-OF-THE-HARBOUR TAX AVOIDANCE SCHEMES.

Smithsonian Agreement. Agreement reached by the Group of Ten (q.v.) countries in Washington in December, 1971, to re-establish a system of fixed rates of exchange embodying a major re-alignment of parities and a widening of the margins of exchange rate fluctuation. It was also agreed to consider reform of the international monetary system. The gathering was held at the Smithsonian Institution. Under the Agreement, the U.S. dollar was devalued in terms of gold by 7.9 per cent, the 'official' gold price being raised from $35 to $38 per fine ounce. Within the total permitted range of fluctuations against the dollar of 4½ per cent ('the tunnel'), the rates for the participating currencies at any one time were restricted to a band of 2¼ per cent ('the snake'). Hence the expression 'the snake in the tunnel'.

The 1972 snake had an awkward career. Exchange market pressures forced Britain and Ireland to withdraw within 6 weeks. Italy followed at the beginning of 1973. In March, 1973 all foreign exchange markets were closed for a few days, and the European Economic Community (q.v.) countries decided to abandon their attempts to keep any limits against the dollar. The tunnel disappeared, though the snake survived, though only just. France left in January, 1974; rejoined in July, 1975; then left for good in March, 1976. Only West Germany and a few small countries continued.

The snake was succeeded in March, 1979, by the European Monetary System (E.M.S.) (q.v.), and a new currency, the E.C.U. (European Currency Unit) was created.

Smokestack America stocks. In the United States, a term descriptive of basic industrial stocks and shares, compared with glamour stocks which may have shorter lives. It also infers frostbelt (N.E.) stocks compared with sunbelt (S.W.) stocks.

Snake in the tunnel. *See* SMITHSONIAN AGREEMENT.

Social account. An organised arrangement of all transactions, actual or imputed, in an economic system.

Social accounting. The compilation of accounts for particular groups within the nation—the sectors of the economy. The organisation of statistics into a set of social accounts has become normal practice and is the framework on which is built the presentation of the statistics for the United Kingdom.

Social benefits. Private plus external communal benefits; the value of gains accruing to the community as a consequence of the establishment of an industry, factory or facility, although the new development may not have taken place with that aim or purpose. Benefits may include increased opportunities for employment, steadier employment, improved roads, improved shops and amenities, elimination of a swamp or removal of unsightly existing premises.

Social capital. Assets belonging to the community as a whole, rather than to private persons or industries, e.g. schools, hospitals, roads, etc.

Social contract. A voluntary incomes policy agreed between the trades unions and the British Labour Government in 1973. The Government promised social and industrial policies favourable to workers, while the unions promised to moderate their wage claims according to agreed guidelines. However, wages rose by 32 per cent during the period of the 'social contract', an all-time record, and the policy collapsed in ruins. *See* NATIONAL INCOMES POLICY.

Social costs. Costs which do not appear in the accounts of a company, e.g. the costs to the public caused by air pollution, water pollution, noise and congestion, or the provision and maintenance of roads by the public for private distribution purposes. If a company is required by legislation to prevent or minimise its contribution to, say, air pollution then the cost of doing this will appear in the accounts of the company. In this instance a general and difficult to measure social cost will have been converted into a specific and accurately measured private cost.

Social indicator. An attempt to measure by means of an index the degree of human welfare or quality of life in a given area, national or regional. The need for such an index has arisen from widespread discontent with the use of the concept of gross national product as a measure of human well-being. An integrated social indicator reflects a set of social and environmental indices, as well as conventional economic indices. It is influenced by such factors as real income; employment, housing, educational and cultural characteristics; ease of access to social, community and transport services; recreational opportunities; depletion of non-renewable resources; air, water, and noise pollution. In regional terms, a social indicator becomes a basis of comparison, and an important element in the development of urban and regional policies and the determining of priorities within and between programs. Subjective social indicators deal with the degree of satisfaction felt by people with various aspects of their lives. Work on social indicators, both objective and subjective, has been conducted in several countries. The subject of social indicators is reviewed in the publication *Social Trends No. 4* (London: H.M.S.O., 1974).

Social insurance. The collective insurance of members of a community through the State for a variety of social benefits in times of illness, old-age and unemployment. The development of social insurance in Britain dates from the National Insurance Act 1911, which provided insurance against sickness and disablement on a compulsory and contributory basis for most lower paid workers, and introduced a limited scheme of unemployment insurance which was subsequently widened. In 1925 the Widows', Orphans' and Old Age Contributory Pensions Act provided the first national scheme of contributory pensions. Following the Second World War, a more comprehensive scheme of social insurance was introduced which embraced the whole population. The scheme was based on a plan prepared by Sir William (late Lord) Beveridge, which appeared in his famous Report on Social Insurance. The scheme embodied in the National Insurance Act 1946 was compulsory and contributed to by employees, employers and the State; the 'self-employed' also became compulsory contributors. Benefits are payable in respect of sickness, unemployment, widowhood and old-age; retirement pensions are payable to men at 65 and women at 60 years of age; maternity grants and funeral grants are also payable.

Social Security Act 1935. A United States measure of social insurance involving old-age, survivors, disability and health insurance, welfare and unemployment payments; payroll taxes to finance the social security programme are the second largest source of federal tax revenues.

Social service. A service, subsidy or payment rendered by, or on behalf of, the community to an individual or to a family for his or its exclusive use. A social service contains an element of redistribution of income and resources. Social services in Britain include the following: (a) education; (b) insurance; (c) housing (subsidising and provision of), (d) health (hospital, medical, dental services, etc.); (e) national assistance; (f) old people's services; (g) children's services; (h) family allowances (although these are subject to income tax); (i) food subsidies; (j) rent restriction; and (k) legal aid and advice.

Social survey. A first-hand investigation and analysis of the economic, sociological and other related aspects of a selected community or group. A survey may have as its object: (a) the provision of material scientifically gathered from which social theorists may draw conclusions, and/or (b) the formulation of a programme of amelioration of the conditions of life and work of a particular group or community. Well-known reports include those of: (a) Le Play, who in the 19th century studied European working men's family budgets; (b) Charles Booth and associates who undertook in 1886 studies reported in 'Life and Labour of the People in London'; (c) the Kellogg Survey in the United States in 1909; (d) the Rowntree surveys of the City of York in 1900, 1936 and 1950; (e) the 1934 London School of Economics 'New Survey of London Life and Labour'; (f) the Rowntree and Lavers surveys of 'English Life and Leisure' published in 1951. Many social surveys conducted today are confined to the investigation of a particular phase of community life, such as crime and delinquency, housing, health, education or recreation.

Social time preference rate. The relative value which the community as a whole, through government decisions, assigns to present as opposed to future consumption at the margin.

Social transformation function or social production frontier. Represents the amount of any one output which can be produced given all other outputs; inputs are regarded as negative. A society on its production frontier is achieving its production potential given the state of the arts; there is general maximisation of production. The concept does not imply that consumer wellbeing may not be raised through various techniques such as production redistribution or lump sum payments.

Socialisation of losses. A primary aim of the private sector (q.v.) in times of economic difficulty; the objective is to secure arrangements whereby the public at large carry the losses of a company or industry, through a variety of devices including direct subsidies, increased trade protection and tariffs, restrictions on competitors, tax relief and concessions of various sorts, wage and salary freezes, market guarantees, and the arbitrary placing of orders by the public sector which would otherwise have been placed overseas. Major corporations and companies holding key positions in the national economy and employing large labour forces incorporate schemes for the socialisation of losses into their corporate plans. Beyond a certain size and importance some industries 'cannot lose'. If in the end the community takes over ownership of the lame industry or company, the internal strategy is to ensure a smooth transition and continuing employment of the top echelons of management who continue to thrive and prosper within a somewhat different ownership environment.

Socialist economics. As defined by G. D. H. Cole, a form of practical economics concerned not merely with attempts to describe and analyse what happens under certain underlying conditions but also with the discovery of what ought to happen in the interests of the general well-being of society and of its members. For socialists, he argued, the traditional distinctions between 'pure' and 'applied' economics, and between economics proper and welfare economics, simply do not exist. *See* SCHOOLS OF ECONOMICS.

Society for Worldwide Inter-bank Financial Telecommunication (S.W.I.F.T.). A non-profit, co-operative company owned by the member banks using the network; it was established in 1973 by 239 European and American banks. By 1982, the system served more than 1,000 banks in western Europe, Hong Kong, Singapore, Australasia, Japan, Latin America, South Africa, North America, and Australia. S.W.I.F.T. members are able to transmit transactions among themselves using computer-based telecommunications technology.

Sociosphere. The area of study of the social scientist; analogous to the hydrosphere as the area of study of the oceanographer, the biosphere as the area of study of the biologist, and the lithosphere as the area of study of the geologist. The sociosphere embraces people, their roles and patterns of behaviour, their organisations and groups, and social interactions.

Soft commodities. Commodities such as coffee, cocoa, sugar and tea; hence the term 'soft commodities futures markets'.

Soft company. A company engaging in analysis and consultancy, as distinct from the actual development, production and marketing of a range of products. Some soft companies develop to a point where they become major product companies, i.e. hard companies. Soft companies require low capital and management expertise; hard companies require major up-front investments in manufacturing equipment and distribution before the first sales are made, and depend on venture capital.

Soft currency. A currency with a relatively unstable or declining value in international exchange. For many years following the Second World War, sterling and most European currencies were 'soft', while the United States dollar was recognised as 'hard'.

Soft loan. A loan with more generous terms than the prevailing market level, such as a loan containing a period of grace from interest payments, an extended repayment period, or a rate of interest below commercial rates; mixed credit schemes (q.v.) may also soften a loan.

Sole proprietor, the. The commonest type of business unit in which a single person is responsible for raising the capital, organising and managing the business, and undertaking the risk. A very high proportion of the 700,000 shops and service establishments in Britain are in the hands of sole proprietors. A similar position exists in the United States and Canada. The main advantages of this type of business unit are (a) the self-interest of the owner can be a great driving force making for efficiency; (b) changes can be introdued without the need to consult anyone else; and (c) the proprietor knows both his staff and customers personally. Sole proprietorship has been described as an opportunity 'to work as hard as you like, for as long as you like, for as little as you like'. Many small firms have very short lives—the main cause of failure is insufficient capital.

Southern African Development Co-ordinating Conference (S.A.D.C.C.). An association of southern African nations formed in 1980 in an attempt to reduce the degree of economic dependence on South Africa; South Africa has been the region's cheapest and most efficient supplier of food, fertiliser, and transport. The southern African nations have been members of a customs union with South Africa since 1910. The membership of S.A.D.C.C. comprises Angola, Botswana, Lesotho, Malawi, Mozambique, Swaziland, Tanzania, Zambia and Zimbabwe.

Special deposits. A monetary control device first used in the summer of 1960 as a counter measure against inflationary pressure. The London Clearing and Scottish banks were required to make 'special deposits' with the Bank of England amounting to 1 per cent ($\frac{1}{2}$ per cent for the Scottish banks) of their total deposits; these 'special deposits' were not classified as 'liquid assets' and the capacity of the banks to extend credit to customers was reduced. Special deposits were required between June 1960, and December, 1962; they were again required in May, 1965, and July, 1966. Deposit requirements have risen as high as 3 per cent of total deposits. Such deposits are not at free disposal of the banks lodging them, and can only be withdrawn with Bank of England permission. The measure was introduced as a means of making traditional weapons more effective by preventing the commercial banks from defeating open-market operations (q.v.) by selling their holdings of Treasury Bills.

Special Drawing Rights (S.D.R.s). An international reserve currency system created by the International Monetary Fund (q.v.) in October, 1969. It provides for a new type of money (known as 'paper gold') to serve by agreement of the free world nations as the first international legal tender. S.D.R.s are used along with gold and dollars as monetary reserves; they are not held by individuals or private businesses but used in transactions between governments and central banks.

The first allocation of S.D.R.s by the International Monetary Fund took place on 1 January 1970. S.D.R.s, as international assets, can be used between central banks in cases of balance-of-payments difficulties. S.D.R.s bear interest and have a gold value guarantee.

While originally the S.D.R. was fixed to the official price of gold, from 1 July 1974, it became a composite unit reflecting the value of 16 major currencies, weighted by their relative importance in international transactions. The currencies in the 'basket' valuation are those of countries with a share in world exports of goods and services in excess of 1 per cent.

The complexity of S.D.R.s has been reduced; from January, 1981, the system became based on five instead of sixteen currencies. However, S.D.R.s still amounted to only 5 per cent of the world total.

Special Economic Zones (China). Areas designated by the People's Republic of China for accelerated economic development. The most important, Shenzhen, is just over the border from Hong Kong; the other three are Zuhai, Shantou, and Ziaman. Shenzhen is by far the most successful.

Specialist. A member of the New York Stock Exchange (q.v.). The specialist has two primary functions: (a) to maintain an orderly market, insofar as reasonably practicable, in the stocks in which he is registered as a specialist, and to buy and sell for his own account when there is a temporary disparity between supply and demand, and (b) to act as a broker's broker. In 1982, there were some 400 specialists on the Exchange.

Speculation. The buying of something cheap at one time for the purpose of selling the same thing dearer at another time. Speculation may be described as 'arbitrage through time'; instead of buying in one place and selling in another, commodities are bought at one time and sold at another. The difference between arbitrage through space and arbitrage through time is that in the former the prices in the various markets are known, while in the latter prices at future dates can only be estimated. Whilst in a sense all deals are speculations the term is generally limited to circumstances where profit is made because the same thing has different prices at different times. John Maynard Keynes in his *General Theory* commented, 'Speculators may do no harm as bubbles on a steady stream of enterprise. But the position is serious when enterprise becomes the bubble on a whirlpool of speculation.'

Speculative demand. The demand for money for the purchase of financial assets, as distinct from the transactions demand (q.v.) for money. The two financial variables, the transactions and speculative demand for money, are influenced by income and interest rates respectively. Higher interest rates mean a higher return on holding bonds, and a larger opportunity cost (q.v.) against holding cash or interest-free bank deposits.

Speculator. One who attempts to anticipate forthcoming commodity and share prices, and attempts to profit through the considered purchase and sale of those commodities; the purpose of the speculator is to achieve income and wealth regardless of whether this adds anything to the income and wealth of the nation. A person entering into futures contracts for any purpose other than hedging. *See* SPECULATION.

S.P.I. contracts. *See* SHARE PRICE INDEX FUTURES.

Split (U.S.). The division of the outstanding shares of a corporation into a larger number of shares; thus a 3-for1 split by a company with 1 million shares outstanding would result in 3 million shares outstanding.

Split pricing. The practice of selling a product uniform in quality and other characteristics at different prices, because it is branded or packed differently, or distributed through different channels, or both.

Spot commodity. An actual commodity as distinct from a futures contract; synonymous with 'actuals' or 'cash commodity'.

Spot market. A market in which goods are sold for immediate delivery. Also includes the nearest delivery month on a futures contract.

Spot month. The next possible delivery month available for each type of futures contract.

Spot price. The price quoted for an actual physical commodity; same as cash price. It also refers to a futures contract for the current month, in which case the trading is still in 'futures' but delivery is possible at any time.

Spread. In respect of futures contracts, the purchase of one futures contract against the sale of another in the expectation that the price relationship between the two will change to realise a profit; the difference can be in the commodity itself, the month, or in the exchange. There are four major types of spread: (a) the *interdelivery or intra-commodity spread.* This consists of futures contracts for the same commodity between two different delivery months; for example, Short July Wheat against Long December Wheat; (b) *intermarket spread.* This comprises futures contacts for the same commodity in the same month but spread between two different exchanges; for example, Short Chicago Silver against Long New York Silver; (c) *intercommodity spread.* This comprises futures contracts traded on the same exchange for the same delivery month but spread between two different commodities; for example, Long Corn against Short Oats; and (d) *commodity-product spread.* This consists of two futures contracts spread between a commodity and the product or products derived from it and traded on the same exchange; for example, soyabeans and soyabean oil.

Spread trading. The buying of one forward contract and the simultaneous selling of another of similar quality and term on a commodity market; the two contracts are terminated by reversing this buy/sell action.

Squeeze. Stock exchange term to describe a situation in which 'bears' (q.v.) are forced into losses. A situation in which a lack of supply on a futures market tends to force prices upwards to the disadvantage of those who are short (q.v.).

Stabilisation policy. A policy to alter systematically certain variables controlled by government, such as the growth of the monetary base and the size of the budget deficit, in response to movements in key economic variables such as inflation and output. Two types of stabilisation policy have emerged: feedback policies where, as new information arrives, the authorities alter their targets for the future (e.g. raise the deficit or money supply target); and automatic policies, where in response to unexpected developments, the current outcomes for the target variables are allowed to diverge from targets to some extent. Following the Second World War, most Western capitalist nations actively used stabilisation policies in an endeavour to secure high employment levels without inflation; they met with varying degrees of success until about 1974, subsequently meeting with various degrees of failure.

Stag. A person who applies for a number of shares (q.v.) in a new issue, with the intention of selling quickly to make a profit.

Stagflation. A high rate of inflation (q.v.) associated with industrial stagnation and a high level of unemployment. The co-existence of these two elements appears to contradict the 'Phillips curve' thesis by which the rate of increase of prices is expected to fall when unemployment rises. However, in a country with a developed arbitration system, such as Australia, an important consideration is the rate of increase in award wages as a determinant of the rate of increase of prices, independently of the state of the labour market. Stagflation has been experienced in several countries including the United States of America and the United Kingdom.

Stagflation created a dilemma for Keynesian economics; should demand be stimulated in order to reduce unemployment, inflation simply accelerates; and if demand is deliberately restricted to combat inflation, unemployment may well rise. *See* CAMBRIDGE SCHOOL.

Stagnation thesis. An argument developed in the 1930s that in a rich country continuing to increase in wealth (through accumulation of capital and technical improvements), opportunities for further profitable capital development will tend to decline, while the propensity to save will be at least maintained, and that this combination of circumstances is likely to produce a chronic tendency to under-employment of the country's resources.

Stagnationist theory. Theory prominent in the 1940s that the United States faced a future of increasing unemployment unless the government took a more active role in sustaining the economy, especially through a vigorous fiscal policy (q.v.). The theory was based on the view that the slowing of population growth, the vanishing of the frontier, associated with reduced investment opportunities, created increasing difficulties while the propensity to save could be expected to remain high.

Stamp duties. Classified in Britain as expenditure taxes, a motley assortment of fees on transactions in, for example, property and shares, and on documents such as life insurance contracts.

Standard and Poor's credit ratings. Credit ratings maintained by Standard and Poor in respect of corporations; in respect of what is called senior debt or long-term rating the designations are AAA, AA, A, BBB, BB, B, etc. with plus or minus in the intermediate cases; in respect of commercial paper or short-term debt, the ratings are A-1, A-2, B-1 etc. again with plus or minus as appropriate.

Standard and Poor's indexes. Indexes computed and published by Standard and Poor of the United States; over 130 stock price indexes are published covering a variety of individual industries such as cement, copper, chemicals and so on. Five indexes are particularly well-known: these are the indexes covering 400 industrial stocks, 20 transportation stocks, 40 utility stocks, and 40 financial stocks, with a composite index covering the whole of these 500 stocks.

Staples. Commodities with a large natural resource content, e.g. furs, wheat, timber and minerals.

State and local government bonds. Debt obligations incurred by way of the issue of bonds for the financing of capital projects such as schools, highways, and water and sewerage schemes. Such bonds may be general, simply resting upon the 'full faith and credit' of the issuer for the payment of interest and the ultimate repayment of capital. On the other hand, bonds may be limited obligation or revenue bonds depending upon the revenue gained from the asset financed (for example, a bridge, tunnel or turnpike) for the payment of interest and repayment of capital.

Statics. The study of the economy in a state of rest. The range of available productive resources, the state of technology, and the desires and tastes of individuals, are given; statics is concerned with how the resources will be divided among alternative uses, what prices will be established for them as factors of production, and what prices will be established for the goods and services finally flowing from them. It is assumed that equilibria will be established.

Statutory Reserve Deposit (S.R.D.). The deposits which the Australian trading banks must keep with the Reserve Bank; in 1984, the required deposit was 7 per cent of total deposits. The deposits at the Reserve Bank earned an interest rate of 5 per cent. *See* AUSTRALIAN BANKING SYSTEM.

Statutory Sick Pay scheme (S.S.P.). A new sickness benefit scheme which became operational in Britain in April, 1983; all employers were required to contribute directly to the scheme, whether employing just one person or many hundreds.

Sterling M3. *See* MONEY SUPPLY.

St. James's Group. A forecasting club of leading British industrial, commercial and financial companies in both the public and the private sectors; the London journal, *The Economist*, is also a member. The club is run by the economic assessment unit of that journal's Economic Intelligence Unit, which prepares forecasts with the aid of the Treasury's own macro-economic model of the British economy.

Stock. Equity (q.v.) or ownership in a company or corporation (q.v.). In the United States, stock is classified as either common or preferred. *See* COMMON STOCK; PREFERRED STOCK.

Stock dividend. A dividend (q.v.) paid in securities rather than cash; the dividend may be additional shares of the issuing company, or shares of another company (usually a subsidiary) held by the company.

Stock exchange. An auction market for the purchase and sale of securities such as stocks, bonds and shares. It thus provides a convenient arrangement for persons to invest money in large business enterprises and to liquify their investments at any time by selling their securities. In the United States there are three national stock exchanges accounting for some 90 per cent of the total trading on exchanges throughout the nation. These are: (a) the New York Stock Exchange, the principal security market in the United States, whose beginnings may be traced back to 1792; (b) the American Stock Exchange, formerly known as the Curb Exchange as its early trading was conducted for many years in the open street; and (c) the National Association of Securities Dealers. All three exchanges are located in New York City. The principal exchange in the United Kingdom is the London Stock Exchange. *See* AMERICAN STOCK EXCHANGE; BOSTON STOCK EXCHANGE; LONDON STOCK EXCHANGE; NATIONAL ASSOCIATION OF SECURITIES DEALERS; PHILADELPHIA STOCK EXCHANGE; NEW YORK STOCK EXCHANGE; OVER-THE-COUNTER MARKET; UNLISTED SECURITIES MARKET.

Stock Exchange Compensation Fund. A fund introduced by The London Stock Exchange (q.v.) to provide additional protection for clients in the event of the default of a stock exchange firm. The affairs of the defaulting firm are taken over by the official assignee appointed by the Council of the Stock Exchange, who acts in a manner similar to a Trustee in a bankruptcy case. As the official assignee winds up the firm's affairs, the amounts due to clients who are creditors of the firm for either securities or cash are confirmed. These clients may then apply to the Council for compensation, and the Council may pay them the amount of that loss.

Stock Exchange Daily Official List (S.E.D.O.L.). A daily publication of The London Stock Exchange (q.v.) showing the closing prices of shares traded and full details of the previous day's trading.

Stock Exchange Introduction. The introduction of one or more classes of the securities of a company on to The London Stock Exchange (q.v.). A company seeking this privilege must instruct its broker to submit an application, setting out the particulars of the securities for which a quotation is sought. Such an application must ultimately have the approval of the Stock Exchange Regulations relating to the advertisement of an introduction, arranging for supplying jobbers with shares to make a free market, etc. must be carefully complied with.

Stock Exchange of Great Britain and Ireland. *See* LONDON STOCK EXCHANGE, THE.

Stock index futures options. A financial instrument that is available to investors for personal and corporate money management. They are traded in the United States on the New York Futures Exchange (N.Y.F.E.), the Chicago Mercantile Exchange (C.M.E.), and the Chicago Board Options Exchange (C.B.O.E.); and in Australia on the Sydney Futures Exchange (S.F.E.). The strike price (q.v.) is at-the-money, the option term is variable (according to the delivery month), and the option premium is variable (according to the strike price, the option period, and overall market volatility). Stock index futures options in the United States markets are equivalent in character to traded share options in Australia, in as much as they have a range of fixed strike prices, fixed maturity dates, and can be bought and sold in secondary markets. *See* ORDINARY AND TRADED OPTIONS (AUST.).

Stock manipulation. The buying or selling of securities for the purpose of creating a false or misleading appearance of active trading, or for the purpose of raising or depressing a price to induce purchase or sale by others.

Stock market flotation. The placing of stocks and shares into the free market by private companies; in Britain this may be achieved by a Stock Exchange Introduction (q.v.) (an 'S.E. listing'); by entering the Granville Over-the-Counter Market (O.T.C. market); the Unlisted Securities Market ('U.S.M.') (q.v.); and general over-the-counter trading. *See* OVER-THE-COUNTER MARKET.

Stockbroker. On The London Stock Exchange, (q.v.) an agent buying or selling securities on behalf of his clients. He also gives advice to his clients on request and attends to the transfer of the legal title to securities. When negotiating a transaction on the Stock Exchange, a broker does not disclose whether he has buying or selling instructions. The broker makes enquiries regarding the price of a security with stockjobbers dealing in that particular stock. Two prices are quoted by a stockjobber, the lower being the price at which he is prepared to buy from the broker and the higher being the price at which he is prepared to sell. The stockbroker charges a commission on the shares which he sells and buys for his clients.

This single-capacity arrangement is abolished in 1986 giving way to a dual-capacity arrangement in which members can, if they wish, perform the role of both stockbroker and stockjobber (q.v.).

Stock-index future. A futures contract (q.v.) on stock market indices; in 1982, traded on three United States exchanges. The buyer of a stock-index future pays a fixed amount for each point of the underlying index. In 1982, for the Standard and Poor's 500 index the price was $500 a point. The buyer normally had to put up only 10 per cent of the contract amount when he bought. All settlements were made in cash when the contract expired; the underlying securities in the index never changed hands. Options on stock-index futures were also available.

Stockjobber. Member of The London Stock Exchange who buys and sells stocks and shares. Stockjobbers are essentially 'wholesalers' and have no direct dealings with the public, as distinct from stockbrokers (q.v.) who buy and sell on behalf of members of the public. In 1920 there were 411 jobbing firms in London; in 1960, 100; in 1966, 49; and in 1976 only 15.

Most jobbers specialise in one of the main groups of the 9,000 or so different securities (q.v.) quoted on the floor of the Exchange. Some deal in the 'gilt-edged' market, others in the 'Kaffir' market, or in steel, bank, shipping, oil, property and brewery shares.

The spread between the buying and selling price which a jobber quotes is known as the 'jobber's turn'—but profit is not automatic and the market highly competitive.

This single-capacity arrangement is abolished in 1986 giving way to a dual-capacity arrangement in which members can, if they wish, perform the role of both stockjobber and stockbroker (q.v.).

Stocks and shares. Terms which tend to be used interchangeably, the distinction becoming blurred. Stocks, however, denote generally money lent to a government, local council, or company and involving a fixed rate of interest; shares denote part-ownership of a company's capital, issued on a variety of terms, and yielding variable returns. The main groups of stocks and shares are: (a) gilt-edged, i.e. government issues and a number of securities grouped with them; (b) foreign government bonds; (c) American and Canadian shares; (d) banking, insurance and shipping; (e) breweries; (f) commercial and industrial; (g) iron, coal and steel; (h) financial, land and property; (i) investment trusts; (j) rubber and tea plantations; (k) oil; (l) mining—South African, Rhodesian, Canadian, Australian, West African and others; (m) cables and transport.

Stocks and shares prefixed or affixed 'A', 'B' etc. Stocks or shares which carry special rights, or a special limitation of rights, such as being 'non-voting'. *See* NON-VOTING SHARES.

Stop limit order. A stop order (q.v.) which becomes a limit order (q.v.) after the specified stop price has been reached.

Stop-loss order. An order to sell securities when a stipulated price has been reached on a falling market. By using 'stops', holders of securities limit their losses in a declining market.

Stop order. An order for the purchase of securities on an exchange placed at a limit above the prevailing market price in the case of a buy stop, or below the existing level in the case of a sell stop. By using a sell stop, holders of securities limit their losses in a declining market. The order will not be executed until the stop price has been reached; then the stop order becomes a market order. A stop order offers some protection against a possible change of trend. However, prices may react outside the day-to-day pattern for a short time only leading to premature selling or buying, requiring corrective buying or selling later.

Straddle also known as a spread (q.v.). The purchase of one future month against the sale of another future month of the same commodity. A straddle trade is based on a price relationship between the 2 months and a belief that the 'spread' or difference in price between the 2 contract months will change sufficiently to make the trade profitable.

Straddle option. A combination of a 'put' option and a 'call' option which may be exercised in both respects at a common specified price before the expiry date. *See* DOUBLE OPTION; SHARE OPTIONS.

Street name. Securities held in the name of a broker instead of his customer's name; such securities are said to be 'carried in street name'. This occurs when the securities have been bought on margin, or when the customer wishes the security to be held by the broker. *See* NEW YORK STOCK EXCHANGE.

Strike price. The price at which an option (q.v.) can be converted by exercise into the underlying futures contract.

Strong, hard and firm prices. Stock exchange (q.v.) terms meaning prices are rising.

Structural unemployment. *See* UNEMPLOYMENT, TYPES OF.

Sub-index futures contracts. A variation of a stock index future (q.v.) being related only to a segment of the index. The Philadelphia stock exchange trades options contracts on two sub-indices: gold and silver stocks, and gaming and hotel stocks. The gold and silver contract offers the right to buy or sell a 'basket of stocks' within a certain time at a specific exercise price (q.v.). The sub-index is based on the stock prices and capitalisation of the seven companies that represent the industry. The gaming and hotel sub-index is based on the stock prices and capitalisation of nine major companies in the industry. Both these sub-index futures contracts were introduced in December, 1983. The American Stock Exchange (q.v.) has also introduced a computer technology sub-index.

Substitution effect. The change in the quantity demanded of a good or service which results solely from a change in its price relative to the prices of other goods and services. If the price of a commodity falls it becomes more attractive relative to its substitutes, the rate of substitution depending on the closeness of the substitutes. *See* INCOME EFFECT.

Sunrise industries. Industries in the forefront of developments and which may become large industries in the future, e.g. industries engaged in high technology, biotechnology, and solar energy.

Sunset legislation. Legislation embodying measures which cease to have effect after a specified time; self-destructive measures. In 1982, the Australian Government introduced legislation for the freezing of federal public service salaries for a period of 12 months. The principal of sunset legislation is by no means new.

Supplementary financing facility. A facility extended by the International Monetary Fund (q.v.) utilising funds obtained from some oil producers and industrial countries. Also known as the 'Witteveen facility'.

Supply. The amount of a commodity or service which will be offered for sale at a given price per unit of time. *See* DEMAND; ELASTICITY OF SUPPLY.

Supply and demand curves. A graphical presentation of supply and demand functions, showing on the one hand how much of a commodity will be supplied per unit of time at any given price, and on the other how much of a commodity will be bought per unit of time at any given price; the equilibrium price is the price at which there will be just sufficient demand to take the whole of the supply off the market. If conditions change, and more will be offered for sale at any given price than before ('an increase in supply'), the equilibrium price will be lower than before. Conversely, if less is offered at any given price ('a decrease in supply'), the equilibrium price will be higher than before. Corresponding changes in the equilibrium price will take place if there is an increase or decrease in demand. Figure 21 shows a combination of two normal supply and demand curves, with the equilibrium price shown at P. *See* SUPPLY CURVE; DEMAND CURVE.

Supply and demand, laws of. In respect of goods and services:

(a) If, at the price ruling, demand exceeds supply, the price tends to rise; con-

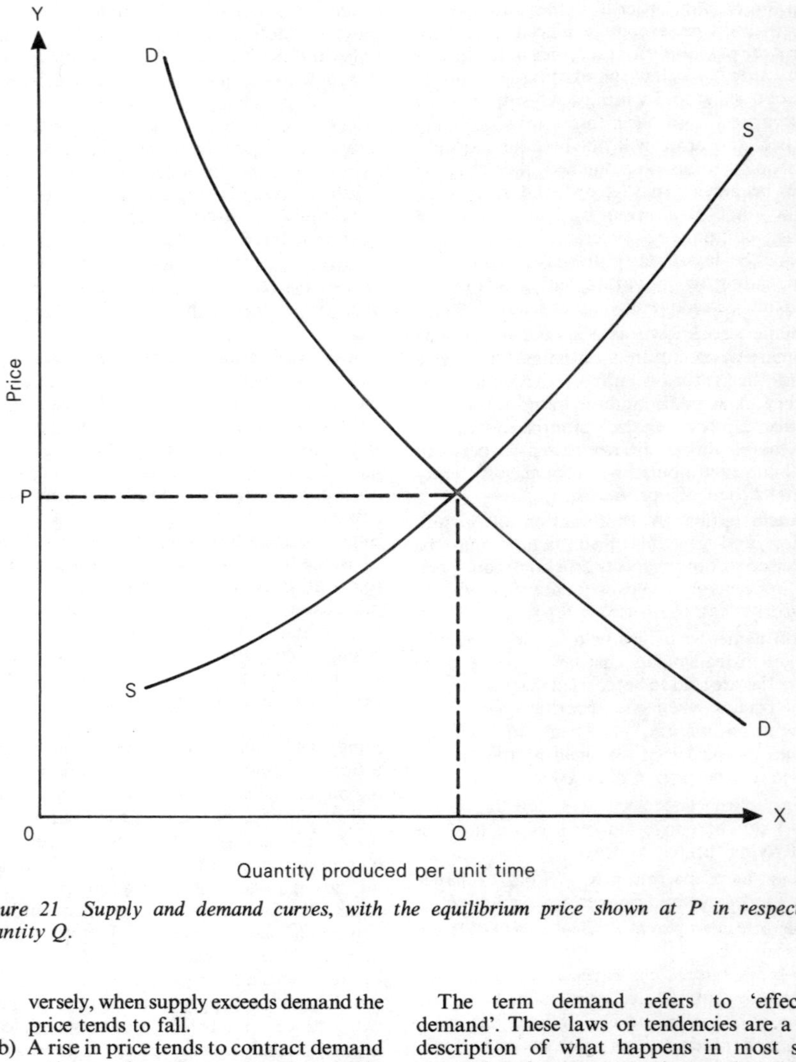

Figure 21 Supply and demand curves, with the equilibrium price shown at P in respect of quantity Q.

versely, when supply exceeds demand the price tends to fall.

(b) A rise in price tends to contract demand and expand supply; conversely, a fall in price tends to expand demand and to contract supply.

(c) Price tends to a level at which the demand is equal to the supply, i.e. to an 'equilibrium price'.

(d) The greater the increase in price, the greater the expansion in supply;

(e) For any given price increase, the expansion in the quantity supplied will be greater, the longer the time the market is allowed to adjust.

The term demand refers to 'effective demand'. These laws or tendencies are a fair description of what happens in most situations; but there are exceptions, at least in the short term. In a period of growing shortages (due to famine or national emergencies) a rise in price of a certain commodity might be accompanied by an increase in demand, if it is feared that the price will rise higher still for a long period. A fall in share prices may not be accompanied by an immediate increase in demand if potential buyers are confident that prices will fall lower still; conversely a rise in share prices might not stimulate an increase in the quantity for sale, if potential sellers have grounds for believing that prices will rise higher still. *See* PRICE MECHANISM.

Supply curve. A graphical presentation of a supply function, $x = \phi(p)$, showing how much of a commodity will be supplied per unit of time at any given price, providing that the other influences governing supply remain unchanged. The supply curve is referred to axes OY and OX along which prices and supplies are respectively measured. It is an economic convention that supply curves are referred to a vertical price axis. In normal supply curves x increases as p increases, i.e. the supply function, $x = \phi(p)$, is monotonic increasing. The shape is generally concave to the origin, but the precise form depends on the commodity and the elasticity of supply. Generally supply expands with an increase in price, although a trend cannot continue, of course, if production is unable to keep pace with demand or there is no more of a commodity available. In exceptional circumstances supply curves may be regressive, less being offered at a higher price. This could happen if supplies were withheld because of an expectation that prices will rise even higher; the expectation of an even higher future price may shift the supply curve temporarily to the left (less being offered at any given price than previously). Figure 22 shows a normal supply curve under condition of perfect competition (q.v.). The terms 'expansion' and 'contraction' of supply are reserved for changes in supply attributable to changes in the price of the commodity only; the amount supplied at any given price remaining constant. The terms 'increase' or 'decrease' in supply are reserved for changes in supply attributable to changes in the state of supply; more or fewer goods being supplied at any given price than formerly.

Supply curves, regressive, or backward sloping. A graphical presentation of an abnormal market situation in which the fall in the price of a good or service leads to an increase in the supply of that good or service, or conversely an increase in price leads to a fall in supply, at least in the short term. A fall in price shifts the supply curve to the right, more being offered at the lower prices; or conversely an increase in price leads to a fall in supply at least in the

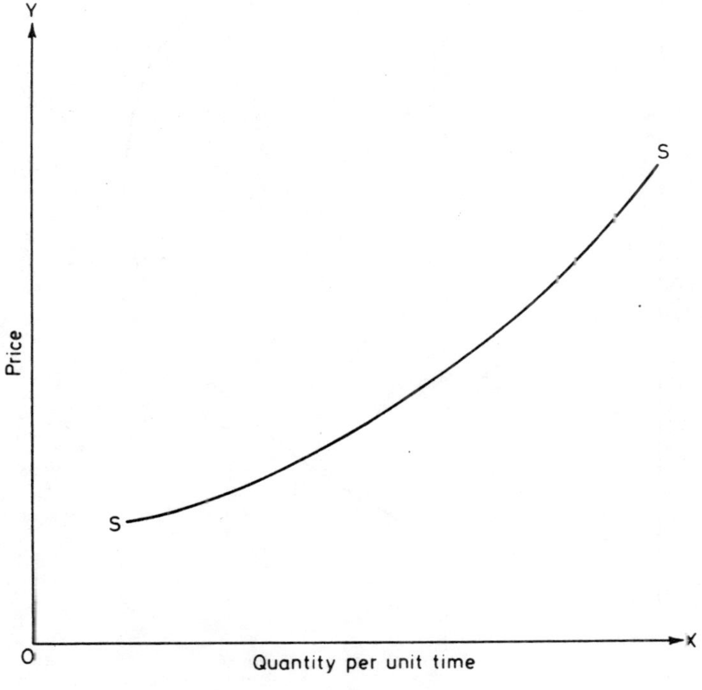

Figure 22 Supply curve.

short-term, the supply curve shifting to the left. For example, it has been observed that a fall in the price of an agricultural product has resulted in increased production. The explanation may be that if prices are low a farmer may work with greater energy to produce a large crop with the object of maintaining his standard of living. Conversely, when prices are likely to be high he may plan a smaller output. In the longer term, poor prices will tend to reduce the number of farmers in business, while high prices will have the reverse effect. To take another example, an increase in wages in a particular occupation may result in a reduction in the number of hours worked (by way of reduced overtime) and total output may be reduced, at least until such time as the total labour force has been increased as a result of the more attractive wages. *See* FIGURE 23.

Supply function. For an individual producer, the expression of the quantity produced and supplied as a function of output and input prices; profit maximisation is assumed. An aggregate supply function is obtained by summing the supply functions of all the individual producers.

Supply side economics. The forces considered by many economists to determine output; the availability or supply of capital and labour, and the state of technology. Hence the volume of money should grow in line with the growth of output generated by capital accumulation and labour force growth. Flexible wages and prices would automatically ensure full employment and an appropriate level of aggregate demand. There would still be a natural rate of unemployment due to frictional, structural and technological unemployment, but no more.

Swap deposits. A technique developed in Hong Kong for evading a withholding tax on Hong Kong dollar deposits; an individual performs a swap by purchasing foreign currencies with Hong Kong dollars and then taking a forward contract to cover the transaction. The depositor's Hong Kong dollar funds appear as foreign currency deposits in the books of the deposit-taking institution. The withholding

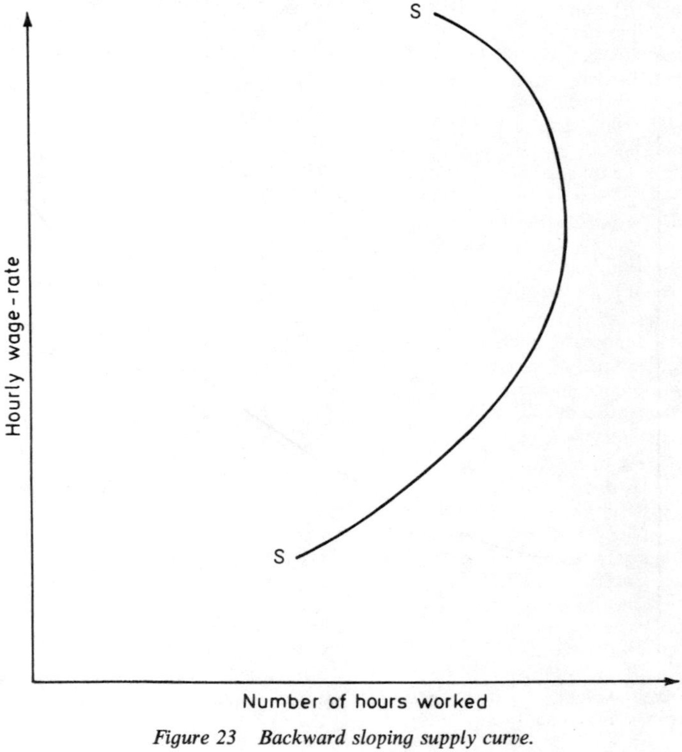

Figure 23 Backward sloping supply curve.

tax (q.v.) of 10 per cent on interest paid on Hong Kong dollars was thus evaded. The system was facilitated by banks raising Hong Kong dollars by selling foreign currencies and then buying them back on a forward basis.

S.W.I.F.T. *See* SOCIETY FOR WORLDWIDE INTER-BANK FINANCIAL TELECOMMUNICATIONS.

Swiss numbered accounts. Anonymous accounts permitted in the banking system of Switzerland; secrecy is protected not only by civil but also by the criminal law. The identity of clients is known only to selected members of the bank's management. Tax evaders can profit from Swiss bank secrecy, tax evasion not being considered a crime (as distinct from tax fraud). The Swiss banking system has been described as a well-protected edifice of banking discretion existing in one of the leading financial centres of the world with a reputation for political and economic stability and a high concentration of banking expertise. Although banks everywhere are expected to keep their client's secrets, at least to a considerable degree, Swiss banking secrecy has been of an unusual order.

Switch dealer. A dealer (q.v.) who disposes to others goods that one trading party does not wish to receive from another trading party under, say, a bilateral trade agreement. The activities of these dealers injects some flexibility into bilateral trade agreements which oblige trading partners to keep their trade with each other in approximate balance. *See* BILATERAL TRADE.

Switch order—contingent order. An order for the purchase (sale) of one stock and the sale (purchase) of another stock at a stipulated price difference.

Switch selling. Advertising one model and trying to sell a more expensive one. The offer or advertisement of a 'cheap' commodity is used to arouse consumer interest; persuasive salesmen then concentrate on selling dearer models to customers who have shown interest.

Switching. The transfer of investment between different classes of securities. Switches are of four fairly distinct kinds:

(a) Policy switching—made to take advantage of future possibilities in relation to an investor's requirements. It may involve the redistribution of a portfolio.

(b) Coupon switching—made to take advantage of immediate possibilities of profit.

(c) Anomaly switching—switching between securities of comparable maturity to profit from some fleeting anomaly in their prices. The purpose is always a profit on trading without any change in the broad pattern of an investor's portfolio. Large stakes are needed to show a profit on the fine margins available.

(d) Simultaneously buying a contract for futures delivery in 1 month while selling a contract of the same commodity in another delivery month, on the same exchange.

Generally, switching helps to even out prices and makes a contribution to the smooth functioning of the gilt-edged market.

Sydney Futures Exchange. A commodity exchange which began operating in May, 1960, located in Sydney, Australia. Trading in futures contracts occurs on the floor of the Exchange in a similar manner to the stock exchange; all transactions are by 'open outcry' as opposed to private treaty. All transactions are guaranteed by an independent clearing house and the identity of all buyers and sellers remains undisclosed. Trading in wool futures has been prominent. The introduction of a live cattle contract was approved by members late in 1974. The exchange now trades futures contracts in silver, fat lambs, export bullocks, 90-day bank accepted bills and U.S. dollars.

Sydney International Options Market. Established in 1984, an options market based at the Sydney Stock Exchange, Australia, trading in gold, silver, and foreign currencies. Through the use of an electronic order book, an order placed with a limit is automatically transferred from centre to centre throughout the world until the trigger price is struck and the transaction executed. Trading and settlement is in U.S. dollars, settlement occurring in London, England. Clearing work is done through the international options clearing corporations, with final processing being done in Sydney. The system embraces the European Options Exchange in Amsterdam, and the Montreal and Vancouver stock exchanges.

Syndicate. (a) An association between two or more firms to carry on together a joint activity without the formation of a separate legal entity.

(b) A ring formed by London discount houses for the purpose of tendering for agreed quotas of Treasury bills at uniform rates. The practice of tendering at a 'syndicate price' was discontinued in 1971.

Syndicated loans. Loans involving several banks joining together to raise massive sums (say$1 billion or more) for a single borrower.

T

T-notes. *See* TREASURY NOTES.

Taker. The buyer or purchaser of an option (q.v.).

Takeover bid. An offer addressed to the shareholders of a company by an individual or company, to buy their shares at a named price with a view to securing control of the company. If a company earns a smaller return on its shareholders' capital than can be found elsewhere, its share price will fall, eventually encouraging a bidder who believes that he can manage the company more profitably or can close it down and sell off its assets for more than the company cost to buy from the original shareholders. In Britain, the monopolistic dangers inherent in take-over bids when control of an industry or service is passing into fewer and fewer hands are scrutinised by the Office of Fair Trading (q.v.).

Talisman. The computerised settlement system of The London Stock Exchange (q.v.). The letters stand for Transfer Accounting, Lodging for Investors, and Stock Management for Jobbers.

Talon. A slip attached to dividend and interest coupons for the purpose of applying for further coupons when necessary. *See* COUPON BOND.

Tap issue. The issue of bills and securities by the Treasury direct to Government Departments and other buyers at a special price, without going through the market. *See* TREASURY BILLS.

Tap stocks. Securities (q.v.) which are always available; the term is applied also to government securities which are sold by the government departments holding them when they reach a certain market price. Tap stocks may be short- or long-dated.

Tare. The weight of the packing or container of an article. This must be deducted from the gross weight to find the actual or net weight of the article.

Target prices. In respect of the European Economic Community (q.v.), prices set by the Commission for each agricultural product, the aim being to keep the market price throughout the Community at a level which will help farmers plan their production. *See* COMMON SUPPORT PRICES; INTERVENTION PRICES.

Target return pricing. The setting of prices at a level that will ensure an adequate return on investment by a company, if achieved. *See* ANTICIPATORY PRICING, FULL COST PRICING, SUPPLY AND DEMAND, LAWS OF.

Tarif de combat. A tariff used as a bargaining counter in attempting to secure trade advantages.

Tariff. (a) A duty or tax charged by a country on its imports from other countries; a customs duty (q.v.). The duty may be imposed on an 'ad valorem' basis, as a percentage of the value of the goods, or by way of a specific amount per unit of weight or volume. The tariff may be used to protect home industries from the competition of foreign producers, or it may be adopted to reduce the total imports bill a country has to pay. (b) A method of charging for services, e.g. supplies of gas or electricity.

Tax avoidance scheme. A business scheme which seeks to avoid or minimise the payment of tax; it is basically lawful and conducted within the framework of existing legislation however deficient or inadequate that legislation may be. *See* TAX EVASION SCHEME.

Tax based incomes policy (T.I.P.). A policy suggested to influence prices through tax incentives to firms and workers to keep price or wage rises low. In 1978, the Carter administration proposed real wage insurance as a means of reducing the rate of wage increase; the proposal was that unions contracting for a wage increase which proved less than the rate of inflation would be compensated by the government for any fall in real wages. Payment might be direct or by way of a reduction in taxes. Congress did not accept the proposal.

Tax based leases. Leases designed to take advantage of tax concessions such as investment allowances and accelerated depreciation rates; these can amount to more than 50 per cent of the equipment cost in the first year. The concessions are equivalent to an additional source of funding. There are essentially two types of tax based leases—equity and leveraged leases. *See* EQUITY LEASING; LEASE; LEVERAGED LEASING.

Tax break. A situation providing some relief from tax, in whole or part. *See* TAX HAVEN; TAX SHELTER.

Tax evasion scheme. A business scheme which seeks to avoid or minimise the payment of tax; it is basically unlawful infringing the framework and principles of existing legislation. *See* TAX AVOIDANCE SCHEME.

Tax haven. A country offering special opportunities for tax minimisation by way of free zones, cash grants, and tax incentives, in order to obtain additional employment and gain votes. All havens are not equally useful to all users or tax refugees. Countries which have reputations for offering special advantages to investors or immigrants include France, Monaco, Italy, Spain, the Channel Islands, Malta, the Caribbean, Latin America, the Bahamas, Bermuda, Cayman Islands, Hong Kong, Liechtenstein, Luxembourg, the Isle of Man, the Netherlands, Antilles, Panama, Switzerland, Vanuatu and the British Virgin Islands.

Tax, marginal rate of. The amount of tax a person pays on the last unit or increment of income received.

Tax, progressive. *See* INCOME TAX, PROGRESSIVE.

Tax, regressive. A tax which takes a larger percentage of income from people the smaller their income.

Tax-rort account. False bank accounts, opened for the purposes of tax evasion; a financial institution may open such false bank accounts with money on deposit from the public. The accounts are opened in false names by bank officers, or employees of other financial institutions.

Tax sharing. Proposals that a federal government share some part of its tax collections with state and local governments.

Tax shelter. A medium or process intended to reduce or eliminate the tax burden of the individual. Tax shelters range from tax exempt municipal securities to sophisticated partnerships in real estate, cattle raising, equipment leasing, oil drilling, research and development activities.

Taxation, Adam Smith's canons of. Smith's canons of taxation were as follows:

(a) the amounts people paid in taxes should be equal, i.e. proportional to their incomes;
(b) there should be certainty with regard to the amount to be paid;
(c) there should be convenience of payment and collection;
(c) economy should be observed so that taxes should not be imposed of a kind where the cost of collection was excessive.

Taxation, purposes of. The purposes of direct and indirect taxation are broadly:

(a) To provide the public authorities with the revenue required for meeting the cost of defence, social services, interest payments on the national debt (q.v.), municipal services, etc.
(b) To give effect to economic policy, the objects of which may include:
  (i) increasing the economic welfare of the community as a whole by reducing the inequality of incomes;
  (ii) reducing or increasing purchasing power through increasing or reducing purchase taxes;
  (iii) checking the imports of a commodity from abroad in order to help to correct an adverse balance of payments;
  (iv) influencing the rate of economic growth of the nation;
  (v) to reduce or increase the money supply.

Taxation schemes, fraudulent. Schemes designed to minimise or avoid the payment of taxes using illegal means and procedures. Schemes may involve simply the concealment of income, or they may involve ways of 'annihilating' income by the creation of fictitious debts. Schemes are devised by entrepreneurs and marketed by tax advisers. *See* BOTTOM-OF-THE-HARBOUR TAX AVOIDANCE SCHEMES; CASH ECONOMY.

Taxes. A compulsory financial contribution by a person or body of persons towards the expenditure of a public authority. Taxes on income (i.e. on wages, salaries, profits, dividends, rent and interest) and on capital are known as 'direct' taxes. In Britain, direct taxes accounted for about 32 per cent of receipts in 1981–82. Income tax accounted for 77 per cent of all direct taxation, followed a long way behind by corporation tax and petroleum revenue tax (a special tax on North Sea oil).

Taxes on commodities or services are known as 'indirect' taxes. In Britain, the indirect taxes on tobacco, oil and alcoholic drinks account for over 70 per cent of the revenue from this source. Other indirect taxes include purchase taxes, entertainment taxes and import duties. Purchase taxes are *ad valorem* (q.v.) taxes and were first introduced into Britain during the Second World War. Indirect taxes yielded some 39 per cent of the public sector's 1981–82 receipts. Value-added tax provided more than a quarter of the indirect tax total, followed by excise duties on oil, tobacco, alcohol and motor cars. Indirect taxes also included local authority rates, which raised almost as much as value-added tax (q.v.).

Technical analysis. A term in use in the futures and stock markets for the analysis of the patterns of price changes, rates of change, and changes in the volume of trading; one of the best known forms is 'chartism'.

Technical Development Capital Ltd. (T.D.C.). A company formed in 1962 to provide finance for the commercial exploitation of technical developments and innovations. Its formation was among the recommendations of the Radcliffe Committee (q.v.). The company's shareholders comprise over forty leading insurance companies, investment trusts and merchant banks. The primary objective is to help medium-sized and small businesses to accelerate the commercial exploitation of technical innovations rather than to finance research or development. The company is therefore prepared to support at an early stage projects having attendant high risks. Usually most of the finance required is made available on secured loan terms, repayable over a reasonable period. While a share in the equity of any project is expected, majority control is seldom sought. In 1983, renamed Investors in Industry, Ventures Division. *See* FINANCE CORPORATIONS; INVESTORS IN INDUSTRY, PLC.

Technical position. A term used in the futures markets to indicate internal market conditions which have been created as a result of past actions. When the market is sold out or oversold, its technical position is said to be strong; conversely, after a sharp advance when a market is clearly over-bought, its technical position is said to be weak.

Technical rally. Price variations in futures markets arising from such technical factors as trading volume, open interest, delivery conditions, or chart configurations, as distinct from movements resulting from any fundamental change in supply and demand.

Technological change. *See* TECHNOLOGICAL PROGRESS.

Technological effects or 'real' effects. Effects which alter the total production possibilities or the total welfare opportunities for consumers in the economy. The effects are described as economies when they are favourable, and diseconomies when they are unfavourable. Classical examples of external real diseconomies are air and water pollution; the effects are borne by persons and firms other than those who cause the pollution and in consequence production and consumption opportunities elsewhere in the economy are reduced.

Technological progress. Progress characterised by (a) improvements in the methods of production, achieved through more effective management, more advanced specialisation, better utilisation of labour, equipment and materials and in the rationalisation of productive processes in general; (b) improvements in the quality of resources in the form of more highly skilled labour and functional differentiation of capital; (c) improvements in the quality of products; and (d) a rising capital-labour ratio, i.e. an increasing amount of productive fixed capital per worker.

Technology. A body of information and techniques, and of skills and experience, developed for the production and use of goods and services.

Technology stocks. Stocks and shares in corporations specialising in high technology, e.g. Apple Computer.

Technostructure. Described by Professor John Kenneth Galbraith as the complex of professions and skills which comprises the structure of the modern business firm and gives it a measure of 'commanding power'. The primary affirmative purpose of the technostructure is the growth of the firm; in a growing firm it is possible for all members of the technostructure to advance; all can succeed. Growth also assists the business to protect itself against sources of intrusion: owners and creditors, workers through their unions, consumers, and government. Galbraith considered it often easier for the business to cope with the intrusion of owner and creditor (and even consumer) than to cope with the intrusion of union and government. He described the technostructure as the complex of scientists, engineers, and technicians; of sales, advertising, and marketing personnel; of public relations experts, lobbyists, lawyers, and people with a specialised knowledge of the bureaucracy and its manipulation; and of co-ordinators, managers, and executives.

Tender offer. A public offer to buy shares from existing stockholders of a public corporation by another company or organisation; stockholders are asked to tender (surrender) their holdings for a stated value, usually at a premium above current market price, subject often to the tendering of a minimum and maximum number of shares.

Tender to Contract Cover (T.T.C.). An option (q.v.) which allows exporters to fix forward exchange rates on which to base their tender prices. If an exporter wins a contract, the deal must proceed at the agreed price; if not, there is nothing lost save the fee. In this way, the customer only enters into a commitment to trade at the agreed rates if a contract is awarded.

Tenderable grades. Sometimes called deliverable grades. The actual grades for commodities which may be delivered under exchange rules in settlement of a futures contract.

Term assurance. A form of insurance life cover; the life office agrees to insure the policyholder's life for a fixed term (usually 25 years or more) for a fixed annual premium; if the policyholder outlives the term of the policy, nothing is payable.

Term loans (U.K.). Conventional loans for a period of up to 20 years and may be at fixed or variable rates of interest related to current yields in the gilt-edged market. When arranging a long-term loan, the borrower usually has to provide comprehensive information on the firm's past performance and future prospects. A loan will normally be secured against an existing fixed asset of the business. In some cases, the owners of the smaller business seeking such a loan may be required to supplement this security, and the lender will require an independent valuation of the assets securing the loan. Costs of such valuation and investigation are paid by the borrower. A term loan is not an overdraft.

Terminal markets. In London, markets in which trading is confined to 'futures', i.e. the making of contracts for the delivery of commodities at some specified future date.

Terms of trade. The relationship between the prices of exports and imports. It may be expressed as an index:

$$\text{Index of Terms of Trade} = \frac{\text{Price Index of Exports}}{\text{Price Index of Imports}}$$

The price index of exports measures the change in the aggregate value of a representative selection of exports as compared with the corresponding value in a base year; similarly the price index of imports measures the change in the aggregate value of a representative selection of imports as compared with the corresponding value for the same base year. If the prices of imports rise in relation to the prices of exports, then the terms of trade have moved against the exporter.

Tertiary industry. The provision of a wide range of services required by the primary and secondary industries and by individual consumers, e.g. the provision of transport and communication; commercial and financial services such as insurance and banking; the provision of health, legal and educational services; and the wholesale and retail trade. *See* PRIMARY INDUSTRY; SECONDARY INDUSTRY.

Thin market. A relatively inactive market with a low-volume, low-value turnover.

Third market. The trading of stock exchange listed securities in the over-the-counter market by non-exchange member brokers and all types of investors.

Thrifts. Financial institutions in the United States such as savings and loans associations, mutual savings banks, and credit unions.

Throughput economy. An economy in which resources are continuously used up without replacement or recycling.

TIC. The minimum price movement in the gold futures market at the Chicago Board of Trade (q.v.); it is 10 cents per troy ounce, rounded to $3.22 per contract. The daily limit or maximum price movement is $50 per troy ounce. Thus the price of a contract can move 500 tics in either direction before it reaches the maximum permitted daily limit. The fluctuation of $50 per troy ounce is $1,607.50 per contract, above or below the previous day's settlement price.

Ticket or name day. Day prior to settlement or account day (q.v.) on The London Stock Exchange (q.v.) when stockbrokers make out tickets bearing the names of their clients and details of shares brought during the previous account period (q.v.). These tickets are passed on to the stockjobbers from whom the shares were obtained. The stockjobbers pass on the tickets which finally reach the stockbrokers who first sold the shares. Arrangements are then made for payment for the shares and their legal transfer. The following day, accounts are settled.

Tight money. A monetary policy (q.v.) regarded as retarding economic activity. Opposite of easy money (q.v.).

Time deposit. An interest-bearing deposit for a

fixed period of time; in Eurodollar contracts the period is 3 months.

Time order. An order for securities which becomes a market or limited price order at a specified time.

Time preference. The relative evaluation of present versus future goods; usually the preference given a present as distinct from a future good of the same nature. It may be possible to apply a discount rate to a given situation.

Time sharing. An arrangement in which the financial contribution towards the purchase of an asset is related to the use of that asset in terms of time; thus a group of purchasers may share the cost of a 'second home', each enjoying the right to occupy it for a prescribed period of the year.

Time spread. *See* OPTION SPREAD.

To-arrive contracts. Contracts for cash grain or other commodity which allow for shipment or arrival at some specified time in the future. These contracts specify amount, grade, price and origin of the commodity.

Tokyo economic summit meeting. A meeting of the representatives of seven major industrial nations held in Tokyo in June 1979 to debate the energy crisis and devise means for restricting the growth in demand for oil, principally by the control of imports and by conservation measures. The summit meeting was a response to growing oil shortages and the pricing policies of the Organisation of Petroleum Exporting Countries (O.P.E.C.). The countries involved were the United States of America, West Germany, Britain, France, Japan, Italy and Canada.

Tokyo Round. A round of international discussions under the auspices of the General Agreement on Tariffs and Trade (q.v.) which led to tariff cuts in the early 1970s. The Tokyo Round embraced not only further tariff reductions but also new codes covering trading practices, e.g. non-tariff measures, subsidies, government procurements, and so on. The Tokyo Round of talks followed the Kennedy Round (q.v.).

Trade bill. A commercial bill used in transactions actually involving goods. A trade bill is drawn by the seller and accepted by the buyer, and is payable on a set date in respect of goods purchased. It can be offered for discount to a discount house or to the seller's own bank. The rate of discount charged depends upon the credit standing of the traders and occasionally upon the goods concerned. Trade bills guaranteed by a credit insurance company will command a finer rate of discount.

Trade cycle. Alternating periods of trade boom and depression, especially characteristic of 19th century business activity in Britain when cycles of this nature occurred at fairly regular intervals. Lord Beveridge in his *Full Employment in a Free Society* (1944) examined the cycles of business activity from 1792 to 1913 revealing intervals of from 5–11 years between one boom and the next, with an average of 8 years. During boom periods employment, wages, prices, profits and production rise together, only to decline during the ensuing slump. While all, or nearly all, industries are simultaneously prosperous or depressed, fluctuations occur most sharply in the production of capital goods. The long drawn out depression from 1920–39, between the two World Wars, differed in character from previous periods. A short period of boom after the First World War was followed by acute depression. Unemployment in the years 1920–28 averaged 1½ million. Superimposed on this came the Great Depression of 1929–35 in which unemployment rose to the unprecedented heights of almost 3 million, declining only slowly. By 1939 unemployment had decreased to about 1¼ million. The Great Depression was more severe and more worldwide than any other. All capitalist countries were affected. In very marked contrast, the period following the Second World War was for many years one of boom; unemployment in Britain rarely exceeded 500,000 or 2 per cent of the working population. *See* UNEMPLOYMENT.

Trade cycle, theories of the. Theories adduced by economists to explain fluctuations in trade have included:

(a) '*Real causes*' *theories.* (i) Attempts to explain the trade cycle in terms of harvest fluctuations attributable to the weather. One of the most famous of these theories was the 'sunspot' theory of William Stanley Jevons (1835–1882). Jevons traced cyclical trade fluctuations to cycles in harvest yields; in turn he correlated the harvest fluctuations with the appearance of spots on the face of the sun, it being argued that sunspots influence the weather and hence harvest yields. This and other climatic theories are no longer accepted as primary explanations of trade movements. (ii) Theories that fluctuations in capital-producing industries are due to the fact that the demand for their products is a derived demand (q.v.). *See* ACCELERATOR, THE.

(b) *Psychological theories.* Theories that business persons are influenced alternately by waves of optimism and pessimism. When trade is good people are optimistic, buying more while prices rise and production is stimulated. When trade is poor pessimism prevails buying is reduced, prices fall and production is depressed. The importance of these theories lies in the light they throw on the forces which tend to accentuate fluctuations, even if they do not themselves produce them. John Maynard Keynes (1883–1946) attached great importance to the psychological influences affecting the propensities to consume and save (q.v.).

(c) *Monetary theories.* Theories that stress the role of the quantity of money and credit, and the rate of interest, in influencing business activity. The view that the trade cycle (q.v.) is a purely monetary phenomenon has been held by Ralph G. Hawtrey (1879–1975) who regarded the Bank Rate (q.v.) as the mainspring of cyclical change. A reduction in Bank Rate and other short-term interest rate encouraged merchants to carry larger stocks of goods and stimulates trade generally; an increase in interest rates had the reverse effect. Hawtrey argued that by raising the Bank Rate a stop could be put to any boom, and by reducing the Bank Rate we could end nearly all depressions. The first proposition finds agreement in the Government White Paper on Employment Policy of 1944, although the Paper expressed doubt that changes in the rate of interest at the bottom of a depression will have any decisive effect on the course of trade.

(d) *Over-production and under-consumption theories.* Numerous and diverse theories but all may be described as theories of the deficiency of effective demand. John A. Hobson (1858–1940) argued that in good times profits increase without a corresponding increase in the wages level and the purchasing power in the hands of the general public. Surplus profits are invested and productive capacity is greatly enlarged; but there is no market to carry off the increased supply of consumers' goods and a crisis persists until the surplus of stocks is worked off.

(e) *Saving-investment theory.* A theory that consumption depends on the level of income, and that this in turn depends on real investment. Now saving, i.e. the abstention from the purchase of consumers' goods, is a pre-requisite for investment. Thus saving, consumption and investment depend on one another, together determining the level of total income. For full employment of resources to be maintained it is essential that the effective demand for goods and services should be sufficient to absorb all the output of the economic system. When saving is not translated into investment, the demand for goods is insufficient to cover all that is being produced; output falls and unemployment results. Between the two World Wars savings tended to exceed investment with adverse effects on employment. In these circumstances, incomes tend to fall until saving is once more brought into equality with investment. This may be at a level which is socially unacceptable. The solution lies in stimulating investment and hence incomes and effective demand.

Traded options. The buyer (taker) acquires the right to buy or sell a futures contract at one of several fixed base (or strike) prices for a fixed delivery month. The premium paid by the buyer will vary according to the length of time taken to buy, and the distance from the current price to the base (or strike) price of the option.

Trader. An individual who buys and sells for his own account on an Exchange for short-term profit; also an employee of a broker or financial institution who specialises in handling purchases and sales of securities for the firm or its clients.

Trades Union Congress. A body representing most British trade unions (q.v.); its objects are to further the interests of its members and improve the economic and social conditions of workers. Founded in 1868 it is an important channel of communication and consultation between the Government and unions. The Scottish Trades Union Congress has objectives similar to those of the T.U.C.

Trade unions. Combinations of workers formed for the purpose of taking collective, as distinct from individual, action against their employers for the improvement of pay and other working conditions. Most unions also develop 'friendly society' activities offering their members additional insurance against sickness and accident. There are two types of union; (a) craft unions, members of which are all engaged in the same—or one or two closely associated—occupations; (b) industrial unions, members of which come from branches of a particular industry. Of the British workforce of 25.5 million, about half belong to trade unions; of these over 11 million belong to unions affiliated to the Trades Union Congress (q.v.). *See* AMERICAN FEDERATION OF LABOUR AND CONGRESS OF INDUSTRIAL ORGANISATIONS.

Trading post. A structure on the floor of the New York Stock Exchange (q.v.) at which stocks are bought and sold; about 100 stocks are traded at each post.

Training board. *See* INDUSTRIAL TRAINING ACT, 1964.

Transactions demand. The demand for money that people need to have available for spending, as distinct from the speculative demand (q.v.) for money. For convenience, people need cash and a bank account, to meet living expenses as they arise and occasional emergencies. The two financial variables, the transactions and speculative demand for money, are influenced by income and interest rates respectively.

Transfer payments. Payments made by public authorities which are not made in consideration of goods and services currently produced, e.g. national assistance payments, unemployment benefit, grants to students, family allowances, interest paid on the national debt.

Transfer pricing. The pricing of goods and services which are merely being transferred from one part to another part of the same organisation, e.g. movements, including international movements, of goods and services within a multinational corporation. Transfer pricing manipulation has been suggested as a source of tax avoidance. Some countries adopt an "arm's length" pricing principle for tax assessment purposes, i.e. a price may be substituted into the accounts which is what would have been charged in an international deal between two entirely different companies. A 1979 O.E.C.D. report identified three main methods of arriving at proper transfer prices: the comparable uncontrolled price which promotes the idea that there is a price at which independent groups would transfer the same product; resale price method, which starts with the price at which the goods finally leave the group if bought by a genuinely independent purchaser—the price is then reduced by the turn which the seller would have to make to cover his costs and make a reasonable profit; and the cost-plus method, which defines the right transfer price as cost plus a suitable mark-up. All methods have their difficulties, both in principle and in application. Often, the actual method used is called the 'residual method' in which the company and the taxation officials sit round a table and negotiate over the size of the tax cheques which the company will have to pay; this method avoids court litigation while multinationals are able to keep their names out of the newspapers in relation to alleged tax avoidance.

Treasury, the. The central department in the British Civil Service, functioning as the technical controller of the public purse with responsibility for macro-economic policy, exchange rate policy, and overseas public spending. A 10 year campaign by Sir Warren Fisher in the 1920s left the Treasury, through its control of the public purse, at the commanding heights of the British bureaucracy.

Treasury bills. (a) *U.K.* Short-term bearer securities, with a maturity usually of 91 days, issued by the British Treasury. Tenders are invited every Friday for the bills to be issued in the following week. The effective yield is the discount at which they are sold, that is to say the difference between the price at which they are sold and their redemption value. These are known as 'market' Treasury bills. They must be distinguished from 'tap' Treasury bills which are those bills issued directly, not through the tender, to Government departments, including the Issue Department of the Bank of England (q.v.) and the National Debt commissioners. The raising of money by the Treasury through the issue of Treasury bills enables the British Government to meet its weekly commitments which are ultimately paid for by taxation. The taxes do not come in at an even rate, however, a large part coming in at the end of the financial year; hence the need for short-term borrowing. The discount houses apply each week for a total amount of Treasury bills sufficient to cover the amount offered at the tender, but from September, 1971, discontinued their long-standing practice of tendering at a common, agreed price.

(b) *U.S.* Financial instruments (q.v.) of the United States government with original maturities of 1 year or less. They are issued with 3, 6, 9 or 12 month maturities at auctions held on a weekly basis by the Federal Reserve Banks acting as fiscal agents for the U.S. Treasury. Treasury bills are a sound form of short-term investment, without credit risk. Potential lenders to the government submit bids at the auctions; these may be competitive bids specifying the price the purchaser is willing to pay, or they may be non-competitive bids stating that the purchaser will accept the average yield at the auction in question. The holders of these bills can sell them easily before maturity if desired, as a large secondary market exists for Treasury securities; the price may be higher or lower than that initially paid depending upon changes in market interest rates.

Treasury bond (T-bond) futures contract (U.S.). A firm commitment by two parties: the seller who agrees to make delivery of $100,000 face amount of U.S. Treasury bonds, and the buyer who agrees to take delivery of these bonds at a certain time in the future. The price of the contract is determined by open outcry (q.v.) on the trading floor of futures exchanges, and fluctuates daily. The contract price is predicated on the possibility of delivery, but actual delivery rarely occurs. The vast majority of futures positions are liquidated by offsetting trades before contracts expire.

Trading also takes place in options on T-bond futures contracts. These are also contracts involving a buyer and seller, but options are unilateral contracts. Anyone buying (holding) an option on a bond futures contract acquires the right, though not the obligation, to assume a long or short position in one T-bond futures contract for a fixed price (the exercise or strike price set by the Exchange) at any time during the life of the option. Buyers may or may not exercise this right. Anyone selling (writing) an option on T-bond futures undertakes a firm commitment to perform if the option is exercised.

Treasury bond tender. A method of sale of government treasury bonds, adopted by some governments. A tender usually makes provision for two types of bidders—'competitive' and 'non-competitive'. The return on such an investment is called the 'yield', this being determined by the outcome of competitive bids in the tender. A yield higher than the announced interest rates means that bonds are issued at a discount (i.e. at less than face value). A lower yield than the announced interest rates means the bonds have been issued at a premium. Following the result of the competitive bidding, the non-competitive bidders may have to make an additional payment, or may receive a refund, for the return to non-competitive bidders is comparable to that paid to professional and institutional investors.

Treasury bonds, sale by tender of. A method of selling bonds used by some governments in which competitive tenders are called for bonds at a given face value and a fixed coupon interest rate (q.v.); the market determines the actual yield on treasury bonds under the tender system as they may sell at a premium or discount depending on the purchasers' perception of prospective future interest rates.

Treasury Department (U.S.). One of the original departments of the United States created by Act of Congress in 1789. The appointment of the Secretary of the Treasury and the political appointees serving under him are subject to Senate confirmation. The Treasury is directly responsible for taxation policy and for some aspects of monetary policy; it has a strong voice in United States international economic policy. In practice, the functions of the Department depend on the power actually wielded by the Secretary. Under recent Secretaries, the Department has had a predominant voice in economic policy formulation.

Treasury Deposit Receipt. Largely replaced the Treasury bill (q.v.) in Britain during the Second World War. Each week the Banks were advised as to the amount of Treasury Deposit Receipts they were to take up. The system declined in post-war years. By the beginning of 1952, the Treasury Deposit Receipt had disappeared.

Treasury Directive. Instruction or request by the British Treasury to the banks in respect of the volume of bank advances. It has become an important additional instrument of monetary policy.

Treasury Growth Investment Receipts (T.G.I.R.s). Zero coupon bonds (q.v.), first launched in the United States by Merrill Lynch in August, 1982.

Treasury notes (U.S.). Financial instruments (q.v.) of the United States government with original maturities of between 1 and 10 years; for this reason they are not classified as bonds, as a bond (q.v.) usually matures in a period of more than 10 years.

Treasury securities (U.S.). *See* TREASURY BILLS; TREASURY NOTES.

Treasury stock (U.S.). Stock issued by a company but later re-acquired; it may be held in the treasury of a company indefinitely, reissued to the public, or retired. No dividend is payable in respect of treasury stock and it carries no voting rights.

Tripartite Agreement 1936. An agreement which achieved a *de facto* stabilisation between the major currencies (sterling, franc, and dollar); it represented a major step towards what became the Bretton Woods Agreement (q.v.) with its return to fixed par values against a gold-dollar exchange standard. The collapse of the gold standard (q.v.) in the face of the severe world-wide recession at the beginning of the 1930s, and exchange rate instability which followed, had allowed individual currencies to fluctuate wildly against each other.

Trust. A combination or amalgamation of

large firms exercising monopoly control over the commodity produced. Government legislation may be introduced to protect consumers, e.g. the anti-Trust legislation in the U.S.A. The Sherman Anti-Trust Act 1890, dissolved the great oil and tobacco trusts, although both were later reconstituted. *See* INVESTMENT TRUST COMPANIES; UNIT TRUST.

Trust stripping. A tax avoidance scheme the essence of which is that the income of a family trust is diverted, through a chain of trusts, to people who do not pay tax on it. Family trusts have been widely used as a method of minimising income tax, but some of the methods used such as trust stripping have come to be regarded as blatant tax evasion. Promoters have often advertised these schemes for sale.

Trustee companies. Specialised companies which perform a wide range of services for clients, notably by way of acting as executor or trustee under a will when they administer a person's estate after death, distributing the assets according to the will. A trustee company may also act as a guardian of infant children or guardian of their estates; it may also act as an agent in the collection of rents and dividends.

Trustee status (U.K.). Used in reference to the ordinary shares of those companies which meet the requirements of the 'wider range' investments defined by the Trustee Investments Act 1961. Briefly, such a company is United Kingdom registered, has paid-up capital of at least £1 million, and has paid a dividend for at least the last 5 years.

Truth-in-lending Act 1968 (U.S.). An Act which requires creditors to furnish borrowers with certain basic information, in a uniform manner, regarding the cost of the credit they are seeking; the Act also lays down rules for disclosure in the advertising of credit terms. The Board of Governors of the Federal Reserve System (q.v.) administers this Act.

Turn. A Jobber's 'turn' is the difference between his buying and his selling price. He may make a profit or loss.

Twin deficits. In the mid-1980s, a reference to the U.S. Federal Budget deficit and the U.S. current balance of payments deficit.

Two-dollar broker (U.S.). A broker who makes a livelihood by executing orders for commission brokers during busy periods. The broker charges commission for his services, which at one time was $2 for every 100 shares or stocks bought or sold.

U

Uncalled capital. Authorised capital remaining uncalled on shares issued to the public. The uncalled capital may be regarded as reserve capital. *See* CAPITAL—AUTHORISED, NOMINAL OR REGISTERED.

Uncertainty. In economics, non-insurable business risk; the unpredictability of the outcome of much of business activity. The risks of theft, fire and flood to a large number of businesses can be calculated and insurance offered against them. In this way this class of risk can be converted through insurance into a known cost to the firm. Other business risks cannot be so provided against, e.g. the unforeseeable effect of political decisions on the markets for certain goods. These risks or uncertainties must be borne by the entrepreneur (q.v.). In private competitive enterprise profit is regarded as the reward for bearing uncertainties. *See* RISK.

Undated security. *See* DATED SECURITIES.

Underground economy. *See* CASH ECONOMY.

Underlying security. The shares subject to purchase upon the exercise of an option. *See* SHARE OPTIONS.

Underwriting. The act of insuring or guaranteeing. In the new issues market, underwriters guarantee, for a commission, that the money required will be forthcoming; if the public does not subscribe fully to the new issue the underwriters take up the remaining shares or stock.

Unemployment. A condition of involuntary idleness. Officially in Britain, the concept of 'unemployment' is confined to the total of those people (counted on 1 day in each month) who are registered with local employment offices as out of work and looking for jobs and who, in the judgment of employment officers, are 'capable and available' for work. The definition of 'capable and available', is based on national insurance case law going back to 1922. In some countries, unemployment is measured on a survey or sample date basis rather than on the basis of official registration statistics. Unemployment in the United States is calculated on a survey basis, and tends to give a higher figure than a narrower measure would reveal.

In October, 1982, 11,551,000 people were out of work in the United States, amounting to 10.4 per cent of the labour force. In the same month there were 99,093,000 persons employed, a decline of 630,000 since the previous month and a total drop of 1.8 million since the recession began in July, 1981. There were also more than 1.6 million 'discouraged workers' who had stopped looking for work because it was believed that none was available. More than 6.6 million persons worked only part time, an increase of 2.2 million since the recession began. The average length of time people were out of work rose to 17.2 weeks. However, in 1933 in the depths of the Great Depression, the unemployment rate reached 24.9 per cent; even in 1940, it stood at 14.6 per cent. Unemployment in the United States fell from 10 per cent in June, 1984, to 7.1 per cent 1 year later.

Unemployment, costs of. The direct and indirect economic and social costs to society of unemployment of labour: these comprise (a) the cost to the nation in unemployment pay and subsistence allowances, (b) the loss to the nation of tax revenue, both by way of income tax and indirect taxes; (c) the loss in output due directly to the waste of resources; (d) the adverse effect on health and the consequent additional burden on the health services; and (e) the social, family, and individual impacts which are serious yet incalculable.

Unemployment rate. The number of persons capable of working and willing to work but unable to find suitable employment, expressed as a percentage of the total number of persons available for employment at any time. The rate of unemployment may be calculated:

$$\frac{u}{e+u} \times 100$$

where

u = numbers unemployed
e = numbers employed
e + u = labour force

Unemployment, types of. Economists distinguish the following types of unemployment:

(a) *Disguised unemployment.* A slackening of total effective demand may not be fully reflected in the increase of persons registered as unemployed for two reasons: (i) workers may be put on 'short-time', thus reducing the number of hours worked per person and avoiding redundancy, and (ii) employers may retain a greater number of men than they require during what is believed to be a temporary recession in order to keep teams together and to have sufficient labour available when demand revives. (iii) In addition, some workers become discouraged and drop out of the labour force (and the statistics) in the belief that work is not available. *See* ACTIVITY RATE; PAYROLL TAX.

(b) *Unemployables.* Individuals who, suffering from a mental, temperamental or physical disability, are unable to find or follow any normal employment. The number of such individuals is relatively small. They are no longer included in the figures for unemployment.

(c) *Frictional unemployment.* This type of unemployment consists of individuals who are temporarily unemployed, although there may be an overall unsatisfied demand for labour in the country, because they are not offering the right skills at the right time in the right place to meet that demand. Mobility or retraining may provide a solution. A more stubborn problem exists if the person displaced by the introduction of a labour-saving device, such as a computer, is too old to find another place, and perhaps another kind of work, in industry.

(d) *Seasonal unemployment.* Unemployment which arises in particular trades and industries through seasonal variations in activity. For example, bad weather often causes a temporary suspension of work in the building industry; seaside resorts offer little employment during the winter season; agriculture provides seasonal employment at times of harvesting, potato-lifting and fruit gathering.

(e) *Structural unemployment.* Unemployment which arises in particular industries through a major and more or less permanent fall in demand for the products of those industries. Between the two World Wars, this type of unemployment was prevalent in three declining industries—coal-mining, ship-building and cotton. On Clydeside, Scotland, unemployment never fell below 12 per cent during the inter-war period, averaged 17 per cent and often exceeded 30 per cent.

(f) *Mass unemployment.* Unemployment affecting many trades and industries arising from a fall in the total volume of effective demand for goods and services of all kinds. It is associated with the trade cycle (q.v.) and is sometimes called 'cyclical unemployment'. The Great Depression, 1929–35 (q.v.), and indeed the whole period between the two World Wars, provided an unprecedented example of this type of unemployment. The problem was not confined to Britain, affecting all industrial countries.

Unemployment trap. A situation in which middle and older aged persons retrenched during a recession are passed over during the subsequent economic recovery, employers tending to hire the younger short-term unemployed and new job seekers; the predicament of those caught in the unemployment trap worsens notwithstanding considerable experience and competence previously greatly valued.

Unincorporated businesses. In Britain, sole proprietorships, sole traders, or partnerships; businesses in which individuals are personally liable for any business debts. *See* INCORPORATED BUSINESSES; PARTNERSHIP, THE; SOLE PROPRIETOR, THE.

Unit trust. A method of investment by which money subscribed by many people is invested on their behalf by a management company; the investment and management is subject to the strict legal provisions of a trust deed. The investments acquired are held by a trustee which may be a bank or an insurance company. The management company and the trustee are parties to the trust deed which defines their respective responsibilities and contains the rules for the operation of the trust. Unit trusts in Britain are subject to the Prevention of Fraud (Investments) Act 1958. Net income is paid to all investors in the trust in proportion to the size of their holdings. *See* INVESTMENT TRUST COMPANIES.

United Arab Emirates (U.A.E.). A sovereign federal state formed in December, 1971, with the following members: Abu Dhabi, Dubai, Sharjah, Umm al-Qaiwan, Fujairah and Ajman, Ras al-Khaimah joined the federation in 1972. The federal capital is Abu Dhabi. The United Arab Emirates is today an oil-rich country with vast resources, although a little more than 10 years ago it had one of the lowest incomes per head in the world; it is a member of the Organisation of Petroleum Exporting Countries (q.v.). *See* ABU DHABI FUND FOR ARAB ECONOMIC DEVELOPMENT.

United Kingdom and the European Communities, The (Cmnd. 4715). A White paper published on 7 July 1971, outlining the case for Britain's entry into the European Economic Community (q.v.).

United Nations Conference on Trade and Development (U.N.C.T.A.D.). An organisation set up by the United Nations to assist the less developed nations, defined as those countries with a gross national product per head of less than $600 a year. It seeks to accelerate the growth rate of the less developed countries to not less than 5 per cent per annum. The Conference endeavours to do this by arranging aid and finance, and by promoting trade. In respect of finance, special drawing rights have been made available at the International Monetary Fund (q.v.) to assist the less developed countries when faced with an unexpected slump in their export receipts. The first U.N.C.T.A.D. meeting was held in Geneva in 1964. The sixth meeting was held in 1983. By then, virtually all industrial nations and Third World nations considered that the organisation had become an indispensable forum for North-South dialogue. However, the sixth conference was considered to have achieved little beyond emphasising the need for a stronger commitment to overcoming protectionism and for continuing financial flows to the south; the Action Plan of 1981 was, however, re-affirmed. It was recognised by many that only an increase in the value of exports from debt-ridden countries could ease the basic problems. *See* BRANDT COMMISSION.

United Nations Economic Commission for Latin America (E.C.L.A.). A regional economic commission serving the Economic and Social Council of the United Nations; it is mainly concerned with the utilisation of resources. In 1983, E.C.L.A. proposed a 'debtors club' or 'cartel of the penniless' aimed at giving the Latin American countries a new leverage with their banking creditors in the West. An information centre was also proposed where debtors could pool their knowledge of the financial world; the centre would not only collect financial data, but would also help those governments engaged in renegotiating their foreign debts.

United States banking system. *See* FEDERAL RESERVE BANKS; FEDERAL RESERVE BOARD; FEDERAL RESERVE SYSTEM.

Unlisted company. A company which has not signed the listing agreement of a stock exchange (q.v.); without this status, a company does not have the advantages of a regulated market in its securities.

Unlisted Securities Market (U.S.M.). Established in November, 1980, a market designed to provide easier access to sources of long-term funds for small companies in Britain with outstanding growth prospects; the market enables their shares to be traded before they are able to satisfy the rigorous criteria for a Stock Exchange listing. The U.S.M. must necessarily be regarded as carrying a higher element of risk than the traditional market in listed securities.

Unlisted security. A security which has not been admitted to the official list of a stock exchange. *See* SECURITIES.

Unload. Withdraw by selling shares, commodities, or futures; a journalistic expression, e.g. 'Since the price fell only in the last hour there may be many who have not yet unloaded their positions'.

Unsecured creditors. Persons to whom debt is owing, but who are uncovered or unprotected by prior claims on land, property, and other assets. In the event of a business failure, an unsecured creditor may expect a return of funds in whole or part when all prior claims have been met; hence an unsecured creditor may lose all. *See* CREDIT; FIRST MORTGAGE BOND; LIQUIDATION; PREFERENCE SHARE; PREFERRED STOCK.

Up-market. That part of a market which caters for the demands of the higher socio-economic groups.

Up tick. Descriptive of a transaction made at a price higher than the preceding transaction; also called a 'plus-tick'. A 'zero-plus' tick is a term used for a transaction at the same price as the preceding trade, though higher than previously. Conversely, a down tick or 'minus' tick is a term used to designate a transaction made at a price lower than the preceding trade. A plus sign or a minus sign is displayed throughout the day next to the last price of each stock at the trading post (q.v.) on the floor of the New York Stock Exchange (q.v.).

U.S. dollars futures contract. A futures contract (q.v.), the main purpose of which is to protect importers and exporters from unfavourable fluctuations in exchange rates between say the Australian dollar and the American dollar. To illustrate its use, take the case of an Australian exporter who expects to receive $U.S.100,000 in June as payment for goods despatched to Japan. He can take a contract to sell U.S. dollars in the appropriate delivery month, thus protecting himself from a devaluation of the U.S. dollar against the Australian dollar.

User cost. (a) A term introduced by Lord Keynes to describe the reduction in the value of capital equipment due to its being used as compared with its not being used; if a machine could be sold now for £10,000, but instead is used for a time in the production process and is then sold for $9,000, then the user cost is £1,000. (b) In cost-benefit analysis (q.v.), the total costs incurred by users in their use of a facility, including social as well as private costs, e.g. the costs of using alternative road systems including such factors as the costs of petrol, wear-and-tear on vehicles, time, pollution, and social intrusion.

Usurious loans. Loans at exorbitant rates of interest. There is a strong demand in the small business community for monies to be available when required, albeit at usurious rates, when ordinary forms of finance are not available. Profits from organised crime are often amplified through the usurious loan market.

Utility. The capacity of a good or service to satisfy a human want. Utility cannot be measured in any definite quantitative form; it is sufficient to be able to say, however, that the utility of commodity A > B > C, and so on.

Utility, ordinal. A concept of utility (q.v.) based on the idea of a preference ordering; it is assumed that a consumer compares alternative bundles of goods deciding whether he prefers one to others, or is indifferent between them. *See* INDIFFERENCE CURVE.

V

Valuation ratio. The stock-market valuation of a firm's ordinary shares as a ratio of the book value of assets due to ordinary shareholders.

Value. To an economist, the 'exchange value' or price of a commodity or service, i.e. the power it possesses of acquiring other goods or services by means of exchange. However treasured a thing may be to an individual, if that thing cannot be exchanged then as far as the economist is concerned it has no value. Value depends in the first instance on demand in relation to supply. Alfred Marshall (1842–1924) likened value to the keystone of an arch, balanced in equilibrium between the contending pressures of its two opposing sides, the forces of demand on the one side and those of supply on the other. He visualised the amounts and prices of the several agencies of production as mutually determining one another—'when several balls are lying in a bowl, they mutually determine one another's position'.

Value added. The value added to a commodity at each stage of its manufacture; for example, the value added by a flour miller to the final value of the flour, minus the cost of the wheat. The value added at each stage of processing equals the final value of the bread sold.

Value-added tax. A tax levied on net business turnover. It differs from a turnover tax in eliminating from the taxable 'base' the cost of inputs such as material and labour. it is a tax on the 'value added' to a group of inputs by the operations of the firm. This 'value-added' is the difference between the untaxed selling price of an article or service and the unit cost of production. Value-added tax is collected, not in a single stage like purchase tax but in instalments at each stage of the production and distribution process. Each manufacturer, wholesaler or retailer is accountable for tax on the full value of what he sells, but is allowed to take credit for tax already paid on his purchases. The value-added tax has been adopted throughout the European Economic Community (q.v.) as a means of sales taxation. Value-added tax was invented in France and first introduced there in 1954; eight European countries have adopted it. It was adopted in Britain at a single rate of 10 per cent from 1 April 1973, replacing both purchase tax and selective employment tax. In 1982 the main rate in Britain was 15 per cent, in West Germany 13 per cent, and in Denmark 22 per cent.

Value judgment. A decision involving basic issues of fairness, justice or morality. An economist is no more fitted to make such judgments than anyone else; he is concerned solely with the relationship between means and ends, whatever the nature of those ends might be. However, the economist can point out the feasible alternatives and the true costs that may be involved in different decisions.

Value Line Average Stock Index (V.L.A.). An index of general stock market trends; published by Arnold Bernhard since 1961, it is an unweighted geometric average of the prices of nearly 1,700 stocks being blue chip and second tier stocks listed on both the American Stock Exchange (q.v.) and the New York Stock Exchange (q.v.). The V.L.A. has the reputation of being the most volatile and most sensitive of all stock market indexes, due to the inclusion of many second tier stocks. The V.L.A. is the index on which Value Line Futures are traded, e.g. it is the basis of the Kansas City Board of Trade (q.v.) value line futures contract. The beta factor (q.v.) of the index is 1.2.

Value line futures contract. A firm commitment between a buyer and a seller to make or take delivery of an amount of money equal to the value of the Value Line Average Stock Index (q.v.) at a specific time in the future. The vast majority of these futures positions are closed-out by offsetting trades before contracts mature; cash settlement rarely occurs.

Value line investment survey. A survey conducted by the largest U.S. investment advisory service embracing some 1,700 stocks ranked one to five in descending order on the basis of their expected performance over the next 6–12 months.

Value of service principle. A basis for charging for services which may be adopted by a monopolist who enjoys the power to discriminate between markets. A monopolist adopting this principle will divide the total market served by him into a number of minor markets, exacting the maximum gain from each market. In respect of railway rates, this principle has led to elaborate schemes of classification, both for passenger and for goods traffic. *See* COST OF SERVICE PRINCIPLE.

Value, theories of. Theories devised to explain the exchange value or price of commodities and services. These have included:

(a) *Labour theory of value.* A theory that commodities are sold in ratios determined by the amount of labour expended on producing them. This was a fair observation for freely reproducible goods in a labour-intensive economy, but confused cause and effect. This theory was expounded by Adam Smith (1723–1790), David Ricardo (1772–1823), Karl Marx (1818–1883) and others.

(b) *Cost of production theory of value.* A theory which states that the value of a commodity is governed by the cost of the various factors employed in its production. This theory is simply a restatement of the labour theory of value expressed in monetary terms. Again the argument is from the side of supply, i.e. that cost determines price. The plasusibility of this theory arises from the fact that under free competition between freely reproducible goods, a high rate of profit on any class of commodity will attract new producers into the field. The addition to the supply will tend to reduce the price until it is equal to the cost of production, including normal profit (q.v.). Conversely, low profits or a loss will drive producers out of the market, and once again will tend to equal the cost of production, including normal profit. The theory does not account, however, for the value of goods which are not freely reproducible, or for the depressed value of goods due to a change in taste or fashion, or for the price of goods supplied under monopolistic conditions.

(c) *Marginal theory of value.* A theory expounded by William Stanley Jevons (1835–1882), Léon Walras (1834–1910) and Carl Menger (1840–1921) which states that the value of any commodity or service is determined by its marginal utility for any particular purpose. Thus value depends on relative scarcity, or on demand in relation to supply. This theory satisfactorily explains the value of all goods whether freely reproducible or not, and whether the goods are supplied in highly competitive conditions or not; yet it does not preclude the view that in the case of freely reproducible goods, produced in competitive-conditions, their values in the long-run are derived from the values of the factors of production which enter into their manufacture. Thus, although costs do not determine values or prices directly, they have an indirect influence through their effect on the supply curve (q.v.).

Vanilla product. A standard product, e.g. a straightforward Eurobond fixed-interest issue, without the sophistication of options or swaps.

Variable costs. Costs which vary directly with variations in the volume of output. The major variable costs involved are those of labour and material. Also known as 'prime costs'.

Variable proportions, law of. If the quantity of one productive service is increased by equal increments, from zero, the quantities of the other essential productive services remaining fixed, the resulting increments of product will increase for a period, then become constant, and then decrease. Thus increasing, constant and diminishing returns may be regarded as an aspect of the law of variable proportions—as a movement towards or away from the optimum. The law relates to quantities per unit of time and is essentially technological.

Variables, endogeneous and exogenous. An endogenous variable is a variable explained within a theory; thus the price of oranges is an endogenous variable being determined within the framework of the theory of price. An exogenous variable is one that impinges on a theory from the outside; thus the state of the weather is an exogenous variable which will influence the price of oranges. Exogenous variables are sometimes referred to as autonomous variables.

Variation margin. *See* INTERNATIONAL COMMODITIES CLEARING HOUSE LIMITED.

Velocity of circulation. The average number of times that each unit of money (whether in the form of coins, notes or bank deposits) changes hands in the course of a year. In other words:

$$\text{Average velocity of circulation} = \frac{\text{Volume of spending per year}}{\text{Total volume of money}}$$

The velocity of circulation is taken into account in the Quantity Theory of Money (q.v.). In the 'equation of exchange' MV=PT, where M is the quantity of money, V the velocity of circulation, P the price level, and T the total volume of transactions. With T constant, an increase in the quantity of money will not raise the price level proportionately if V falls. The velocity of circulation is not constant, changing in boom and depression. A feature of the Great Depression, 1929–35 (q.v.), was a reduced velocity of circulation. Those who thought recovery could be stimulated by increasing the quantity of money were disappointed by the unexpected decline in the velocity of circulation of the new money. Money became less active. The velocity of circulation is influenced by such fundamental factors as savings and investment, the total quantity of money and the amount of new money, the movement of interest rates and security prices, and many other factors.

The income velocity of money differs from the transactions velocity above as it excludes both financial transactions and a considerable volume of intermediate transactions. It takes account only of payments to dealers for goods and services. Income velocity measures the number of times per year that a unit of currency completes the circuit from income to purchase of goods and services and back to income again. Sometimes called circuit velocity. In the United States in 1979, the gross national product was about $2,369 billion while the money stock was $360 billion (i.e. M1); hence the velocity was about 6.6.

Vendor placing. (1) A means of financing acquisitions which may be adopted instead of a rights issue (q.v.); the new equity of a company, with the approval of shareholders, is placed with a small number of institutional investors, equivalent of up to 30 per cent of the total equity. This may be to the disadvantage of small investors who are excluded from the expansion of the equity.

(2) Employed in takeovers, when the bidding company issues shares to the target company (the vendor) which promptly exchanges them for cash with the bidder's bank. The bank, in turn, will already have agreed a sale of its shares to institutions.

Versailles Economic Summit. A conference of seven leading industrial nations held in 1982 at Versailles, France. The gathering split on the issue of whether currency intervention was an appropriate means of stabilising exchange rates; eventually there was agreement that co-ordinated intervention in foreign exchange markets was occasionally appropriate. *See* WILLIAMSBURG ECONOMIC SUMMIT.

Vertical distintegration. An opposing trend to vertical integration, being a situation in which an isolated process has an optimum scale of operation much greater than that required by the other processes of manufacture and, therefore, tends to be undertaken by a specialist firm which supplies a number of firms in the main industry. *See* HORIZONTAL INTEGRATION; VERTICAL INTEGRATION.

Vertical integration. The amalgamation of firms engaged in the different stages of production of the same commodity to achieve greater economic strength and profitability. Although the units may be far apart, geographically, both the sources of raw materials and the outlets for the products are assured. The American Steel Trust consists of firms engaged in transport, coal and iron-mining, steel production and rolling. A high degree of vertical integration may occur within the same establishment. An integrated iron-and-steel works provides a leading example of integration in so far that coke-ovens, blast furnaces, steel-making furnaces and rolling equipment are all in close proximity to each other. A considerable saving in fuel is effected by passing metal from one stage to another while it is still hot. In addition, gases produced in blast furnaces and coke ovens can be used to provide heat and power for other parts of the plant. Metal scrap can be readily returned to the steel-making processes. Transport savings are also considerable. Some British breweries are integrated backwards into the ownership and management of their own maltings, and forward into the control of large numbers of retail outlets. Also known as 'vertical combinations'. *See* HORIZONTAL INTEGRATION; VERTICAL DISINTEGRATION.

Vertical spread. *See* OPTION SPREAD.

Vertical supply curve. A market situation in which output cannot be permanently expanded by a fiscal or monetary expansion of demand, for total output cannot be expanded without improvements in productivity (q.v.).

Vintage capital models. Models of economic growth in which capital is not treated as one homogeneous stock, but as a series of layers of past investment, each layer having its own unique characteristics and representing a more efficient technology than its predecessors. Such models have provided theoretical insights into the determinants of productivity dispersion within industries and the rates at which new technological innovations are adopted.

Vintage pricing. The charging of higher prices during the early years of the life of a plant because uncertainty about the fugure makes distant prospective profits too speculative to count on; because of uncertainty, short 'pay-off periods' are adopted and the price level in the early years reflects this. On the whole, the more dynamic an industry, the shorter the pay-off periods and the higher the price.

Volume. The number of shares traded in a security or an entire market during a given period; volume on exchanges is usually considered on a daily basis and a daily average is computed for a longer period.

Voting trust. A permanent form of trust (q.v.) in which a number of competing companies agree to assign the whole of their stock to a group of trustees, receiving in exchange trust certificates representing the valuation of their properties. The trustees are thus able to exercise complete control over all the companies. This form of organisation was prevalent at one period in the United States until held to be illegal by the Courts. Perhaps the most familiar example was that of the Standard Oil Company which adopted this form of control during the years 1879–92. Following a decision of the Supreme Court in 1892 the organisation was reconstructed to take the form of a holding company (q.v.).

W

Wage drift. The gap between nationally-negotiated wage-rates and actual earnings which tend to be higher; this difference is due to overtime payments, bonuses and other incentives. In view of the significance of the trends in wage-rates and actual earnings in the national economy, variations are often expressed in percentage form. This is calculated:

$$\left(\frac{E}{M}-1\right)100$$

where E = ratio of average earnings at end of period to those at the beginning; and M = corresponding ratio in respect of wage-rates.

Wage freeze. *See* NATIONAL INCOMES POLICY.

Wage-fund theory. *See* WAGES, THEORIES OF.

Wage indexation. The adjustment of wages in line with changes in the cost-of-living; in this way real incomes can be maintained during inflationary periods. In Brazil, wages are adjusted every year in this manner. In several European countries, the practice of including cost-of-living adjustment clauses in collective agreements is widespread. In Belgium and Denmark it has been common practice since the Second World War; in the Netherlands since 1969. It is common practice also in Norway and Italy. In Australia, the principle was adopted by the conciliation and Arbitration Commission in 1975, though not always strictly applied.

Wage leadership. A characteristic of industries in which productivity is rising and firms find it easier for a variety of reasons to concede demands for wage increases than to reduce prices; the wage increases gained in one trade or industry tend to stimulate pressures for similar increases in other branches. These are the wage-following branches of the economy.

Wage-price controls. Mandatory regulation of wages and prices applied to certain segments of the United States economy during the period 1971–74.

Wage-price guideposts. Wage-price standards set by the President's Council of Economic Advisers (q.v.) in the 1960s to help curb inflation; the standards were based on the principle that wage increases should be no greater than increases in productivity and that prices should be stable on average. The guideposts were not mandatory.

Wages councils. *See* MINIMUM WAGE LEGISLATION.

Wages, theories of. Theories seeking to account for the level of wages in a community. The main theories which have been advanced are as follows:

(a) *Subsistence theory.* Of French origin, this 'iron law' of wages asserted that if wages rose above subsistence level an increase in population would inevitably follow, thus forcing wages down again to subsistence level. In many parts of the world, in which the standard of living is very low, this problem persists; nevertheless, the advanced industrial countries have demonstrated that this 'law' is not inevitable and that rising wages can be associated with a falling birth rate.

(b) *Wage-fund theory.* A theory advanced in the early 19th century that the amount available for wages is limited by the amount of capital; thus there is a definite 'fund' from which wages are paid, and if some get more, others get less. Wages depend, therefore, upon the proportion that the working population bears to capital. The idea of a fixed wages fund is a fallacy, but the proportion between labour and capital does influence directly the productivity of labour, and ultimately the level of real wages.

(c) *Marginal productivity theory.* A current theory that wages tend to be equal to the value of the marginal product of labour. The marginal product is the additional income that would accrue to an organisation from the employment of one extra person (or alternatively the decline in total income from the dismissal of one person). It is profitable to employ additional people until the value of the marginal product is equal in value to the wages. If wages are increased, workers will tend to be dismissed until the value of the marginal product is equal to the higher wage, other things remaining the same. In equilibrium, the marginal cost of the variable factor equals the marginal revenue product of that factor. If the firm buys its factors in a perfect market, then the marginal cost of the factor is its price; if it sells in a perfect market the marginal revenue is the going price.

In Western economies wages have tended to dictate, rather than be dictated by, the prices of what they produce; prices are pushed too high in inefficient industries and demand for their products and services collapses when exposed to international competition from more efficient producers.

The neoclassical theory of the demand for labour relates labour demand only to the real wage, given the quantity of other factors the firm is using. Competitive firms that are able to change the quantity of labour they employ, costlessly and immediately, will hire labour up to the point where the real wage is equal to the marginal product of labour.

Wagner Act. *See* NATIONAL LABOUR RELATIONS ACT 1935.

Waiter. Uniformed attendants stationed about The London Stock Exchange, or 'House'. A derivation from the old coffee house days.

Waiting line theory. *See* QUEUING, THEORY OF.

Walks. Cheques payable at the London Offices of branches of banks which are not members of the clearing house, e.g. overseas and foreign banks and merchant banking houses.

Wall Street. Or simply 'the Street', a reference to the New York financial community concentrated in the Wall Street area of Manhattan, New York City. *See* WALL STREET CRASH (1929).

Wall Street Crash (1929). The collapse of prices on the New York Stock Exchange in 1929 which precipitated the Great Depression, 1929–35 (q.v.), in the United States and throughout the capitalist world. Excessive speculation in stocks and shares had raised prices to abnormal heights.

Walters scheme. One of the new employment schemes introduced in Britain in 1982, the Walters scheme (named after Professor Alan Walters, the prime minister's economic adviser) offered a subsidy of £15 a week to any employer paying less than £40 a week to anyone aged between 16 and 18; employers paying between £40 and £45 got half the subsidy. The scheme aimed at cutting the price to employers of teenage labour, though leaving the employers free to hire or not to hire.

Warrant. A document which gives the holder a right to subscribe to the shares of a company as from some future date at some stated price. They are quoted, like the underlying shares, and move in a relationship with them. If the shares of a company are standing at 100p and the warrant is exercisable at 80p in the near future, then the warrant would be worth 20p.

Warranted rate of growth. The rate of economic growth (q.v.) at which desired saving is equal to required investment; a concept developed by Sir Roy Harrod in his *Economic Dynamics* using the equation:

$$G_w = \frac{S_d}{C_r}$$

where:

G_w = warranted growth rate;
S_d = fraction of income representing the amount of saving that people currently want to make;
C_r = fraction in which the values of the numerator and denominator are such that people find that the amount of capital goods on hand, fixed and circulating, is just what is required.

Traditionally, monetary and fiscal policies have been regarded as correctives to be used to check movements away from the warranted rate. If unchecked, such movements create conditions of inflation or deflation. The warranted rate may be entirely different from the natural growth rate.

Watering stock. The issue of securities to an extent unwarranted by the assets of a company.

Ways and means advances. Short-term loans made by the Bank of England (q.v.) to the British Government. These loans form part of the Government's short-term or 'floating debt'.

Wealth. Goods and other assets in existence at any time which command a market value (i.e. price) if offered for sale; this implies that such assets have utility and scarcity value, and that it is possible to transfer their ownership from one person or body to another. Economic science is concerned with the production and distribution of wealth defined in this way, and not with assets which have value in the mind of the owner only. Wealth is a fund of goods which can be consumed; it represents stored up facilities for the satisfaction of future wants. The Royal Commission on the Distribution of Income and Wealth estimated that at the end of 1973 the value of individually owned wealth in Britain exceeded £200 billion. Of this physical assets, such as houses and consumer durables, were valued at £140 billion. Bank deposits and ordinary shares accounted for much of the rest.

France introduced a wealth tax for the first time in 1981, though with numerous exemptions. Initially, the wealth tax only affected fortunes exceeding $500,000; the starting rate was 0.5 per cent a year, rising to a maximum of 1.5 per cent for personal wealth of more than $1.8 million. Less than 200,000 people were affected. Exemptions in whole or part embraced the owners of companies, art owners, farmers and the owners of forests and woods, and finally the champagne, cognac and fine wine makers.

Welfare economics. A branch of economics (q.v.) concerned with studying the extent to which economic activity maximises human welfare, and the evaluation of public policies relating to the economy designed to achieve that end. A term first associated with the work of the British economist. A. C. Pigou. The subject is concerned with defining economic efficiency (q.v.); with evaluating the economic efficiencies of individual systems of resource allocation; and analysing the conditions under which economic policies may be regarded as having improved human or social welfare.

Welfare frontier. A concept which represents the maximum well-being any person can enjoy, given the levels of welfare enjoyed by the remaining members of the community. Given the state of the arts, there is no position within the frontier which can be regarded as one of maximum social welfare; conversely there is no point outside the frontier attainable by society.

Welfare State. A nation that provides minimum standards in respect of education, health, housing, pensions and other social benefits, etc. when the individual means of certain sections of the population may be inadequate to provide these standards. The development of welfare in Britain had its origins in the 19th century with early factory legislation.

West German banking system. A banking system consisting of a central government bank (Deutsche Bundesbank), a few large commercial banks which operate nationwide branch systems, and about 300 other banks, mainly local or regional. The largest commercial banks are the Deutsche Bank, the Dresdner Bank and the Commerzbank. Commercial banks take sight, time and savings deposits, and lend not only at short-term but also through medium- and long-term credits and loans. The banks are required to maintain a 'minimum reserve ratio' with the Bundesbank by way of a specified proportion of their deposits. West German banks are active in the security markets, acting as issuing houses, brokers and dealers on the stock exchange.

When issued market. A market for bonds about-to-be-issued; when purchases are made, the bonds are acquired in advance even though no money may change hands for a week or two or even longer after the trade. The U.S. Treasury typically announces coming bond issues, up to 2 weeks before being available. Active trading in these not-yet-issued bonds begins, though no formal settlement is made until several days after the bonds are auctioned. The purchases made are real, even though at that time no money is put up.

Wholesale banks. Banks that concentrate on 'big-ticket' deposit-taking and lending (such as Morgan Guaranty and Bankers Trust). Banks such as Citibank and Bank of America tailor their lending more to individuals. In Britain, specialisation is not so marked; probably the Midland Bank is the most wholesale and Lloyds the most retail.

Wieser's law of costs. A law formulated by Friedrich von Weiser (1851–1926), an Austrian economist, that the cost of a commodity is the alternative foregone in producing it. *See* OPPORTUNITY COST.

Wild card. *See* SELLER' PUT.

Wildcat banking (U.S.). Term originally applied to United States banks which were located 'where only wildcats could find them'. Inaccessibility made the redemption of their paper money in species extremely difficult. Wildcat banks sprouted between the fall of the Second Bank of the United States and the introduction of a national banking system.

Williamsburg Economic Summit. The ninth annual economic summit of the seven major Western industrial powers, known as the 'Big Seven': the United States of America, Japan, the United Kingdom, France, West Germany, Italy, and Canada. The Conference was held in 1983 at Williamsburg, Virginia.

The final Declaration stressed the need to reduce interest rates further, cut budget deficits, promote non-inflationary growth, encourage a convergence of economies, and to roll-back protectionism. Ways and means of improving the international monetary system were to be investigated. The Declaration conceded that a coordinated intervention by government in the exchange markets was warranted where it was 'agreed that such intervention would be helpful'. The growth of the money supply should be disciplined and non-inflationary. *See* VERSAILLES ECONOMIC SUMMIT.

Wilson Report. A committee, under the chairmanship of Sir Harold Wilson, which reported in 1980 on the functioning of British financial institutions. The Committee identified three main issues that had developed since the Radcliffe Committee (q.v.) of 1959: the impact of inflation, the growth of financial institutions (particularly the pension funds and insurance companies), and the part they can play in encouraging industry to invest. Institutions, such as the above, were found to own more than half the shares listed on The London Stock Exchange, compared with only 21 per cent in 1957. The committee found that inflation sets a bias against long-term borrowing or lending; the long-term fixed-interest debenture market had dried up. The committee considered the scope for issuing index-linked securities and mortgages, the index being that of average earnings. The committee recommended the removal of impediments to issuing long-term industrial securities index-linked to earnings. There was no support for an American-style Securities and Exchange Commission (q.v.), though some support for the establishment of a new review body to keep a watching brief on the regulation of all parts of the financial system. The building societies and their cartel were severely criticised. The cartel was considered to protect inefficient societies and encourage them to engage in 'wasteful non-price competition in areas like the number of branches'. Between 1968 and 1978, building society branches had increased by 175 per cent to almost 4,600. The Wilson Committee recommended the scrapping of the cartel with a view to more competition. The Committee agreed, on balance, that there was no case for nationalising financial institutions such as clearing banks and insurance companies.

Windows. Opportunities for profitable investment in markets or transfers between markets; for raising capital in different markets; or for profitable arbitrage (q.v.) taking advantage of fluctuations in interest rates and exchange rates.

Wire house. A business house operating a private wire to its own branch officers, or to other firms.

Withholding tax. A tax imposed on the gross receipts of companies or the incomes of individuals in advance of normal tax assessment. For many years, until 1984, the United States imposed a 30 per cent tax at source on income paid to foreign investors who held U.S. domestic bonds issued by either companies or the U.S. Treasury; this deterred many Europeans from buying U.S. bonds. the Eurodollar bond market issuing bonds in bearer form with interest paid gross. In 1983, the Australian Government imposed a withholding tax on gross payments for labour and services in an attempt to reduce rampant tax avoidance in the cash economy (q.v.).

Witteveen facility. *See* SUPPLEMENTARY FINANCING FACILITY.

Workable competition. A concept first put forward by Professor J. M. Clark (1884–1963) in 1940 which asserted the widespread existence of competition notwithstanding equally widespread monopoly elements in the real world. Even within what appeared to be monopolistic or oligopolistic market structures, important elements of competition may be found. The emphasis should not therefore be on structure or even on conduct but on actual performance in respect of price, profits, products, and technical progress. Thus the more workably competitive an industry, it may be argued, the more prices will approach those which would rule in conditions of perfect competition (q.v.), allowing for the fact that internal economies of scale might make perfect competition impossible.

Working control over a corporation or company comprises, theoretically, ownership of at least 51 per cent of the total voting shares; however, effective control can sometimes be exercised through ownership, individually or by a group acting in concert, of less than 50 per cent of the shares.

World Bank. A group of three institutions: the International Bank for Reconstruction and Development (q.v.), the International Development Association (q.v.) and the International Finance Corporation (q.v.). The common objective of these institutions is to help raise standards of living in developing countries by channelling financial resources from developed countries to the developing world. The Bank was established in December, 1945.

In 1946, the World Bank had 38 members; in 1960, 68 members; in 1970, 113 members; and in 1982, 143 members. The members range from the Seychelles (population 67,000) to China (population 1 billion). Lending has expanded from $3.4 billion in 1972–73 to $13 billion in 1981–82, an increase in real terms of about 6 per cent per annum. In 1982, the Bank had a staff of 2,600; the headquarters is in Washington, D.C. Despite many criticisms, the World Bank has been the largest single source of development funds for the world's poorer nations.

World Development Fund. *See* BRANDT COMMISSION.

'World Development Report'. An annual publication of the World Bank (q.v.); publication began in 1978. The report surveys the state of the world in terms of poverty and wealth, health and general well-being, and describes the nature and character of the projects supported in whole or part by the Bank.

World Financial System. *See* EUROPEAN MONETARY AGREEMENT; GENERAL AGREEMENT ON TARIFFS AND TRADE; INTERNATIONAL BANK FOR RECONSTRUCTION AND DEVELOPMENT; INTERNATIONAL DEVELOPMENT ASSOCIATION; INTERNATIONAL FINANCE CORPORATION; INTERNATIONAL MONETARY FUND; ORGANISATION OF PETROLEUM EXPORTING COUNTRIES; WORLD BANK.

Writing a call. Selling a call option (q.v.).

Writing a put. Selling a put option (q.v.).

Writing an option. Selling an option (q.v.).

XYZ

XC. The abbreviation for ex-capitalisation (q.v.).
XD. The abbreviation for ex-dividend (q.v.).
XR. The abbreviation for ex-rights (q.v.).
Yankee bonds. Bonds denominated in U.S. dollars, issued in the United States by a foreign borrower.
Yearling bonds. Bonds issued with only twelve months to maturity.
Yield. The percentage return on capital. The gross flat yield on a security is the annual amount receivable in interest expressed as a percentage of the purchase price; the net flat yield is the gross flat yield less income tax at the standard rate.

If, as is nearly always the case, the market price of a share differs from the nominal value, the yield is calculated according to the following formula:

$$\frac{\text{Nominal Value} \times \text{Dividend}}{\text{Market price}} = \text{Yield per cent}$$

For example: 'A' Co. £1 shares, market price £1.75, dividend 14 per cent:

$$\frac{1.00 \times 14}{1.75} = 8 \text{ per cent yield.}$$

If securities are redeemed at a known date, the gross redemption yield comprises the gross flat yield together with an annual apportionment of the calculated capital gain or loss; the net redemption capital gain or loss; the net redemption yield is similar to the gross redemption yield except that income tax at the standard rate is deducted from dividends, and any capital gains tax (q.v.) from the capital appreciation. *See* TABLE 5.
Yield to maturity. The yield of a bond (q.v.) related to its market value as distinct from face value; it is greater than the current yield when the bond is selling at a discount and less than the current yield when the bond is selling at a premium.
Youth Opportunity Programme (Y.O.P.). A British government programme, introduced in 1978, to allow some access for school leavers to work experience; school leavers are paid and offered training and work experience on employees' premises or on socially useful projects. In 1981, some 360,000 unemployed young people were in Y.O.P. schemes.
Zaibatsu. Large Japanese firms with interlocking interests in banking, industry, and shipping, e.g. Mitsubishi and Mitsui.

TABLE 5
INTEREST YIELDS ON STOCKS

Interest rate quoted in title of stock (i.e. the 'coupon' rate)	Annual interest on £100 nominal of stock	Purchase price per £100 nominal of stock (examples only)	Annual interest yield and method of calculation
12%	£12	£110	10.9% ($12 \times 100 \div 110$)
$2\frac{1}{2}$%	£2.50	£25	10.0% ($2\frac{1}{2} \times 100 \div 25$)

Zero coupon bonds. Issued by companies in 1981, bonds which pay no interest but are priced at a discount of their redemption price; they offer the promise of reward through capital gains, which are normally taxed at a lower rate than income received as interest.

Zero coupon bonds may be created by physically separating the interest coupons from the bond principal itself; the principal and each coupon may be sold individually. *See* DEEP DISCOUNT BONDS; DISCOUNTED INVESTMENT IN NEGOTIABLE GOVERNMENT OBLIGATION; TREASURY GROWTH INVESTMENT RECEIPTS.

Zero energy growth. An objective commended by a number of economists, conservation bodies, and interested citizens who share a conviction that the natural resources of the world, and most notably non-renewable energy resources, should be conserved in the interests of present and future generations.

Zero opportunity cost. A situation which may arise in conditions of substantial unemployment of resources; these resources may be directed into public projects without any reduction in production elsewhere in the economy, that is without opportunity cost (q.v.).

Zero population growth. An objective commended by a number of economists, demographers, conservation bodies, and interested citizens who share a conviction that only with a stable world population can modern society survive and moderately prosper over the long-run. A number of countries, including the People's Republic of China, have encouraged family planning programmes to limit the size of families.